Advances in Tourism Economics

Álvaro Matias · Peter Nijkamp · Manuela Sarmento
Editors

Advances in Tourism Economics

New Developments

Physica-Verlag
A Springer Company

Editors
Professor Álvaro Matias
Universidade Lusíada de Lisboa
School of Economics and Business
Rua da Junqueira, 188-198
1349-001 Lisboa
Portugal
amatias@edu.ulusiada.pt

Professor Manuela Sarmento
Universidade Lusíada de Lisboa
School of Economics and Business
Rua da Junqueira, 188-198
1349-001 Lisboa
Portugal
manuela.sarmento@bizturis.com

Professor Peter Nijkamp
Free University of Amsterdam
Faculty of Economics and
Business Administration
Department of Spatial Economics
De Boelelaan 1105
1081 HV Amsterdam
The Netherlands
pnijkamp@feweb.vu.nl

Publication sponsored by the Portuguese Association for Tourism Research and Development (APIDT):

apidt
Associação Portuguesa para a Investigação
e Desenvolvimento em Turismo

ISBN 978-3-7908-2899-3 ISBN 978-3-7908-2124-6 (eBook)
DOI 10.1007/978-3-7908-2124-6
Springer Dordrecht Heidelberg London New York

Cover design: WMXDesign GmbH, Heidelberg

Printed on acid-free paper

Springer is part of Springer Science+Business Media (www.springer.com)

Preface

With the advent of rising mobility and leisure time together with a structural tendency for declining airfares, tourism has become a sector of major significance in modern economies. There is a wealth of literature on the motives of tourists, on the sustainability aspects of large-scale tourism, on the expected economic and social consequences of tourism in host countries and regions, on the attractiveness of different localities and tourist sites (e.g., beaches, historico-cultural heritage, nature etc.), or on local or regional initiatives to promote tourism (e.g., through tourism packages, e services etc.). Tourism research has indeed become a booming and timely research approach in contemporaneous economics.

There is indeed a host of descriptive, qualitative and policy-oriented research, but applied and quantitatively-oriented economic research is still underrepresented. Fortunately, we have witnessed in the past years an upsurge of model-based economic research in the tourist sector, which builds on powerful research tools in quantitative economics, such as discrete choice models, social accounting matrices, data envelopment analysis, impact assessment models or partial computable equilibrium models including environmental externalities. The present volume originates from this novel research spirit in tourism economics and aims to offer an attractive collection of operational research tools and approaches in tourism research. Originality and advanced methodology have been the major criteria for selecting these contributions. They form an appealing record of modern tourism economic research and position tourism economics within the strong tradition of quantitative economic research, with due attention for both the demand and supply side of the tourism sector, including technological and logistic advances in the sector. This volume offers thus examples of pioneering research in tourism economics.

Lisboa, Portugal *Álvaro Matias*
December, 2008

Amsterdam, Netherlands *Peter Nijkamp*
December, 2008

Lisboa, Portugal *Manuela Sarmento*
December, 2008

Contents

Contributors

António Almeida Department of Management and Economics, University of Madeira and CEEAplA, Funchal, Portugal, amma@uma.pt

Francis Aubert ENESAD, UMR Cesaer, Dijon, France, francis.aubert@enesad.inra.fr

Paul Belleflamme CORE and IAG-Louvain School of Management, Université Catholique de Louvain, Louvain, Belgium, paul.belleflamme@uclouvain.be

Ester Blanco University of the Balearic Islands, Edifici Jovellanos, Palma de Mallorca, Balears, Spain, ester.blanco@uib.es

Ana Bobirca Faculty of International Business and Economics, Academy of Economic Studies, Bucharest, Romania, Ana.Bobirca@rei.ase.ro

José Cabral Vieira Department of Economics and Business, University of the Azores and CEEAplA, Ponta Delgada, Portuga, jvieira@notes.uac.pt

Massimiliano Castellani Department of Economics, University of Bologna, Bologna, Italy, castellani@rimini.unibo.it

Houssine Choyakh Faculty of Economics and Management MODEVI, University of Sfax, Tunisia, choyakh@gmail.com

Gualter Couto Business and Economics Department, University of the Azores, CEEAplA, Ponta Delgada, Azores, Portugal, gcouto@notes.uac.pt

Cristiana Cristureanu Faculty of International Business and Economics, Academy of Economic Studies, Bucharest, Romania, cristiana.cristureanu@rei.ase.ro

Jean-Christophe Dissart Cemagref, UR DTM, Grenoble, France, jean-christophe.dissart@cemagref.fr

Paolo Figini Department of Economics, University of Bologna, Bologna, Italy, paolo.figini@unibo.it

António Gomes de Menezes Department of Economics and Business, University of the Azores and CEEAplA, Ponta Delgada, Portugal, menezesa@notes.uac.pt

Norsiah Kadir Faculty of Business and Management, Universiti Teknologi MARA, Perlis, Malaysia, Norsiahkadir6699@yahoo.com

Mohd Zaini Abd Karim Faculty of Economics, Universiti Utara, Sintok, Malaysia, zaini500@uum.edu.my

Valerio Lacagnina Faculty of Economics, University of Palermo, Palermo, Italy, ricopa@unipa.it

Eveline van Leeuwen Faculty of Economics and Business Administration, VU University Amsterdam, Amsterdam, The Netherlands, eleeuwen@feweb.vu.nl

Gang Li University of Surrey, School of Management, Guilford, UK, g.li@surrey.ac.uk

Javier Lozano University of the Balearic Islands, Edifici Jovellanos, Palma de Mallorca, Balears, Spain, javier.lozano@uib.es

Álvaro Matias School of Economics and Business, Lusíada University, Lisbon, Portugal, amatias@edu.ulusiada.pt

Jan Møller Jensen Department of Marketing, University of Southern Denmark, Odense, Denmark, jmj@sam.sdu.dk

Ana Moniz Department of Economics and Management, University of the Azores, Ponta Delgada, Portugal, amoniz@notes.uac.pt

Nicolas Neysen CRECIS and IAG-Louvain School of Management, Université Catholique de Louvain, Louvain, Belgium, nicolas.neysen@uclouvain.be

Peter Nijkamp Faculty of Economics and Business Administration, VU University Amsterdam, Amsterdam, The Netherlands, pnijkamp@feweb.vu.nl

Pedro Telhado Pereira Department of Management and Economics, University of Madeira and CEEAplA, Funchal, Portugal, ppereira@uma.pt

Pedro Miguel Pimentel Business and Economics Department, CEEAplA, University of the Azores, Ponta Delgada, Azores, Portugal, ppimentel@notes.uac.pt

Clemente Polo Department of Economics and Economic History, Universidad Autónoma de Barcelona, Barcelona, Spain, clemente.polo@uab.es

Davide Provenzano Faculty of Economics, University of Palermo, Palermo, Italy, davidepro@yahoo.com

Javier Rey-Maquieira University of the Balearic Islands, Edifici Jovellanos, Palma de Mallorca, Balears, Spain, javier.rey@uib.es

Piet Rietveld Faculty of Economics and Business Administration, VU University Amsterdam, Amsterdam, The Netherlands, prietveld@feweb.vu.nl

Carlos Santos Business and Economics Department, University of the Azores, CEEAplA, Ponta Delgada, Azores, Portugal, csantos@notes.uac.pt

Manuela Sarmento School of Economics and Business, University Lusíada, Lisbon, Portugal, manuela.sarmento@bizturis.com

Shujie Shen Institute for Transport Studies, University of Leeds, Leeds, UK, s.shen@its.leeds.ac.uk

Haiyan Song Hong Kong Polytechnic University, Hong Kong SAR, China, hmsong@polyu.edu.hk

Susanna Teles Department of Management and Economics, University of Madeira, Funchal, Portugal, s_teles@sapo.pt

Stéphanie Truchet Cemagref, UMR Métafort, Clermont-Ferrand, France, stephanie.truchet@cemagref.fr

Elisabeth Valle Applied Economics Department, University of the Balearic Islands, Balearic Islands, Spain, elisabeth.valle@uib.es

Laura Vici Department of Economics, University of Bologna, Bologna, Italy, laura.vici@unibo.it

Chapter 1
Research Needs on the Tourist Nexus

Álvaro Matias, Peter Nijkamp, and Manuela Sarmento

1.1 Prologue

The tourist sector has witnessed a drastic transformation in the past years. Until a few decades ago, tourism was mainly a privileged activity for the "happy few" or a period of relaxation during a few weeks a year for the population at large. Nowadays it is almost a "normal" activity pattern, as witnessed by the fact that most aircraft seats are tourist class seats. As a consequence, tourism is increasingly becoming a major source of revenues for many countries and regions. Since the Second World War the rise in tourism has been significantly higher than the average world economic growth, while the average annual rise in tourist expenditures was approximately 10%. This considerable increase in tourist activities is a result of many underlying factors such as (see also Bossel-Hunterman et al. 1999, Bull 1991, Cater and Lowman 1994, Hunter and Green 1995, De Kadt 1979, Lindberg 1991, Ritchie and Goeldner 1987, and Weierman and Fuchs 1998):

- the rise in general economic welfare, so that a relatively higher proportion of discretionary income could be spent of recreational and tourist purposes;
- the rise in leisure time, so that a higher proportion of a consumer's time budget could be allocated to recreation and tourism (cf. Klaassen 1968, Patmore 1973);
- the rise in transportation facilities and mobility, so that many worthwhile places received a high degree of accessibility (cf. Coccossis and Nijkamp 1995);
- the rise in (tele)communication (e.g. the use of ICT and Internet services) between countries, so that many foreign and remote countries were able to exert an increased attractiveness upon potential tourists (cf. Tsartas 1998);
- the quality of life in many industrialised countries (pollution, urbanisation, e.g.), so that more and more people were inclined to flee heir home country during the holidays ("get away from it all") (cf. Honey 1999);

Á. Matias (✉)
School of Economics and Business, Lusíada University, Lisbon, Portugal
e-mail: amatias@edu.ulusiada.pt

Á. Matias et al. (eds.), *Advances in Tourism Economics*,
DOI 10.1007/978-3-7908-2124 6_1, © Physica Verlag Heidelberg 2009

- the increased supply of many high quality tourist accommodations and services in certain countries, so that many tourists were stimulated to visit the country in question (cf. Eadington and Redman 1991, Johnson and Thomas 1990, Lee et al. 1996, and Tribe 1997).

The rise in tourism and its growth potentials have attracted increasing attention from development agencies, particularly in lagging regions and in the developing world. Tourism is frequently considered as an important expedient for an accelerated endogenous regional or national growth, since it provides a developing economy with foreign exchange needed for financing other economic sectors. The general idea is that the existence and attractiveness of tourist areas – in combination with fine tuned investments – will generate tourist flows of a sufficient size to act as a self-accelerating growth engine.

In order to delimitate here tourism from other economic activities, it will be conceived of as a short-term movement of people to and as activities at destinations outside their usual living and work places for other than business reasons (cf. also Burkart and Medlik 1974). Tourist activities have a multiplicity of effects at the places (or countries of destination:

- a rise in supply of foreign exchange, since tourism is an important foreign exchange earner (at least, if tourist facilities are built and controlled by the country itself or by local agents);
- a creation of new incomes, not only in the tourist sector itself, but also in all other sectors owing to intersectoral multiplier-effects (cf. Bryden 1973);
- a rise in employment (both direct and indirect), even though it has to be recognized that tourist activities have frequently no higher labour effectiveness per unit of investment than comparable activities (in particular, owing to the seasonal character of tourism);
- a rise in socio-economic frictions (particularly in developing countries), because of deviating behavioural patterns and of different expenditures patters (the so-called demonstration or conspicuous consumption effect).

An important advantage of tourism is the fact that it has in general a rather high income elasticity with respect to the demand for tourist services (see Baretje and Defert 1972). A serious drawback is that a concentration on tourist activities may imply a rather vulnerable economic structure, since there are in general no firm links with respect to the industrial sector of the national economy. It is obvious, that a promotion of a balanced economic development requires a detailed insight into the determinants and effects of the tourist sector.

A matter of major significance in tourism development is the increased demand for tourist facilities and the compatibility of increased tourism with the natural and cultural characteristics of the areas concerned. An unlimited growth of tourism affects frequently attractive natural or cultural resources (for example, in the Mediterranean), so that tourism development in certain areas is in serious competition with alternative uses of these areas (see also Brandon et al. 1997, and Gössling

1999). A large-scale tourism development poses serious ecological problems owing to damage to interesting places, generates an increased claim on land for use and enjoyment, and leads to air pollution, noise and congestion owing to increased traffic. Therefore, an unplanned and uncontrolled tourism development can lead to the deterioration of fragile ecosystems and attractive landscapes through overbuilding and excessive densities of tourists. The expanded demand for tourist facilities may at certain places lead to a destruction of the environment which is the very source of tourist attractiveness.

Tourism is essentially a double-edged sword that exploits local beauty and historico-cultural heritage as an attraction force for generating socio-economic benefits for society at large, but on the other hand, it may easily lead to over-exploitation of these local resources and hence erode the foundations of local or regional attractiveness (e.g., in the form of negative externalities such as noise, diseconomies of density, social tension, water pollution etc.)

The analysis of all forces at work prompts the need for an appropriate toolbox on both the supply and the demand side, as well as from a policy perspective.

This volume intends to present a collection of mainly methodological advances in tourism economic research focussing on various agents in the sector. Not only behavioural aspects, but also sustainability and competitiveness factors are dealt with as well as policy responses. The emphasis is mainly on applied modelling experiments and phenomena, with the aim to assess in quantitative form the importance of the various key factors at work.

A focussed and detailed investigation of the relevance of tourism calls thus for an advanced set of statistical and modelling tools supported by a paper data set on drives and implications of tourist behaviour. These tools may be multi-faceted in nature, as they are concerned with the complex interactions between supply, demand, locational conditions, transport systems, private investments, and policy initiatives. The aim of the present volume – the second in a series – is to offer a collection of appropriate and sophisticated analysis tools for studying tourist behaviour in a complex local-environmental system from both the demand and supply side. The volume is organized in three major parts which will concisely be presented here.

1.2 Organization of the Book

This volume centres around three major focal points, viz. (i) methodological innovation in tourism economic research, (ii) quantitative assessment of various impacts caused by the tourist sector, and (iii) trend analysis in the modern tourist market.

In Part A, on advances in the methodology of tourism economics, five contributions are included. The first article in Part A, written by Eveline van Leeuwen, Peter Nijkamp and Piet Rietveld, offers a meta-analytic contribution to the estimation of output multipliers in the tourism sector. Stakeholders need to know the magnitude of the impact of international and domestic tourist expenditures on the economy in order to make decisions about budget allocations for the development of tourist facilities. But there is a great deal of variation, and the question emerges whether such variations can be ascribed to systematic factors. Therefore, in this chapter the authors perform a meta-analysis on tourism multipliers. As multiplier values reflect the size of the multiplier effect, with respect to a specific feature of the economy such as income or employment, these values can help policy makers to learn something about the magnitude of tourist expenditures. Within a meta-analysis the empirical outcomes of studies with similar research questions are analysed. The research question addressed in this sector is: which characteristics of the tourism sector, the research area, or the type of publication in which a study was published can explain variations in the size of the tourism multiplier? The authors briefly describe the input–output model and its multipliers, and explain next the order of magnitude of the multipliers, followed by an initial analysis of the empirical data. Then they perform a linear regression on the available data, followed by another meta-analytical method, viz. rough set analysis. They then use the obtained insights to assess – and reflect upon – tourism multipliers for six Dutch towns.

The next chapter is written by Valerio Lacagnina and Davide Provenzano and offers a dynamic optimization framework for hotel chain management. In this work, the authors the authors combine the System Dynamics (SD) methodology with Data Envelopment Analysis (DEA) in order to investigate the path taken by the hotels of a chain as they move towards the efficient frontier. Periodically a centralized decision maker collects multiple input/output data of the hotel chain to judge the relative efficiency of each hotel and to figure out the policies to be implemented to increase the total system's performance. The relative efficiency is measured by making use of DEA, while the economic effect of the policies implemented is integrated into a dynamic framework in order to enhance the usefulness of the efficiency analysis. SD offers a readily accessible methodology for making this integration operational. Differently from the static approach, the study shows that in a dynamic framework DEA has to be run more than one time in order to push the hotels of the chain towards the efficient frontier. Moreover, the more the market is reactive to the policies implemented, the more the efficiency analysis will not be completely effective to increase the total performance of the system.

A new demand approach – based on cointegration and error correction – is adopted by Norsiah Kadir and Mohd Zaini Abd Karim in Chap. 4. Their study examines the effect of some selected factors on tourist arrivals from the long-haul markets (US and UK) to Malaysia by using cointegration and error correction model approach. Analyses are conducted with quarterly data over the period of 1995:1 through 2005:2 on international tourism flows to Malaysia from the US and the UK. Results of the study indicate that there is a long-run relationship between tourist arrivals from the US and the UK and income, relative price of tourism in Malaysia and price of tourism in the competing destinations. Both the long-run and short-run results show that income is positively related with tourism demand in Malaysia. As in most previous empirical studies, relative prices of tourism and the price of tourism in competing destination were found to have a significant effect on tourist arrivals in Malaysia. The "Malaysia ... Truly Asia" promotion campaign also have a positive impact on tourist arrivals from the U.S and the UK, while the spread of SARs in Asia tends to have a negative effect on tourist arrivals from the UK only.

However, the 1997/98 Asian financial crisis tends to have a negative effect on both tourist arrivals from the US and the UK. Nevertheless, the September 11, 2001 terrorist attacks in the US tend to have a negative effect on tourist arrivals from the US only.

Another paper in the same vein is presented by Houssine Choyakh in the next chapter, using again an error correction model. This paper investigates the relationship between the demand of Europeans for international travel to Tunisia and the factors that affect holiday visits such as income in origin countries, relative prices and substitute prices. For this purpose, the Johansen's maximum likelihood procedure and error correction models has been applied. The main conclusion is that income is the most significant factor of tourism demand to Tunisia, while relative prices do not have an important effect on the motivation of Europeans to visit Tunisia except the British tourists. Also, substitute prices play an important role on tourism demand of British and Italian tourists, but not the German and the French ones.

The final paper in Part A, written by António Gomes de Menezes, José Cabral Vieira and Ana Isabel Moniz, uses a parametric survival analysis to estimate the determinants of length of stay of tourists. Length of stay Length of stay is one of the most important decisions made by tourists as it conditions their overall expenditure and stress caused on local resources. This paper estimates survival analysis models to learn the determinants of length of stay as survival analysis naturally lends itself to study the time elapsed between arrival and departure. It is found that socio-demographic profiles, such as nationality and gender, and trip attributes, such as repeat behavior, travel motive and satisfaction, are important determinants of length of stay. This paper's results can be used to estimate the probability that a target group experiences a stay longer than a given threshold. This is important to design marketing strategies that effectively influence length of stay.

Part B of the present volume is concerned with the assessment of tourist impacts. The first contribution in this part is offered by Shujie Shen, Gang Li and Haiyan Song. It deals with the use of the time-varying parameter model in making tourism demand forecasts. Comparisons of forecasting performance amongst different tourism demand models have been carried out in numerous studies over the past two decades. Empirical studies have consistently shown that the time-varying parameter (TVP) model outperforms its static counterpart, based on conventional non-statistical measures of forecast accuracy, such as the mean absolute percentage error (MAPE) and root mean square percentage error (RMSPE). However, whether the differences in forecasting performance amongst these models are statistically significant has rarely been tested in the tourism context. The current paper aims to bridge this gap by applying statistical means to test the forecast accuracy of the TVP and static models in the context of Thai inbound tourism demand by seven major countries – Australia, Japan, Korea, Malaysia, Singapore, the UK and the US. Two statistical tests are employed: the Morgan-Granger-Newbold (MGN) test and Harvey-Leybourne-Newbold (HLN) test. The forecast accuracy of the TVP and static models using one- to four-periods-ahead forecasting horizons is examined. The empirical results show that the improvements in the forecast accuracy of the TVP model relative to its static counterpart are statistically significant in most cases.

This study provides robust evidence to suggest that the TVP model is the preferred model in tourism demand forecasting practice.

The next chapter is written by Clemente Polo and Elisabeth Valle and presents an impact analysis of the tourism sector based on input–output and SAM models. According to the official Tourism Studies Institute, the Balearic Islands (BI), a Spanish region with just over one million inhabitants, received 9.6 million international arrivals in 2005 out of 55.8 million for the entire country. Although a rather impressive figure, it is 4.8% below the 10.1 million recorded in 1999 which might explain partially why the BI region has recorded the worst growth performance of all 17 autonomous Spanish regions since 2000. A look at the 1997 regional input–output table, confirms the BI as a service oriented economy highly specialized in the production of services for tourism. The main contribution of this paper is to provide the first assessment of the weight of tourism in the BI using input–output techniques and several alternative assumptions on endogeneity of final demand components. The paper also estimates the effects of a 10% fall in tourism flows using input–output and social accounting matrix models.

Next, a new contribution on the basis of choice modelling is provided by Paolo Figini, Massimiliano Castellani and Laura Vici. During their holidays, tourists produce direct and indirect effects on local residents, which can either be positive or negative. In this paper the authors investigate how residents of Rimini, a popular Italian seaside resort hosting more than ten million national and foreign overnight stays every year, internalise such effects. They use a stated preference approach and, in particular, a discrete choice modelling technique; within this framework, they are able to test some conjectures about residents' welfare, by measuring their willingness to pay for alternative scenarios regarding the use of the territory. Tourist policies and public investments in the destination affect the residents' welfare, and the results suggest areas of potential synergies and trade-off with tourists, leading to important policy implications.

Another important analytical tool is formed by stated choice experiments. In their study, the authors, Pedro Telhado Pereira, António Almeida, António Gomes de Menezes and José Cabral Vieira, apply this approach to estimate the willingness to pay for airline services. They implement a stated preferences choice game to estimate passengers' willingness to pay for airline services attributes, in the air corridor from Funchal to Las Palmas. And they find that the willingness to pay for improvements in service levels, such as punctuality warranties, hinge on the reasons why passengers undertake the trip, namely for work or tourism. The gains for airlines from patronizing non-marginal changes in service levels are large, and, concomitantly, stated choice experiments like ours are a powerful tool to devise effective service differentiation strategies that cater for the heterogeneous preferences of passengers.

Finally, the last contribution in Part B is written by Carlos Santos, Gualter Couto and Pedro Miguel Pimentel. The authors develop a statistical model to make forecasts of overnights subdivided by country of origin as compared to the total overnights in the tourist area concerned. Based on extensive data for the Azores, they perform measurement error analysis using various time series techniques.

A final part of this volume, Part C, is devoted to the analysis of structural development and trends in the tourism industry. The first chapter in this part, written by Ana Bobirca and Cristiana Cristureanu, studies the international competitiveness of trade in tourism services. The main purpose of this chapter is to examine the international competitiveness of the Romanian tourism services trade and its structure of specialization on both the EU-25 and the world tourism markets. To this end, the paper addresses the need for competitiveness indicators that cover the tourism sector and attempts to suggest a framework for assessing the international competitiveness of Romania's tourism services trade. Against this background, the first part of the paper introduces the concept of international competitiveness. The second part includes an overview of Romania's international trade in tourism services, while the third part of the paper sets out in detail the framework for calculating the proposed measures of competitiveness. The paper concludes by illustrating Romania's competitive position on the European tourism services market and by identifying research issues that require further study.

The next chapter is devoted to electronic ticket purchases. The author, Jan Møller Jensen, aims to investigate whether travellers' shopping orientations influence their tendency to purchase travel products online. A conceptual model is developed by the author and a number of hypotheses are forwarded and tested. Linear structural equation modelling is utilised to investigate expectations and test hypotheses. The results support several of the stated hypotheses. Most of the explained variance in intentions to purchase travel products online is produced by travellers' perceived loss of experience from not visiting an agency, but also convenience and preferences for better product variety are important predictors. The results provide travel and tourism marketers with important insights on travellers' tendency to purchase travel products online.

A subsequent chapter deals with the importance of Internet use for the tourist industry. Since the economic and managerial fields have integrated the Internet tool, new opportunities have been created. Among them, information management aiming at helping to make the "best choices" became a central topic in e-management. New types of intermediaries appeared in the virtual world. Actors who join these intermediation places and take part in their development play an atypical game: on the one hand, they cooperate in the same virtual entity of reticular form and, on the other hand, they remain individually in competition with one another since they are active on the same market. How should we address this competitive game? As an answer to the latter question, the authors suggest to rely on coopetition theory to describe the collaboration between members of a same platform. Moreover, in order to avoid any confusion, they propose a distinction between "electronic marketplaces" and "online information platforms". To illustrate their work, they apply their general analysis to the case of e-tourism.

The question of sustainable tourism is also an important issue in tourism research. In Chap. 15, Esther Blanco, Javier Lozano and Javier Rey-Maquiera review the state of the literature on economic incentives of tourism firms to undertake voluntary environmental initiatives. Contributions in this respect are embedded within the broader debate on "pays to be green" for the manufacturing industry. Differences between the service sector in general and tourism firms in particular are discussed, and the main findings of this literature are stressed. Overall, it can be defended that, for at least a certain proportion of firms in the tourism industry, it pays to undertake voluntary environmental action. When conceptualizing this evidence under a game theoretic perspective, it is shown that empirical results do not seem to support general free-riding, which would be expected according to the tragedy of the commons. This result has implications for the management of natural resources for tourism-related uses. These implications are presented as reflections on governance considerations.

An important trend in modern tourism is the emergence of the aviation sector in the framework of a modern leisure society. In this context, Susana Teles, Manuela Sarmento and Álvaro Matias offer a contribution on tourism and strategic competition in the air transport industry. Competition is often regarded as the ultimate solution for market efficiency. In certain sectors, however, market imperfections together with scale and scope economies lead market participants to establish some sort of cooperation efforts in order to maximize the common benefit of the cooperating partners. The authors argue that this is increasingly the case with the air transport industry in Europe and elsewhere. They analyse the economic rationale behind strategic alliances in the air transport sector, namely emphasizing the individual contributions and collective benefits of airlines when merged within a specific alliance for cooperation purposes. The several possibilities of cooperation agreements between air carriers are also analysed, as well as some of their managerial implications. Finally, the implications for tourism and the prospective medium-term trends for the airline sector are also taken into consideration for the immediate future of this competitive market, notwithstanding the competitive pressures ahead, namely the ones stemming from IT innovation and increasing energy costs.

The final chapter in Part C is concerned with the importance of tourism in rural areas. The authors, Jean-Christophe Dissart, Francis Aubert and Stéphanie Truchet, aim to estimate the importance of tourism in the economies of rural areas. Considering previous analyses of rural dynamics, the study (i) focuses on tourism activity, (ii) analyzes the situation of Functional Economic Areas (FEAs), and (iii) takes into account socioeconomic indicators as well as landscape attributes. Using statistical analysis of secondary data, resource-like regions are defined, the local share of tourism employment is estimated, key results regarding tourism indicators by cluster are presented, tourism-dependent FEAs are identified, and the relation between, on the one hand, tourism indicators and resource variables, and on the other hand, regional growth indicators and tourism dependence, is studied. This study aims to present the wealth of effects of tourism on rural development.

1.3 Retrospect and Prospect

Tourism economics has become an important research field in modern economics. Tourism reflects the mobility drive in our global society and has significant economic impacts, not only on major urban agglomerations, but also on regions, rural areas and developing countries. It is often regarded as the spearhead of new socio-economic developments. The drastic changes in human behaviour – with a higher frequency of leisure travelling, and long-distance movements –, make tourism a popular economic sector for intensified growth initiatives.

Nevertheless, tourism has also intrinsic weaknesses as a growth strategy, in particular because of its seasonal and volatile character and its threat to vulnerable local ecologies. And therefore, the development of a solid methodology and a sophisticated analysis toolbox is a sine qua non for a reliable impact assessment in the tourist sector, in order to gauge the anticipated impacts of tourism developments on both the supply and the demand side. The range of such impact studies exhibits a wide variation and may cover such fields as attractiveness of tourist sites, socio-economic effects of tourism, multi-faceted policy responses to new tourism challenges, the expected effects of new logistic and electronic services, the drastic structural changes in the airline industry (e.g., the emergence of low cost carriers), the incorporation of environmental externalities in tourist-economic research, and so forth.

Thus, there is a need for advanced and appropriate research tools that are able to serve the new research challenges in tourism economics. Applications of discrete choice models, spatial input–output and social accounting matrices, techniques from industrial organization and efficiency analysis (such as data envelopment analysis), dynamic optimization tools, statistical cointegration and error correction analysis, time-varying parameter models, or stated preference methods reflect the rich potential of sophisticated research tolls, in this rapidly emerging field. This volume just aims to offer an appetite of this fascinating new domain.

References

Baretje R, Defert L (1972) Aspects economiques du tourisme. Berger Levranit, Paris

Bosselman FP, Peterson CA, McCarthy C (1999) Managing tourism growth. Island Press, Covelo, California

Brandon P, Lombardi P, Bentikegna V (eds) (1997) Evaluation of the built environment for sustainability. Chapman & Hall, London

Bryden JM (1973) Tourism and development. Cambridge University Press, Cambridge

Bull A (1991) The economics of travel and tourism. Longman Cheshire, Australia

Burkart AJ, Medlik S (1974) Tourism. Heinemann, London

Cater E, Lowman G (eds) (1994) Ecotourism – A sustainable option? John Wiley, Chichester, UK

Coccossis H, Nijkamp P (eds) (1995) Sustainable tourism development. Avebury, Aldershot, UK

Eadington WR, Redman M (1991) Economics and tourism. Ann Tourism Res 18(1):41–56

Gössling S (1999) Ecotourism. Ecol Econ 29:303–320

Honey M (1999) Ecotourism and sustainable development. Island Press, Covelo CA

Hunter C, Green H (1995) Tourism and the environment: A sustainable relationship? Routledge, London/NewYork

Johnson P, Thomas B (1990) Measuring the local employment impact of a tourist attraction: An empirical study. Reg Stud 24(5):395–403

de Kadt E (1979) Tourism – The passport to development? Oxford University Press, Washington DC

Klaassen L (1968) Social amenities in area economic Growth. OECD, Paris

Lee CK, Var T, Blaine TW (1996) Determinants of inbound tourist expenditures. Ann Tourism Res 23(3):527–524
Lindberg K (1991) Policies for maximizing nature tourism′s ecological and economic benefits. World Resource Institute, Washington DC
Patmore JA (1973) Recreation: Evaluating the human environment. In: Dawson JA, Doornkamp JC (eds) Evaluating the human environment. Edward Arnold, London, pp 224–248
Ritchie JR, Goeldner CR (eds) (1987) Travel, tourism and hospitality research. John Wiley, New York
Tribe J (1997) The economics of leisure and tourism-environments, markets and impacts. Butterworth-Heinemann, Oxford
Tsartas P (1998) Sustainable development and tourism. In Laskaris C (ed) Sustainable development. National Technical University, Athens, pp 121–155
Weierman K, Fuchs M (1998) On the use and usefulness of economics in tourism. Int J Dev Plann Lit 13(3): 255–275

Part I
Methodological Advances

Chapter 2
A Meta-analytic Comparison of Regional Output Multipliers at Different Spatial Levels: Economic Impacts of Tourism

Eveline S. van Leeuwen, Peter Nijkamp, and Piet Rietveld

2.1 Introduction

On a local (town) scale, tourism is more and more being regarded as a possible instrument to change the future. With decreasing employment in agriculture, tourism is often seen as a new activity in the rural economy, generating employment and income and at the same time embracing local tradition and (landscape) qualities.

Over the last decades, tourism has become a major activity in our society and an increasingly important sector in terms of economic development (Giaoutzi and Nijkamp 2006). Higher incomes and a greater amount of leisure time, together with improved transport systems have resulted in a growing flow of tourists, travelling more frequently and over longer distances. According to Pearce (1981), the socio-economic effects of tourism are very diverse. When focusing on small and medium-sized towns, important effects are regional development, diversification of the economy and employment opportunities. Because tourism also addresses more rural and peripheral areas, it allows the spread of economic activities more evenly over a region. In the peripheral areas, tourism can be helpful in improving the multifunctionality of the local area, leading to more robust economic development. Finally, as tourism is a rather labour-intensive sector, also requiring unskilled labour, it can be a good employment opportunity for small and medium-sized towns.

This has recently prompted much policy and research interest in the benefits of tourism for regional income and employment. Policy makers in the government need to know the magnitude of the impact of international and domestic tourist expenditures on the economy in order to make decisions about budget allocations for the development of tourist facilities (Freeman and Sultan 1999). But there is a great deal of variation, and the question emerges whether such variations can be ascribed to systematic factors.

E.S. van Leeuwen (✉)
Faculty of Economics and Business Administration, Department of Spatial Economics, VU University, Amsterdam, The Netherlands
e-mail: eleeuwen@feweb.vu.nl

Á. Matias et al. (eds.), *Advances in Tourism Economics*,
DOI 10.1007/978-3-7908-2124-6_2, © Physica-Verlag Heidelberg 2009

Therefore, in this chapter we will perform a meta-analysis on tourism multipliers. As multiplier values reflect the size of the multiplier effect, with respect to a specific feature of the economy such as income or employment, these values can help policy makers to learn something about the magnitude of tourist expenditures. Within a meta-analysis the empirical outcomes of studies with similar research questions are analysed (Baaijens et al. 1997). The research question we want to answer in this paper is:

Which characteristics of the tourism sector, the research area, or the type of publication in which a study appeared can explain variations in the size of the tourism multiplier?

Therefore, first, in Sect. 2.2, we elaborate on the meta-analytic approach. Then, in Sect. 2.3, we will briefly describe the input–output model and its multipliers. In Sect. 2.4, we explain the order of magnitude of the multipliers, followed by an initial analysis of the empirical data. After this, in Sect. 2.5, we perform a linear regression on our available data. Another meta-analytical method, viz. Rough set analysis, will be applied in Sect. 2.6. We then use the obtained insights to develop and reflect upon tourism multipliers for six Dutch towns in Sect. 2.7. Finally, in Sect. 2.8, some research conclusions will be drawn.

2.2 Meta-analysis

Meta-analysis can be defined as the "study of studies" (Glass et al. 1981). It refers to the statistical analysis of individual studies with the same research question in order to integrate the findings. In meta-analysis, outcomes from a collection of studies are combined in order to draw general conclusions. It was initially applied in the medical and natural sciences, where it was used to compare the result of (semi-) controlled experiments. Meta-analyses can be performed in almost all thinkable research fields. In the economic sciences, examples are: Nijkamp and Vindigni (2000) who studied the agricultural sector in several countries; Nijkamp and Pepping (1998) and Holmgren (2007) who all analysed public transport demand; van den Bergh et al. (1997) Who dealt with environmental economics; and Baaijens et al. (1998) and Brander et al. (2007) who studied tourism-related subjects.

Meta-analysis is very useful when there is a need to systematize results that differ in magnitude and sometimes in direction. The problem of different studies resulting in different answers is particularly problematic for decision makers who are actually trying to use existing research as a basis for decisions (Holmgren 2007). One reason for different outcomes is that different variables are taken into account to answer the same research question. Especially in economics, the effect of several variables is often considered simultaneously which results in different outcomes when the set of independent variables are not the same. Also the scale level can affect the results: the effect of tourism on a national level will be different compared with the effect on a city-level. In a meta-analysis all the characteristics of a study are taken into account together when comparing the results. Furthermore, there can be a publication bias:

In meta-analysis there is often a concern that it is only studies which have obtained significant and expected results (at least the right sign) that are being published. It is possible that studies using sound methods and good data will not be reported because the results are not as expected (Begg 1994). Therefore, for a meta-analysis, it is important to be aware of this bias, and if possible to search for publications in all kind of fields and from different sources (such as refereed journals, research papers, or reports).

2.3 Input–Output Analysis and Multipliers

The use of input–output models in estimating economic impacts of recreation and tourism has increased considerably in the past decades because of their ability to provide accurate and detailed information and the ease of interpreting the results (Fletcher 1989).

As described in Chap. 4, the basic information dealt with in input–output analysis concerns the flows of products from each industrial sector considered as a producer to each of the sectors considered as a user (Miller and Blair 1985). When the demand changes in one of the sectors, this can affect many other sectors as well, especially when they deliver or buy intermediate products from the sector concerned.

Multipliers can be seen as summary statements of predicted effects of changes in demand (Armstrong and Taylor 2000). They are based on the estimated recirculation of spending within the region; recipients use some of their income for consumption spending, which then results in further income and employment (Frechtling 1994).

The size of the multiplier depends on several factors. First of all, it depends on the overall size and economic diversity of the region's economy. Regions with large, diversified economies which produce many goods and services will have high multipliers, as households and business can find most of the goods and services they need in their own region. Also the geographic scale of the region and its role within the broader region plays a role. Regions with a large geographic coverage will have higher multipliers, compared with similar small areas, as transportation costs will tend to inhibit imports (imports are seen as leakage and have a negative effect on a multiplier). Regions that serve as central places for the surrounding area will also have higher multipliers than more isolated areas. Furthermore, the nature of the specific sectors concerned can have a significant effect. Multipliers vary across different sectors of the economy based on the mix of labour and other inputs and the tendency of each sector to buy goods and services from within the region (hence less leakage to other regions). Tourism-related businesses tend to be labour-intensive. They, therefore, often have larger induced effects, because of household spending, rather than indirect effects. Finally, the year of the compilation of the input–output table should be taken into account. A multiplier represents the characteristics of the economy at a single point in time. Multipliers for a given region may change over time in response to changes in the economic structure as well as to price changes (Stynes 1998).

In the meta-analysis undertaken in this study, we look at output multipliers. The reason for this is that, in the sample of studies that we found, these multipliers are most often used.

2.4 Data Analysis of Tourist Multipliers

For our meta-analysis we were able to collect 32 case studies from 27 publications, which contain estimates of tourist multipliers including a (type II) output multiplier (see Appendix 1 for the references). A precondition was that the multiplier had to be derived with the help of input–output analysis. Also a (brief) description of background factors concerning, for example, the area and the tourist activities had to be given. Appendix 2 shows the characteristics we used together with the classification.

2.4.1 The Database

More than half of the case studies are (non-refereed) reports found on the Internet. These reports are often written by researchers to give local authorities insight into tourist situation of the area concerned. A fifth of the case studies collected are papers written for scientific conferences. In addition, several articles from refereed journals have been included. As Fig. 2.1a shows, conference papers estimate, on average, the highest multipliers, whereas the articles give relatively low values. We also incorporate the year in which the data was gathered in order to build the input–output table. In two instances this was before 1990, and in six instances it took place in 2000 or later. On average, as Fig. 2.1b shows, the oldest multipliers are the highest and the newer ones the lowest.

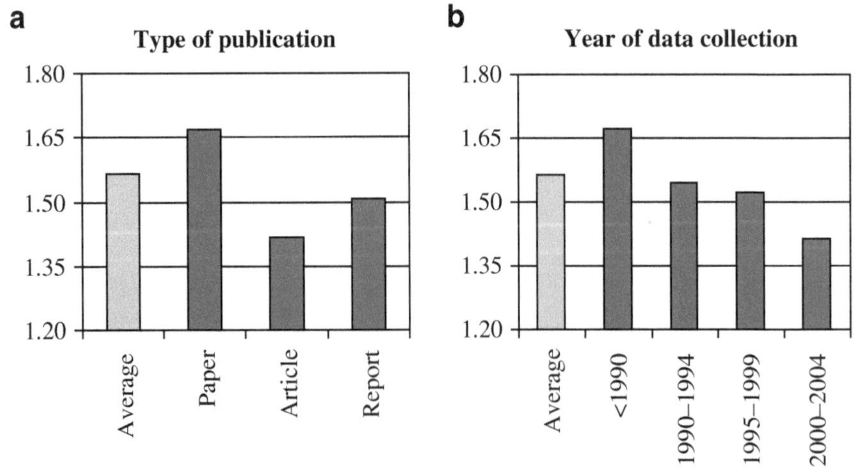

Fig. 2.1 Average multipliers according to type of publication (**a**) and years of data gathering (**b**)

Of course, not only characteristics of the reports affect the size of the output multiplier but also the characteristics of the areas which are described. Around half of the areas have a population density below 100 persons per km^2. Even a third of the studies have a population density of less than 30 persons per km^2. These areas are often the places with high nature values. The parts of the studies with the highest population density are related to urbanized areas or cities.

Figure 2.2a shows that, under type of area, multipliers concerning countries are higher on average than, for example, the average multiplier values of a city. This is partly because a city has to import a large part of its inputs, which lead to leakages. This also applies to a region or national park.

However, Fig. 2.2b shows that not only the size (here in terms of population) matters; the areas with the smallest population do not necessarily have the lowest multipliers. Nevertheless, the areas with a large population (8 studies) do have on average the highest multiplier.

Besides the publication and area-specific characteristics, tourism itself also has to be included in this multiplier analysis. The next two graphs (Fig. 2.3a and b) show the average multiplier values related to the type of attraction, as well as to the expenditures per square kilometer (*1,000$/km^2). In many studies, the visitors are attracted to their holiday destination by a beautiful landscape. A slightly smaller number of studies relate to tourists visiting an area because of the cultural values. Furthermore, we distinguish a group of studies in which people visit a place, because they want to enjoy the sun or because of a mix of values.

According to Fig. 2.3a, areas with tourists who want to enjoy the sun are related to the highest output multipliers. An explanation for this could be that people who visit areas to enjoy the sun often do not travel around a lot but stay in the village or hotel and spend all their money locally. On the other hand, visitors searching for culture have (very) small multipliers.

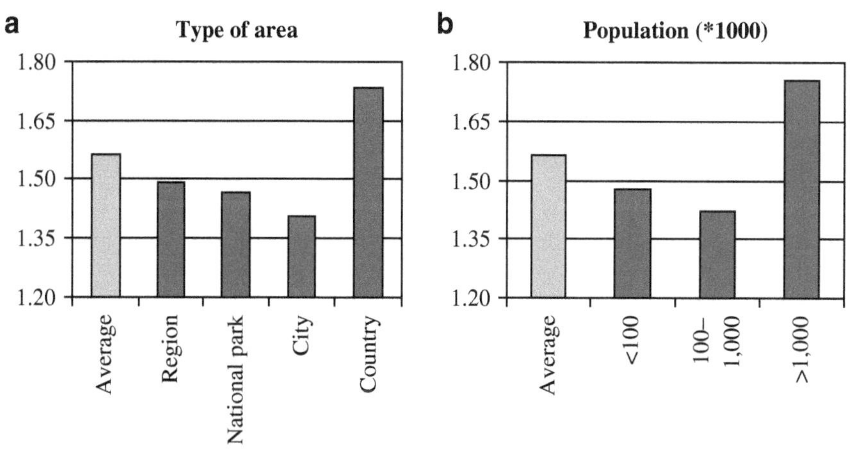

Fig. 2.2 Average multipliers according to type of area (**a**) and population (*1000) of the area (**b**)

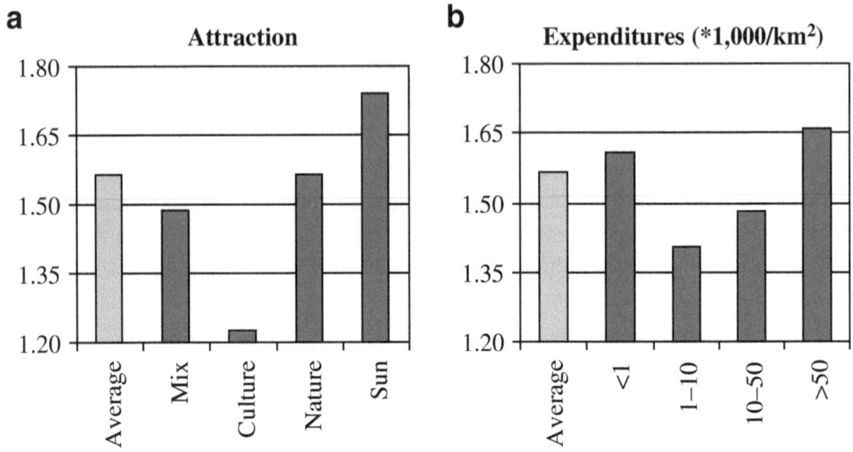

Fig. 2.3 Average multiplier values according to kind of attraction and total expenditures per year

From the data, it appears that areas with large expenditures have the highest multiplier values. However, this is partly related to the scale effect. Figure 2.3b shows the average values of the multipliers according to total tourist expenditures per year related to the size of the area. When looking at expenditures per km^2, it appears that there is no clear linear effect: both areas with the smallest amount of expenditures and those with the largest amounts have high multipliers. Obviously, we need to keep in mind that the multipliers themselves describe the effect of expenditures.

Of course, all these figures only show average multiplier values and they do not reveal anything concerning any relationship or coherence between the different indicators and the size of the output multipliers.

2.5 Linear Regression Results

2.5.1 Introduction

Linear regression is a standard technique that can also be used in meta-analytical experiments, insofar as statistical results from a sample of previous studies are analysed. This statistical model presupposes that there is a one-way causation between the dependent variable Y and the independent variable X. However, because we have only a limited number of studies available, it is not plausible that the assumptions of the standard linear regression are satisfied, for the variances of the distant multiplier values are not equal (see also Baaijens and Nijkamp 1996).

The analysis starts with the formulation of a set of hypotheses, which we will verify with the help of the linear regression model.

- Hypothesis 1: The larger the economic base, the higher the multiplier. As described in the section on multipliers, a larger economic base needs less import.

Import can be seen as a leakage of money to other regions. Therefore, it may be expected that the size of the land area or the size of the population has a positive effect on the multiplier. In particular, countries as a whole will have lower imports.
- Hypothesis 2: The more visitors or expenditures of visitors, the higher the multiplier. The visitors or at least the expenditures of the visitors may cause a higher multiplier as a result of cluster effects.
- Hypothesis 3: The longer ago the multiplier has been derived, the higher the multiplier. If we assume that the tourism sector has changed over the years and becomes more internationally oriented, the "older" multipliers should be higher

2.5.2 Results of the Regression Analysis

The estimation results for the output multiplier equations can be found in Table 2.1. When looking at the correlation between the variables with help of a bi-variate Pearson correlation, we find that several variables are related. We find, for example, a positive significant correlation between population and area or visitors and expenditures. Therefore, the variables size of area and number of visitors are excluded from the regression analysis.

The first equation focuses on the meta-variables. If we take into account R^2, which describes the proportion of the total variation in the dependent variable (the output multiplier) explained by the regression of the variables, we see that the meta-variables describe only 12%. The equation shows us that the year of data collection is of significant importance: the more recent the data, the lower the multiplier. Furthermore, multipliers published in an article are lower than those published in a report, and those published in a paper are higher. However, in this equation these documentation variables are not significant.

The second equation uses the variables related to the characteristics of the area concerned. It appears that, in particular, the size of population is significant, the larger the population, the higher the output multiplier. Furthermore, the country dummy is significant. This dummy variable has the value 1 if the area is a country, and a 0 if the area is for example a region or a city. Because the country dummy shows a positive coefficient, this can indicate that the boundaries of countries prevent, to a certain extent, leakages.

When looking at the next column, with the tourism-specific variables we find again that the year of data is of importance, and so is the expenditures variable. This last variable indicates that more expenditures lead to higher multipliers, when no area-specific variables are taken into account. The dummies that describe the factor which attracts visitors, e.g. nature values, cultural values, or sun, are not significant in this equation.

The final equation includes all variables distinguished for the regression analysis. We find five variables that show significant coefficients. As can be found in the table, the year of data has a negative effect on the multipliers. This means that when the data are younger, the multipliers get lower. It also appears that when a multiplier

Table 2.1 Regression equations of the output multiplier

Variable	Meta-variables	Area-specific	Tourism-specific	All variables
	1	2	3	4
Constant	1.95***	1.484***	1.480***	1.720***
t-value	10.016	23.647	8.738	11.63
Year of data (0 = 1980)	–0.025*		–0.019*	–0.018**
t-value	–1.673		–1.819	–2.147
Conference paper (dummy)	0.143			0.012
t-value	0.936			0.120
Article (dummy)	–0.071			–0.426***
t-value	–0.431			–3.789
Density (100 inh/km^2)		0.005		0.013**
t-value		1.15		2.522
Population (1E 07)		0.010***		0.014**
t-value		4.972		5.912
Country (dummy)		0.200*		0.191
t-value		1.881		1.425
City (dummy)		–0.165		–0.139
t-value		–1.268		–1.087
National park (dummy)		–0.019		0.030
t-value		–0.193		0.283
Expenditures (1E 07)			0.076***	–0.015
t-value			4.383	0.563
Nature (dummy)			0.109	–0.07
t-value			1.072	–0.669
Sun (dummy)			0.049	0.202**
t-value			0.400	2.177
Culture (dummy)			–0.069	0.103
t-value			0.466	0.832
R^2	0.12	0.64	0.50	0.86
N	33	33	32	32

*** Correlation is significant at the 0.01 level (2-tailed).
** Correlation is significant at the 0.05 level (2-tailed).
* Correlation is significant at the 0.10 level (2-tailed).

is published in an article in a scientific journal, the value will be lower than when published in a paper or report. According to the values of the parameters, we may say that the output multiplier published in an article is 0.43 lower than the multiplier found in an average report commissioned by a client. Furthermore, the population density and the population size show positive coefficients with the output multiplier. In this equation, the expenditures variable has a negative sign. It is also insignificant. This indicates that the relation between output multipliers and expenditures is not easy to explain. Furthermore, in this broader context the "attraction" sun has an significant effect on the output multiplier. This is in line with what was found in an earlier similar publication (van Leeuwen et al. 2006), in which fewer tourism multipliers were included.

Looking back at the three hypotheses, we can conclude that Hypothesis 1 can be accepted; the larger the economic base, the higher the multiplier. The effect of the size of population, as well as of the density variable is positive significant. However, second Hypothesis 2 is rejected. Although the amount of expenditures is significant when only variables related to the tourism sector are taken into account, it is not significant in the total model. Furthermore, we can accept Hypothesis 3; the longer ago the multiplier has been derived, the higher the multiplier.

2.6 Rough Set Analysis

2.6.1 Introduction

Rough set analysis was developed in the early 1980s by Pawlak (1991). The method generally serves to pinpoint regularities in classified data, in order to identify the relative importance of some specific data attributes and to eliminate less relevant ones, and to discover possible cause-effect relationships by logical deterministic inference rules (van den Bergh et al. 1997). It is essentially a classification method devised for non-stochastic information. This means that categorical information (qualitative data) can be taken into consideration. Quantitative data must first be converted into qualitative or categorical data by means of a codification (Nijkamp and Pepping 1998). However, this classification of the values of the attributes is a somewhat problematic issue in the application, as the use of thresholds implies some loss of information, and the thresholds are chosen subjectively (Bruinsma et al. 2000).

The difference between the outcomes of linear regression and rough set analysis is that the first method indicates a potential causal relationship between the dependent and the independent variable. The relationship between a decision attribute (the dependent variable) and the condition attribute (the independent variable) of the rough set analysis refers to the statistical frequency at which a certain category of the decision attribute occurs in certain categories of the condition attributes (Oltmer 2003). An important product of rough set analysis is decision rules of an "if ... then ..." nature. The method aims to determine which combinations of a classified set of attributes that characterize the objects are consistent with the occurrences of variation in the dependent variable or the decision attribute (Bruinsma et al. 2000).

For this analysis we aim to describe the relationship between the decision attribute, the output multiplier, and seven condition attributes. The condition attributes are first considered as one group, and then divided into three sub-groups. The first of those subgroups describes the characteristics of the information source; the so-called "meta-variables", the second subgroup describes the characteristics of the area and the third subgroup describes the characteristics of the tourism sector. Table 2.2 shows the relevant attributes per group. Attribute classes can be found in Appendix 2.

According to van den Bergh et al. (1997), the categorization of data is seen as the most problematic issues in taxonomic experiments. For example, a loss of information of continuous variables is involved because they have to be translated into discrete ones. Another aspect of classification is that it can affect the outcomes. Different classifications can lead to different outcomes. In this study, we categorize the

Table 2.2 Attributes per group

Information source	Area	Tourism
Year of data collection Type of documentation	Size of population Geographic entity Kind of attraction to tourists Population density	Year of data collection Kind of attraction to tourists Total expenditures per year

data according to the "equal-frequency binning", in only two groups (Witten and Frank 2000). This method implies an even distribution of the attribute values over a predetermined number of bins, in this case two bins. As rough set analysis deals with monotonic relationships, and a significant number of our variables are ordinal in nature, the best option is to use two classes: relatively low and relatively high values. This will improve the interpretation of the results.

2.6.2 The Minimal Set of Reducts

First, we examine the minimal set of reducts together with their frequencies of appearance. The minimal subset of attributes, called a "reduct", ensures the same quality of classification as the total set of attributes. Often, a number of reducts can be found. However, the minimal set of reducts contains no redundant information. In an optimal situation, only one reduct occurs because, the fewer possibilities for minimal sets, the higher the "predictive power" of the information (Pawlak 1991). If an attribute appears in all reducts it is called a "core" attribute. This core attribute is the most meaningful attribute and the common part of all reducts.

When analysing the relationship between the tourism output multiplier and the seven condition attributes, it appears that three of those nine are the most important ones: year of data, kind of attraction, and geographic entity. All three variables are core variables and with no other attributes apparent in the minimal set of reducts it means that there is only one reduct which has a high predictive power. It also means, that in theory, only these three variables are necessary to predict high or low multiplier values.

If, however, we derive the reducts for the separate groups of attributes, concerning the area, the tourism sector, and the information source, we find that all seven attributes are core attributes, and therefore of equal importance.

2.6.3 The Decision Rules

To obtain decision rules we use the Rose program (Predki and Wilk 1999) to calculate the basic minimal covering. We only use those rules with a strength of 2 or more. This means that the relation described in the rule appears at least twice in the

Table 2.3 Output multiplier rules when distinguishing two equal classes

Rules related to all the attributes

	Year of data	Documentation	Population	Density	Geo-graphic	Attraction	Expenditures	Multiplier
1	2		–		2			1
2		1	–		1			1
3			–		3	4		1
4			–	1	3		1	1
5	1		–		2			2
6			–	1	4			2
7			–			1		2

Rules related to meta-data

	Year of data	Documentation	Multiplier
1	1	3	2

Rules related to the area

	Attraction	Population	Geographic	Multiplier
1	4	–	3	1
2	1	–		2
3	2	–	4	2
4	4	–	4	2

Rules related to tourism sector

	Attraction	Expenditures	Year data	Multiplier
1	4	1	2	1
2	1			2
3	2	2	1	2

data set, but in some cases it also appears seven times. Table 2.3 shows the decision rules for the output multipliers. For example, the first rule, when including all the attributes, means: IF the year of data attribute has value 2 and the geographic entity attribute has a value 2, THEN the income multiplier has a value 1. If we take a look at the classification of the data in Appendix 2, we can see that the decision rule can also be stated as: IF the year of data collection is after 1997, and the geographic entity is a national park, THEN the income multiplier has a value between 1.10 and 1.50.

The first part of Table 2.3, shows the rules when using all the attributes. Although year of data, kind of attraction and geographic entity are the most relevant ones, we are also interested in the influence of the other variables in order to be able to compare the rough set analysis results with those of the linear regression. Table 2.3 also indicates that more recent data is related to lower multipliers, and that a sunny destination relates to high multipliers and a destination with a mix of attractions to lower ones. Furthermore, multipliers published in an article and dealing with cities are related to low multipliers.

The rules which only include variables related to the publication show that, when the data is older, and the multiplier is described in a conference paper, its value is higher.

The rules including the area-specific attributes do not include the population attribute. They show that regions, especially when they have no specific attraction but a mix, often have low multiplier values. On the other hand, a country with a mix of attractions is related to higher multipliers; apparently the size of the area has a stronger effect than the kind of attraction. Furthermore, the tourism multipliers tend to be higher in sunny areas. Finally, the tourism-related rules again confirm the importance of the year of data, as well as of the attraction variable. In addition, tourism-related Rules 1 and 3 (as well Rule 4 related to all attributes) implicate that higher expenditures are related to higher multipliers.

Recalling the three hypotheses described in Sect. 2.5, it appears that from the rough set analysis we can (again) accept Hypothesis 1: "the larger the economic base, the higher the multiplier", but with less certainty. Although the size of population did not appear in any of the rules, we did find that countries relate to higher multipliers than regions or cities do. From the rough set analysis, we can also accept Hypothesis 2: Greater expenditures are related to higher multiplier values. The explanation for this can be that when the tourism sector becomes an important sector, with many visitors and expenditures, the economy as a whole is more involved with these kind of activities, resulting in higher multipliers. Furthermore, we can again accept the Hypothesis 3; the older the data from which the multiplier was derived, the higher the multiplier.

The results from the rough set analysis confirm the results from the linear regression analysis. In addition, it suggests the acceptance of Hypothesis 2 which was rejected by the linear regression analysis. However, we have to keep in mind that the method has its limitations and that it is not really suitable to draw conclusions about the complicated relationships that seem to exist (see also Fig. 2.3b) between the amount of expenditures and the tourism output multiplier.

2.7 Tourism Multipliers for Dutch Towns

The transferability of research findings is an often-mentioned problematic issue related to meta-analysis, but, at the same time, it is also one of its greatest potentials (Baaijens et al. 1997). In their study describing a meta-analysis of tourism income multipliers, Baaijens et al. state that in 1997 the transfer of existing knowledge to a similar situation had not been investigated before. Also nowadays, these kind of studies are very rare. In the Baaijens study, an interval of plausible values of unknown tourist income multipliers is derived by using the regression equations estimated from the meta-analysis. This, of course, requires the availability of data related to the variables used in the regression analysis. In this section, we want to estimate output multipliers for six Dutch towns. Although, no information is available about the number of visitors or expenditures of visitors per town, we did find information about the expenditures of tourists in several other large Dutch cities, as well as in Zandvoort, a town located at the seaside with around 16,000 inhabitants (Gemeente Zandvoort 2004), and in Heusden a small town of 6,000 inhabitants in the south of the Netherlands (www.Heusden.nl). Together with information about the relative importance of the tourism sector in the six (case-study) towns, it is possible to estimate plausible expenditures for each of them.

With this information we can use the regression equation to estimate the multiplier values. In the next step, we will first estimate tourism multipliers with the linear regression model, and then we will calculate tourism multipliers using local input–output models. This enables us to evaluate the usefulness of the results of the meta-analysis to transfer the outcomes to a similar situation.

2.7.1 Expectations Resulting from the Meta-analysis

The meta-analysis pointed out the important factors affecting the size of tourism output multipliers. Of course, for the Dutch towns, some of the factors are more relevant than others. First of all, the meta-variables are the same for all towns. However, the year of data collection, 2003, points to lower multiplier values than the average 1.56 of the meta-analysis. In addition, the (small) size of the population of the towns, between 7,000 and 20,000 inhabitants, also suggests low multiplier values. On the other hand, the attractiveness of the towns could result in a diversification of the outcomes per town: Oudewater and Bolsward, for example, are two historic towns with more cultural attractiveness, while Nunspeet is perhaps less appealing as a town but it is located near a highly appreciated nature area, "De Hoge Veluwe" which has many recreation facilities.

Table 2.4 shows the different characteristics of the towns, relevant for the value of the tourism multiplier. All towns are considered as "a city", except for Nunspeet which is regarded as being a national park, because most visitors stay in or close to De Hoge Veluwe. Furthermore, Table 2.4 also shows the multiplier value derived with help of the linear regression model.

According to the town characteristics, it would be expected that Schagen and Nunspeet would have higher multipliers because of their medium-sized population and the relatively large share of firms in tourism-related sectors. The municipality of Bolsward also has a relatively large share of firms in tourism-related sectors, but its population is relatively small. Given its relatively low population, its impacts on the multiplier values are small.

Table 2.4 Town characteristics and the estimated relative multiplier value of the six Dutch towns (2003)

Town	Population size town	Density (pop/km^2)	Share of firms in tourism related sectors (%)*	Expenditures ($ *106)**	Attraction	Multiplier values from regression model
Dalfsen	6,570	2,900	17	20	Nature+ Culture	1.08
Schagen	17,214	3,900	33	100	Culture	1.16
Bolsward	9,378	3,700	32	100	Culture	1.13
Nunspeet	19,215	3,200	27	100	Mix	1.16
Oudewater	7,745	2,800	17	50	Culture	1.09
Gemert	14,815	3,800	20	40	Mix	1.13

* Retail, catering and culture/recreation sector in 2003 (Source: own calculations from CBS data)
** Based on the share of firms in tourism related sectors and expenditures in Zandvoort, which is a seaside resort of 16,000 inhabitants receiving $300*106 of tourism expenditures (Gemeente Zandvoort, 2004), and in Heusden, a small town of 6,000 inhabitants receiving $20*106 of tourism expenditures (www.Heusden.nl).

2.7.2 Composition of Local Tourism Multipliers

To be able to evaluate the above-estimated multipliers with help of the linear regression model, we will now develop local tourism multipliers ourselves.

As mentioned in the introduction, it is important to be aware that no such thing exists as "the tourism sector" in any usual statistical definition. First of all, even sectors that are strongly oriented towards leisure activities also serve non-leisure business activities. Furthermore, different kinds of tourism require different inputs and provide different outputs. Day trippers, for example, have different expenditures than visitors who stay overnight.

According to the Dutch corporation for "Continuous Holiday Research" (Stichting Continu Vakantie Onderzoek, 2002), visitors to Dutch city-centres (day-trippers) spend on average 40% of their expenditures on shopping, 40% on catering services, and the rest, 20%, on other services.

For visitors staying overnight, it is more difficult to predict their expenditures. However, in some of the studies used for the meta-analysis, it is described how the tourism multipliers are derived. Table 2.5 shows the distribution of tourism expenditures over several sectors, as described in 7 studies. The last column shows the distribution estimated for the Dutch towns. The first two studies describe the distribution of expenditures of tourists visiting a region in Spain and Denmark. These tourists spend most of their money on accommodation, around 60%. The other studies focus on cities, of which Christchurch and Akaroa in New Zealand are the smallest and most similar to the Dutch towns. In these cities, around 30% of total expenditures are spent on accommodation, another 19–24% on shopping and around 23% on restaurants and catering. Taking all this information together resulted in the estimated distribution of expenditures in the Dutch towns. This is in line with the "general" distribution that Chang (2001) proposes in his dissertation about variation in tourism multipliers.

Table 2.5 Distribution of tourism expenditures of visitors staying overnight over different sectors, as described in 7 studies, and estimated for Dutch towns

	Galicia	Denmark	Washington	Christ-church	Akaroa	Amsterdam	Edinburgh	Dutch towns
	Region	Island	City	City	Town	City	City	Town
Accommodation	60	60	30	28	28	50	26	30
Recreational Facilities	9	6	8	9	19	–	6	10
Shopping	7	7	12	24	19	35	22	20
Restaurants and catering	–	23	40	24	22	–	41	25
Transport (local)	2	4	6	8	1	–	–	2
Other	22	0	4	7	11	15	5	13

2.7.3 *Tourism Output Multipliers for the Six Dutch Towns and their Hinterland*

In this thesis, we derived output multipliers for several sectors located in the six Dutch towns (by using SAM tables). The exact method was described in Sect. 2.5. However, Table 2.6 shows the type II output multipliers for the sectors which are related to tourism, and which are thus necessary to estimate a tourist multiplier.

Table 2.7 shows that, on average, the tourism multiplier for the Dutch towns is 1.13 for day trippers, and 1.14 for visitors who stay overnight. This value is relatively low, even when taking into account the small area and the year of data, but it is not implausible. In addition, Butcher et al. (2003) derive a tourism multiplier for a town of less than 1,000 inhabitants in New-Zealand (Akaroa), and that multiplier also has a value of 1.13.

The tourism multiplier values per town are quite diverse. First of all, the multiplier of Dalfsen is relatively low: only 1.08 for day trippers, and 1.10 for visitors staying overnight. But, according to the relevant factors which resulted from the meta-analysis (Table 2.4), this was expected. The estimated multiplier form the linear regression model has the same value. It was also expected that the tourism multiplier of Oudewater would be relatively low which can be confirmed by our calculations. Both towns have a small population and a low share of firms related to

Table 2.6 Estimated type II output multipliers for tourism related sectors in six Dutch towns

	Transport Services	Retail Services	Hotels and catering	Public administration and recreation*	Average of all sectors
Dalfsen	1.36	1.02	1.14	1.02	1.10
Schagen	1.42	1.24	1.16	1.09	1.20
Bolsward	1.29	1.15	1.14	1.09	1.17
Nunspeet	1.03	1.07	1.43	1.06	1.10
Oudewater	1.02	1.20	1.02	1.10	1.05
Gemert	1.04	1.04	1.11	1.02	1.04
Average	1.19	1.12	1.17	1.06	1.11

* Public administration, education, recreation and other services

Table 2.7 Tourism output multipliers for the six Dutch towns

	Day trippers	Visitors staying overnight
Dalfsen	1.08	1.10
Schagen	1.18	1.17
Bolsward	1.13	1.13
Nunspeet	1.23	1.28
Oudewater	1.11	1.08
Gemert	1.07	1.08
Average	1.13	1.14

the tourism sector. Furthermore, in line with our expectations, Schagen has a high multiplier value and Bolsward a medium one. However, the linear regression model does not predict the multiplier for Nunspeet very well. Although, the regression model does predict a relatively high multiplier value (1.16), the actual value is even higher. Furthermore, the multiplier value of Gemert is lower than was expected from the regression model. In spite of the larger population of Gemert, the actual tourism multiplier is the lowest of all the towns.

This indicates that for these small towns, the regression model predicts the multiplier values quite well, but there are some discrepancies.

2.8 Conclusions

In this chapter we have performed a meta-analysis on tourism output multipliers. The basic research question we addressed in this paper is: "Which characteristics of the documentation source, the research area, or the tourism sector affect the size of the output tourism multiplier?"

After the first analysis in which we considered average multiplier values according to relevant characteristics, a linear regression analysis and a rough set analysis were performed. Therefore we formulated three hypotheses:

1. The larger the economic base, the higher the multiplier.
2. The more visitors or expenditures of visitors, the higher the multiplier.
3. The longer ago the multiplier has been derived, the higher the multiplier.

Trying to answer the basic research question in this paper, it appears first of all that the characteristics of the documentation source do have an effect on the size of the multiplier. According to all three analyses we found that especially conference papers estimate higher multipliers than articles do. We also found that recently derived multipliers often have lower values. This can be related to the increasing openness of local economies that is characteristic of many economies nowadays.

As can be found in many other publications, it appears that multipliers for countries are higher, and so are multipliers for areas with large populations, which is consistent with the expectation that higher multiplier values are expected for larger economies. In addition, national multipliers are higher than regional multipliers, probably because country boundaries decrease import leakage (Hypothesis 1). The year of data has a negative impact, which confirms Hypothesis 3.

Seemingly, the outcomes of the rough set analysis are complementary to the outcomes of the linear regression because, besides accepting Hypotheses 1 and 3, Hypothesis 2 can be accepted as well.

Finally, we tried to transfer our findings to a similar situation: six Dutch towns. Therefore, we used the total linear regression model to predict the multiplier values of the towns, taking into account the population, density, expenditures, kind of attraction and importance of the tourism sector per town.

It appeared that the relative multiplier values for the tourism sector in six Dutch towns could be "predicted" quite well by the linear regression model. The predicted multiplier for Nunspeet was underestimated and for Gemert overestimated by the regression model. This seems to result from the variables "nature" and "expenditures", which are both positively related to the output multiplier, when only tourism-specific variables are included, and negatively for the total regression model. Apparently, further research on these two variables is needed in order to find out how they exactly affect tourism output multipliers.

Furthermore, both the explorative analysis and the rough set analysis showed that the amount of expenditures has an effect on the output multipliers. However, in which way is not exactly clear.

Appendix 1: Publications Used for the Meta-analysis

Butcher G, Fairweather JR, Simmons DG (2003) The economic impact of tourism on Christchurch City and Akaroa Township. Tourism Recreation Research and Education Centre, Report No. 37

Castanon L, Pereira X (2007) Measuring the impact of tourism on production by means of an Input–Output Model of interior flows: An application to Galicia. In: Matias A, Nijkamp P, Neto P (eds) Advances in modern tourism research, economic perspectives. Physica-Verlag, Heidelberg

Enlish DBK, Kriesel W, Leeworthy VR, Wiley PC (1996) Economic contribution of recreating visitors to the Florida Keys/Key West. National Oceanic and Atmospheric Administration, Strategic Environmental Assessments Division, Silverspring MD

Fretchling DC, Horvath E (1999) Estimating the multiplier effects of tourism expenditures on a local economy through a regional Input–Output Model. J Travel Res 37:324–332

Hiles G, Webb R (1995) The economic impact of tourism in Guam. Bureau of Labor Statistics, Guam Finance Commission, Guam

Hjerpe EE, Kim YS (2007) Regional economic impacts of Grand Canyon river runners. J Environ Manag 85:137–149

Khan H, Seng CF, Cheong WK (1990) Tourism multiplier effects on Singapore. Ann Tourism Res 17(3):408–418

Kweka J, Morrissey O, Blake A (2001) Is tourism a key Sector in Tanzania? Input–output analysis of income, output, employment and tax revenue. TTRI Discussion paper 2001/1

Limburg B van (1997) Overnight tourism in Amsterdam 1982–1993 – a forecasting approach. Tourism Manag 18(7):465–468

McDavid H (2003) An input–output analysis of the Jamaican hospitality and tourism sector. Soc Econ Stud 52(1):161–184

McDonough M, Fried J, Witter-Potter K, Stevens J, Stynes D (1999) The role of natural resources in community and regional economic stability in the Eastern Upper Peninsula. Michigan Agricultural Experiment Station. Michigan State University. Research Report 568

NSW National Parks and Wildlife Service (2000) The Contribution of Warrumbungle national park to regional economic development. NPWS Environmental Economics Series

NSW National Parks and Wildlife Service (2001) The contribution of Sturt national park, Kinchega national park and Mutawintji national park to regional economic development. NPWS Environmental Economics Series

Parlett G, Fletcher J, Cooper C (1995) The Impact of Tourism on the Old Town Edinburgh. Tourism Manag 16(5):355–36

Propst D, Stynes DJ, Sun Y (2002) Economic impact of Badlands national park, visitors on the local economy, 2000. Michigan State University, Dept of Park Recreation and Tourism Resources, East Lansing MI

Saayman M, Saayman A, Naudé W (2000) Economic and sectoral effects of tourist spending in South Africa: Regional implications. Paper presented at the ABAS International Conference, 10–12 July, Prague, Czech Republic

Smyth D (1999) Economic impact of national visitor spending. Gleaning visitor spending patterns from secondary data, Glacier national park-1990. Michigan State University, Dept of Park Recreation and Tourism Resources, East Lansing MI
Stynes D (2002) Bay county, economic impacts of visitor spending 1999–2001. Michigan State University. Dept of Park Recreation and Tourism Resources
Stynes D (2002) Economic impact of great smoky Mt. national park, visitors on the local region 1997–2000. Michigan State University. Dept of Park Recreation and Tourism Resources, East Lansing MI
Stynes D (2002) Michigan Statewide Tourism Spending and Economic Impact Estimates 1998–2000. Michigan State University. Dept of Park Recreation and Tourism Resources, East Lansing MI
Stynes D, Warzecha C (2002) Washtenaw county, summary of tourism impacts 1999–2001. Michigan State University. Dept of Park Recreation and Tourism Resources, East Lansing MI
Sun Y, Stynes DJ, Propst D (2002) Economic impact of visitors to Rainier national park 2000. Michigan State University. Dept of Park Recreation and Tourism Resources, East Lansing MI
Var T, Quayson J (1985) The multiplier impact of tourism in the Okanagan. Ann Tourism Res 12:497–514
Wood N, Halbrendt C, Liang C (2000) The role of tourism in a small economy of Montpellier, Vermont. Paper presented in the ICSB World Conference, Australia, June 7–10, 2000
Wood N, Liang K (2001) The impact of the tourism sector on the Vermont economy 1999–2000. Dept of Community Development and Applied Economics, University of Vermont. Burlington, Vermont
Yan M, Wall G (2001) Economic perspectives on tourism in China. Tourism Hospitality Res 3(3): 257–275
Zhang J, Rassing CR (2000) Tourism impact studies, the case of Bornholm. Research centre of Bornholm, Denmark

Appendix 2: Attribute Classes When Using Two Equal Classes

Decision attribute	Classes		
Output multiplier			
1	1.10–1.50		
2	1.51–2.75		
Condition attribute	Classes	Condition attribute	Classes
Population	(#)	Publication	
1	0–323,000	1	Article
2	323,000–123,000,000	2	Report
		3	Conference Paper
Expenditures	(Mil. $/year)		
1	0–300	Attraction	
2	300–13.000	1	Sun
		2	Nature
Density	(Inh/km^2)	3	Culture
1	0–50	4	Mix
2	51–4.000		
		Geographic	
Year of data	(Year)	1	City
1	1980–1997	2	National Park
2	1998–2004	3	Region
		4	Country/State

References

Armstrong H, Taylor J (2000) Regional economics and policy. Blackwell, Oxford

Baaijens SR, Nijkamp P (1996) Meta-analytic methods for comparative and exploratory policy research, an application to the assessment of regional tourist multipliers. J Policy Model 22(7): 821–858

Baaijens SR, Nijkamp P, van Montfoort K. (1997) Explanatory meta-analysis of tourist income multipliers an application of comparative research to island economics. Tinbergen Institute discussion paper 97-017/3, Rotterdam

Begg CB (1994) Publication bias. In: Cooper H, Hedges LV (eds) The handbook of research synthesis. Russell Sage Foundation, New York

van den Bergh JCJM, Button KJ, Nijkamp P (1997) Meta-analysis in environmental economics. Kluwer, Dordrecht

Brander LM, van Beukering P, Cesar HSJ (2007) The recreational value of coral reefs: A meta-analysis. Ecol Econ 63(1):209–218

Bruinsma F, Nijkamp P, Vreeker R (2000) Spatial planning of industrial sites in Europe: A benchmark approach to competitiveness analysis about the suitability of sites for economic activities. Research Memorandum 2000-7, VU University, Amsterdam

Butcher G, Fairweather JR, Simmons DG (2003) The economic impact of tourism on Christchurch City and Akaroa Township. Tourism Recreation Research and Education Centre, Report No. 37

Chang WH (2001) Variations in multipliers and related economic ratios for recreation and tourism impact analysis. Dissertation submitted to Michigan State University, Department of Park, Recreation and Tourism resources

Fletcher JE (1989) Input–output analysis and tourism impact studies. Ann Tourism Res 16: 514–529

Frechtling DC (1994) Assessing the economic impacts of travel and tourism – Introduction to travel economic impact estimation. In: Ritchie JRB, Goeldner CR (eds) Travel, tourism and hospitality research, second edition. Wiley, New York

Freeman D, Sultan E (1999) The economic impact of tourism in Israel: A multi regional input–output analysis. In: Rietveld P, Shefer D (eds), Regional development in an age of structural economic change. Ashgate, Aldershot

Gemeente Zandvoort (2004). Zandvoort in economische en toeristische cijfers 2003. Bespiegelingen over economische en toeristische ontwikkelingen. Gemeente Zandvoort, Zandvoort, The Netherlands

Giaoutzi M, Nijkamp P (2006) Emerging trends in tourism development in an open world. In: Giaoutzi M, Nijkamp P (eds) Tourism and regional development: New pathways. Ashgate, Aldershot

Glass GV, McGaw B, Smith ML (1981) Meta-analysis in social research. SAGE Publications, Beverly Hills

Holmgren J (2007) Meta-analysis of public transport demand. Trans Res A Policy Pract 41(10): 1021–1035

van Leeuwen ES, Nijkamp P, Rietveld P (2006) Economic impacts of tourism: A meta-analytic comparison of regional output multipliers. In: Giaoutzi M, Nijkamp P (eds) Tourism and regional development: New pathways. Ashgate, Aldershot

Miller RE, Blair PD (1985) Input–output analysis: Foundations and extensions. Prentice Hall, Englewood Cliffs NJ

Nijkamp P, Pepping G (1998) Meta-analysis for explaining the variance in public transport demand elasticities in Europe. J Trans Stat 1(1):1–14

Nijkamp P, Vindigni G (2000) A multidimensional comparative assessment methodology for policy analysis: a multi-country study of the agricultural sector. J Environ Syst 28:71– 90

Oltmer K (2003) Agricultural policy, land use and environmental effects, studies in quantitative research synthesis. Dissertation. Tinbergen Institute Research Memorandum no. 318, Amsterdam

Pawlak Z (1991) Rough sets: Theoretical aspects of reasoning about data. Kluwer Academic Publishers, Dordrecht

Pearce D (1981) Tourist development. Longman, New York

Predki B, Wilk S (1999) Rough Set Based Data Exploration Using ROSE System. In: Ras ZW, Skowron A (eds) Foundations of intelligent systems, lecture notes in artificial intelligence 1609. Springer-Verlag, Berlin, pp 172–180

Stichting Continu Vakantie Onderzoek (2002) Onderzoek 'Toeristisch bezoek aan steden 2001'. NBTC-NIPO Research, Leidschendam

Stynes DJ (1998) http://www.msu.edu/course/prr/840/econimpact/multipliers.htm

Witten IH, Frank E (2000) Data mining: Practical machine learning tools and techniques with Java implementation. Morgan Kaufman, San Francisco

Chapter 3
An Optimized System Dynamics Approach for a Hotel Chain Management

Valerio Lacagnina and Davide Provenzano

3.1 Introduction

The proposed model consists of an integrated system dynamics-data envelopment analysis approach to value, in a dynamic framework, the effects over time of the policies implemented according to the relative efficiency analysis. Rooms' price and competing facilities (the hedonics) are the decision variables to move in order to push the hotels towards a higher relative efficiency at the end of the observation periods.

In fact, in competitive markets as tourism, hotels compete for money offering differentiated quality. Moreover, according to the microeconomic theory, a producer of differentiated goods is not a price taker but a price maker. Therefore, we assume that the decision maker of the hotel chain can freely set the rooms' price and the hedonics that will increase the relative economic efficiency of all the hotels of the chain.

The proposed model treats the rooms' pricing and the hedonic setting problem in an environment characterized by uncertainty of the customers' preferences.

The relative efficiency analysis is carried out by making use of data envelopment analysis that identifies the peer group and targets for the inefficient units. The dynamic analysis of the effects over time of the policies implemented is carried out using system dynamics methodology.

This combined approach will help the decision maker in answering the following questions: which hotels of the chain will be attractive, and which ones will be efficient? What adjustments on prices and hedonics will attract more tourism demand? What are the dynamic effects of the DEA policies?

The remaining sections of this paper are organized as follows. Section 3.2 is devoted to a brief survey of the theoretical background with particular attention to data envelopment analysis and system dynamics. Section 3.3 describes our model both from the customer side and the hotel management side. Section 3.4 shows the

V. Lacagnina (✉)
Faculty of Economics, Universitd di Palermo, Palermo, Italy
e-mail: ricopa@unipa.it

Á. Matias et al. (eds.), *Advances in Tourism Economics*,
DOI 10.1007/978-3-7908-2124-6_3, © Physica-Verlag Heidelberg 2009

parameters of the model and the results of the conducted experiments. Finally, Sect. 3.5 concludes the paper.

3.2 State of the Art and Theoretical Background

The analysis of the hotels' efficiency up to now represents a neglected area. There is just a small number of studies among which the earliest ones make use of ratios to evaluate the performance of the lodging industry (Baker and Riley 1994), or use the break even analysis to discern the effectiveness of tourism management (Wijeysinghe 1993) or the yield management (Brotherton and Mooney 1992; Donaghy et al. 1995) to enhance hotels' profitability. In the efficiency context, DEA techniques have been applied by Anderson et al. (1999), Hwang and Chang (2003), Barros (2004, 2005), and Barros and Mascarenhas (2005).

System dynamics methodology is also very new in this research field. The only recent example we know is Georgantas (2003) who uses a system dynamics simulation model to test Cyprus' hotel value chain and profitability. An example of integration of system dynamics with an economic model is illustrated by Smith and van Ackere (2002).

Two papers, Png, (1988) and Scott et al. (1995) share a common theme with our study: the optimal hotel pricing cum capacity-utilization problem within an uncertain demand environment. They both deduce that optimal strategy leaves some unused capacity.

3.2.1 Data Envelopment Analysis

Data envelopment analysis is a linear programming based technique for measuring the relative performance of organizational units where the presence of multiple inputs and outputs makes comparisons difficult. Indeed, when the activity of measuring and comparing the efficiency of relatively homogeneous units (authority departments, schools, hospitals, shops, banks, and so on) involves multiple inputs and outputs related to different resources, activities and environmental factors, the usual measure of efficiency

$$\text{efficiency} = \frac{\text{output}}{\text{input}}$$

is often inadequate.

In fact, the initial assumption is that the measure of technical efficiency requires a common set of weights to be applied across all decision making units (DMUs). This immediately raises the problem of how such a set of weights can be obtained. Such a problem was addressed the first time by Farrell (1957) and developed by Farrell and Fieldhouse (1962), focusing on the construction of a hypothetical efficient unit, as a weighted average of efficient units, to act as a comparator for an inefficient one. Later, Charnes et al. (1978) recognized the legitimacy of the proposal that each unit might value inputs and outputs differently and therefore it should be allowed to adopt a set of weights which shows it in the most favourable light in comparison to the other units.

Therefore, by making a generalization of the Farrell's technical efficiency measure, Charnes, Cooper, and Rhodes first introduced the data envelopment analysis to describe what is a mathematical programming approach to the construction of production frontiers and the measurement of efficiency of developed frontiers. In their general-purpose DEA they assumes constant return-to-scale (CRS) and an input orientation. A few years later Banker et al. (1984) developed a variable returns-to-scale (VRS) model. Other models are the additive model (Charnes et al. 1985), the multiplicative model (Charnes et al. 1982), the cone-ratio DEA model (Charnes et al. 1990, the assurance region DEA model (Thompson et al. 1990), and Thompson et al. 1986), and the super-efficiency model (Anderson and Peterson 1993).

Since 1978 over 4000 articles, books and dissertation have been published and DEA has rapidly extended to dummy or categorical variables, discretionary and non-discretionary variables, incorporating value judgments, longitudinal analysis, weight restrictions, stochastic DEA, non-parametric Malmquist indices, technical change in DEA and many other topics.

Up to now the DEA measure has been used to evaluate and compare educational departments (schools, colleges and universities), health care (hospitals, clinics), prisons, agricultural production, banking, armed forces, sports, market research, transportation (highway maintenance), courts, benchmarking, index number construction and many other applications.

One of the main characteristics of DEA is its flexibility in the choice of weights for the different inputs and outputs. Therefore, DEA may be appropriate where units can properly value inputs or outputs differently, or where there is a high uncertainty or disagreement over the value of some inputs or outputs. The heart of the analysis lies in finding the "best" virtual producer (a single peer or a peer group) for each real producer (virtual because this producer does not necessarily exist and two or more DMUs can be combined to form a composite producer). If the virtual producer is better than the original producer by either making more output with the same input or making the same output with less input then the original producer is inefficient. By identifying the efficiency score of each DMU in the sample, the slack variables in inputs and outputs of the inefficient DMUs and the peer group of efficient ones, DEA is one of the most promising techniques for the improvement of efficiency.

Yet, the same characteristics that make DEA a powerful tool can also create problems. An analyst should keep these limitations in mind when choosing whether or not to use DEA. First of all, since DEA is an extreme point technique, noise (even symmetrical noise with zero mean) such as measurement error can cause significant problems. Second, DEA is good at estimating "relative" efficiency of a DMU but it converges very slowly to "absolute" efficiency. In other words, it can tell you how well you are doing compared to your peers but not compared to a "theoretical maximum". Thirdly, DEA is a nonparametric technique and, therefore, statistical hypothesis tests are difficult. Finally, since a standard formulation of DEA creates a separate linear program for each DMU, large problems can be computationally intensive.

More detailed reviews of the methodology are presented by Seiford and Thrall (1990), Ali and Seiford (1993), Lovell (1994), Charnes et al (1994), Seiford (1988, 1996), Thanassoulis and Dyson (1988), Dyson and Thanassoulis (1988), and Thanassoulis et al. (1987).

3.2.2 System Dynamics

System dynamics is a methodology for modelling, studying and managing complex feedback systems by making use of a feedback-based, object-oriented approach. SD was developed initially by Jay W. Forrester and his seminal book Industrial Dynamics (Forrester 1961) is still a significant statement of philosophy and methodology in the field. Since its publication, the span of applications has grown extensively and now encompasses works in corporate planning and policy design, public management and policy, biological and medical modelling, energy and the environment, theory development in the natural and social sciences, dynamic decision making, complex nonlinear dynamics. According to Simonovic and Fahmy (1999), system dynamics is based on a theory of system structure and a set of tools for representing complex systems and analyzing their dynamic behaviour.

The most important feature of system dynamics is that it helps to elucidate the endogenous structure of the system under consideration, and demonstrates how different elements of the system actually relate to one another. This then facilitates experimentation as relations within the system are changed to reflect different decisions. Unlike other scientists, who study the world by breaking it up into smaller and smaller pieces, system dynamicists therefore look at things as a whole. A system can be anything from a steam engine, to a bank account, to a basketball team.

What makes system dynamics different from other approaches used for studying complex systems is the use of *feedback loops*, where a change in one variable affects other variables over time, which in turn affects the original variable, and so on. A typical system dynamics model is composed of four basic building blocks: *stock*, *flow*, *connector* and *converter*. Stocks (levels) are used to represent anything that accumulates; for instance water stored in storage or dams. Flows (rates) represent activities that fill and drain stocks; an example includes releases or inflows. Connectors (arrows) are used to establish the relationship among variables in the model while the direction of the arrow indicates the relationship of the dependency. They carry information from an element to another one in the model. Converters transform input into output. Stocks and flows help to describe how a system is connected by feedback loops which create the nonlinearity found in real systems. Models are built by making use of a computer software to run the simulations. As long as such a dynamic model is a good representation of the problem being studied, running "what if" simulations to test certain policies on such a model can greatly aid understanding how the system changes over time. Moreover, since the resulting structure of the model and the way it actually works is the result of the hypothesis made in building the model, the inherent flexibility and transparency of the model is particularly helpful to understand the underlying dynamics in the observed behaviour of the system. Therefore, compared with the conventional simulation approaches, system dynamics can better represent how different changes in basic elements can affect the dynamics of the system in the future.

3.3 The Model

Let us suppose to have an economic system composed by a hotel chain on one side and its potential customers on the other side. Each hotel of the chain has a certain number of single, double and familiar rooms and a set of attractive factors. The room's price depends on the hotel chain management policies and on the hedonics as well. The latter are the result of external factors, like tourism attractiveness, and internal factors as the facilities offered by the hotel. Customers rationally choose the hotel according to a quality/price ratio and matching the price for the room to book with the price she/he wants to pay.

We develop a dynamic model combining customer side with the hotel management side to analyse the interaction between demand and supply in the lodging industry and to evaluate the effect of the efficiency policies adopted by the decision makers on the attractiveness of each hotel.

Figure 3.1 depicts the system dynamic model (SD) as composed by the two sides. The hotel management registers bookings and lodgings and periodically conducts a relative efficiency analysis (DEA) to identify how to modify rooms' price and the hedonics of the inefficient hotels. The SD model is developed using Powersim Studio 2005 while DEA is carried out by EMS ver 1.3.0.

We suppose to have N hotels belonging to the chain (with $i = 1,2,\ldots,N$). Let r be the type of the room where $r = 1, 2, 3$ indicates single, double and familiar room

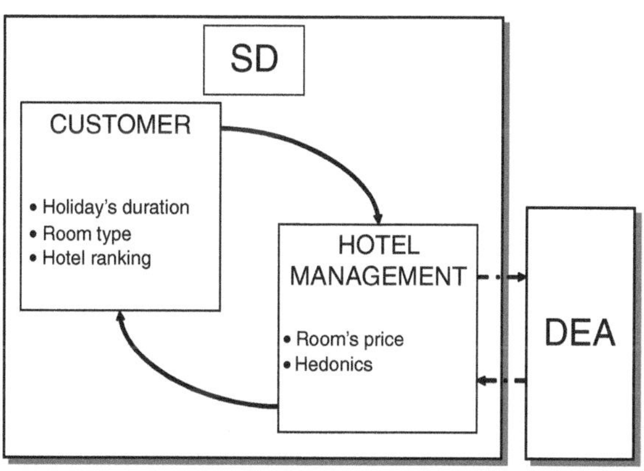

Fig. 3.1 The system dynamics-DEA model

respectively. We use to indicate the price of the room type r for the i-th hotel, while p_c^r is the price the customer wants to pay for the room type r. Let h_i be the hedonics and n_i^r the number of rooms of type r for the i-th hotel of the chain. We also define $p_{\min}^r$, $p_{\max}^r$ the minimum and the maximum price of room type r, and $h_{\min}$, $h_{\max}$ the minimum and the maximum hedonics value of hotels of the chain. The d_c^r variable indicates the number of nights the customer wants to book for room type r. Let T be the number of simulation days (with $t = 1, 2, \ldots, T$) and K the maximum number of bookings within a day. DEA is run at the end of each semester.

3.3.1 Customer Side

The potential customer enters the market of lodging having already chosen the room type r and the duration of the holiday d_c^r. She/He is assumed to have complete information regarding both the hedonics and the rooms' price for each of the hotels of the chain. This hypothesis is not really far from reality due to the development of the Information Technology and, therefore, she/he has only to decide which of the hotels of the chain is the best according to her/his preferences expressed in terms of priceand quality h_i. In fact, on the demand side, h_i represents an important decision factor because room comfort, quality of service, hotel facilities, measure the attractiveness of the hotel i, whereas rooms' price works in the opposite direction. Each visitor balances hedonic and price factors and ranks the hotels belonging to the chain as follows:

$$\text{rank}(i,r) = QI(i) \times PI^r(i)$$

where $QI(i)$ is the quality index function of the hotel i, and $PI^r(i)$ is the price index function of the hotel i for the room type r.

The function QI: $[h_{\min}, h_{\max}] \rightarrow [0,1]$ is defined as:

$$QI(i) = \frac{h_i}{h_{\max}}, \quad i = 1,2,\ldots,N$$

The set of functions PI^r:$[p_{\min}^r, p_{\max}^r] \rightarrow [0,1]$ is defined as:

$$PI_i^r = \begin{cases} \frac{p_{\max}^r - p_i^r}{p_{\max}^r - p_{\min}^r} & \text{if} \quad p_c^r = p_{\min}^r \le p_i^r \le p_{\max}^r \quad \text{(a)} \\ \frac{p_i^r - p_{\min}^r}{p_{\max}^r - p_{\min}^r} & \text{if} \quad p_{\min}^r \le p_i^r \le p_{\max}^r = p_c^r \quad \text{(b)} \\ \frac{1}{2}\frac{p_i^r - p_c^r}{p_c^r - p_{\min}^r} + 1 & \text{if} \quad p_{\min}^r \le p_i^r \le p_c^r \le p_{\max}^r \quad \text{(c)} \\ \frac{p_{\max}^r - p_i^r}{p_{\max}^r - p_c^r} & \text{if} \quad p_{\min}^r < p_c^r \le p_i^r \le p_{\max}^r \quad \text{(d)} \\ 0 & \text{otherwise} \end{cases} \tag{3.1}$$

Figure 3.2 depicts the $PI^r(i)$ function for the different values of p_c^r and . In particular, case (a) represents condition (3.1a) where the customer wants to book the

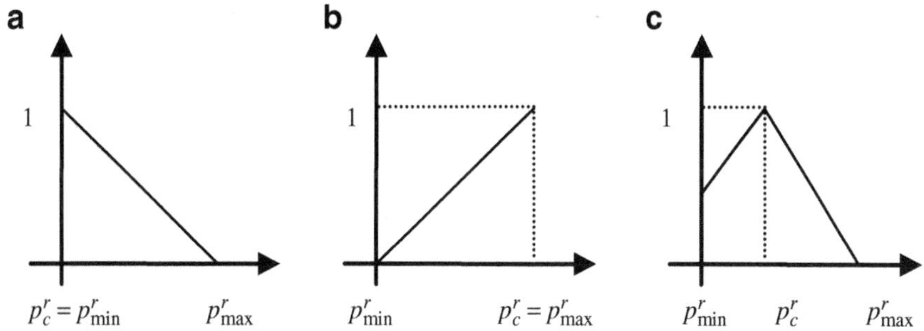

Fig. 3.2 $PI^r(i)$ function

room with the lowest price, case (b) condition (3.1b) where the customer wants to book the room with the highest price, and finally case (c) conditions (3.1c) and (3.1d) together where the customer wants to book a room with a price between the lowest and the highest with a weight of 0.5 assigned to the minimum room's price in the hotel chain to take into consideration that the customers prefers to pay less than more.

The rank(i,r) is used to sort the hotels, in a way to put the hotels with the higher hedonic value h_i and price close to or lower than p_c^r in the highest positions. If the chosen hotel has no vacancies the customer selects the next one with a lower rank. A maximum of K bookings per day are allowed.

Without loss of generality, we assume that every potential guest of the hotel chain is looking for a room to be available since the following day. We also assume that cancellations are not allowed.

3.3.2 Hotel Management Side

Figure 3.3 depicts the structure of the hotel management side as composed by the booking system, the room management and the centralized hotel chain management.

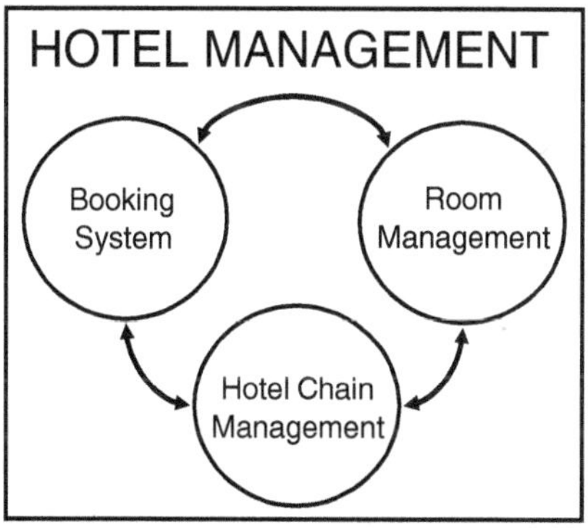

Fig. 3.3 The structure of the hotel management side

Each hotel possesses n_i^r rooms for each type. If a reservation is made, the booking system of the hotel chain immediately update the vacancies in the hotel selected by the client reducing the available rooms. According to the reservation received by the booking system, the rooms management assigns the first vacant room in the selected hotel to the client and keeps the room taken for all the holiday period. When the reservation period elapses, the room management system increases the vacancies of the hotels with the room again available.

Looking at the rooms taken every day the system dynamics model, which implements the hotel management structure, calculates the daily revenues for each hotel as follows:

$$\text{Rev}(i,t) = \sum_{r=1}^{3} \sum_{j=1}^{n_i^r} b_i^r(t) p_i^r(t)$$

with $b_i^r(t)$ a binary variable indicating if the room r in the i-th hotel is busy or not. An index of revenue efficiency is computed every day for each hotel:

$$I_{\text{Rev}}(i,t) = \frac{\sum_{r=1}^{3} \sum_{j=1}^{n_i^r} b_i^r(t) p_i^r(t)}{\sum_{r=1}^{3} \sum_{j=1}^{n_i^r} p_i^r(t)}$$

Such an index is the ratio between the hotel's actual daily revenues and its maximum potential daily revenues as if it were fully booked. Therefore the higher this index, the higher the revenue efficiency, and the higher the operational level of the hotel will be. The manager may decide to vary room's prices and hedonics in order to improve the attractiveness of each hotel and to increase its relative efficiency.

At the end of each semester of the time horizon T, a DEA optimization is carried out to identify the peer group and the inefficient hotels. We utilise a *dual, variable return to scale, input oriented, radial model with weights restrictions* formalized as follows:

$$\begin{aligned}
&\min_{\theta_i,\lambda} \theta_i \\
\text{s.t.}& \\
&-y_i + \mathbf{Y}\lambda \geq 0 \quad i = 1,2,\ldots,N \\
&\theta_i \mathbf{x}_i - \mathbf{X}\lambda \geq \mathbf{0} \\
&\mathbf{1}\lambda = 1 \\
&\lambda \geq \mathbf{0}
\end{aligned} \tag{3.2}$$

where θ_i represents the efficiency score for the hotel i, $\mathbf{X}$ is the $4 \times N$ input matrix with prices ($r = 1,2,3$) and the hedonics h_i in the rows, $\mathbf{Y}$ is the $1 \times N$ output matrix of the hotels' economical efficiency, $\mathbf{x}_i$ is the input vector of the hotel to score and

y_i the scalar representing the output value of the same hotel. $\boldsymbol{\lambda}$ is the $N \times 1$ vector of weights of the inputs and the output in the i-th linear program. **1** is a vector of ones.

The dual form has been used to reduce the computational effort required by the optimization. Moreover the dual solution returns inputs and outputs' values that are directly comparable to the original data. The Variable Return to Scales model allows us to capture measures of scale inefficiency as we will see in the next section, whereas the input oriented measure quantifies the input reduction needed for the hotel to become efficient holding the outputs constant. Dual, input oriented, radial models give the measure θ_i that reduces the input vector proportionally (radially) to a value as small as possible holding the actual output level. This means that the efficiency frontier is reached from the inefficient unit by a proportional reduction of all the input variables. Finally, in order to control the variability of both the double and familiar rooms' prices and the hedonics, weights restrictions are imposed as follows:

$$\begin{aligned} \alpha_{\min}^{2,1} &\leq \frac{p_i^2}{p_i^1} \leq \alpha_{\max}^{2,1}, \\ \alpha_{\min}^{3,1} &\leq \frac{p_i^3}{p_i^1} \leq \alpha_{\max}^{3,1} \\ \alpha_{\min}^{h,1} &\leq \frac{h_i}{p_i^1} \leq \alpha_{\max}^{h,1} \end{aligned} \tag{3.3}$$

where $\alpha_{\min}^{\bullet,\bullet}$ and $\alpha_{\max}^{\bullet,\bullet}$ are the lowest and the highest value allowed for each ratio respectively. The use of weights restriction allows us to define an assurance region limiting the feasible region to some special area.

3.4 Experimental Results

Data used to run our simulations are displayed in Table 3.1. The number of hotels in the chain has been fixed according to the DEA convention that the minimum number of DMUs is greater then three times the sum of the number of inputs and outputs (Raab and Lichty 2002).

The time horizon T for the simulations has been set in two years but, since the efficient analysis is run at the end of each semester, data collected refer to four observation periods which are sufficient to illustrate trends and to get the purpose of the study. A longer time horizon would not provide further relevant information. Table 3.2 shows the room distribution per hotel.

The results of our simulations are depicted in Fig. 3.4. It is clear that from the first semester to the fourth, there is a substantial improvement of the scores values obtained. This result is supported not only by the increasing trend of the revenue efficiency (showing a better allocative efficiency) but also by the reduction of its volatility, as depicted in Fig. 3.5. Moreover, this result shows an homogenization of the hotels' revenue efficiency together with the DEA scoring (technical efficiency).

An interesting result coming from the dynamic analysis conducted is shown in Table 3.3.

Table 3.1 Simulation data

Variable name	Simulation value
T	2 years of 364 days
K	256 per day
N	16
$\sum_{r=1}^{3} n_i^r$	100
$[p_{\min}^1, p_{\max}^1]$	[85,125]
$[p_{\min}^2, p_{\max}^2]$	[150,240]
$[p_{\min}^3, p_{\max}^3]$	[240,340]
$[h_{\min}, h_{\max}]$	[5,10]
R	{1,2,3} with probability 0.5, 0.3, and 0.2 respectively
d_c^r	{1,2,. . .,7} with the same probability
p_c^r	Uniform($p_{\min}^r, p_{\max}^r$)
$\alpha_{\min}^{2,1}$	1.5
$\alpha_{\max}^{2,1}$	2
$\alpha_{\min}^{3,1}$	2.5
$\alpha_{\max}^{3,1}$	3
$\alpha_{\min}^{h,1}$	0.057
$\alpha_{\max}^{h,1}$	0.082

The Variable Return to Scale (VRS) efficiency score provides an upper bound to the Constant Return to Scale (CRS) efficiency measure. The difference between the two measures of efficiency is defined as the measure of scale inefficiency. It expresses the additional gain in efficiency that could be obtained if the hotels were

Table 3.2 Single, double and familiar rooms per hotel

Hotel	Single room	Double room	Familiar room
1	58	30	12
2	44	36	20
3	59	17	24
4	48	41	11
5	58	31	11
6	56	18	26
7	47	36	17
8	54	31	15
9	65	18	17
10	69	8	23
11	51	39	10
12	55	18	27
13	58	16	26
14	61	22	17
15	59	22	19
16	46	33	21

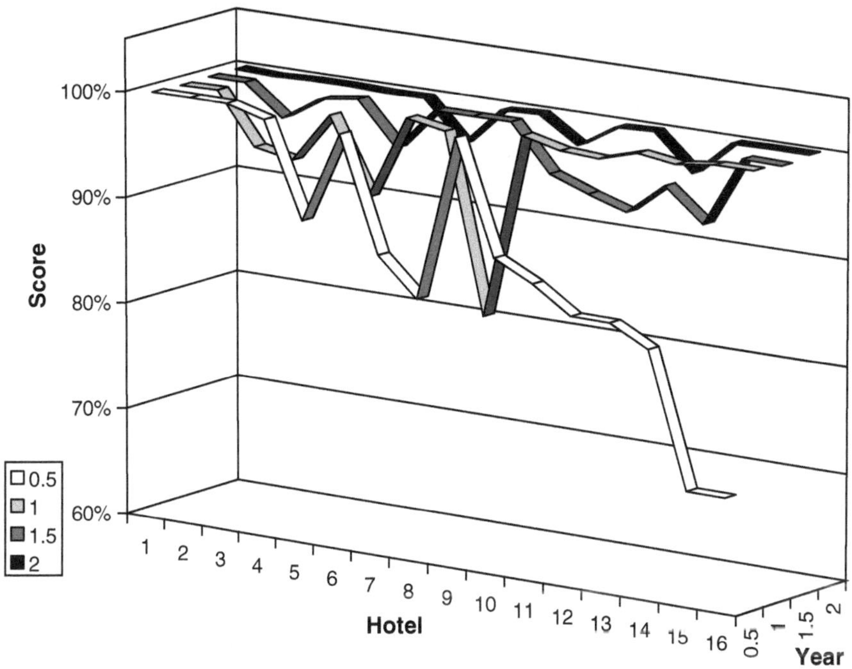

Fig. 3.4 Scores values per hotel per DEA optimization

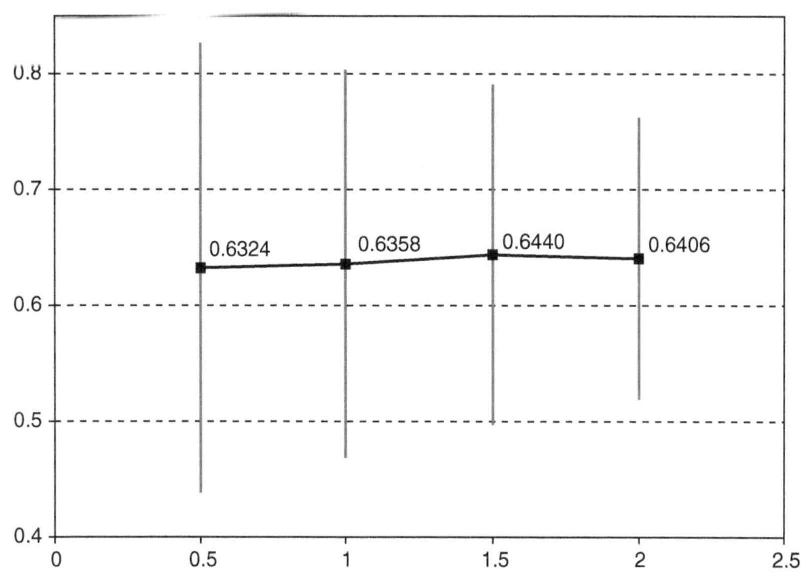

Fig. 3.5 Mean revenue efficiency and its volatility in the four periods

Table 3.3 Mean differences between VRS and CRS in the four periods

Semester	VRS vs CRS
First	0.1520
Second	0.1674
Third	0.1858
Fourth	0.1944

operating at the long run equilibrium constant return to scale. The experimental results show an increasing pattern in the average difference between VRS and CRS scores over time indicating that the scale inefficiencies grow every time we adjust the values of the input variables according to the results of DEA. This result is consistent with the analysis carried out by Png (1988) and Scott et al. (1995) namely, optimal strategy leaves some unused capacity.

Figure 3.6 represents the efficient frontier at the end of the first and the last semester. The values in the horizontal axis are the single rooms' prices whereas the vertical axis shows the revenue efficiencies.

The dynamic reiteration of DEA shows that the redistribution of the total demand over the hotels of the chain, caused by the adjustment of prices and hedonics implemented by the decision maker in accordance with the efficiency analysis, first of all changes the efficient frontier (the peer group) calculated at the end of every observation period and, because of that, such adjustments could not be completely effective to increase the total system's performance.

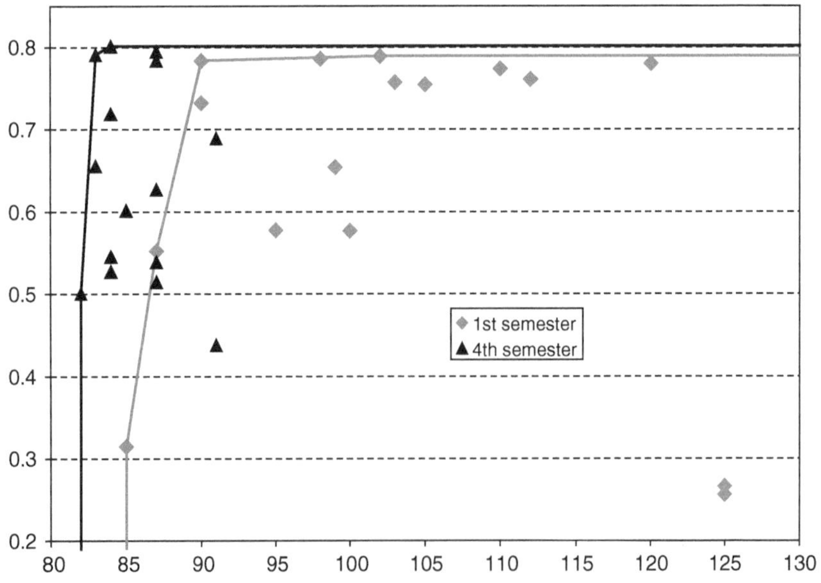

Fig. 3.6 Efficient frontiers at the end of the first and the fourth semester

3.5 Conclusions

In this work we combined System Dynamics methodology with Data Envelopment Analysis in order to investigate the path taken by the hotels of a chain as they move towards the efficient frontier.

The relative efficiency is measured by making use of DEA whereas the economic effect of the policies implemented are investigated by making use of system dynamics methodology.

The results of the model show that reiterating DEA there is a substantial improvement of the VRS scores values together with allocation efficiency.

Nevertheless, the mean differences between VRS and CRS scores show that scale inefficiencies grow every time we adjust the values of the input variables according to the results of DEA.

Finally, the dynamic analysis shows that the redistribution of the total demand after a DEA adjustment changes the peer group and, because of that, the implemented policies are not completely effective to push all the hotels towards the efficient frontier. Therefore, the study shows that, differently from the static approach, in a dynamic framework DEA has to be run more than one time in order to push the hotels of the chain towards the efficient frontier. Moreover, the more the market is reactive to the policies implemented, the more the analysis could not be completely effective to increase the total efficiency of the system. This is the main result of the study and our contribution to the field.

References

Ali AI, Seiford LM (1993) The mathematical programming approach to efficiency analysis. The measurement of productive efficiency: Techniques and applications. Oxford University Press, New York, pp 120–159

Anderson RI, Peterson N (1993) A procedure for ranking efficient units in data envelopment analysis. Manage Sci 39:1261–1264

Anderson RI, Lewis D, Parker M (1999) Another look at the efficiency of corporate travel management departments. J Travel Res 37:267–272

Anderson RI, Fish M, Xia Y, Michello F (1999) Measuring efficiency in the hotel industry: A stochastic frontier approach. J Hospitality Manage 18(1):45–57

Baker M, Riley M (1994) New perspectives on productivity in hotels: Some advances and new directions. Int J Hospitality Manage 13:297–311

Banker RD, Morey RC (1986) Efficiency analysis for exogenously fixed inputs and outputs. Oper Res 34:513–521

Banker RD, Charnes RF, Cooper WW (1984) Some models for estimating technical and scale inefficiencies in data envelopment analysis. Manage Sci 30:1078–1092

Barros CP (2004) A stochastic cost frontier in the Portuguese hotel industry. Tourism Econ 10: 177–192

Barros CP (2005) Measuring efficiency in the hotel sector. Ann Tourism Res 32(2):456–477

Barros CP, Mascarenhas MJ (2005) Technical and allocative efficiency in a Chain of small hotels. Hospitality Manage 24:415–436

Brotherton B, Mooney S (1992) Yield management progress and prospects. Int J Hospitality Manage 11(1):23–32

Charnes A, Cooper WW, Rhodes E (1978) Measuring the efficiency of decision making units. Eur J Oper Res 2:429–444
Charnes A, Cooper WW, Huang W (1990) Polyhedral cone-ratio DEA with an illustrative application to large commercial banks. J Econom 46:73–91
Charnes A, Cooper WW, Seiford L, Stutz J (1982) A multiplicative model of efficiency analysis. Socioecon Plann Sci 16:223–224
Charnes A, Cooper WW, Lewin A, Seiford LM (1994). Data envelopment analysis: Theory, methodology and applications. Kluwer, Boston
Charnes A, Cooper WW, Gollany B, Seiford L, Stutz J (1985) Foundations of data envelopment analysis for pareto-koopmans efficient empirical productions functions. J Econom 30(1/2): 91–107
Donaghy K, McMahon U, McDowell D (1995) Yield management: An overview. Int J Hospitality Manage 14(2):1339–1350
Dyson RG, Thanassoulis E (1988) Reducing weight flexibility in data envelopment analysis. J Oper Res Soc 39:563–576
Farrell MJ (1957) The measurement of productive efficiency. J R Stat Soc Ser A 120(III):253–281
Farrell MJ, Fieldhouse M (1962) Estimating efficient production functions under increasing returns to scale. J R Stat Soc Ser A 125:252–267
Forrester JW (1961) Industrial dynamics. Productivity Press, Cambridge MA
Gat D (1998) Toward a theory of the intraurban market for hotel services. J Real Estate Financ Econ 17(2):199–211
Georgantas NC (2003) Tourism dynamics: Cyprus's hotel value chain and profitability. Syst Dynam Rev 19(3):175–212
Hwang S, Chang T (2003) Using data envelopment analysis to measure hotel managerial efficiency change in Taiwan. Tourism Manage 24:357–369
Lovell CAK (1994) Linear programming approaches to the measurement and analysis of productive efficiency. Technical report. Dept of Economics, Georgia-College of Business Administration, Georgia
Morey RC, Dittman DA (1995) Evaluating a hotel GM's performance: A case study in benchmarking. Cornell Hotel Restaur Adm Q 36(5):30–35
Powersim Studio 2005 (2006) Academic kit, powersim software – The business simulation company. http://www.powersim.com/
Png IPL (1988) Pricing capacity without precommitment by likelihood of availability. Technical Report 87-4. School of Management Business Economics, University of California, Los Angeles
Raab R, Lichty R (2002) Identifying sub-areas that comprise a greater metropolitain area: the criterion of county relative efficiency. J Reg Sci 42:579–594
Scheel H (2000) EMS: Efficiency measurement system. User's manual. Version 1.3. http://www.wiso.uni-dortmund.de/lsfg/or/scheel/ems/
Scott R, Sattler E, Highfill J (1995) A hotel capacity utilization model. J Econ XXI(2):101–105
Seiford LM (1988) A bibliography of data envelopment analysis. Technical report. Dept of Industrial Engineering and Operations Research, University of Amherst, Arnherst
Seiford LM (1996) Data envelopment analysis: The evolution of the state of the art (1978–1995). J Productivity Analysis 7:99–137
Seiford LM, Thrall RM (1990) Recent developments in DEA: The mathematical programming approach to frontier analysis. J Econom 46:7–38
Simonovic SP, Fahmy H(1999) A new modeling approach for water resources policy analysis. Water Resour Res 35(1):295–304.
Smith PC, van Ackere A (2002) A note on the integration of system dynamics and economic models. J Econ Dyn Control 26:1–10
Thanassoulis E, Dyson RG (1988) Setting target input output levels for relative efficiency under different priorities over individual input output improvements. Technical Report 25, University of Warwick, Warwick

Thanassoulis E, Dyson RG, Foster MJ (1987) Relative efficiency assessments using data envelopment analysis: An application to data on rates departments. J Oper Res Soc 38:397–412
Thompson L, Langemeier R, Lee C, Thrall R (1990) The role of multiplier bounds in efficiency analysis with application to Kansas farming. J Econom 46:93–108
Thompson R, Singleton F, Thrall R, Smith B (1986) Comparative site evaluation for locating a high-energy physics lab in Texas. Interfaces 16(6):35–49
Wijeysinghe B (1993) Breakeven occupancy for hotel operation. Manage Account 712:23–33

Chapter 4
Demand for Tourism in Malaysia by UK and US Tourists: A Cointegration and Error Correction Model Approach

Norsiah Kadir and Mohd Zaini Abd Karim

4.1 Introduction

The travel and tourism industry is one of the world's largest and most diverse industries. Many nations rely on this dynamic industry as a primary source for generating revenues, employment, infrastructure development and economic growth. Over the last few years, tourism has become one of the fastest growing industries in the service sector and the second largest gross domestic product (GDP) contributing industry for Malaysia. The industry performed favorably as reflected in the growth of tourist arrivals and tourist receipts. According to the Malaysia Tourism Promotion Board (MTPB),[1] total tourist arrivals reached a high record of 20.7 million in 2007 as compared to 1.2 million in 1974. The share of tourism revenue in total earnings of the services account of the balance of payment increased from 32.7% in 2000 to 43% in 2005 while net contribution by tourism improved by RM11.2 billion to RM18.1 billion for the same period.[2]

Despite the important role of tourism industry in the Malaysian economy, the industry faces several issues and challenges such as decline in tourist arrivals from the short-haul, and regional markets such as South Korea, Japan, Thailand and Indonesia as the *won, yen, baht* and *rupiah* suffered from the recent regional currency crisis. The Malaysian tourism industry also faced increasing competition from other developing countries within the Asian region to gain market share in the tourism industry. At the same time, well-known industry players such as Thailand, Hong Kong, Indonesia and Singapore are launching aggressive promotions to attract tourists particularly from the long-haul markets (the US and Europe). In addition, a series of mishaps such as the Asian financial crisis (1997), avian influenza (1997),

[1] The Malaysia Tourism Promotion Board (MTPB), more popularly known as "Tourism Malaysia", was formally established with the primary objective to stimulate and increase the number of tourist arrivals to Malaysia.
[2] See Ninth Malaysia Plan 2006–2010.

N. Kadir (✉)
Faculty of Business and Management, University Teknologi MARA, Perlis, Malaysia
e-mail: Norsiahkadir6699@yahoo.com

Á. Matias et al. (eds.), *Advances in Tourism Economics*,
DOI 10.1007/978-3-7908-2124-6_4, © Physica-Verlag Heidelberg 2009

the September 11 incident in the United States (2001), Bali blasting on October 12 (2002), the Iraq War (2003), JW Marriot Hotel bombing in Jakarta (2003), the SARs (2002) and the Tsunami aftermath (2004), have adversely affected the tourism industry. The number of tourist arrivals declined substantially because foreign tourists are concerned about their safety and security when traveling in the Asian region.

Even though the global tourism industry had gradually recovered since then, the economic recovery was not strong as expected. Hence, international tourism remains in a precarious situation. Even without the complication of disaster, tourists or potential tourists still have preconceived ideas of the risk associated with travel to certain areas where uncertainty is high. Perceived danger has a negative effect to tourism industry.

Given the highlighted issues, the challenge faced by the Malaysian tourism industry is to increase and sustain the growth in tourist arrivals since Malaysia is the second most-visited country in Asia.[3] In order to increase and sustain arrivals, it is important to understand the factors that influence tourism demand in Malaysia. Hence, the main objective of this study is to investigate the long-run relationship between tourism demand and factors that influence tourism demand in Malaysia using a battery of cointegration tests and error correction models.

The short-run error correction model is then estimated to obtain the short-run elasticity of income, relative price of tourism in Malaysia and the price of tourism in the competing destinations. Modelling the short-run dynamics will provide information concerning how rapid is the adjustment taking place among the various variables to restore long-run equilibrium in response to short-term disturbances in the demand for tourism in Malaysia.

The paper proceeds as follows: Section 4.2 provides an overview of the Malaysian tourism industry. Section 4.3 reviews related literature. Section 4.4 explains the data and methodology used, followed by Section 4.5 which presents the empirical results and discussion. Finally, Section 4.6 concludes the paper.

4.2 Overview of the Malaysian Tourism Industry

Over the last 30 years, the tourism industry has contributed significantly to the Malaysian economy, particularly in terms of foreign exchange earnings and job creation. From 1974 to 2007, the numbers of tourist arrivals have increased almost 20-fold from 1.2 million to 20.9 million. Likewise, gross earning for the same period has also increased from RM0.35 billion to RM45.7 billion. The positive growth was sustained throughout the period, with the exception of 2003 when the number of tourist arrivals was adversely affected, particularly by the outbreak of Severe Acute Respiratory Syndrome (SARs), as well as geopolitical uncertainties worldwide.

[3] See the New Straits Time, December 24, 2005.

Table 4.1 Selected tourism indicators 2000–2010

Indicator	2000	2005	Prevision of 2010
Number of tourist arrivals (million)	10.2	16.4	24.6
By country of origin (%)			
ASEAN	70.4	76.8	65.0
China	4.2	3.8	6.1
Japan	4.5	1.9	2.2
Australia	2.3	1.5	2.7
United Kingdom	2.3	1.5	2.8
Taiwan	2.1	1.3	2.7
India	1.3	1.2	1.8
West Asia	0.5	1.0	2.7
Others	12.4	11.0	14.0
Total tourist receipts (RM billion.)	17.3	31.0	59.4
Per capita expenditure (RM)	1,696	1,890	2,417
Average length of stay (nights)	5.8	7.2	8.7
Number of hotels	1,492	2,256	3,218
Number of hotel rooms	124,413	170,873	247,008
Average occupancy rate of hotel (%)	59.2	63.5	66.4
Employment	390,600	451,000	520,700

Source: Ninth Malaysia Plan, 2006–2010

In 2005, tourist from the Association of South East Asian Nations (ASEAN) contributed for more than 70% of total arrivals. While, total tourist arrivals from China accounted for 3.8%, followed by Japan 1.9% as well as Australia and the UK 1.5% (Table 4.1).

In terms of growth of tourist arrivals, total tourist arrivals from ASEAN recorded an increase of 6.0% or 9.9% increase in total tourism receipts in 2005. While total tourist arrivals from the UK recorded an increase of 17.4% or 47.8% in receipts, the number of tourist arrivals from the US in 2005 recorded an increase of 4.3% or 4.5% in receipts (Table 4.2).

4.3 Review of Literature

Tourism can be defined in a variety of ways, but the broad focus is on travelers away from home and the services they utilize, including trans-portation modes, food and lodging services, entertainment, and tourist at-tractions (Sharpley and Telfer 2002). The United Nations World Tourism Organization (UNWTO) defines tourism as any activity that occurs when tourists travel, which encompasses everything from

Table 4.2 Tourist arrivals and receipts 2005/2004

Country of residence	Tourist arrivals 2004	Tourist arrivals 2005	Growth(%)	Tourist receipts (RM MIL) 2004	Tourist receipts (RM MIL) 2005	Growth (%)
Brunei	453,664	486,344	7.2	1,153.7	1,286.5	11.5
Indonesia	789,925	962,957	21.9	1,125.8	1,447.7	28.6
Philippines	143,799	178,961	24.5	282.6	348.8	23.4
Singapore	9,520,306	9,634,506	1.2	16,826.9	17,715.0	5.3
Thailand	1,518,452	1,900,839	25.2	1,362.7	2,005.6	47.2
Vietnam	42,088	52,543	24.8	62.1	79.3	27.7
Other Area	22,796	22,748	−0.2	33.5	38.4	14.8
Total Area	**12,491,030**	**13,238,898**	**6.0**	**20,846.3**	**22,921.3**	**9.9**
China	550,241	352,089	−36.0	1,329.2	787.0	−40.8
Taiwan	190,083	172,456	−9.3	458.0	343.6	−25.0
Hong Kong	80.326	77,528	−3.5	183.4	233.9	27.5
Japan	301,429	340,027	12.8	760.4	651.8	−14.3
South Korea	91,270	158,177	73.3	206.6	305.5	47.9
India	172,996	225,789	30.5	323.3	557.5	72.4
Saudi Arabia	39,432	53,682	36.1	222.3	420.9	89.4
U.A.E	21,161	29,606	39.9	91.9	176.3	91.8
Canada	32,822	31,167	−5.0	70.7	69.8	−1.2
USA	145,094	151,354	4.3	400.2	418.2	4.5
Australia	204,053	265,346	30.0	554.2	1,032.8	86.4
New Zealand	23,855	33,846	41.9	72.0	93.8	30.3
Denmark	11,884	11,681	−1.7	25.9	27.2	4.8
Finland	11,308	13,172	16.5	26.3	34.4	30.7
Norway	9,437	9,823	4.1	19.3	23.4	21.1
Sweden	25,960	32,408	24.8	59.2	80.9	36.7
UK	204,406	240,031	17.4	618.7	914.6	47.8
Italy	20,036	21,561	7.6	42.9	58.7	36.8
Spain	19,229	17,064	−11.3	45.4	43.8	−3.6
Belgium	7,449	9,386	26.0	17.9	30.7	71.6
Netherlands	28,112	40,494	44.0	64.3	138.9	116.0
France	32,562	40,474	24.3	67.8	107.2	58.1
Germany	53,783	59,344	10.3	127.1	152.3	19.9
Switzerland	15,584	17,701	13.6	41.1	47.7	16.2
South Africa	16,511	16,381	−0.8	58.3	54.9	−5.8
Other Asia	145,573	167,457	15.0	451.9	487.7	7.9
Other America	939,85	92,394	−1.7	236.2	183.6	−22.3
Other Europe	94,426	98,376	4.2	276.8	277.2	0.1
Other	561,029	413,343	−26.3	1,918.1	1,278.6	−33.3
Total non Area	**3,212,376**	**3,192,157**	**-0.6**	**8,804.1**	**9,032.8**	**2.6**
Grand total	**15,703,406**	**16,431,055**	**4.6**	**29,651.4**	**31,954.1**	**7.8**

Source: Tourism Malaysia, Profile of Tourists by Selected Markets 2005

the planning of the trip, traveling to the place, the staying itself, returning and reminiscences.

There exists a wide variety of published works on tourism demand modelling, which can be classified according to: (i) those that use single-equation estimation techniques; (ii) more complete models; and (iii) panel data studies (Saayman and Saayman 2008); however, majority of tourism studies have employed single-equation techniques, the most popular are log-linear and cointegration analyses (for example, Kulendran 1996, Kim and Song 1998, Lathiras and Syriopoulos 1998, Song and Witt 2000, Vanegas and Croes 2000, and Dritsakis 2004). Moreover, the choice of the log-linear functional form is often preferred because it is easy to interpret as elasticity and yielded superior empirical results in terms of "correct" coefficient signs and model fit.

The investigation of demand for tourism has generally involved the estimation of the relative importance of particular variables, which determine the level and pattern of tourist expenditure, such as income, relative prices, exchange rates and transport costs (Sinclair and Stabler 1997). Dritsakis (2004) in his study of German and British tourism demand for Greece using cointegration analysis, found that real income per capita, tourism prices, transportation cost and exchange rate are the main determinants of tourism demand in Greece. While, Song et al. (2003) in their study on demand for tourism in Hong Kong found that the most important factors affecting tourism demand are the cost of tourism in Hong Kong, income of tourist's country of origin, the cost of tourism in competing destinations and the "word of mouth".

Narayan (2003a) in examining the determinants of tourist expenditure in Fiji by using cointegration analysis and error correction models found that in the long-run real GDP of the origin country, relative price and transport costs (airfares) are significantly affect tourists spending in Fiji. In addition, coup d'etat negatively impact on tourist expenditure in the short-run. Meanwhile, Ishak (2006) in investigating factors that influence inbound tourists from Japan and Korea to Malaysia found that income of the origin country, the cost of tourism in Malaysia and exchange rates are important factors that influence the demand for tourism in Malaysia.

Special events or government policy are also important in influencing tourism demand. This factor was included as dummy variables in the international tourism demand functions to allow for the impact of "one-off" events (Witt and Witt 1995). Crouch (1994), found out more than half of the tourism studies have included dummy variables to account for various disturbances that might have biased the estimated parameters if they had been ignored. Such disturbances includes political factors and social conflict, terrorism, travel restrictions, exchange restrictions, changes in duty-free allowances, economic recessions, special events, oil crises and other disturbances that are difficult to quantify. Garin-Muňoz and Amaral (2000) used the 1991 Gulf War as a dummy variable in their study on International tourism flows to Spain. The results showed that the 1991 Gulf War had a significant negative effect on the international tourism flows to Spain.

In addition, Salman (2003) used the Chernobyl nuclear accident and the 1991 Gulf War as dummy variables in estimating the long-run relationship between monthly tourists flows to Sweden from American, European and Scandinavian countries. However, the results did not indicate any statistically significant effect of the Chernobyl nuclear accident, or the 1991 Gulf War on the international tourism demand to Sweden. Katafona and Gounder (2004) used coups and major cyclones in Fiji as dummy variables in modeling tourism demand for Fiji. The results of the study showed that coups are a major deterrent for tourism demand in Fiji, while major cyclones were not significant in influencing tourism demand for Fiji.

4.4 Data and Methodology

Most of tourism demand models borrow from consumer theory which assumes that the optimal consumption level depends on the consumer's income, the price of good, the prices of related goods and other factors. The Marshallian demand for tourism product can be derived as follows:

$$TAR_{ji} = f(Y_j, P_j, P_i, P_s, X) \tag{4.1}$$

where TAR_{ji} = demand for tourism in destination i by consumer from origin Country j; Y_j = the income of origin country j; P_j = the price of other goods and services in the origin country j; P_i = the price of tourism in destination i; P_s = the price of tourism in competing destinations; X = the vector of other factors affecting tourism demand.

When homogeneity is assumed, demand can be expressed as a function of income in constant domestic and destination prices and prices of substitutes in relative terms,

$$TAR_{ji} = f\left(\frac{Y_j}{P_j}, \frac{P_i}{P_j}, \frac{P_s}{P_j}, X\right) \tag{4.2}$$

Our tourism demand model is based on the above theory and follows that of Narayan (2003a). The study covers a period of 1995:1 through 2005:2 using quarterly data. Most tourism demand studies have either used tourist arrivals or tourist expenditure as a dependent variable in their model. For the purpose of this study, tourist arrivals will be employed as the dependent variable. The selection of independent variables are based on previous empirical studies (among others, Kulendran 1996, Lee et al. 1996, Song and Witt 2000, Salman 2003). In a survey of 80 empirical studies on international tourism demand, Crouch (1994) found that income, relative prices, transportation cost and exchange rates were the most commonly used explanatory variables.

The tourism demand function is estimated in a log-linear single equation model, where both the dependent and independent variables are expressed in logarithms. The choice of the log-linear form is often preferred because the coefficients are interpreted as elasticity. Recent empirical studies have adopted this functional form (Song and Witt 2000, Vanegas and Croes 2002, Kulendran and Witt 2001, Lim and McAleer 2002, Dritsakis 2004).

The method involved estimation of the following reduced-form function:

$$Y = \beta_0 + \beta_1 X + \beta_2 Z + \varepsilon \tag{4.3}$$

The dependent variable (Y) in this study will be the number of tourists who travel from origin country j (US and UK) to country i (Malaysia). X represents the set of explanatory variables that are significant determinants of tourism demand and are included in most studies. It consists of the level of real gross domestic product of country j during year t, the relative price of tourism for a tourist from country j to Malaysia in year t and the price of tourism in the substitute destinations k (Singapore, Thailand and the Philippines). Z represents dummy variables that are used to determine the effect of the Asian financial crisis, the "Malaysia ... Truly Asia" promotion campaign, the spread of the Severe Acute Respiratory Syndrome Virus (SARs) in Asia and the September 11 incident in the United States. ε is the white noise error terms, with a zero mean and constant variance.

In this study, the relative price of tourism is defined as a ratio of the consumer price index of the host country (CPI_{it}) to that of the country of origin (CPI_{jt}) adjusted by the relative exchange rate (ER_{ijt}) to obtain a proxy for the real cost of living (Kulendran 1996, Salman 2003). Hence, the relative price of tourism in Malaysia is defined in proxy terms by the relative CPIs as follows:

$$PR_{it} = \frac{CPI_{it}/ER_{ijt}}{CPI_{jt}} \tag{4.4}$$

where PR_{it} = relative price of tourism in country i (Malaysia), CPI_{it} = consumer price index for country i (Malaysia), CPI_{jt} = consumer price index for country j (tourist's country of origin), ER_{ijt} = exchange rate between currency country i (Malaysian Ringgit), and currency country j (foreign currency) in real term.

The price of tourism in other destinations (k) refers to the relative price of tourism in Singapore, Thailand and the Philippines. It is assumed that an increase in the price of tourism in Malaysia will increase demand for tourism in Singapore, Thailand and the Philippines, if these countries are substitute destinations for Malaysia, but otherwise demand for tourism in these countries will decrease, if they are complementary destinations for Malaysia.

Hence, the price of tourism (relative price of tourism) in Singapore, Thailand and the Philippines are calculated using the following formula:

$$PS_{kt} = \frac{CPI_{kt}/ER_{kjt}}{CPI_{jt}} \tag{4.5}$$

where PS_{kt} = price of tourism in destination k (k refers to Singapore, Thailand and the Philippines), CPI_{kt} = consumer price index for destination k, CPI_{jt} = consumer price index for foreign country (country j), ER_{kjt} = exchange rate between destination k and foreign currency (country j)

Our estimation is then based on the following long-run model:

$$\begin{aligned}\ln TAR_{jt} = {} & \beta_0 + \beta_1 \ln Y_{jt} + \beta_2 \ln P_{Mit} + \beta_3 \ln P_{Skt} + \beta_4 \ln P_{Tkt} + \beta_5 \ln P_{Pkt} \\ & + \beta_6 D_{AFC} + \beta_7 D_{MTA} + \beta_8 D_{SAR} + \beta_9 D_{S11} + \varepsilon_{it}\end{aligned} \tag{4.6}$$

where the subindex j is for countries, t is for time and ln denotes natural logarithm (log).

$\ln TAR_{jt}$	=	Log of the number of tourist who travel from the country of origin j to country i (Malaysia).
$\ln Y_{jt}$	=	Log for the real gross domestic product of country j (in dollars) during year t.
$\ln P_{Mit}$	=	Log for the cost of living in relative prices for a tourist from country j to Malaysia at time t.
$\ln P_{Skt}$	=	Log for the price of tourism in the competing destination k (Singapore) for tourists from the country of origin j, in year t.
$\ln P_{Tkt}$	=	Log for the price of tourism in the competing destination k (Thailand) for tourists from the country of origin j, in year t.
$\ln P_{Pkt}$	=	Log for the price of tourism in the competing destination k (the Philippines) for tourists from the country of origin j in year t.
D_{AFC}	=	Dummy variable to capture the effect of Asian financial crisis, taking the value of 1 if observation in 1997:3 to 1999:4, and 0 if otherwise.
D_{MTA}	=	Dummy variable to represent the "Malaysia ... Truly Asia" promotion campaign, taking the value of 1 if observation in year 1999:4 to 2005:2 and 0 if otherwise.
D_{SAR}	=	Dummy variable: to capture the effect of the SARs in Asia, taking the value of 1 if observation in 2002:4 through 2003:4 and 0 if otherwise.
D_{S11}	=	Dummy variable: for the September 11 terrorist attacks in the US (2001), taking the value of 1 if observation in 2001:4 through 2002:4 and 0 if otherwise.

The expected signs for coefficients of explanatory variables are as follows:

$$\beta_1, \beta_7 > 0;\ \beta_2, \beta_3, \beta_4;\ \beta_5, \beta_6, \beta_8, \beta_9 < 0$$

The data used in this study were obtained from Malaysia Tourism Promotion Board (Planning and Research Division), *Key Performance Indicator of Tourism in Malaysia* (various issues), *Annual report of Bank Negara Malaysia* (various issues), *Economic Report 2005–2006* and *International Financial Statistics Yearbook* of the IMF.

In this study, we attempts to investigate the long-run relationship between tourism demand in Malaysia and the factors that influence tourism demand from the long-haul markets. We use cointegration and error correction models to analyze the tourism data for Malaysia and her partners the US and the UK.

4.4.1 Unit Root Tests

In carrying out the cointegration analysis, the first step is to implement the unit root tests. The unit root tests are conducted to verify the stationary properties of the time series data so as to avoid spurious regressions. A series is said to be integrated of order 1, denoted by $I(1)$, if it has to be differenced 1 time before it becomes stationary. If a series, by itself, is stationary in levels without having to be first differentiated, then it is said to be $I(0)$. For the purpose of this study, we use tests proposed by Dickey and Fuller (ADF 1979, 1981) and Kwiatkowski et al. (KPSS 1992) in testing the properties of unit root for all variables used. If all of the series are non-stationary in levels, it should be stationary in first difference with the same level of lags. For appropriate lag lengths, we use the Akaike Information Criterion (AIC) and Schwartz Bayesian Criterion (SBC).

4.4.1.1 Augmented Dickey-Fuller Test

The ADF test (Dickey and Fuller 1979) takes the following form:

$$\Delta Y_t = \alpha_0 + \delta T + \beta Y_{t-1} + \sum_{i=1}^{p} \theta_i \Delta Y_{t-i} + \mu_t \qquad (4.7)$$

The ADF auxiliary regression tests for a unit root in Y_t, namely the logarithm of tourist arrivals, real GDP, the relative price of tourism in Malaysia and the price of tourism in the competing destinations; T denotes the deterministic time trend; ΔY_{t-i} is the lagged first difference to accommodate a serial correlation in the error, μ_t; α, δ, β, and θ are the parameters to be estimated.

4.4.1.2 KPSS Test

In the first method, the unit root hypothesis corresponds to the null hypothesis. If we are unable to reject the presence of a unit root, meaning that the series are integrated of order one. However, Kwiatkowski et al. (1992) argued that not all series for which we cannot reject the unit root hypothesis are necessarily integrated of order one. Therefore, to circumvent the problem that unit root tests often have low power, they offer the KPSS test as an alternative test. Where stationarity is the null hypothesis and the existence of a unit root is the alternative. The KPSS test is shown by the following equation

$$y_t = x'_t \beta + \mu \qquad (4.8)$$

The LM statistics is given by:

$$\mathrm{LM} = \sum_{t=1}^{T} \mathrm{S}_t^2 / \sigma_\varepsilon^2 \qquad (4.9)$$

where, ${\sigma_\varepsilon}^2$ is an estimator for the error variance. This latter estimator ${\sigma_\varepsilon}^2$ may involve corrections for autocorrelation based on the Newey-West formula. In the KPSS test, if the null of stationarity cannot be rejected, the series might be cointegrated.

4.4.2 Cointegration Tests

The cointegration tests are applied to detect the presence of any long-run relationship between the variables. For the two series to be cointegrated, both need to be integrated of the same order. If both series are stationary or integrated of order zero, there is no need to proceed with cointegration tests since standard time series analysis will then be applicable. If both series are integrated of different orders, the two series could be cointegrated. Lack of cointegration implies no long-run equilibrium among the variables so that they can wander from each other randomly. Their relationship is thus spurious (Narayan 2003b).

In this study, if there is a long-run relationship between tourist arrivals and the explanatory variables in Eq. (4.6), then all variables should be cointegrated. To estimate the cointegrating relationship between tourist arrivals to Malaysia and its determinants (Income, relative price of tourism and the price of tourism in the competing destinations), Johansen's (1988, 1991) Full Information Maximum Likelihood (ML) technique is used. Given that it is possible to have multiple long-run equilibrium relationships between tourist arrivals and their determinants, the techniques described by Johansen (1988, 1991) and Johansen and Juselius (1990) allows one to determine the number of statistically significant long-run relationships. The Johansen approach to cointegration is based on Vector Autoregression (VAR). Consider the unrestricted VAR model represented by the following equation:

$$Y_t = \alpha + \sum_{k=i}^{p} \Pi_k Y_{t-k} + \varepsilon_t, t = 1, \ldots, \mathrm{T} \tag{4.10}$$

where ε_t is a i.i.d. P-dimensional Gaussian error with mean zero and variance matrix $\wedge$, Y_t is an $(\mathrm{n}\times 1)$ vector of I(1) variables, and α is an $(\mathrm{n}\times 1)$ vector of constants. Given that Y_t is assumed to be non-stationary, specifying $\Delta Y = Y_t - Y_{t-1}$.

4.4.3 Error Correction Model

An error correction model is used to capture adjustments in a dependent variable that depend on the extent to which an explanatory variable deviates from an equilibrium relationship with the dependent variable. It captures the dynamics of both short-run and long-run adjustments (Banerjee et al. 1993).

Equation (4.10) can be expressed in error correction form as follows:

$$\Delta Y_t = \sum_{k=i}^{p-1} \Gamma_k \Delta Y_{t-k} + \Pi Y_{t-k} + \varepsilon_t \tag{4.11}$$

where Y_t is a column vector of m variables, Γ and Π represent coefficient matrices, Δ is the first difference operator, and P represents the lag length. There exists no stationary linear combination of variables if Π has zero rank. If, however, the rank r of Π is greater than zero, then there exists r possible stationary linear combination. According to Engle and Granger (1987), Π may be decomposed into two matrices α and β, such that $\Pi = \alpha\acute{\beta}$. The cointegration vector β has the property that $\acute{\beta}Y_t$ is stationary even though Y_t is non-stationary. The cointegration rank, r, can be formally tested using the maximum eigenvalue (λ_{max}) test and the trace test (λ_{tr}). The asymptotic critical values are provided in Johansen and Juselius (1990).

According to the Granger representation theorem, in the presence of a cointegration relationship among variables, a dynamic error correction representation of the data exists. Following Engle and Granger (1987), we estimate the following short-run model:

$$\begin{aligned}\Delta \ln TAR_t = \beta_0 &+ \sum_{i=0}^{p} \beta_1 \Delta \ln Y_{t-i} + \sum_{i=0}^{p} \beta_2 \Delta \ln P_{Mt-i} + \sum_{i=0}^{p} \beta_3 \Delta \ln P_{St-i} \\ &+ \sum_{i=0}^{p} \beta_4 \Delta \ln P_{Tt-i} + \sum_{i=0}^{p} \beta_5 \Delta \ln P_{Pt-i} + \beta_6 D_{AFC} + \beta_7 D_{MTA} \\ &+ \beta_8 D_{SAR} + \beta_9 D_{S11} + \delta_1 EC_{t-1} + \mu_t\end{aligned} \tag{4.12}$$

where μ_t is the disturbance term; EC_{t-1} is the error correction term generated from Johansen multivariate procedure, and P is the lag length. Equation (4.13) captures both the short-run and long-run relationship between tourist arrivals and a set of explanatory variables. The long-run relationship is captured by the lagged value of the long-run error correction term and it is expected to be negative in reflecting how the system converges to the long-run equilibrium, which implied by Eq. (4.6). Convergence is assured when δ_1 is between zero and minus one.

4.5 Empirical Results

In order to estimate the long-run relationship of the variables using the cointegration approach, firstly we need to examine the stationary properties of the time series data, to avoid spurious regression. Tables 4.3 and 4.4 summarize the outcome of the ADF and KPSS tests performed on all the series for the two countries (US and UK). It is evident from the table that the calculated ADF statistics are less than their critical values (obtained from Mackinnon 1991 tables), suggesting that the variables are not level stationary for all cases. This suspicion finds evidence of support when the results on the first difference of the series are examined. Which prove the hypothesis

Table 4.3 Augmented Dickey Fuller test (ADF) for individual countries

US

	t_μ			t_τ		
Variables	Level	First-Difference	Conclusion	Level	First-Difference	Conclusion
$\ln TAR$	−1.4951[2]	−8.3698[2]**	$I(1)$	−2.8602[2]	−8.2572[2]**	$I(1)$
$\ln Y$	−2.8279[1]	−6.4679[1]**	$I(1)$	−3.4603[1]	−6.3791[1]**	$I(1)$
$\ln P_m$	−1.4194[1]	−3.6139[1]**	$I(1)$	−1.4720[1]	−3.7578[1]*	$I(1)$
$\ln P_s$	−2.1153[1]	−4.1473[1]**	$I(1)$	−2.6430[1]	−4.1416[1]*	$I(1)$
$\ln P_T$	−1.7571[1]	−4.3758[1]**	$I(1)$	−2.3615[1]	−4.3225[1]**	$I(1)$
$\ln P_p$	−1.8371[1]	−4.4119[1]**	$I(1)$	−1.8731[1]	−4.6682[1]**	$I(1)$

UK

	t_μ			t_τ		
Variables	Level	First-Difference	Conclusion	Level	First-Difference	Conclusion
$\ln TAR$	−1.4950[2]	−8.4884[2]**	$I(1)$	−2.5144[2]	−8.2572[2]**	$I(1)$
$\ln Y$	−2.1021[1]	−6.8659[1]**	$I(1)$	−3.1799[1]	−6.7839[1]**	$I(1)$
$\ln P_m$	−1.7393[1]	−4.4270[1]**	$I(1)$	−1.5604[1]	−4.5051[1]**	$I(1)$
$\ln P_s$	−2.8134[2]	−4.2429[2]**	$I(1)$	−2.8061[2]	−4.2483[2]**	$I(1)$
$\ln P_T$	−2.4917[1]	−4.9834[1]**	$I(1)$	−2.5109[1]	−4.9363[1]**	$I(1)$
$\ln P_p$	−1.5142[1]	−6.4681[1]**	$I(1)$	−2.6685[1]	−6.7355[1]**	$I(1)$

Note: The t-statistics refer to the ADF test, where the subscripts μ and τ indicate the model that allows for a drift term and model with both a drift and a deterministic trend respectively. ** and * denote rejection of a unit root hypothesis based on MacKinnon (1991) critical values at 1% and 5% respectively. Figures in the square brackets indicate the lag length. The ADF test examines the null hypothesis of a unit root against the stationarity alternative.

that the series being stationary or $I(1)$. This finding is corroborated by the η_μ and η_τ of the KPSS test. The results of KPSS test as reported in Table 4.4, rejects the null hypothesis of level and trend stationarity. However, the KPSS statistics does not reject the $I(0)$ hypothesis for the first differences of the series at different levels of significance. Therefore, the combined results from both tests (ADF and KPSS) suggest that all series under consideration appear to be integrated of order 1, $I(1)$.[4]

Having established that the variables are integrated of the same order of $I(1)$, we then proceed with the cointegration tests in testing for the cointegration among the series. The Johansen and Juselius (JJ) approach is employed to test whether there is any cointegrated relationship among the selected variables. The results of the Johansen test for cointegration are summarized in Table 4.5.

[4]The Phillips and Perron (1988) test that allows for ϵ_t to be weakly dependent and follow heterogeneously distributed process has also been computed for all the series in this study. Since their verdict is in agreement with the ADF and KPSS, the procedure is not reported for reason of brevity.

Table 4.4 KPSS test for individual countries

US

	η_μ			η_τ		
Variables	Level	First-Difference	Conclusion	Level	First-Difference	Conclusion
ln*TAR*	0.7640[1]**	0.03007[1]	*I*(0)	0.1468[1]*	0.0295[1]	*I*(0)
ln*Y*	0.8111[3]*	0.1723[3]	*I*(0)	0.1498[3]*	0.1156[3]	*I*(0)
lnP_m	0.5357[2]*	0.1652[2]	*I*(0)	0.1679[2]*	0.0646[2]	*I*(0)
lnP_s	0.5346[4]*	0.0454[4]	*I*(0)	0.1465[4]*	0.0449[4]	*I*(0)
lnP_T	0.5786[4]*	0.1588[4]	*I*(0)	0.2158[4]*	0.0458[4]	*I*(0)
lnP_p	0.4878[1]*	0.2152[1]	*I*(0)	0.1535[1]*	0.0650[1]	*I*(0)

UK

	η_μ			η_τ		
Variables	Level	First-Difference	Conclusion	Level	First-Difference	Conclusion
ln*TAR*	0.3353 [1]*	0.2159[1]	*I*(0)	0.1465[1]*	0.0227[1]	*I*(0)
ln*Y*	0.4635[2]*	0.1404[2]	*I*(0)	0.1659[2]*	0.0645[2]	*I*(0)
lnP_m	0.3128[2]*	0.0688[2]	*I*(0)	0.1748[2]*	0.0668[2]	*I*(0)
lnP_s	0.1557[3]*	0.0889[3]	*I*(0)	0.1489[3]*	0.0682[3]	*I*(0)
lnP_T	0.5926[4]*	0.1214[4]	*I*(0)	0.1658[4]*	0.0276[4]	*I*(0)
lnP_p	0.4780[4]*	0.0834[4]	*I*(0)	0.1941[4]*	0.0786[4]	*I*(0)

Note: The η-statistics refer to the KPSS test, where the subscripts μ and τ indicate the model that allows for a drift term and model with both a drift and a deterministic trend respectively. ** and * denote rejection of a unit root hypothesis based on Kwiatkowski et al. (1992) critical values at 1% and 5% respectively. Figures in the square brackets indicate the lag length. KPSS tests the stationarity null hypothesis against the alternative hypothesis of a unit root.

The calculated Trace statistics and the maximum eigenvalue statistics indicate the existence of more than one cointegrating vector for each model (US and UK). Therefore, the hypothesis of no cointegrating vector is rejected at conventional significance levels for both countries. Rejecting the null hypothesis of no cointegration between the $I(1)$ variables implies that the variables do not drift apart in the long-run. Therefore, there is a long run relationship.

Table 4.6 reports the results of long-run elasticity estimates, which is obtained by normalizing with respect to total tourist arrivals. The results are consistent with the previous studies (Narayan, 2003a; Salman 2003). The results reveal that incomes in the tourists' country of origin have a positive influence on tourist arrivals to Malaysia. The income elasticity is greater than one in both cases. A 1% increase in income of tourists' country of origin, increases tourist arrivals to Malaysia by 1.73% and 2.35% from the US and the UK respectively. The results also indicate that tourists from these markets are sensitive to the relative price of tourism in Malaysia.

Table 4.5 Cointegration tests using the Johansen and Juselius (JJ) approach

Ho	λ_{trace} test	5 % CV	λ_{max} test	5 % CV
U S:	301.1134*	95.7537	158.1061*	40.0766
r=0	143.0073*	69.8189	79.0839*	33.8769
r≤1	63.9234*	47.8561	35.7045*	27.5843
r≤2	28.2189	29.7971	15.6839	21.1316
r≤3	12.5349	15.4947	10.1579	14.2646
r≤4	2.3769	3.8415	2.3769	3.8415
r≤5				
K:	224.1717*	95.7537	81.8466*	40.0766
r=0	142.3251*	69.8189	62.6724*	33.8769
r≤1	79.6527*	47.8561	39.3821*	27.5843
r≤2	40.2705*	29.7971	27.5690*	21.1316
r≤3	12.7015	15.4947	11.8937	14.2646
r≤4	12.7015	3.8415	0.8078	3.8415
r≤5				

Note:
r stands for the number of cointegrating vectors.
Column 1 lists the null hypothesis of zero, at least one, two, . . .,five cointegrating vector; column 2 lists the trace statistics; column 3 lists the critical values for trace statistics at 5% significance level; column 4 lists the maximum eigenvalue statistics; column 5 lists the critical values for maximum eigen statistics at 5% significance level.
3. * indicates statistical significance at 5% level.

Moreover, tourists from the UK are more responsive to changes in relative prices of tourism in Malaysia than tourists from the US.

In terms of prices in the competing destinations, the findings reveal that Thailand and the Philippines are complementary destination for Malaysia, while Singapore is Malaysia's substitute destination. The results indicate that a 1% increase in the relative prices of tourism in Singapore will increase tourist arrivals from the US and the UK to Malaysia by 1.71% and 2.74% respectively. On the other hand, an increase in the relative prices of tourism in Thailand and the Philippines will decrease tourist arrivals from the US and the UK to Malaysia.

Table 4.6 Long-run elasticities of Malaysia's tourism demand

Tourist arrivals from:	Y	Pm	Ps	Pt	Pp
US	1.7317*	–1.8101**	1.7089**	–1.7016*	–1.9213**
	(0.6490)	(0.2242)	(0.5923)	(0.7421)	(0.2840)
	[2.6683]	[–8.0738]	[2.8852]	[–2.2929]	[–6.7642]
UK	2.3477**	–3.2029**	2.7359**	4.9342**	–3.3585*
	(0.2965)	(0.7844)	(0.7072)	(1.6108)	(1.3144)
	[7.9164]	[–4.0832]	[3.8686]	[–3.0633]	[–2.5753]

Note: Figures in the parentheses indicate standard errors and figures in the square brackets indicate t-statistics. ** and * denote significance at 1% and 5% level respectively.

Using the information provided by the Johansen cointegration test, an error correction model (ECM) is constructed to obtain the short-run elasticities. The coefficient of the error correction term represents the speed of adjustment back to the long-run relationship among the variables. In other words, this shows how quickly the system will return to equilibrium after a random shock. It is expected to be negative to ensure convergence. As stated by Hendry (1995), in general to specific modeling approach, the initial step is to set the value of lags of the explanatory variables, and then delete the most insignificant differenced variables. Therefore, in this study we start the estimates by using 4 lags and tried various values of lags. After several estimations, the model that fits the data best is presented in Table 4.7.

Table 4.7 Error correction model for tourism demand in Malaysia

Variable	US	UK
Constant	0.1452**	0.0207***
	(2.3992)	(4.4895)
$\Delta \ln TAR_{t-1}$	0.1404**	0.0108*
	(2.3253)	(1.8786)
$\Delta \ln Y_{t-1}$	0.0730	0.0911***
	(1.4192)	(3.2059)
$\Delta \ln Pm_{t-1}$	–0.5799***	–2.0286***
	(–6.1002)	(–5.0407)
$\Delta \ln Ps_{t-1}$	0.3639**	3.2011***
	(2.770)	(3.8687)
$\Delta \ln P_{T\,t-1}$	–2.7078**	–0.4707**
	(–2.2463)	(–2.1988)
$\Delta \ln Pp_{t-1}$	–0.2929***	–0.3583***
	(–2.8257)	(–5.6414)
D_{AFC}	–0.1252***	–0.5381**
	(–3.3404)	(–2.4781)
D_{mta}	0.2182** (2.0476)	0.0665** (2.0764)
D_{SARs}	–0.0007	–0.0736**
	(–0.0439)	(–2.0986)
D_{s11}	–0.1165***	–0.1375
	(–5.2778)	(–0.8081)
Ec_{t-1}	–0.1877***	–0.6153***
	(–11.5827)	(–2.9913)
R^2	0.9415	0.9429
Adjusted R^2	0.8829	0.8859
Jarque-Bera	472.8841	132.7277
(and probability)	(0.0000)	(0.0000)
Durbin-Watson	1.90	1.98
Serial Correlation	2.31	2.35
LM	(0.52)	(0.54)

Note:
1. ***, ** and * indicate significance at 1%, 5% and 10% levels respectively.
2. The figures in parentheses are the t-statistics.

The final results of the error correction term (EC_{t-1}) as presented in Table 4.7 passed the diagnostic tests. The Jarque-Bera statistics fails to reject the null hypothesis at 1% significance level confirming the normality of residuals. In addition, the Breusch-Godfrey's Lagrange Multiplier (LM) test statistic rejects the existence of serial correlation and therefore accepts the null hypothesis (no correlation exists between variables) at 5 percent significance level.

From Table 4.7, the estimated error correction term (EC_{t-1}) for the US and the UK are –0.1877 and –0.6153, respectively and are statistically significant. The negative values of the coefficients ensures that the series are not explosive and that in the long-run, equilibrium can be attained. The results also imply that the adjustment capacity is faster in the case of the UK compared to the US.

In the short-run, as expected, income is positively related to tourism demand. However, in this study, income is only significant in the case of tourist arrivals from the UK. A 1% increase in the income raised tourism demand (tourist arrivals) from the UK by 0.0911%% as compared to 0.0730% from the US.

The relative price of tourism in Malaysia is statistically significant in influencing tourist arrivals from both the US and the UK. The estimated coefficient of price elasticity is between 0 and 2 showing that a 1% increase in relative price of tourism in Malaysia decrease tourist arrivals from the US and the UK by 0.580 and 2.003% respectively. The results indicate that tourists from the UK are more sensitive to changes in prices of tourism than are the US.

In terms of price of tourism in the competing destinations, the price of tourism in Singapore is statistically significant in affecting tourist arrivals from the US and the UK to Malaysia. The positive sign indicates that tourists from the long-haul market (the US and the UK) regarded Malaysia and Singapore as substitute destinations. Therefore, increase in prices of tourism in Singapore will increase tourist arrivals from these markets to Malaysia.

On the other hand, the price of tourism in Thailand and the Philippines are negatively significant in explaining tourism demand from the US and the UK. This shows that tourists from these markets regarded Thailand and the Philippines as complementary destinations for Malaysia. Increase in tourism demand for Thailand and the Philippines will also increase demand for tourism in Malaysia. In other words, the demand tourism in Malaysia, Thailand and the Philippines are considered as a package. Tourists from these markets will visit Malaysia, Thailand and the Philippines together in one trip.

The 1997/98 Asian financial crisis tends to have a significant negative effect on tourist arrivals from the US and the UK. Tourist arrivals from UK decreased more than from US. This could be explained by the fact that Malaysia is not only a major tourism destination, but also an important industrial and trading partner for the US and the UK. As a result, the slowdown of businesses during the 1997/98 Asian financial crisis causes business traveling to decrease, adversely affecting the tourism industry.

The "Malaysia ... Truly Asia" promotion campaign dummy variable tends to have a significant positive effect on both tourist arrivals from the US and the UK. Tourist arrivals from the US and the UK increases because of this promotion campaign. However, the spread of SARs in Asia did have a significant negative impact on tourist arrivals from the UK only. Tourist arrivals from the UK decreased more than from the US because of this factor. The results indicate that tourists from the UK are more sensitive to the presence of any breakdown of diseases as compared to the US.

The September 11, 2001 terrorist attack in the US as expected tends to have a significant negative effect on tourist arrivals from the US. Tourist arrivals from the US decreased because of this factor. This could be due to the fact that tourists from the US are more concerned about their safety and security after the September 11 incidents, particularly when traveling in the Asian region. On the other hand, the September 11, 2001 incidents in the US do not defer tourist arrivals from the UK to Malaysia. This could be explained by the fact that tourists from the UK regarded Malaysia as a safe and pleasant place to visit because of the long-term historical relationship between the two countries. Moreover, the commitment by the Malaysian government in combating terrorists to ensure the safety of tourists has further increased the confidence of tourists to travel within Malaysia.

4.6 Conclusion

This study uses cointegration analysis and error correction models in estimating a tourism demand model for Malaysia by US and UK's tourists. Before proceeding to the cointegration analysis, the unit root tests (using ADF and KPSS tests) were conducted to verify the stationary properties of the data so as to avoid spurious regression. The combined results from both tests (ADF, KPSS) suggest that all the series under consideration appear to be integrated of order 1 or $I(1)$.

Further, the results of the cointegration indicate that there is a long-run relationship between tourist arrivals and its main determinants. The existence of cointegration allowed for the application of error correction models to determine the short-run elasticities. The results of the error correction model shows that income and the relative price of tourism in Malaysia significantly affects tourist arrivals from the US and the UK. The estimated coefficient of income variable for both countries is positive and less than 1 ($0 < Ey < 1$). This suggests that the demand for tourism in Malaysia is regarded as a normal necessity by tourists from the US and the UK.

The estimated price elasticity of demand for tourism in Malaysia by the US and the UK's tourists are –0.57 and –2.02 respectively. The results reveal that higher prices are likely to discourage the US and the UK's tourists from traveling to Malaysia. According to a survey of 71 cities worldwide by Swiss banking giant UBS (2006), they found that Malaysia's capital city, Kuala Lumpur, has the most competitive prices when they comes for food, electronic goods, clothes, public transport, hotel rates and entertainment.[5] With regard to this, in order to attract more tourist

[5]See The Star, November 7, 2006.

arrivals, Malaysia needs to maintain its price competitiveness especially in relation to other ASEAN countries.

In terms of price of tourism in the substitute destinations, tourism price in Singapore, Thailand and the Philippines are significant in influencing tourist arrivals from the US and the UK. The effect of the Asian financial crisis, as expected, tends to have a significant negative effect on tourist arrivals from the US and the UK. This could be explained by the fact that these two countries are Malaysia major trading partners. As a result, the slowdown of businesses during the Asian financial crisis causes business travelers to decrease, adversely affecting the tourism industry.

The "Malaysia ... Truly Asia" promotion campaign also appears to be significant in affecting tourism demand in Malaysia by tourists from these two markets. The results have important policy implication for Malaysia. The Malaysian authority should focus more on promoting Malaysia in the overseas markets as a quality, premier and value-for-money destination in order to increase tourists' arrivals. However, the spread of SARs in Asia has a significant negative impact on tourist arrivals from the UK only.

The effect of the September 11, 2001 terrorist attacks in the US tends to have a significant negative effect on tourist arrivals from the US only. Based on the results, it is recommended that in order to increase tourist arrivals from the long-haul markets, especially the US and the UK, Malaysia should also focus on safety and security of tourists, because tourists from these markets considered safety and security as an important factor for choosing destination. In addition, government should ensure that every necessary step will be taken in order to protect tourists in cases when there is a breakdown of diseases.

References

Banerjee A, Dolado JJ, Galbraith JW, Hendry DF (1993) Cointegration, error correction, and the econometric analysis of non-stationary data. Oxford University Press, Oxford

Bank Negara Malaysia, Annual Report of Bank Negara Malaysia (1995–2005). Bank Negara Malaysia, Kuala Lumpur

Crouch GI (1994) The study of international tourism demand: a survey of practice. J Travel Res 14:41–55

Dickey DA, Fuller WA (1979) Distribution of the estimators for autoregressive time series with a unit root. J Am Stat Assoc 74:427–431

Dickey DA, Fuller WA (1981) Likelihood ratio statistics for autoregressive time series with a unit root. Econometrica 49:1057–1072

Dritsakis N (2004) Cointegration analysis of German and British tourism demand for Greece. Tourism Manage 22:111–119

Engle RF, Granger CWJ (1987) Cointegration and error correction: representation, estimation and testing. Econometrica 55:251–276

Garin-Munoz T, Amaral TP (2000) An econometric model for international tourism flows to Spain. Appl Econ Lett 7:525–529

Government Malaysia (2006) Ninth Malaysia Plan 2006–2010. Economics Planning Unit, Prime Minister's Department, Kuala Lumpur

Hendry DF (1995) Dynamic econometrics. Oxford University Press, Oxford

International Monetary Fund (various years) International Financial Statistics, IMF, Washington DC
Ishak NZ (2006) Tourism and economics sustainability. Paper presented at the international borneo business conference 2006, Sarawak, Malaysia
Johansen S (1988) Statistical analysis of cointegration vectors. J Econ Dyn Control 12: 231–254
Johansen S (1991) Estimation and hypothesis testing of cointegration vectors in Gaussian vector autoregressive models. Econometrica 59:1551–1580
Johansen S, Juselius K (1990) Maximum likelihood estimation and inference on cointegration with applications to the demand for money. Oxf Bull Econ Stat 52:169–210
Katafona R, Gounder A (2004) Modelling tourism demand in Fiji. Economic Department, Reserve Bank of Fiji
Kim S, Song H (1998) Analysis of tourism demand in South Korea: a cointegrration and error correction approach. Tourism Anal 3:25–41
Kulendran N (1996) Modeling quarterly tourism flows to Australia using cointegration analysis. Tourism Econ 2:203–222
Kulendran N, Witt SF (2001) Cointegration versus least squares Regression. Ann Tourism Res 28(2):291–311
Kwiatkowski D, Phillips PCB, Schmidt P, Shin Y (1992) Testing the null hypothesis of stationarity against the alternative of a unit root. How sure are we that economic time series have a unit root? J Econom 54:159–178
Lathiras P, Syriopoulos C (1998) The demand for tourism to Greece: a cointegration approach. Tourism Econ 4(2):171–185
Lee C, Var T, Blain TW (1996) Determinants of inbound tourists expenditures. Ann Tourism Res 23:527–542
Lim C, McAleer M (2002) A cointegration analysis of annual tourism demand by Malaysia for Australia. Math Comput Simul 59:197–205
MacKinnon JG (1991) Critical value for cointegration test. In R.F. Engle and C.W.J. Granger (eds) Long-run economic relationships: reading in cointegration. Oxford University Press, Oxford
Malaysia Tourism Promotion Board (MTPB), Planning and Research Division, PWTC, Kuala Lumpur, Malaysia
Ministry of Finance (2006) Economic report 2005/2006. Putrajaya, Malaysia
Narayan PK (2003a) Determinants of tourist expenditure in Fiji: a co-integration approach. Pac Tourism Rev 6:159–167
Narayan PK (2003b) Tourism demand modeling: some issues regarding unit roots, cointegration and diagnostic tests. Int J Tourism Res 5:369–380
New Straits Times (2005) Malaysia Second Most Visited, December 24
Phillips PCB, Perron P (1988) Testing for a unit root in times series regression. Biometrika 75: 335–346
Saayman A, Saayman M (2008) The determinants of inbound tourism to South Africa. Tourism Econ 14(1):81–96
Salman AK (2003) Estimating tourist demand through cointegration analysis: Swedish data. Curr Issues Tourism 6(4):323–339
Sharpley R, Telfer DJ (2002) Tourism and development: concepts and issues. Channel View Publications, Clevedon
Sinclair MT, Stabler M (1997) The economics of tourism. Routledge, London.
Song H, Witt S (2000) Tourism demand modeling and forecasting. Elsevier, Oxford.
Song H, Wong KF, Chon KK (2003) Modeling and forecasting the demand for Hong Kong. Tourism Hospitality Manage 22:435–451
The Star (2006) Tourism boom seen in 2007. November 7, 2006
Tourism Malaysia (various years) Key Performance Indicators (various issues), Kuala Lumpur

Tourism Malaysia (2005) Profile of tourists by selected market 2005. Planning and Research Division, Tourism Malaysia, Kuala Lumpur

Vanegas M, Croes RR (2000) Evaluation of demand: US tourists to Aruba. Ann Tourism Res 27(4):946–963

Witt SF, Witt CA (1995) Forecasting tourism demand: a review of empirical research. Int J Forecast 11:447–475

Chapter 5
Modelling Tourism Demand in Tunisia Using Cointegration and Error Correction Models

Houssine Choyakh

5.1 Introduction

Tunisia is considered as a popular destination for the European tourists because of lots of factors such as the geographic proximity to Europe, the natural attractions like the sunny weather, the nice beaches, the Sahara and also for the cultural heritage of the country which vary from Carthaginian and Roman past to the Arab and Islamic history. Some 6.5 million of tourists visited Tunisia in 2006 and have spent over 2 billion dollars, which represents more than 6% of Tunisian GDP. Moreover, tourism employs 100,000 people and the revenue generated by this sector amounts to 74% of the commercial trade deficit.

Over the last four decades, tourist arrivals in Tunisia have grown at an average rate of 9% per annum. The Europeans' arrivals form the main part of foreign visitors to Tunisia. European nights represent 95% of overnights in Tunisian hotels. Furthermore, receipts from European market have exceeded 85% of the total tourism income. Within the European market, there are four countries which are considered as the major generating tourist countries to Tunisia: France, Germany, the UK and Italy. In terms of arrivals, they contribute to half of the total number of visitors and 70% of total hotel's nights and receipts from these countries exceed 68% of the total tourism revenue. According to their significant market shares, it seems realistic to study European tourism demand in Tunisia with regard to these four countries.

Since the works of Syriopoulos (1995) and Kulendran (1996), the number of international tourism demand papers using cointegration analysis has grown considerably (Seddighi and Shearing 1997; Song and Witt 2000; Kulendran and Witt 2001; Lim and McAleer 2002; Song et al. 2003a, b; Dritsakis 2004; Ouerfelli 2008 ...). These studies showed the importance of using econometric models to find tourism demand elasticities which represent a meaningful tool of elaborating strategies for

The econometric results are available upon request from the author

H. Choyakh (✉)
Faculty of Economics and Management MODEVI, University of Sfax, Tunisia,
e-mail: choyakh@gmail.com

Á. Matias et al. (eds.), *Advances in Tourism Economics*,
DOI 10.1007/978-3-7908-2124-6_5, © Physica-Verlag Heidelberg 2009

destinations and providing researchers with valuable insights in which tourists make their decision about the destination choice.

In this study, we will construct an economic model of tourism demand to find demand elasticities for the four major tourist's market of Tunisia and compare results of these countries. At last, we will examine the causes of the limited tourism receipts and suggest some solutions to this problem.

The paper is structured as follows. Section 5.2 examines the specification of tourism demand model. The third section outlines the estimation results of the Johansen's maximum likelihood procedure and the fourth one will be reserved to the Error correction models (ECM) results. The concluding remarks will be discussed in the final section.

5.2 Determinants of Demand and Model Specification

The first step in constructing an econometric model is the definition of the economic theory basis. According to microeconomic theory, tourism demand is defined as the amount of tourist goods that a customer is willing and able to buy at a certain time and under certain conditions (Croes and Vanegas 2005). In this way, demand is a function of a set of variables such as consumers' income, price of tourism goods and prices of substitute goods.

Within international level, tourism demand is often measured by number of tourist arrivals or by tourist expenditures. In some cases, the number of tourist nights is used. We have selected this proxy because it is more appropriate in the case of Tunisian tourism product which is based on hotel activity and offered principally as an inclusive package (including the main tourism services such as accommodation and travel).

5.2.1 The Determinants of Tourism Demand

In a latest review of literature, Song and Li (2007) stated that recent econometric studies of tourism demand have shown that tourists' income, tourism prices in a destination relative to those in the origin country, tourism prices in the competing destinations (i.e., substitute prices) and exchange rates are the most important determinants of tourism demand. Such result is consistent with the previous reviews such as Li et al. (2005) and Lim (1997, 1999). In our study, the tourism demand determinants can be summarized in four categories: income per capita in origin, prices of tourism goods, substitute prices and qualitative factors.

5.2.1.1 Income Per Capita in Origin

The income is considered as the most important determinant of tourist's motivation to travel. Lim (1997) argued that discretionary income, defined as the income remaining after spending on necessities in the country of origin, should be used as the appropriate measure of income in the demand model, but such variable cannot be easily obtained in practice. Hence, past studies have used a range of alternative income measures such as per capita national disposable income, gross domestic product, gross national product, permanent income, total personal income and consumption expenditure. It has been found that income variable is generally highly elastic (Crouch 1994, 1996) which means that tourism is a luxury item.

5.2.1.2 Prices of Tourism Goods

Crouch (1992) pointed that a potential international visitor to a particular country has the option of spending his vacation in his own country or in other international destinations. Hence, the price of domestic tourism products and the international one (relative prices) may well influence the demand for travel. However, it is difficult to have a good approximation of tourism prices in the tourism demand models because tourism regroups many heterogeneous activities and services that could not be easily measured. Ideally a tourist price index should be used in order to measure tourism prices; but, such an index is not available. According to the review of literature of tourism demand studies of Crouch (1994) and Lim (1997), prices of tourism goods are measured generally with the consumer price index (CPI) of destination divided by the CPI of origin and adjusted by the nominal exchange rate.

5.2.1.3 Substitute Prices

In the last years and because of the intensive competition among countries to improve tourism services and the development of transport and communication systems, consumers have a greater choice of destinations and tourism products. Consequently, before travelling, tourists may compare prices (and quality) of tourism services between a set of destinations rather than considering a single international destination. Tourism demand studies like Martin and Witt (1988) and Divisekera (2003) have shown the importance of including the effect of substitute destinations in the demand model and the necessity of investigate the cross price effects.

5.2.1.4 Qualitative Factors

There is a large number of noneconomic factors that affect tourism demand which are impossible to quantify such as special events, terrorism, and political instability. For this reason, the majority of tourism demand models use dummy variables to pick up the effects of qualitative factors that affected tourism.

5.2.2 The Model Specification and Data

According to our variable description and to the previous works, the model of European tourism demand in Tunisia can be expressed in a log-linear functional form as follows:

$$LogNT_{j,T,t} = a_1 + a_2 \log Y_{j,t} + a_3 \left[\frac{CPI_T}{CPI_j \times EX_{T/j}}\right]_t + a_4 \log \left[\frac{CPI_T}{\sum_{C=1}^{4} \alpha_C (CPI \times EX_{T/C})}\right]_t + a_5 D86 + a_6 D91 + a_7 D02 + \mu_t \quad (5.1)$$

In a simple form, Model (5.1) can be written such as:

$$LogNT_{j,T,t} = a_1 + a_2 \log Y_{j,t} + a_3 \log RP_{T/j,t} + a_4 \log SP_{T/j,t} + a_5 D86 + a_6 D91 + a_7 D02 + \mu_t \quad (5.2)$$

The data used in this study are annual times series for the period 1965–2005, and are collected from three sources. For the number of nights, data is taken from the Tunisian National Tourism Office, a governmental board under the Ministry of Tourism whose mission is to promote tourism and publish statistics about Tunisian tourism. Data for GDP per capita is collected from the World Bank website. Finally, *CPI* and nominal exchange rate data is collected from the CD-ROM "International Financial Statistics" of the International Monetary Fund (IMF) and the website of IMF (Table 5.1).

5.3 Cointegration Analysis

Most of the empirical works on the least-squares regression (OLS) estimates of tourism demand has used variables in levels rather than first differenced or otherwise filtered data. This method is appropriate for stationary time series data, whereas tourism demand and a lot of explanatory variables such as income and prices are not stationary. The risk of the regression of non-stationary variables is to obtain spurious results consisting on a high value of R^2 and a small value of DW with misleading results of the standard t-tests and F-tests. To avoid the problems of spurious regressions, our study tends to model tourism demand by using cointegration technique and Error Correction Models (ECM).

Cointegration is a technique introduced by Granger (1981), Granger and Weiss (1983) and developed by Engle and Granger (1987) to test common trends in series over the long-run and to find eventual stationary relation by a linear combination of two (or more) non-stationary time series.

To estimate possible long-run relationship between variables, they must have common trends and must move together in the long-run (Kulendran 1996). The existence of common trends among the variables is possible through the application of unit root tests such Augmented Dickey-Fuller test (ADF) or Philips-Perron (PP) test to determine whether variables are stationary or not.

Using the ADF tests, we find that all variables have unit roots in level terms, but are stationary in the first difference; therefore, it is possible to apply the Johansen's likelihood cointegration procedure.

Table 5.1 Definition of the variables used in the model

Variable	Definition
$LNT_{j,T,t}$	the log of the number of nights spent by residents of origin country j = (FR: France; GER: German; the UK or IT: Italy) in Tunisia (T) at the instant t
$LY_{j,t}$	the log of GDP per capita of country j (in constant dollars of the 2000 year)
CPI_T	the consumer prices index of Tunisia (2000 = 100)
CPI_j	the consumer prices index of one of origin country j (2000 = 100)
$EX_{T/j}$	index of Tunisian currency per units of currency of each country j and it measures the units of the country of origin that are needed for the purchase of one Dinar (2000 = 100)
CPI_C*	the consumer prices index of the competing country C; C = {Spain, Morocco, Egypt or Cyprus} (2000 = 100)
$EX_{T/C}$	index of Tunisian Dinar per units of currency of the country C (2000 = 100)
α_c	the weight of the competing destination c
$D86$**	dummy for controlling the effects of the economic recession in Tunisia in 1986
$D91$**	dummy to capture the effects of the Gulf War in 1991
$D02$**	dummy for controlling the effects of the terrorist attack of Djerba in the year 2002
u_t	random disturbance term
a_1	constant term
$a_{i(I=2,\ldots 7)}$	unknown parameters which are expected to have the following signs: $a_2, a_4 \geq 0; a_3, a_5, a_6, a_7 \leq 0$

* Spain, Morocco, Egypt and Cyprus (and Turkey) are considered as the major competing destinations to Tunisia.
** Dummy variable takes a value of 1 in the year of the event took place and 0 otherwise.

5.3.1 Estimation Results by Johansen Cointegration Procedure

To check whether the variables of a system are cointegrated and then identify long-run relationships between them, Johansen (1988) and Johansen and Juselius (1990) provided a maximum likelihood estimation approach to cointegration. This procedure can detect more than one long-run relationship between tourism demand and the explanatory variables.

Using the Eviews 4.0 program, the results of maximum likelihood estimation show that the most appropriate cointegrating models (i.e. that have an expected sign and which are economically significant) of tourism demand for Tunisia are as follow:

$$LNT_{FR,T,t} = 38.59 + 5.43LY_{FR,t} - 0.93LR_{T/FR,t} + 0.20LSP_{T/FR,t} \tag{5.3}$$

$$LNT_{GER,T,t} = 22.73 + 3.84LY_{GER,t} - 0.02LR_{T/GER,t} + 0.35LSP_{T/GER,t} \tag{5.4}$$

$$LNT_{UK,T,t} = 14.15 + 2.86LY_{UK,t} - 1.17LRP_{T/UK,t} + 2.89LSP_{T/UK,t} \tag{5.5}$$

$$LNT_{IT,T,t} = 29.04 + 4.47LY_{IT,t} - 0.03LRP_{T/IT,t} + 1.25LSP_{T/IT,t} \tag{5.6}$$

Taking into account the above results, we can state that all variables exhibit correct sign. In fact, it seems that income elasticity is particularly high and that relative prices do not play a major role in tourism demand, the British model being apart. Moreover, substitute prices are elastic only in the cases of the UK and the Italian models.

5.3.2 Tests for Weak Exogeneity

In order to determine the variables that undergo an adjustment process, we use the exogeneity test. Tables 5.2, 5.3, 5.4 and 5.5 show that dependant variable $LNT_{j,T,t}$ is not weakly exogenous in our four models.

From the tables above, we can observe that all adjustment coefficients of tourist nights in the Tunisian hotels "$LNT_{j,T,t}$" are negative and statistically significant, so the variables $LNT_{FR,T,t}$, $LNT_{GER,T,t}$, $LNT_{UK,T,t}$ and $LNT_{IT,T,t}$ are not weakly exogenous. In others words, they witness a correction of their deviations with respect to the equilibrium level during the estimation period (1965–2005). Also, we can conclude that explanatory variables contribute in the correction of the disequilibrium of

Table 5.2 Model of French demand

	$LNT_{FR,T,t}$	$LY_{FR,t}$	$LRP_{T/FR,t}$	$LSP_{T/FR,t}$
Adjustment coefficients	–0.355568	0.038298	–0.108900	–0.038684
t Student	(–2.40193)	(3.77315)	(–2.09020)	(–0.55150)

Table 5.3 Model of German demand

	$LNT_{GER,T,t}$	$LY_{GER,t}$	$LRP_{T/GER,t}$	$LSP_{T/GER,t}$
Adjustment coefficients	–0.604775	0.003929	0.064350	0.010670
t Student	(–5.71582)	(0.35480)	(1.54250)	(0.23797)

Table 5.4 Model of English demand

	$LNT_{UK,T,t}$	$LY_{UK,t}$	$LRP_{T/UK,t}$	$LSP_{T/UK,t}$
Adjustment coefficients	–0.436130	0.008913	0.040561	0.012305
t Student	(–5.26843)	(1.58971)	(1.22880)	(0.60409)

Table 5.5 Model of Italian demand

	$LNT_{IT,T,t}$	$LY_{IT,t}$	$LRP_{T/IT,t}$	$LSP_{T/IT,t}$
Adjustment coefficients	–0.694616	0.047355	–0.180411	0.006592
t Student	(–3.26026)	(1.98242)	(–1.42772)	(0.07769)

the tourist nights (35% per year in the case of France, 60% in the case of Germany, 43% in the case of the UK, and 69% in the Italian model).

The small values of adjustment coefficients in the cases of France and the UK could be interpreted in such a way that explanatory variables like income and prices do not probably play an important role to equilibrate the variations of the volume of nights in Tunisian hotels from their equilibrium level. It is possible that other factors such marketing efforts undertaken by the authorities or transport coasts could influence more significantly tourism demand.

5.3.3 Empirical Results and Policy Recommendations

5.3.3.1 Income Elasticity

The empirical results indicate that income of the visitors has a positive and significant impact on tourism demand in Tunisia. According to the cointegration equations (5.3), (5.4), (5.5) and (5.6), income elasticities range between 2.46 for the UK and 5.83 for France. The estimated income elasticity shows that an increase of 1% in real GDP per capita of the UK results in a 2.46% increase in stays at Tunisian hotels.

The values of income elasticity are strangely high, which means that Tunisian tourism is largely influenced by the level of revenue in the European countries. In some ways, this result is reasonable; because economic theory considers foreign holidays as "superior goods" so its income elasticity is generally higher than a unit. Also, Crouch (1994) argued that, in many cases the estimated income elasticities of tourism demand studies were well above 2.0. Furthermore, many similar studies of European tourism demand in the Mediterranean countries showed that long-run income elasticity of tourism demand is high. For example, Dritsakis (2004) found that income elasticity for German demand to Greece tourism is 2.16 and 6.03 for the English demand; also, Muñoz and Montero-Martín (2007) found that income elasticity for German demand to Spain is equal to 5.40.

5.3.3.2 Relative Price Elasticities

According to the results of main tourism demand studies which concluded that prices exhibit generally a non-significant elasticity, our results showed that tourism in Tunisia is price inelastic because the value of elasticities is less than a unit (apart from the UK model). This result is possibly due to the limitation of the approximation of tourism prices through CPI. In this case, Divisekera (2003) pointed that "trends in general price levels as implied by Consumer Price Indices measures may not necessarily coincide with that of tourism".

In the cases of Germany and Italy, relative price elasticities are equal to –0.02 and –0.03 respectively, which means that German and Italian tourists choose Tunisia as their destination with almost no regard to the prices of the hotel's night in Tunisia. German tourists are not sensitive to the prices, probably, because they do not have large possibilities of domestic holidaying (essentially in terms of sun and sea).

The little value of price elasticities is compliant with the idea that international tourism is more and more popular. This fact is due to the development of the organized trip and packaged tours, which makes the price of holiday less and less high since tourism operators could minimize their costs through a massive selling.

Tourists from France (–0.93) and UK (–1.17) seem to be more responsive to price changes than tourists from the other countries, which confirms that French and British tourists make arbitration between tourism in their respective countries and tourism in Tunisia before holidaying. This result seems to be realistic in the French case, because it is recognized that France is the first destination in the world and it is common that French holidaymakers choose between a domestic tourism and an international one.

Our results are in line with those of the majority of tourism demand studies. For example, Crouch (1996) found that the average of price elasticity of 77 studies reviewed is –0.63 which is close to our price elasticity-average which is equal to – 0.53.

5.3.3.3 Cross Price Elasticities

The great value of cross price elasticity of British tourists (2.89) is consistent with their relative price elasticity (–1.17) and emphasizes that Spain, Morocco, Cyprus and Egypt are perceived by the British tourists as an important substitute to Tunisia. In other words, they seem to be very sensitive to a change in the rapport of tourism prices between Tunisia and these destinations. Also, there is an important substitution effect in the case of Italian market (1.25).

The little value of cross price in the case of France (0.20) illustrates the loyalty of French tourists to Tunisia. This fact can be interpreted as a natural consequence of a colonialist past and the important links between the two countries, moreover, it is known that Tunisia is one of the first "non-European" destinations of French tourists.

The value of cross price elasticity of tourism demand of Germany (0.35) may indicate that residents of this country are not very sensitive to the prices practised by Tunisia's competing destinations since they decide to visit it. This could signify that an enhancing-price policy might encourage more French and German tourists to travel to Tunisia, ceteris paribus.

5.4 Error Correction Models

5.4.1 Estimation of ECM

Having identified the long-run relationship between economic variables and finding stationary cointegration residual, Error correction models can be constructed and estimated with OLS method to examine the short term dynamics of the model.

Table 5.6 Estimates of ECM (dependant variable $\Delta LNT_{j,T,t}$)

Variable	France	Germany	UK	Italy
Intercept	0.108127 (1.978218)	0.067669 (0.952493)	0.100146 (1.551520)	0.040102 (1.150373)
$\Delta LNT_{j,T,\ t-1}$		0.351211 (2.627539)		
$\Delta LY_{j,\ t}$	2.024834 (1.065961)		0.433345 (0.175635)	
$\Delta LY_{j,\ t-1}$		−2.692343 (−1.671229)		2.830348 (2.308005)
$\Delta LY_{j,\ t-2}$		3.075014 (1.941549)		
$\Delta LRP_{T/j,\ t}$	−0.886663 (−2.238933)		−0.295278 (−0.659020)	−0.886793 (−2.971321)
$\Delta LRP_{T/j,\ t-1}$		0.755670 (2.012499)	0.094744 (0.206529)	
$\Delta LSP_{T/j,\ t}$	0.770335 (2.024012)	0.152299 (0.395649)	2.066152 (2.671250)	1.204668 (2.921999)
$D86$				−0.431153 (−2.495696)
$D91$	−0.929216 (−5.876217)			
$D02$		−0.612688 (−4.483379)		
$U_{j,T,t}(-1)$	−0.447369 (−3.683510)	−0.705395 (−5.066791)	−0.426735 (−4.051897)	−0.655204 (−5.439289)
R^2	0.622283	0.610498	0.429815	0.713801
LM (1)	0.555672	0.947091	0.921015	0.465926
RESET (1)	0.336830	0.563250	0.504185	0.317614
N° of observations	40	39	40	40

LM (1) is the Breusch-Godfrey test for autocorrelation
RESET (1) is Ramsey's test for the functional form of the model.

We use the "general-to-specific" approach of Hendry (1995) which consists on testing significance of variables and then deleting one by one to have a final good model with statistically significant estimators. In other words, "the least significant variable is dropped from the model and the simplified model is re-estimated. This process is repeated until the coefficients are both statistically significant and correctly signed (Song et al. 2003b)". The results of ECM estimates to tourism demand in Tunisia are shown in Table 5.6.

The Error Correction Terms (ECT) $U_{j,T,t}(-1)$ are significant in all models and have expected negative signs. The ECT results show that adjustment capacity is faster in the case of Germany followed by Italy, which means that the loyalty of these tourists to Tunisia as a tourist destination is better than the fidelity of the tourists from France and the UK. The occurrence of a shock in one determined period will have a larger effect on tourism demand from French or British tourists as they present the lowest coefficients (Daniel and Ramos 2002).

The significance and the positive sign of the lagged dependent variable in the German case mean that residents from this country may exemplify a psychocentric profile to a great degree according to the Plog's assumption. In fact, Plog (1974) argued that habits may explain the presence of a psychocentric type of tourist based on the positive relationship between current and past demand.

The values of income elasticity are still elevated in the dynamic model especially in the German and Italian models. In the case of Germany, an increase in income per capita will trigger a 3.07 increase in the number of nights spent in Tunisian hotels at the date t–2, and 2.83 at the date t–1 in the Italian case. These results differ from the long-run estimates where French tourists exhibit the greatest income elasticity. However, the highest elasticities are in accordance with assumption of Crouch (1996) who stated that "estimated income elasticity is significantly higher when income is lagged. This result implies a delay between improvements in income and an increase in international tourism". Also, Ouerfelli (1998) called this fact as a "catalogue effect" which means that tourists prefer to be informed on the prices of tourism services early before travelling.

Contrary to the cointegration results, relative prices have showed a negative and significant sign in the cases of France and Italy; whereas, the model of Germany (positive inconsistent elasticity) and the UK exhibit non-significant coefficients of prices.

The signs of substitute price elasticities are similar to the long-run results in the sense that French and German tourists still not sensitive to the substitute prices oppositely to the British and Italian tourists.

As far as the dummy variables are concerned, *D91* and *D02* are highly significant and have an important negative effect on tourism demand, respectively for French tourists (the Gulf war of 1991) and for German ones (the terrorist attack on German tourists in 2002). The dummy variable *D86* (the economic recession) has also a significant coefficient in the Italian case.

To evaluate model performance, various diagnostic tests are carried out on each model including test for autocorrelation and test for functional form. All of them have passed these tests. Besides, the results of Table 5.6 show that the dynamic models fit the data well according to the R-squared values except the British model. The LM test shows that there are no serial correlations.

5.4.2 Graphical Representation of Long-Run Residuals and Dependent Variables in First Difference Level

Figures 5.1, 5.2, 5.3 and 5.4 allow us to observe the conformity of our long-run model with the real observations. In fact, we can observe two different curves; the dotted curve of long-run residuals *RESIDj* and the curve of dependent variable in first difference level *DLNTj*. From our four figures, we notice that the two curves are relatively parallel which means that the model allows a good estimation of tourism demand in Tunisia.

Fig. 5.1 France model

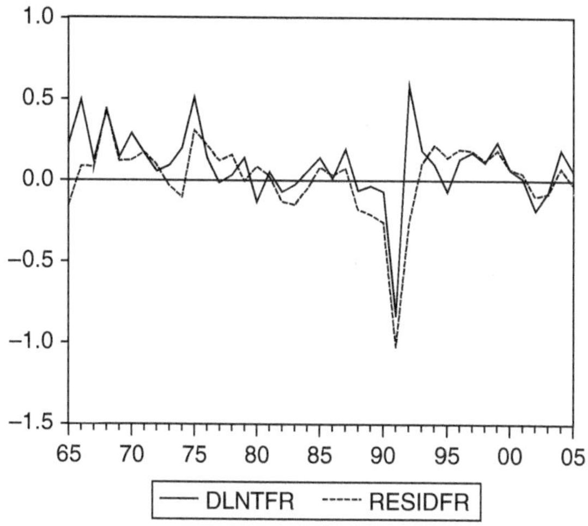

Fig. 5.2 Germany model

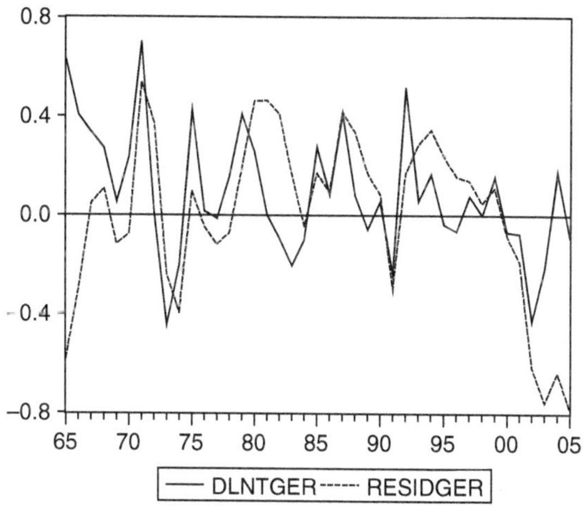

Nevertheless, the periods of divergence between the two curves could be interpreted as follow: when the dotted curve is below the other one, tourism industry in Tunisia is within an empowering phase for the considered market. On the other hand, if the dotted curve is over the dark curve, the tourism industry is in a phase of underperformance.

5.5 Conclusion

In this paper, we have attempted to estimate a model for tourism demand in Tunisia using cointegration technique and ECM. Despite the wrong signs and the high income elasticities, the model performs reasonably well. The results show that income of tourist in origin countries is the most significant factor in determining

Fig. 5.3 UK model

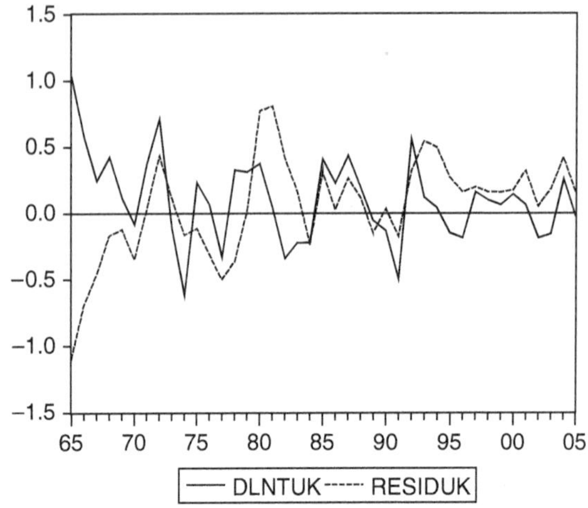

Fig. 5.4 Italy model

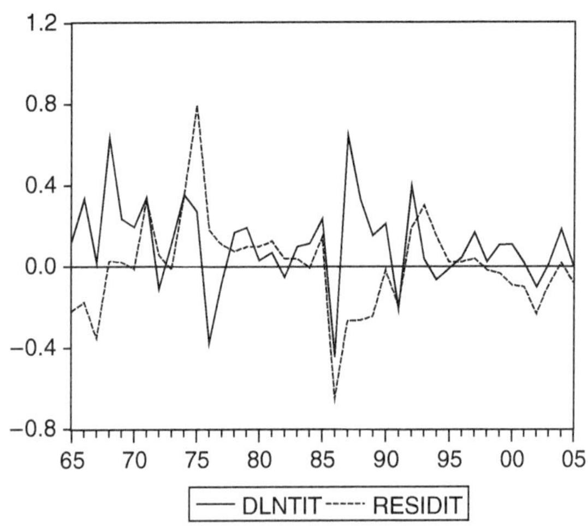

the number of nights spent in Tunisian hotels. The study concurred with previous studies which found that income in the originating countries offers a robust explanation for the changes in tourism demand which means that tourism product is a luxury service. Furthermore, the small values of relative price elasticities confirm the fact that prices do not play an important role to attract tourists. However, the signs of substitute price elasticity showed that tourism demand in Tunisia essentially by the British and the Italian tourists is affected by the competing destinations actions. Finally, the significance of the dummies indicates a great vulnerability of tourism demand in Tunisia with regard to negative events.

According to these empirical findings, a possible explanation of the causes of the limited tourism receipts are the vulnerability of tourism industry in Tunisia to the shocks, and the dependence of tourism demand on the income of the origin's tourist markets. Moreover, the severe competition with the Mediterranean destinations is another negative factor that could affect receipts per tourist. The renowned aspect of a low-cost destination which is perceptible in the small values of price elasticity reinforces this fact. Subsequently, since high prices may be interpreted as signals of high quality and good reputation of the destination, it is possible that a strategy of increasing prices may lead to enhance tourism demand in Tunisia (essentially for the Italian and the German markets).

Finally, such study could be used as an important tool to evaluate tourism demand in Tunisia as well as a good assistance for the authorities operating in tourism. Also, our research was limited to four Europeans countries, but could be extended to all markets of Tunisian tourism and to other south Mediterranean countries; cross sectional comparison also could be undertaken.

References

Croes RR, Vanegas MS (2005) An econometric study of tourist arrivals in Aruba and its implications. Tourism Manage 26:879–890

Crouch GI (1992) Effect of income and price on international tourism. Ann Tourism Res 19: 643–664

Crouch GI (1994) A Meta-Analysis of Tourism Demand. Ann Tourism Res 22(1):103–118

Crouch GI (1996) Demand elasticities in international marketing: A meta-analytical application to tourism. J Bus Res 36:117–136

Daniel AC, Ramos FR (2002) Modelling inbound international tourism demand to Portugal. Int J Tourism Res 4(3):193–209

Divisekera S (2003) A model of demand for international tourism. Ann Tourism Res 30:31–49

Dritsakis N (2004) Cointegration analysis of German and British tourism demand for Greece. Tourism Manage 25:111–119

Engle RF, Granger CWJ (1987) Co-integration and error correction: Representation, estimation and testing. Econom 55(2):251–276

Granger CWJ (1981) Some properties of time series data and their use in. econometric model specification. J Econom 16:121–130

Granger CWJ, Weiss AA (1983) Time series analysis of error correcting models. Studies in econometrics, time series and multivariate statistics. Academic Press, New York, pp 255–278

Hendry DF (1995) Dynamic econometrics. Oxford University Press, Oxford, UK

Johansen S (1988) Statistical analysis of cointegration vectors. J Econ Dyn Control 1988:231–254

Johansen S, Juselius K (1990) Maximum likelihood estimation and inferences on cointegration with application to the demand for money. Oxf Bull Econ Stat 52:160–210

Kulendran N (1996) Modelling quarterly tourist flows to Australia using cointegration analysis. Tourism Econ 2(3):203–222

Kulendran N, Witt SF (2001) Cointegration versus least squares regression. Ann Tourism Res 28:291–311

Li G, Song H, Witt SF (2005) Recent developments in econometric modeling and forecasting. J Travel Res 42:82–99

Lim C (1997) Review of international tourism demand models. Ann Tourism Res 24(4):835–849

Lim C (1999) A meta-analytic review of international tourism demand. J Travel Res 37:273–284

Lim C, McAleer M (2002) A cointegration analysis of tourism demand by Malaysia for Australia. Math Comput Simul 59:197–205

Martin C, Witt SF (1988) Substitute prices in models of tourism demand. Ann Tourism Res 15:255–268

Muñoz TG, Montero-Martín L F (2007) Inbound international tourism to Canary Islands: A dynamic panel data model. Tourism Manage 27:281–291

Ouerfelli C (1998) La demande touristique européenne en Tunisie. Working Paper LATEC Université de Bourgogne, France

Ouerfelli C (2008) Co-integration analysis of quarterly European tourism demand in Tunisia. Tourism Manage 29:127–137

Plog S (1974) Why destination areas rise and fall in popularity? Cornell Hotel Restaur Q 14:55–58

Seddighi HR, Shearing DF (1997) The demand for tourism in north east England with special reference to Northumbria: an empirical analysis. Tourism Manage 18(8):499–511

Song H, Witt SF (2000) Tourism demand modelling and forecasting: Modern econometric approaches book. Pergamon, Oxford

Song H, Wong KF, Chon S (2003a) Modelling and forecasting the demand for Hong Kong tourism. Int J Hospitality Manage 22: 435–451

Song H, Witt SF, Jensen TC (2003b) Tourism forecasting: Accuracy of alternative econometric models. International Journal of Forecasting 19:123–141

Song H, Li G (2007) Tourism demand modelling and forecasting – A review of recent research. Tourism Management (in press)

Syriopoulos T (1995) A dynamic model of demand for mediterranean tourism international. Rev Appl Econ 9:318–336

Chapter 6
Determinants of Length of Stay – A Parametric Survival Analysis

António Gomes de Menezes, José Cabral Vieira, and Ana Isabel Moniz

6.1 Introduction

Length of stay is an important determinant of the overall impact of tourism in a given economy. The number of days that tourists stay at a particular destination is likely to influence their expenditure, for instance, as the number of possible experiences to be undertaken by tourists depends on their length of stay (Davies and Mangan 1992; Kozak 2004; Legoherel 1998). Understanding the determinants of length of stay is, thus, important to fully characterize tourism demand and its impact on a given tourist destination (Gokovali, Bahar and Kozak 2007). In addition, Alegre and Pou (2006) argue that the importance of uncovering the determinants of length of stay and concomitant gains to policymakers and researchers alike has grown with the increasingly pervasive pattern of shorter lengths of stays. Alegre and Pou claim that uncovering the microeconomic determinants of length of stay is critical to the design of marketing policies that effectively promote longer stays, associated with higher occupancy rates and revenue streams. In fact, income from tourism might well be falling in many destinations despite the increase in visitor arrivals, due to a decrease in the length of stay. Length of stay has also aroused interest beyond its importance as an expenditure determinant. For instance, in the tourism sustainability literature, length of stay is important in the context of carrying capacity analysis (Saarinen 2006). However, and as Gokovali et al. (2007) argue, there are relatively few studies that estimate the determinants of length of stay resorting to microeconometric techniques. This paper contributes to fill this gap. The main aim of this paper is to estimate the determinants of length of stay, in particular, how different individual socio-demographic profiles and trip experiences influence length of stay. Length of stay is one of the questions resolved by tourists when planning or while taking their trips (Decrop and Snelders 2004). Hence, it follows that length of stay is best recorded when tourists depart, and, quite

A.G. de Menezes (✉)
Department of Economics and Business, University of the Azores and CEEAplA, Ponta Delgada, Portugal
e-mail: menezesa@notes.uac.pt

Á. Matias et al. (eds.), *Advances in Tourism Economics*,
DOI 10.1007/978-3-7908-2124-6_6, © Physica-Verlag Heidelberg 2009

likely, is influenced by tourists' socio-demographic profiles, on the one hand, and their experiences while visiting their destination, on the other (Bargeman and Poel 2006; Decrop and Snelders 2004). This paper accounts for such insights by employing micro data, rich on individual socio-demographic characteristics and actual trip experiences, built from individual surveys answered by a representative sample of tourists departing from the Azores: the Portuguese tourist region with the highest growth rate in the last decade.

Modeling length of stay poses certain challenges that owe to the fact that length of stay is, necessarily, a non-negative variable. To uncover causal relationships between tourists' socio-demographic characteristics and trip experiences and length of stay, the empirical work must employ some sort of a formal statistical model. However, the most popular statistical tools, such as the linear regression model, are not appropriate to model length of stay, since they do not take into account that length of stay is a non-negative variable, and, hence, lead to biased estimation (Greene 2000). To circumvent such problem, this paper employs survival analysis parametric models in a novel way. This paper argues that survival analysis, or time to event analysis (read, departure), naturally lends itself to the study of length of stay. Quite interestingly, this paper employs a plethora of survival analysis parametric models that display much welcomed features. First and foremost, the survival analysis parametric models accommodate for individual heterogeneity, in the sense that a large number of covariates, pertaining to individual socio-demographic profiles and actual trip experiences, are used to explain length of stay, as suggested by microeconomic theory and a reading of the literature (Decrop and Snelders 2004). It should be noted that controlling for individual heterogeneity allows detailed policy implications, as one is able to quantify the impact of specific individual characteristics or trip attributes on the probability of length of stay exceeding a given threshold for a synthesized, policy relevant individual or target group. Second, the survival analysis parametric models employed are unrestricted and agnostic in the sense that they allow for non-normal data patterns, such as spiky or bimodal data. This is especially important since some lengths of stays are more frequently found in the data than others, such as seven day stays.

Recently, and not surprisingly, several authors have employed microeconometric models to analyze the determinants of length of stay that explicitly deal with the limited nature of length of stay, namely, being a non-negative variable. Alegre and Pou (2006) employ a limited dependent variable discrete choice model, namely, a binary logit, and, thus, collapse length of stay into a binary variable: zero if length of stay is shorter than one week; one if otherwise. By doing so, the ensuing policy implications are less far reaching, in the sense that all length of stays, say, shorter than one week are treated alike, be them one day stays or six day stays. This lost of information may be particularly worrisome when length of stays are not obviously dichotomized or clustered, and are, instead, roughly evenly distributed over several days, leaving the researcher with no obvious cut-off to arbitrarily partition length of stays. To avoid this problem, Gokovali et al. (2007), like this paper, employ survival analysis parametric models to estimate the determinants of length of stay for a sample of tourists departing from a Turkish tourist region. While innovative and informative, the work by Gokovali, Bahar and Kozak is restricted to models of the Proportional Hazards form, and, therefore, with constant or monotone hazard rates: intuitively, the rate at which stays are terminated. This paper capitalizes on Gokovali, Bahar and Kozak yet employs a more general and, concomitantly, richer approach. In particular, this paper employs models not only of the Proportional Hazards form, as in Gokovali, Bahar and Kozak, but also of the Accelerated Failure-Time form, with the former being a special, nested case of the latter. This distinction matters since, and in a nutshell, the Proportional Hazards models, by construction, exhibit constant or monotone hazard rates. The Accelerated Failure-Time models, however, display no such restriction, and, hence, accommodate more general data patterns. This distinguishing feature is especially important in the present context since length of stays may exhibit spiky, multi modal patterns, depending on the destination or the time period under analysis. It should also be noted that this paper's approach leads, ex ante, to models with a better fit to the data. In fact, since the Proportional Hazards models are, in a formal statistical sense, nested cases of Accelerated Failure-Time models, this paper employs a model selection strategy – estimating both Proportional Hazards models and Accelerated-Failure-Time models – that clearly dominates a model selection strategy that estimates only the special case Proportional Hazards model. This turns out to be case, as expected. In fact, the econometric work carried out in this paper selects an Accelerated Failure-Time model as the preferred model, despite the fact that the Proportional Hazards models do display quite satisfactory statistical results.

The theoretical framework underlying the microeconometric work carried out in this paper draws from strands of the social science literature on consumer choice theory, namely microeconomic theory, as they motivate empirical work on the micro determinants of length of stay resorting to econometric techniques. As Alegre and Pou (2006) discuss, discrete choice models as proposed by Dubin and McFadden (1984), Hanemann (1984) and Pollak (1969, 1971) provide a framework that allows one to write the conditional demand function for the length of stay at a given destination, and assuming weak separability between the tourist trip and consumer goods other than tourism, as a function of holiday characteristics, the daily price of the holiday, the total expenditure available for the holiday, maximum time available, the characteristics of the tourist, and a non-observable random effect. On the other hand, and as Hellström (2006) surveys, several authors have recently proposed in the recreational demand literature consumer choice models that endogenously determine time on-site (Berman and Kim 1999; Feather and Shaw 1999; Hellström 2006; Larson 1993; McConnell 1992). In its essence, the aim of this research program is to solve the problem of a utility maximizing consumer whose choices of number of trips per period may be jointly and endogenously determined with the number of nights per trip, in a setting suitable for welfare analysis, that explicitly addresses the unavoidable data problems associated with the integer nature of length of stay (see Hellström (2006) for a theoretical and empirical illustration along these lines; see Papatheodorou (2001) for a critical review of consumer theory in a destination choice context). In addition, the specification of the regressions found in this paper's econometric work draws on consumer behavior models that suggest the factors to include as determinants of length of stay (see Jafari 1987; Mathieson and Wall 1992; Moscardo et al. 1996; Swarbrooke and Horner 2001 and references therein, for discussions on models of consumer behavior).

The empirical work carried out in this paper produced statistically significant and economically important results. Several socio-demographic individual characteristics and trip attributes turn out to be statistically important determinants of length of stay, and, carry, thus, important policy implications. In fact, the results uncovered may be used to aid the design of marketing policies that may promote longer stays. In addition, there are results that shed light on enduring research topics, such as repeat visitor behavior. In fact, it should be noted that repeat visitors display higher probabilities of experiencing longer stays, a fact in line with the findings in Lehto et al. (2004), who claim that repeat visitors exhibit extended length of stays.

6.2 Determinants of Length of Stay: A Parametric Survival Analysis

Length of stay is one of the most useful dimensions used to characterize tourism demand: an enduring research topic (for extensive reviews of research on tourism demand see, among others, Crouch 1994; Crouch and Louviére 2000; Lim 1997; Song and Witt 2000; Witt and Witt 1995). Tourism demand is a broadly defined subject that encompasses a variety of objects, interesting in their own right: tourist arrivals, tourist expenditure, travel exports, nights spend in tourist accommodations and length of stay. Length of stay is an interesting research topic for, at lest, two reasons. First, length of stay conditions the overall socioeconomic impact of tourism in a given economy. In fact, and as Davies and Mangan (1992) and Kozak (2004), among others, argue, an increased length of stay may allow tourists to undertake a larger number of experiences or activities which may affect their overall spending, sense of affiliation and satisfaction. Hence, several authors consider length of stay an important market segmentation variable in estimating the determinants of tourist spending (Davies and Mangan 1992; Legoherel 1998; Mok and Iverson 2000). Second, modeling length of stay is important to tourism sustainability analysis (Saarinen 2006). Sustainability has recently become an important policy issue in tourism. The ubiquitous continuous growth of tourism has fuelled an intense discussion about the socioeconomic and environmental impacts that tourism hinges on destination areas. In the sustainability literature, an important concern focuses on destination areas' carrying capacity, generally defined as the maximum number of people who can use a site without any unacceptable alteration in the physical environment and without any unacceptable decline in the quality of the experience gained by tourists. The concept of carrying capacity occupies a key position with regard to sustainable tourism, in that many of the latter's principles are based on this theory and research tradition. Models of the determinants of length of stay are important to the research on sustainable tourism since they are useful to forecast tourists' on-site time, and, concomitantly, the stress caused by tourism activity on local resources.

Despite the rich literature on tourism demand, Alegre and Pou (2006) argue that most studies on tourism demand fail to pay attention to length of stay, at least at a microeconometric level, where one is able to control for individual heterogeneous behavior. Moreover, the few studies available in the literature on the length of stay are mainly descriptive (Oppermann 1995, 1997; Seaton and Palmer 1997; Sung et al. 2001). These studies show how length of stay varies with nationality, age, occupation status, repeat visit behavior, stage in the family life cycle and physical distance between place of origin and destination, among other variables. While these studies do find interesting results, their descriptive nature hinders formal inference tests on the causal relationships between individual socio-demographic profiles and actual trip experiences and length of stay. Recently, however, some authors have employed microeconometric models to estimate the determinants of length of stay. Fleischer and Pizam (2002) employ a Tobit model to estimate the determinants of the vacation taking decision process for a group of Israeli senior citizens. The Tobit model in Fleischer and Pizam overcomes the fact that several individuals in the study group do not take vacations at all, and, thus, the model allows a corner solution case, with many individuals experiencing zero days of vacation. Fleischer and Pizam conclude that age, health status and income have a positive effect on the length of stay. In the present case, only departing tourists were surveyed, and, hence, all tourists experienced a strictly positive length of stay. Therefore, the Tobit model, employed in Fleischer and Pizam, is not applicable. Alegre and Pou (2006) analyze length of stay for a pooled cross-section of tourists visiting the Balearic Islands. Alegre and Pou employ a logit model, where the explanatory variable is binary (0 if length of stay is shorter than one week and 1 otherwise), and find, among other results, that labour status, nationality and repeat visitation rate are statistically significant determinants of length of stay. Gokovali et al. (2007) estimate parametric survival analysis models of the Proportional Hazards form to learn that, for a cross section of tourists departing from the Turkish region of Bodrum, experience as a tourist, past visits to destination, overall attractiveness and image of destination country, all increase the probability of staying longer.

6.3 Contextual Setting and Data

This section starts with a brief overview of the setting where the questionnaire took place – The Azores – and then describes the data. The Azores are a Portuguese archipelago, with nine islands (from 16 Km^2 – Corvo – to 750 Km^2 – São Miguel), spread between 36°–43° N, 25°–31° W, 1564 km west of Lisbon and 2,300 km east of Nova Scotia, a land area of 2,355 Km^2, a population of 242,000 inhabitants and an autonomous government. The Azores, with their strikingly beautiful nature, are the Portuguese region where tourism has grown more rapidly in the last decade. In fact, the recent stellar performance of tourism in the Azores explains why it is rapidly becoming the most important economic activity in the Azores. Tourist arrivals have increased from 159,000 in 1995 to 260,000 in 2005, while tourists nights spent in tourist accommodations increased from 407,000 in 1995 to 936,000 in 2005 and will well exceed, for the first time ever, the 1,000,000 mark in 2006. Despite the obvious tourist growth potential, until the early 1990s tourism was not promoted by the regional government and the Azores were strapped in an inferior Nash equilibrium with virtually no hotels and no air connections. In the mid 1990s, a change in the regional government led to a change in tourism policy, with the adoption of tourism growth enhancing policies, such as the provision of air connections and the enhancement of brand awareness, that led to a boom in hotel construction, with the total number of hotels beds growing from 3,000 in 1995 to 10,000 in 2005 (data source: SREA statistical office; http://srea.ine.pt).

Traditionally, length of stay has been relatively short – about three to four days – which is explained by the predominant tourists from Mainland Portugal whom routinely took regular flights, mostly over the weekend or around holidays, for short stays. Length of stay has been increasing and is bound to increase even further as the tourist landscape changes. Nowadays, there are several charter carriers offering direct connections and tour packages – one or two weeks, typically – to, among others, the Nordic Countries (Sweden, Norway, Finland and Denmark), Germany, UK, Spain, and the Netherlands, where local people keenly appreciate the Azorean natural surroundings and mild weather year round. Despite the recent successes, several challenges remain. Ranking high among the most pressing issues one finds a desire by public officials and hotel operators to increase average length of stay, which is perceived as critical to increase occupancy rates and make operations smoother to run. Hence, learning the determinants of length of stay is critical to improve the effectiveness of regional tourism policy.

The questionnaire used to construct the data set employed in the empirical part of the paper was carried out in the summer of 2003 and was built as a representative, stratified sample of the tourists who visited the Azores, by nationality, routes and gateways used, in the year of 2002. The total number of questionnaires ministered – 400 – was determined according to the methods discussed in Hill and Hill (2002). In the Summer of 2003 there were three gateways – Ponta Delgada, Lajes, Horta-, in the three main islands of São Miguel, Terceira and Faial, respectively. The questionnaires were carried out at these airports, near the boarding gates, in three languages: Portuguese, English and Swedish. Each questionnaire covered individual socio-demographic profiles – by including variables such as gender, age, education, occupation sector, type of profession, marital status, among others,- and actual trip experiences – by including variables such as travel party composition, travel motive, motives underlying destination choice, alternative destinations considered, repeat visitation rate, tourist experience, overall satisfaction, revisit intention, among others.

Table 6.1 lists the highest frequencies of length of stay. As expected, the highest frequency is seven day stays, typically associated with tourists visiting on tour operator packages, with an in sample frequency of 28%. The combined frequency

Table 6.1 Distribution of length of stays

Length of Stays (days)	Observations (Total = 400)	Frequency (%)	Accum. Frequency (%)
1	1	0.25	0.25
2	6	1.50	1.75
3	12	3.00	4.75
4	11	2.75	7.50
5	14	3.50	11.00
6	16	4.00	15.00
7	114	28.50	43.50
8	21	5.25	48.75
9	7	1.75	50.50
10	38	9.50	60.00
11	7	1.75	61.75
12	15	3.75	65.50
13	4	1.00	66.50
14	65	16.25	82.75
15	19	4.75	87.50
≥16	50	12.50	100.00

of 14–15 day stays is also quite high: about 20%. About half of the stays last no longer than 8 days.

Table 6.2 contains additional selected, self explanatory, descriptive statistics for the data gathered.

Overall, mean stay is about 11 days; median stay is just 10 days while the standard deviation of stays is about 11 days, due to some quite long stays. The largest group of tourists in the sample is tourists from Mainland Portugal, who experience stays similar to those of the overall sample and are the youngest group. Tourists from the Nordic Countries are the second largest group in the sample and exhibit a mean stay of 9 days, a median stay of seven days and a relatively low standard deviation of three days, as most of these tourists visit with either one or two week tour packages. Tourists from Germany experience, typically, longer stays than tourists from the Nordic Countries. In sum, there are interesting differences in length of stays across nationalities.

6.4 Study Methods: An Overview of Survival Analysis

Survival analysis is just another name for time to event analysis. The engineering sciences have contributed to the development of survival analysis, which is called "reliability analysis" or "failure time analysis" in this field since the main focus is in modeling the time it takes for machines or electronic components to break down. Likewise, survival analysis has long been a cornerstone of biomedical research. The analysis of duration data comes fairly recently to the social science literature,

Table 6.2 Selected descriptive statistics

Variables	Observations	Frequency (%)	Average Stay (days)	Median Stay (days)	Sd. Stay (days)	Average Age (years)
		(1) Socio-demographic Profiles				
Portugal (Mainland)	150	37.50	11	10	11	34
Sweden	95	23.75	9	7	3	57
Other Nordic Countries	49	12.25	9	7	3	47
Germany	21	5.25	14	8	24	41
Other Countries	85	21.25	17	14	14	44
Male	203	50.75	11	8	11	44
Marital Status (Married)	264	66.00	11.8	9.5	12	49
Azorean Ascendancy	70	17.50	18.7	15	13.2	43
Education1. Secondary	127	31.75	10.9	10	6.8	40
Education2. Tertiary	183	45.75	10.6	7	10.3	45
Education3. Technical	8	2.00	8.6	7	3	48
Education4. Lesser	82	20.5	16.8	13	17	47
High Level Profession	127	31.75	10.2	8	6.5	48
		(2) Trip Attributes				
Leisure	294	73.50	10.6	8	8.6	45
Visit Friends/ Relatives	57	14.25	17.4	15	14	44
Business	35	8.75	15.6	10	22	36
Other motive	14	3.50	8.5	6	6.2	37
Repeat visitor	141	35.25	16.5	14	16.7	41
Charter flight	150	37.50	11.2	7	6.9	52
Total	400	100.00	11	9	11	43

arguably with a more significant impact on applied economics literature. In fact, economists have recently applied the same body of techniques to strike duration, length of unemployment spells, time until business failure, and so on (for applications of survival analysis in economics, see, among others, Greene 2000; Hosmer and Lemeshow 1999; Kieffer 1998; Lancaster 1990). This section borrows heavily from Cleves et al. (2002).

There are certain aspects of survival analysis data, such as censoring and non-normality that generate great difficulty when trying to analyze the data using traditional statistical models such as the linear regression model. The variable of interest in the analysis of duration is the length of time that elapses between the beginning of some event either until its end or until the measurement is taken, which may precede termination. Hence, it is sometimes the case that durations – the so-called spells – are censored, in the sense that the researcher does not observe the termination of the event.

This framework of analysis naturally lends itself to the study of length of stay, as one is interested in the determinants of the length of time that elapses between the tourist's arrival on a given tourist destination and his departure. The data set employed in the present article was collected at airports from tourists who were departing from their trips. Hence, there is no censoring in the data since all interviewees reported their length of stay. Therefore, the discussion that follows assumes away censoring.

Spell length is, by construction, a non-negative variable. Let spell length be represented by a random variable T, with continuous probability distribution f(t), where t is a realization of T. It is usually the case that one is interested in the probability that the spell is of length at least t, which is given by the survival function $S(t) = \Pr(T \geq t)$. The hazard rate, λ(t), in turn, answers the following question: Given that the spell has lasted until time t, what is the probability that it will end in the next short interval of time, Δ? More formally:

$$\lambda(t) = \lim_{\Delta > 0} \frac{\Pr(t \leq T \leq t + \Delta | T \geq t)}{\Delta} = \frac{f(t)}{S(t)} \tag{6.1}$$

Intuitively, the hazard rate is the rate at which spells are completed after duration t, given that they last at least until t. Armed with the hazard rate, one computes the survival function through backward integration $S(t) = \exp(-\int_0^t \lambda(s)ds)$. Hence, and as a matter of convenience, one usually focuses on estimating the hazard function directly.

Two frequently used models for adjusting survival functions for the effects of covariates are the accelerated failure-time (AFT) model and the multiplicative or proportional hazards (PH) model. In the AFT model, the natural logarithm of the survival time, $\ln t$, is expressed as a linear function of the (1k) vector of time-invariant covariates x, yielding the linear model $\ln t = x\beta + z$, where β is a (k1) vector of regression coefficients to be estimated, and z is the error term with density f(). The distributional form of the error term determines the regression model.

In the proportional hazards model, the concomitant covariates have a multiplicative effect on the hazard function:

$$\lambda(t,x_i) = \lambda_0(t) \exp(x_i\beta) \tag{6.2}$$

where $\lambda_0(t)$ is the baseline hazard function. Intuitively, the baseline hazard function $\lambda_0(t)$ summarizes the pattern of duration dependence and is common to all persons while $\lambda = \exp(x_i\beta)$ is a non-negative function of person specific covariates x_i, which scales the baseline hazard function common to all persons, controlling, hence, the effect of individual heterogeneity.

The PH property implies that absolute differences in x imply proportionate differences in the hazard rate at each t. For some $t = \bar{t}$, and for two persons i and j

identical in all matters except with respect to the kth covariate, then a unit increase in the kth covariate induces the following proportionate change in the hazard rates:

$$\frac{\lambda(\bar{t},x_i)}{\lambda(\bar{t},x_j)} = \exp(\beta_k) \tag{6.3}$$

The above expression lends a natural interpretation to β_k, namely, the log hazard ratio $\beta_k = \partial \log \lambda(t,x)/\partial \log x_k$ which is easily recognized as either a semi-elasticity or elasticity.

The baseline function $\lambda_0(t)$ may be left unspecified, yielding the Cox's PH model, or it may take a specific parametric distributional form, which, and assuming that the correct distributional form is chosen, leads to more efficient estimates.

The choice of a particular distribution matters since it conditions the slope of the hazard function. A particular distribution yields a particular hazard function, which may feature duration dependence, in the sense that the probability that termination of a stay occurs in the next short interval of time may depend on length of stay. Since there is scant or virtual none empirical evidence on the shape of the hazard function of lengths of stays, this paper takes an agnostic view and entertains the possibility of a myriad of shapes of the hazard function. Hence, the hazard function of stays is estimated under the following six alternative distributions – exponential, Weibull, Gompertz, the three most popular PH models; generalized gamma, log-normal and log-logistic, the most widely employed AFT models – which altogether accommodate, ex ante, several possible shapes of the hazard function. It should be noted that this paper's approach – of letting the data speak – allows to formally test some models against others, and, hence, select a model which is formally deemed as more appropriate.

The exponential distribution yields a constant hazard rate $\lambda_0(t) = \lambda$ and hence is suitable to model length of stay when the probability of termination of a stay in the next short interval of time does not depend on the length of the stay. The Weibull distribution, in turn, is a generalization of the exponential distribution and is suitable for modeling data with monotone hazard rates that either increase or decrease exponentially with time. The corresponding baseline function is $\lambda_0(t) = p\lambda t^{p-1}$ where p is an ancillary parameter to be estimated from the data. Note that when $p = 1$ the Weibull model collapses to the exponential model. The Gompertz distribution yields the baseline function $\lambda_0(t) = \exp(\gamma t)$, where γ is an ancillary parameter to be estimated from the data. Like the Weibull distribution, the Gompertz distribution is suitable for modeling data with monotone hazard rates that either increase or decrease exponentially over time. Unlike the PH models – namely the exponential, Weibull and Gompertz models – the lognormal and log-logistic are two AFT models that tend to produce similar results and are indicated for data exhibiting nonmonotonic hazard rates, specifically initially increasing and then decreasing rates. Finally, the generalized gamma, another AFT model, yields a hazard function extremely flexible, allowing for a large number of possible shapes, including as special cases the Weibull, the exponential and the lognormal models. The generalized gamma model is, therefore, commonly used for evaluating and selecting an appropriate model for the data. Note that the lognormal model, the log-logistic model and the generalized gamma model are estimated in AFT form whilst the exponential model, the Weibull model and the Gompertz model are estimated in the PH form, and, therefore, the resulting regression coefficients β are not directly comparable (see Cleves et al. (2002) for more details on survival analysis models). The remainder of this section deals with model estimation and model selection.

6.5 Model Estimation and Model Selection

Model estimation is done via maximum likelihood, given the parametric nature of the six competing models. With respect to model selection, a reasonable question to ask is: "Given that we have several possible parametric models, how can we select one?" When parametric models are nested, the likelihood-ratio or Wald tests can be used to discriminate between them. This can certainly be done in the case of Weibull versus exponential, or gamma versus Weibull or lognormal. When models are not nested, however, these tests are inappropriate and the task of discriminating between models becomes more difficult. A common approach to this problem is to use the Akaike information criterion (AIC), which, in its essence, penalizes the log likelihood to reflect the number of parameters being estimated in a particular model and then comparing them. The AIC is defined as AIC $= -2(\log \text{likelihood}) + 2(c+p+1)$ where c is the number of model covariates and p is the number of model-specific ancillary parameters. Although the best-fitting model is the one with largest log likelihood, the preferred model is the one with the smallest AIC value. Since the log likelihood obtained for any given parametric model depends on the set of covariates used, the set of covariates of interest is defined ex ante and then employed in the estimation of all the six competing models. Overall, 31 covariates were selected given the available data, on the one hand, and a reading of the literature, on the other, and are described at length in the next section, while the rest of this section focuses on model selection. Table 6.3 presents summary results of the log likelihood estimation, ancillary parameters, model discriminating Wald tests and AIC values.

The Weibull model dominates the exponential model in all criteria considered. The log likelihood obtained under the Weibull model is higher than the log likelihood obtained under the exponential model. A Wald test that p, the Weibull model ancillary parameter, is statistically equal to one – the case when the Weibull model collapses into the exponential model – is firmly rejected. In addition, the AIC value obtained under the Weibull model is lower than the AIC value obtained under the exponential model. Hence, the exponential model is not used elsewhere in this paper, since it is dominated by the Weibull model. Note that p has a point estimate of 1.9027, which is indicative of an upward sloping monotone hazard rate.

Like the Weibull model, the Gompertz model is suitable for modeling data with monotone hazard rates that either increase or decrease exponentially over time. Although the Weibull model cannot be formally tested against the Gompertz model,

Table 6.3 Model selection

Model	Statistics	Nested Models Wald Tests	AIC
Exponential (*PH*)	$LL = -455.90$ $\chi^2_{(31)} = 62.36$ $(p.v.{=}0.0007)$	None	977.80
Weibull (*PH*) $(\hat{p}{=}1.9027)$	$LL = -455.90$ $\chi^2_{(31)} = 211.48$ $(p.v.{=}0.0007)$	$H_0{:}p = 1 \rightarrow \chi^2_{(1)} = 162$ $(p.v.{=}0.0000)$ $\rightarrow$ Reject *Exponential*	760.57
Gompertz (*PH*) $(\hat{\gamma}{=}0.0167)$	$LL = -445.17$ $\chi^2_{(31)} = 83.68$ $(p.v.{=}0.0000)$	None	958.34
Lognormal (*AFT*) $(\hat{\sigma}{=}0.5177)$	$LL = -304.23$ $\chi^2_{(31)} = 131.68$ $(p.v.{=}0.0000)$	None	676.47
Log $-$ log *istic* (*AFT*) $(\hat{\gamma}{=}0.2687)$	$LL = -282.01$ $\chi^2_{(31)} = 145.38$ $(p.v.{=}0.0000)$	None	632.03
Generalized Gamma (*AFT*) $(\hat{\kappa}{=}-0.1843; \hat{\sigma}{=}-0.5128)$	$LL = -302.77$ $\chi^2_{(30)} = 127.97$ $(p.v.{=}0.0000)$	$H_0{:}\kappa = 1 \rightarrow \chi^2_{(1)} = 162$, $(p.v.{=}0.0000)$ Reject *Weibull* $H_0{:}\kappa = 0 \rightarrow \chi^2_{(1)} = 2.93$, $(p.v.{=}0.0872)$ *Not* Reject log *normal* $H_0{:}(\sigma,\kappa) = (1,1) \rightarrow \chi^2_{(2)} = 764.41$, $(p.v.{=}0.0000)$ Reject *Exponential*	675.54

it should be noted that the Weibull model yields a higher log likelihood and a lower AIC value than the Gompertz model. Hence, the Weibull model is preferred to the Gompertz model and is the preferred PH model. Quite interestingly, the point estimate of γ, the ancillary parameter of the Gompertz model, is 0.0167, and, hence, the Gompertz's model associated hazard rate displays a monotone and increasing hazard rate: the same result obtained under the Weibull model.

The log-logistic model produces the lowest AIC value of all the six models considered. The log-logistic model also produces the highest log-likelihood value among all the six competing models. The log-logistic model cannot be formally tested against the other models as it is a non-nested case. Hence, it is not possible to reject the idea that the log-logistic model produces the overall best fit to the data.

The lognormal model yields results similar to the log-logistic model, as expected. The generalized gamma model provides an array of discriminating Wald tests, as it nests the exponential model, the Weibull model and the lognormal model. The gamma model dominates the exponential model: not only does the generalized gamma model yields a lower AIC value and a higher log-likelihood but also the Wald test that $(\sigma,\kappa) = (1,1)$ produces a p-value of 0.0000. It is also the case that the generalized gamma model dominates the Weibull model. In fact, the generalized gamma model produces a lower AIC value than the Weibull model and, based on a discriminating Wald test $\kappa = 1$, the Weibull model is strongly rejected as a special case of the generalized gamma model. When the generalized gamma model is compared against the lognormal model, the picture that emerges is not so clear. The lognormal model corresponds to the generalized gamma model in the special case $\kappa = 0$. The Wald test that $\kappa = 0$ yields a p-value of 0.0872, and hence it is not possible to reject the lognormal model at the 10% significance level. In addition, one can also argue in favor of the lognormal case since it produces a slightly lower AIC value than the generalized gamma model.

In conclusion, the Weibull model strictly dominates both the exponential and the Gompertz model, and is kept in the analysis since it is the preferred PH model. With respect to the AFT models considered, the lognormal model produces a slightly lower AIC value than the generalized gamma model and a discriminating Wald test on the generalized gamma model ancillary parameter κ fails to reject the lognormal model at the 10% significance level. Hence, there is some evidence that the lognormal model is preferred to the generalized gamma model. The log-logistic model produces not only the lowest AIC value but also the highest log likelihood of all six competing models, and cannot be formally tested against any other model as it is a non-nested model. Since the lognormal model and the log-logistic models produce remarkably similar results, the regression coefficients are reported only for the log-logistic model, to save on space.

6.6 Results

Table 6.4 reports the results obtained from the Weibull model – the preferred PH model – and the log-logistic model – the preferred AFT model. It should be noted that the coefficients are not directly comparable across models. The Weibull model is presented in PH form and the coefficients may be interpreted as a hazard ratio. Intuitively, and focusing on binary variables, the coefficients presented are of the form $\exp(\beta_k)$ and represent the ratio between the hazard rate when the variable takes the value of one and the hazard rate when the variable takes the value of zero. Hence, a coefficient higher than one means that an increase in the variable leads to an increase in the hazard rate and, thus, to a lower expected duration. In turn, the log-logistic model is presented in AFT form and a negative coefficient is associated with shorter expected time to termination of a stay. Hence, and if one is interested in comparing the qualitative meaning of the coefficients across models, then coefficients higher (lower) than one in the Weibull model correspond to negative (positive) coefficients in the log-logistic model. Inspection of Table 6.4 reveals that, in fact, the Weibull model and the log-logistic model tend to produce the same results, at least at a qualitative level.

Table 6.4 Regression results

Variables	Weibull (PH form; exp(β_k))	Log-logistic (AFT form)
Age1: 25–35 years	0.9455(– 0.27)	0.0071(0.08)
Age2: 35–45 years	0.7867(– 0.98)	−0.0252(– 0.23)
Age3: 45–55 years	1.0353(0.14)	−0.0467(– 0.44)
Age4: ≥55 years	0.8506(– 0.68)	0.0793(0.74)
Male	1.2605(2.03)**	−0.0842(– 1.68)*
Married	1.4595(2.18)**	−0.1111(– 1.68)
Sweden	1.9116(2.19)**	−0.2677(– 2.17)**
Other Nordic country	1.7013(1.82)*	−0.2107(– 1.73)*
Germany	0.5761(– 1.77)*	−0.0777(– 0.64)
Portugal (Mainland)	1.2630(1.32)	−0.1247(– 1.58)
Azorean ascendancy	0.7774(– 1.11)	0.3047(3.12)***
Education1: Secondary	1.6643(2.86)***	−0.0424(– 0.56)
Education2: Tertiary	1.6306(2.69)***	−0.0987(– 1.24)
Education3: Technical	2.6112(1.93)*	−0.2090(– 1.05)
High level profession	1.1833(1.24)	−0.0404(– .065)
Motive1: Leisure	0.6305(– 1.62)*	0.2462(1.84)*
Motive2: Visiting friends or relatives	0.6117(– 1.40)	0.3541(2.23)**
Motive3: Business	0.1864(– 4.49)***	0.3242(1.95)**
Repeat visitor	0.5223(– 3.80)***	0.1427(1.94)**
Considered alternative destination	0.8725(– 0.76)	0.0417(0.55)
Considered alternative island destination	1.009(0.04)	0.0035(0.03)
Azorean circuit (island hopping)	0.8926(– 0.48)	−0.1638(– 1.49)
Number of islands visited	0.7576(– 2.46)***	0.2129(4.00)***
Travel party 1: With spouse	0.9566(– 0.22)	0.0262(0.29)
Travel party 2: With family	0.9834(– 0.08)	0.0774(0.80)
Travel party 3: With other adults	1.7882(2.54)***	−0.1364(– 1.44)
Travel party 4: With business partners	3.1914(3.93)***	−0.1130(– 0.86)
Not coming back off-season	0.8670(– 0.68)	0.1294(1.46)
Highly satisfied with visit	0.7290(– 2.58)***	0.0538(1.02)
Intends to revisit	1.1069(0.59)	0.0683(0.93)
Came in a charter flight	0.5023(– 2.71)***	0.3249(3.14)***
p ancillary parameter Weibull	1.9027***	
γ ancillary parameter log–logistic		0.2687***
Log likelihood	−346.28	−282.01
N	400	400

Figures in parenthesis are t-stats; Weibull coefficients are hazard ratios; Log-logistic coefficients in AFT form; ***, **, and * means significant at the 1%, 5% and 10% level, respectively.

The age coefficients are not individually statistically significant in both models. As Alegre and Pou (2006) suggest, this may owe to the inclusion of other covariates closely related with age. However, and given that the excluded class is less than 25 years, the results suggest that older tourists tend to stay longer, a result in line with Alegre and Pou.

Male tourists tend to experience shorter stays, just like married tourists. These results obtain for both the Weibull model and the log-logistic model. However, they are only significant in the case of the Weibull model.

Tourists from the Nordic Countries, Sweden included, experience shorter stays, under both models. These results are statistically significant and have important policy implications given the strategic importance of these markets in the overall policy context. In turn, German tourists exhibit longer stays. However, this result for German tourists is only marginally statistically significant in the Weibull model and not statistically significant in the log-logistic model. Tourists from Mainland Portugal exhibit shorter stays, under both models. This result has no statistical significance. Overall, the regression coefficients on nationalities do not follow any clear pattern, at least not according to the physical distance between the tourist's place of origin and destination. In fact, ex ante one would imagine that tourists who live far away would experience longer stays, to make up for the increased overall travel cost. Hence, while it is indeed the case that tourists who live close to the Azores, such as tourists from Portugal Mainland, do tend to experience shorter stays than tourists who live farther away as, say, tourists from the Nordic countries, when one controls for socio-demographic profiles and trip attributes, this pattern becomes less blunt. This is indeed the present case. In particular, it is found that the binary variable charter that equals one if the tourist took a (direct) charter flight (and zero otherwise) significantly increases the length of stay. Considering that virtually all tourists from the Nordic Countries took charter flights, it becomes less of a paradox that having a nationality from the Nordic Countries is associated with shorter length of stays. The reverse could be said about tourists from Mainland Portugal. This remark highlights the importance of controlling for a significant number of covariates.

Azorean ascendancy is a binary variable that equals one in case the tourist claims to have some sort of Azorean ascendancy. The Azorean Diaspora far outnumbers the current Azorean population and there are many Azorean descendents, typically residing in North America, who visit the Azores. It is found, in both models, that having an Azorean ascendancy reduces expected time to termination of stays, a result highly statistically significant under the log-logistic model.

With respect to the education variables, it should be noted that the excluded class is other education, an education class associated with a lesser degree of education. Hence, it follows that both models suggest that higher levels of education are associated with shorter stays, albeit with statistical significance only in the Weibull model.

High level profession is a binary variable that takes the value of one for professions associated with high incomes and high social status. In this sense, high level profession proxies top incomes. A first group of 50 tourists were interviewed in a first stage of the field work in order to validate the questionnaire. From this validation exercise, it followed that not all tourists were willing to report directly their income, and, hence, such proxy for income, based on current professional status, was built in the questionnaire. In both models, a high level profession is associated with shorter expected duration of stays; a result with no statistical significance.

Travel motive was divided into four classes: leisure; visiting friends or relatives; business and, the excluded class, other motives (which includes, for instance, religious festivities). It is found that, compared to the excluded class, all travel motives explicitly considered increase expected duration of stays, a result with high statistical significance in the log-logistic model. As Seaton and Palmer (1997) suggest, tourists visiting friends or relatives tend to exhibit longer stays if they are international tourists, as it is generally the case in the Azores.

Repeat visitor is a binary variable that takes the value of one if the tourist visited the Azores at least once in the past, and zero otherwise. Quite interestingly, in both models it is found that repeat visitors stay for longer periods. In fact, everything else the same, being a repeat visitor reduces the hazard rate to half (0.5223) in the Weibull model. Repeat visitor behavior has aroused interest in the recent years (see, among others, Kozak 2001 and Lehto, O'Leary and Morrison 2004; Oppermann 1997), has its relationship with future visiting behavior (destination loyalty) and word-of-mouth recommendation carries important policy and marketing implications. It is interesting to note the strikingly different expected on-site time spent by repeaters from first-timers, as Figure 6.1 documents. Figure 6.1 plots two survival functions, one for repeat visitors and one for first-time visitors. The survival function for repeat visitors is shifted to the right, which means that repeat visitors are associated with a higher probability of experiencing a stay of at least a given duration. For instance, the probability that repeaters stay for at least 14 days is about 45%, more than double the analogous probability for first-timers: about 20%.

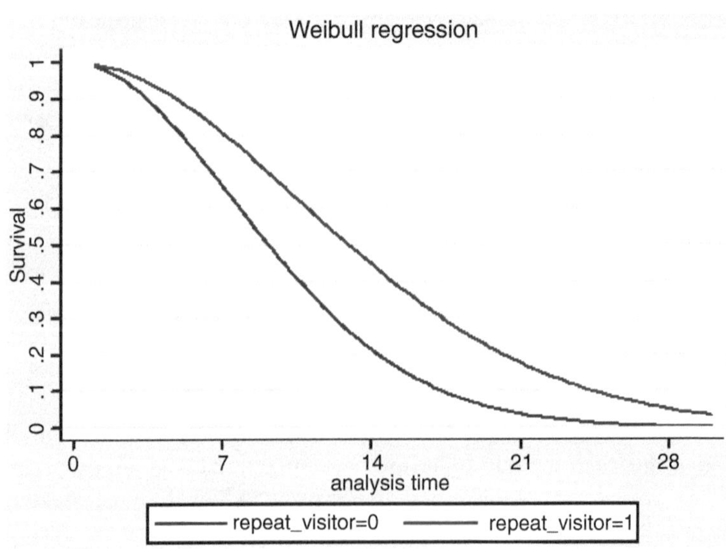

Fig 6.1 Survival functions for repeaters and first-timers

Considered alternative destination and considered alternative island destination are two dummy variables that characterize the destination decision process. However, both variables are not statistically significant in both models.

There are nine islands in the Azores. However, most tourists visit only one island: São Miguel. Azorean circuit is a binary variable that takes the value of one in case the tourist visits more than one island. In both models, engaging in island hopping does not influence expected length of stay, at least in a statistical sense. Number of islands considered, in turn, is a continuous variable ranging from one to 9, since there are nine islands in the Azores. Hence, it can be argued that number of islands embeds richer information then Azorean circuit, since the former is continuous while the latter is binary. While in the Weibull model the number of islands visited is not statistically significant at the conventional levels, in the log-logistic model an increase in the number of islands visited leads to an increase in the expected length of stay, as expected.

The questionnaire was carried out in the summer. To gauge the degree of tourists' satisfaction with their experience in the Azores, it was asked if tourists would consider visiting the Azores off-season (when the weather is arguably not so pleasant). Not coming back off season flags the tourists who answered no. In both models, not coming back off season has no statistical significance. Highly satisfied with visit is a binary variable that directly captures overall tourists' satisfaction with respect their experience. While in the log-logistic model being highly satisfied with the visit has no statistical significance, in the Weibull model being highly satisfied with the visit leads to longer expected length of stays. This result may owe to the fact that highly satisfied tourists prolonged their stays or tourists who report to be highly satisfied are those who were indeed more likely to enjoy their visit and hence planned longer stays from the onset of their visits.

Perhaps not surprisingly, taking a charter flight causes longer expected stays. This result has important policy implications as charter flights are subsidized by the local government.

6.7 Conclusion

One of the most important decisions made by tourists before or while visiting a given destination concerns their length of stay. In fact, length of stay most likely conditions overall tourists' expenditure and stress imposed on local resources; just to name a few of the implications of varying lengths of stays. However, and as Alegre and Pou (2006) document, despite the rich literature on tourism demand, very few studies have resorted to microeconometric models in order to shed light on the determinants of length of stay. This paper estimated a number of alternative microeconometric parametric survival analysis models to learn the determinants of length of stay, in a novel way in the tourism demand literature, featuring non-monotone hazard rates and, concomitantly, accommodating several data patterns: a much welcomed feature, since the pattern of length of stays may vary across destinations and over time. The results suggest that survival analysis may be a fertile ground to analyze tourism demand if time dimension is of the essence, as is obviously the case with length of stay studies. An interesting avenue for future research may lie on tourism demand modeling strategies where time is explicitly modeled, with structural models of consumer demand theory leading to reduced form survival analysis regression exercises, as the ones found in this paper. Arguably, such body of work, rooted on microeconomic foundations, would allow novel tools for welfare analysis, complementary to those recently proposed by researchers who have drawn on discrete choice models based consumer theory and associated count data and logistic models.

The results in this paper are statistically significant and economically important. Quite interestingly, a large number of covariates, pertaining to detailed individual socio-demographic profiles and actual trip experiences of the representative tourists interviewed, were considered in the regressions in order to control for heterogeneous individual behavior. Concomitantly, the richness of the information embedded in the covariates used allows the design of effective marketing policies, in the sense that the regression results allow one to estimate, for a given synthesized, policy relevant individual or target group, not only mean or median expected stays, but also the probability that stays exceed a given threshold. Hence, policymakers and private operators may benefit from such tools that uncover individual socio-demographic profiles and trip attributes that promote longer stays and act or advertise accordingly. Among the several results found, it can be argued that being a repeat visitor and taking charter flights are important criteria to identify tourists who are likely to experience longer stays. In fact, it is shown that repeaters face a 45% probability of experiencing a stay of at least 14 days, which is more than double the analogous probability for first-timers of 20%. Thus, future research should characterize such groups and their economic and activity involvement. Taking a (direct) charter flights also plays a highly statistically significant role in determining length of stay. In particular, taking a charter flight decreases the hazard rate to half, and, hence, leads to longer expected stays. This result is very important as the Azorean government, in its quest to promote air connections to the Azores, subsidizes charter flights, and, must, therefore, assess the socioeconomic implications of such subsidies. Apparently, such policy is successful in terms of promoting longer stays. This is true regardless of nationalities, which were controlled for in the regressions. A higher degree of education is associated with shorter expected stays. It would be interesting to investigate if this result follows from better educated tourists face more stringent time constraints or are purely due to differences in preferences across education levels. Visiting more islands leads to an increase in the expected length of stay. This result suggests that there is no crowding-out behavior from the part of tourists, in the sense that tourists do not trade a larger number of islands visited for a shorter visit per island, keeping, hence, overall length of stay constant. In the contrary: tourists are willing to visit more islands at the expense of longer stays. Hence, future research ought to address tourists' spatial behavior. For instance, what role does inter-island mobility play? By the same token, it is important to note that reporting a high degree satisfaction has a statistically significant positive impact on expected stays. Hence, understanding what causes a high overall degree of satisfaction is also an important future research topic.

References

Alegre J, Pou L (2006) The length of stay in the demand for tourism. Tourism Manage 27: 1343–1355
Bargeman B, Poel V (2006) The role of routines in the decision making process of dutch vacationers. Tourism Manage 27:707–720
Berman, M, Kim H (1999) Endogenous on-site time in the recreation demand model. Land Econ 75:603–619
Cleves M, Gould W, Gutierrez R (2002) An introduction to survival analysis using Stata. Stata Press, College Station Texas
Crouch G (1994) A meta-analysis of tourism demand. Ann Tourism Res 22:103–118
Crouch G, Louviére I (2000) A review of choice modeling research in tourism, hospitality, and leisure. Tourism Anal 5:97–104
Davies B, Mangan J (1992) Family expenditure on hotels and holidays. Ann Tourism Res 19: 691–699
Decrop A, Snelders D (2004) Planning the summer vacation: An adaptable and opportunistic process. Ann Tourism Res 31:1008–1030
Dubin J, McFadden D (1984) An econometric analysis of residential electric appliance holdings and consumption. Econometrica 52:345–362
Feather P, Shaw D (1999) Possibilities for including the opportunity cost of time in recreational demand systems. Land Econ 75:592–602
Fleischer A, Pizam A (2002) Tourism constraints among Israeli seniors. Ann Tourism Res 29: 106–123
Gokovali U, Bahar O, Kozak M (2007) Determinants of length of stay: A practical use of survival analysis. Tourism Manage (in press)
Greene W (2000) Econometric analysis. Prentice Hall, New Jersey
Hanemann W (1984) Discrete/continuous models of consumer demand. Econometrica 52:541–561
Hellström JA (2006) Bivariate count data model for household tourism demand. J Appl Econom 21:213–226
Hill M, Hill A (2002) Research with surveys. Sílabo, Lisbon
Hosmer D, Lemeshow S (1993) Applied survival analysis. Wiley, New York
McConnell K (1992) On-site time in the demand for recreation. Am J Agric Econ 74:918–925
Jafari J (1987) Tourism models: The sociocultural aspects. Tourism Manage 8:151–159
Kieffer N (1988) Economic duration and hazard functions. J Econ Lit 26:646–667
Kozak M (2001) Repeaters' behavior at two distinct destinations. Ann Tourism Res 28:785–808
Kozak M (2004) Destination benchmarking: Concepts, practices and operations. CAB International, Oxon Cab
Lancaster T (1990) The econometric analysis of transition data. Cambridge University Press, Cambridge
Larson D (1993) Joint recreation choices and implied value of time. Land Econ 69:270–286
Lehto X, O'Leary J, Morrison A (2004) The effect of prior experience on vacation behavior. Ann Tourism Res 31:801–818
Legoherel P (1998) Toward a market segmentation of the tourism trade: Expenditure levels and consumer behavior instability. J Travel Tourism Mark 7:19–39
Lim C (1997) An econometric classification and review of international tourism demand models. Tourism Econ 3:69–81
Mathieson A, Wall J(1992) Tourism: Economic, physical and social impacts. Prentice Hall, Harlow
McConnell K (1992) On-site time in the demand for recreation. Am J Agric Econ

Mok C, Iverson T (2000) Expenditure-based segmentation: Taiwanese tourists to Guam. Tourism Manage 21:299–305
Moscardo G, Morrison A, Pearce L, Lang C, O'Leary J (1996) Understanding vacation destination choice through travel motivation and activities. J Vacation Mark 2:109–122
Oppermann M (1995) Travel life cycle. Ann Tourism Res 22:535–552
Oppermann M (1997) First-time and repeat visitors to New Zealand. Tourism Manage 18:177–181
Papatheodorou A (2001) Why people travel to different places? Ann Tourism Res 28:164–179
Pollak R (1969) Modeling conditional demand functions and consumption theory. Q J Econ 83: 60–78
Pollak R (1971) Conditional demand functions and the implications of separable utility. South Econ J 37:423–433
Saarinen J (2006) Traditions of sustainability in tourism studies. Ann Tourism Res 33:1121–1140
Seaton A, Palmer C (1997) Understanding VFR tourism behavior: the first five years of the United Kingdom tourism survey. Tourism Manage 18:345–355
Song H, Witt S (2000) Tourism demand modeling and forecasting: modern econometric approaches. Pergarmon, Oxford
Swarbrooke J, Horner S (2001) Consumer behavior in tourism. Butterworth Heinemann, Oxford
Sung H, Morrison A, Hong G, O'Leary J (2001) The effects of household and trip characteristics on trip types: A consumer behavioral approach for segmenting the US domestic leisure travel market. J Hospitality Tourism Res 25:46–68
Witt S, Witt C (1995) Forecasting tourism demand: A review of empirical research. Int J Forecast 11:447–475

Part II
Assessment of Tourism Impacts

Chapter 7
Is the Time-Varying Parameter Model the Preferred Approach to Tourism Demand Forecasting? Statistical Evidence

Shujie Shen, Gang Li, and Haiyan Song

7.1 Introduction

Over the past 50 years, tourism has become one of the largest and most rapidly growing sectors in the world economy (Eadington and Redman 1991). Accurate forecasts of tourism demand are critical to both private sectors and governments in providing useful information for business strategy formulation and public policy making, respectively. A large body of literature has been published on tourism demand forecasting using regression techniques, and studies in this research stream have made a significant contribution to the understanding of international tourism demand. However, these studies are based on the assumption that the values of the parameters in the demand models are constant over time, an assumption that has been challenged by a number of researchers for being too restrictive (Song and Witt 2000, Song and Wong 2003, Li et al. 2005). A more sophisticated and flexible econometric forecasting method – the time varying parameter (TVP) model – has been developed to overcome the above limitation. Because it takes into account the dynamics of tourist behaviour, the TVP model is likely to generate more accurate tourism demand forecasts than the fixed parameter alternatives (Song and Li 2008). However, applications of the TVP model to tourism demand analysis are still rare. The studies of Riddington (1999), Song and Witt (2000), Song et al. (2003a), Song and Wong (2003) and Li et al. (2006a, b) are the few exceptions. These empirical studies generally suggest that the TVP model outperforms its competitors practically in short-term tourism demand forecasting.

In selecting a forecasting method, the following criteria are relevant: the ease of forecast generation, the cost of model estimation in terms of both financial resources and time and the forecast accuracy (Frechtling 2001). Most researchers and practitioners view forecast accuracy as the most important criterion in forecasting model selection. Accordingly, increasing attention has been paid to the study of tourism forecast accuracy. However, earlier studies that have assessed the prediction

---

S. Shen (✉)
Institute for Transport Studies, University of Leeds, Leeds, UK
e-mail: s.shen@its.leeds.ac.uk

Á. Matias et al. (eds.), *Advances in Tourism Economics*,
DOI 10.1007/978-3-7908-2124-6_7, © Physica-Verlag Heidelberg 2009

accuracy of alternative tourism forecasting models have focused mainly on the error magnitudes, which are commonly judged by non-statistical tools such as the mean absolute percentage error (MAPE) and root mean square percentage error (RMSPE) (see, for example, Li et al. 2005, Song and Witt 2000, Kulendran and Witt 2001), and statistical tools have been rarely employed to examine whether a significant difference exists in the accuracy of different forecasting methods of tourism demand forecasting. The following studies are the few exceptions. De Mello and Nell (2005) applied the Harvey-Leybourne-Newbold (HLN) test proposed by Harvey et al. (1997) and the encompassing test to investigate the differences in forecast accuracy between alternative models. Kon and Turner (2005) applied simple t-tests for the same purpose in their forecast comparison study. Witt et al. (2003) introduced statistics to test for both forecasting unbiasedness and directional changes.

The purpose of this study is to extend the application of the statistical tests by examining the differences in forecasting accuracy between the TVP model and the traditional regression-based static model. This study will provide robust evidence that suggests the TVP model is the preferred model in tourism demand forecasting practice.

7.1.1 The TVP Model

The traditional static regression model is normally specified as

$$y_t = a_0 + a_1 x_1 + a_2 x_2 + \cdots + \varepsilon_t, \tag{7.1}$$

where y_t is the dependent variable, $x_1, x_2 \ldots$ are independent variables, $a_0, a_1, a_2 \ldots$ are the parameters to be estimated and ε_t is the disturbance term. Very often, all variables are transformed into logarithms, by which the coefficients can be interpreted as elasticities.

One of the assumptions behind traditional regression techniques is that coefficients are constant over time. This can be seen from the subscripts of the parameters, which have no time dimension, and implies that the economic structure that generates the data does not change over time (Judge et al. 1985). However, 'a long period of high inflation or a rate of inflation above a certain threshold, for instance, may cause a structural change in the way firms and consumers form their expectations' (Tucci 1995, p. 239). In a logarithm-transformed model, the calculated elasticities are constant over time. Such an assumption is too restrictive to be valid in most cases.

To overcome the limitation of the traditional fixed-parameter regression models, the TVP model was developed, and can be specified in the following state space form (SSF):

$$y_t = x_t \alpha_t + \varepsilon_t, \varepsilon_t \sim N(0, H_t), \tag{7.2}$$

$$\alpha_{t+1} = \Phi \alpha_t + \eta_t, \alpha_1 \sim N(a_1, P_1), \eta_t \sim N(0, Q_t), \tag{7.3}$$

where x_t is a vector of explanatory variables $(x_1, x_2, \ldots)$; α_t is an unobservable vector called the *state vector*; ε_t refers to the temporary disturbance and η_t to the permanent disturbance and ε_t and η_t are Gaussian disturbances, which are serially independent and independent of each other at all time points. Eq. (7.2) is called the measurement, or signal, equation, and Eq. (7.3) is known as the transition, or state, equation. The specification of the transition equation is normally determined by experimentation. The criteria used to determine the structure of the transition equation are the goodness of fit and predictive power of the model. In most economic studies, the random walk process has been proved to be appropriate and sufficient to capture the dynamics of the system under study (see, for instance, Greenslade and Hall 1996, Kim 1993, Song and Witt 2000).

The rationale behind this model is that the measurement equation allows the parameters to be time dependent while the transition equation determines the movement of the parameters. Meanwhile, as the time-varying parameter α_t is an unobservable variable, it has to be estimated using the observed data y_t andx_t. Because α_t varies over time, in a log-transformed model the evolution of demand elasticities over time can be captured.

Once a TVP model has been specified in an SSF, the Kalman filter procedure (Kalman 1960) can be employed to calculate the optimal (minimum mean square error, MMSE) estimator of the state vector at time t, given the information available up to time t–1. Correspondingly, one-step-ahead and multi-steps-ahead forecasts can be generated recursively. A full description of the Kalman filter technique is given in Harvey (1989).

7.2 Significance Tests of Forecast Accuracy

Consider two sets of forecasts, $\{\hat{y}_{it}\}_{t=1}^{T}$ and $\{\hat{y}_{jt}\}_{t=1}^{T}$, of the time series $\{y_t\}_{t=1}^{T}$. Define the forecast errors as

$$e_{it} = \hat{y}_{it} - y_t, \text{ for } i = 1 \text{ and } 2. \tag{7.4}$$

The loss associated with forecast i is assumed to be a function of the actual and forecast values only through the forecast error e_{it}, and is denoted by

$$g(y_t, \hat{y}_{it}) = g(\hat{y}_{it} - y_t) = g(e_{it}). \tag{7.5}$$

Typically, $g(e_{it})$is the square (squared-error loss) or absolute value (absolute error loss) of e_{it}.[1] The loss differential between the two forecasts is then denoted by

$$d_t = g(e_{1t}) - g(e_{2t}). \tag{7.6}$$

[1] Both the squared error and absolute error loss functions are used in the study, i.e., the mean square error (MSE) and mean absolute percentage error (MAPE), respectively.

The null hypothesis of equal forecast accuracy between the two forecasts is $E[g(e_{1t})] = E[g(e_{2t})]$, i.e., $E(d_t) = 0$ for all t.

7.2.1 The Morgan-Granger-Newbold (MGN) Test

Consider the following assumptions.

(i) Loss is quadratic.
(ii) The forecast errors are (a) zero mean, (b) Gaussian, (c) serially uncorrelated or (d) contemporaneously uncorrelated.

Maintaining assumptions (i) and (ii) (a)–(c), Granger and Newbold (1977) developed a test for equal forecast accuracy based on the following orthogonalisation (see Morgan 1939):

$$x_t = e_{1t} + e_{2t} \tag{7.7}$$

$$z_t = e_{1t} - e_{2t}. \tag{7.8}$$

Then, the null hypothesis of a zero mean loss differential is equivalent to the equality of the two forecast error variances or a zero covariance between $x_t$and z_t (i.e., $\rho_{xz} = 0$), and the test statistic is

$$MGN = \frac{r}{[(1 - r^2)/(T - 1)]^{1/2}}, \tag{7.9}$$

where

$$r = x'z/[(x'x)(z'z)]^{1/2} \tag{7.10}$$

and x and z are the $T \times 1$ vectors with tth elements x_t and z_t, respectively. Under the null hypothesis of a zero covariance between x_t and z_t, MGN has a t-distribution with $T - 1$ degrees of freedom. As the test is based on the maintained assumption that forecast errors are white noise, it is only applicable to one-step prediction. In addition, it is valid as a test of the equality of forecast accuracy only under squared error loss (Granger and Newbold 1977).

7.2.2 The Diebold-Mariano (DM) Test

Diebold and Mariano (1995) considered model-free tests for forecast accuracy that can easily be applied to non-quadratic loss functions, multi-step forecasts and forecast errors that are non-Gaussian, non-zero mean, serially correlated and contemporaneously correlated. The basis of the DM test is the sample mean of the observed loss differential series $\{d_t: t=1,2,3,\ldots,T\}$, when assumptions (i) and (ii) (a)–(d) need not hold. Assuming covariance stationarity and other regularity conditions on the process $\{d_t\}$, the test is based on the following statistic:

$$DM = \bar{d}/[2\pi \hat{f}_d(0)/T]^{1/2}, \tag{7.11}$$

where $\bar{d}$ is the sample mean of d_t, and $\hat{f}_d(0)$is a consistent estimate of $f_d(0)$. The null hypothesis that $E(d_t) = 0$ for all t is rejected in favour of the alternative hypothesis that $E(d_t) \neq 0$ when DM, an absolute value, exceeds the critical value of a standard unit Gaussian distribution.

Consistent estimators of $f_d(0)$ can be of the form

$$\hat{f}_d(0) = (1/2\pi) \sum_{k=-m(T)}^{m(t)} w(k/m(T))\hat{\gamma}_d(k), \tag{7.12}$$

where

$$\hat{\gamma}_d(k) = (1/T) \sum_{t=|k|+1}^{T} (d_t - \bar{d})(d_{t-|k|} - \bar{d}) \tag{7.13}$$

$$\text{and } \bar{d} = \sum_{t=1}^{T} [g(e_{1t}) - g(e_{2t})]/T. \tag{7.14}$$

$m(T)$, the bandwidth or lag truncation, increases with T but at a slower rate, and $w(\bullet)$ is the weighting scheme or kernel.[2] One weighting scheme, called the truncated rectangular kernel and used in Diebold and Mariano (1995), is the indicator function that takes the value of unity when the argument has an absolute value less than one:

$$w(x) = I(|x| < 1). \tag{7.15}$$

The DM test has been widely used to test for forecast accuracy equality in the macroeconomic context (see, for example, Swanson and White 1997, Wu 1999, Ocal 2000). An important advantage of the test is its direct applicability to non-quadratic loss functions. In addition, the test is robust to contemporaneous and serial correlations, and when the forecast errors are non-Gaussian, it maintains approximately correct size. However, the condition for this is that the DM test should be applied in large samples, as in small samples it tends to be oversized. Because the forecast samples are small in the present study, the HLN test is used, which is a small-sample modification of the DM test.

---

[2] See, for example, Andrews (1991) for econometric applications.

7.2.3 The Harvey-Leybourne-Newbold (HLN) Test

Harvey et al. (1997) proposed a small-sample modification of the Diebold-Mariano test. The modification concerns an approximately unbiased estimate of the variance of the mean loss differential when forecast accuracy is measured in terms of the mean squared prediction error, and h-steps-ahead forecast errors are assumed to have zero autocorrelations at order h and beyond.

Because the optimal h-steps-ahead predictions are likely to have forecast errors that are a moving average process of order h–1, i.e., MA (h–1), the HLN test assumes that for h-steps-ahead forecasts, the loss differential d_t has autocovariance:

$$\hat{\gamma}(k) = (1/T) \sum_{t=k+1}^{T} (d_t - \bar{d})(d_{t-k} - \bar{d}). \tag{7.16}$$

The exact variance of the mean loss differential is

$$V(\bar{d}) = (1/T)[\gamma_0 + (2/T) \sum_{k=1}^{h-1} (T - k)\gamma_k]. \tag{7.17}$$

The original DM test would estimate this variance by

$$\hat{V}(\bar{d}) = (1/T)[\hat{\gamma}^*(0) + (2/T) \sum_{k=1}^{h-1} (T - k)\hat{\gamma}^*(k)] \tag{7.18}$$

$$\hat{\gamma}^*(k) = T\hat{\gamma}(k)/(T - k). \tag{7.19}$$

With d based on the squared prediction error, the HLN test obtains the following approximation of the expected value of $\hat{V}(\bar{d})$:

$$E(\hat{V}(\bar{d})) \sim V(\bar{d})[T + 1 - 2\,h + h(h - 1)/T]/T. \tag{7.20}$$

Therefore, Harvey et al. (1997) suggested modifying the DM test statistic to

$$DM^* = DM/[[T + 1 - 2\,h + h(h - 1)/T]/T]^{1/2}. \tag{7.21}$$

In addition, Harvey et al. (1997) suggested comparing DM^* with critical values from the t-distribution with (T–1) degrees of freedom instead of the standard unit normal distribution. The current study applies the HLN test to multiple-steps-ahead forecasts of different models based on the MAPE. Similar to the DM test, an important advantage of the HLN test is its direct applicability to nonquadratic loss functions. The loss differential series is defined in this study as

$$d_t = |(\hat{y}_{1,t}/y_t) - 1| - |(\hat{y}_{2,t}/y_t) - 1|. \tag{7.22}$$

Because of the limitations of the MGN test, in this study it is only applied to the one-year-ahead forecasts of different models for each origin country based on the criterion of the MSE. The study also investigates whether the two statistical tests based on different loss functions generate consistent results.

So far, no published study that uses the MGN test has been found in the tourism forecasting literature, and only one study has adopted the HLN test (De Mello and Nell 2005). De Mello and Nell (2005) use the HLN test to examine the forecast accuracy of three vector autoregressive (VAR) models and an almost ideal demand system (AIDS) model, but do not find significant differences in the forecast accuracy between the two kinds of models. The current study employs both statistical tests to test for differences in the forecast accuracy between the TVP and static regression models.

7.3 Empirical Results

This empirical study focuses on inbound tourism demand for Thailand. Thailand is one of the first countries to have developed an international tourism industry, and it has become the third largest tourism receiving country in the East Asia and Pacific region. This study is based on Thai inbound tourism from the following major international markets: Australia, Japan, Korea, Malaysia, Singapore, the UK and the US. The most common measure of tourism demand, the tourist arrivals variable, is used to represent inbound tourism demand for Thailand.

International tourism demand in Thailand can be described by the following double-log function:

$$LTOU_{jt} = f(LGDP_{jt}, LRRCP_{jt}, LRSUB_{jt}, LT_{jt}, DUM74, DUM79, DUM87) \quad (j = 1,2,\&\ 7), \tag{7.23}$$

where the letter L in front of the variable names in Eq. (23) stands for logarithm; TOU_{jt} is tourist arrivals from the origin country j; GDP_{jt} measures the income level of the origin country j; $RRCP_{jt}$ is the relative tourism price level in Thailand, measured by the consumer price index (CPI) in Thailand relative to that in the origin country j, which is then adjusted by the relevant exchange rate; and $RSUB_{jt}$ represents the relative substitute price level of tourism in competing destinations, measured by a weighted average price index of alternative destinations relative to the price level in the origin country, with the shares of tourist arrivals in these potential substitute destinations being the weights. Singapore, Indonesia and the Philippines are chosen as alternative destinations for Malaysia; Malaysia, Indonesia and the Philippines for Singapore; and Singapore, Malaysia, the Philippines and Indonesia for the other origin countries. T_{jt} is the trade volume between the origin country j and Thailand, measured by the sum of their import and export volumes, which is then adjusted by the import and export price indices; *DUM74* and *DUM79* are dummy variables capturing the effects of the two oil crises in 1974 and 1979, respectively; and *DUM87* captures the effect of the 'Visit Thailand Year' campaign in 1987.

The independent variables included in the static regression models and final TVP models are determined by the general-to-specific modelling process. This approach starts with a general model that contains as many variables as possible suggested by economic theory, with an appropriate lag structure, in the form of an autoregressive distributed lag model (ADLM). The insignificant variables are deleted from the model one by one, and then the model is estimated. The process is repeated until all of the remaining variables are significant (Song and Witt 2000). These variables are then included in the static model and final TVP model. Full description of the data and the model specifications can be found in Song et al. (2003b) and Li et al. (2006a). In this study, the data samples cover 1963–2002 for Australia and the UK, and 1968–2002 for the other countries because of data availability.

Plots of the time series (excluding dummy variables) show that all of the variables are trended. The augmented Dickey-Fuller (ADF) test (Dickey and Fuller 1981) and the Phillips-Perron (PP) test (Phillips and Perron 1988) are used in the study to test for unit roots. The results show that all variables are I (1), which indicates that they are stationary after taking first differences. The results from the tests for cointegration suggest that all variables in each country model are cointegrated, which suggests that the static regression model can be regarded as a long-run equilibrium equation based on the Engle-Granger two-stage cointegration and error correction modeling approach.

The estimates of the static regression and TVP models are shown in Tables 7.1 and 7.2, respectively. The estimated coefficients in both of the models have the expected signs except for the trade volume variable in the Australian case and the relative price variable in Japan's TVP model. However, the estimated coefficients of these two variables are insignificant. The gross domestic product (GDP) variable features in the cases of Australia, Singapore and the UK for both the static and TVP models, and the estimated coefficients are all statistically significant. In the static model, the tourism price in Thailand relative to that in the origin country has a significant effect on the international tourism demand for Thailand for Australia, Japan, Korea and the US. However, in the TVP model, the relative tourism price variable features only in the case of Korea.

7.3.1 Dynamic Elasticity Analysis

By plotting the estimated coefficients of the TVP models over the whole sample period, the time paths of demand elasticity evolutions can be observed. Ignoring the first few years in the sample,[3] it can be seen that the most severe fluctuations in the income elasticities amongst the three selected TVP models are observed in the case of the UK, especially during the 1970s and 1980s, which reflects the adverse

[3]To estimate the parameters, the Kalman filter algorithm uses diffuse initialization, which is equivalent to constructing an appropriate prior from the first few observations in the sample (Harvey 1989). Therefore, this period of the sample should not be considered for the elasticity analysis.

Table 7.1 Estimates of static regression models

	Australia	Japan	Korea	Malaysia	Singapore	UK	US
Constant	1.881	16.698*	20.382*	7.450*	0.784	−18.616*	6.713*
	(1.441)	(0.223)	(2.716)	(0.248)	(0.299)	(0.613)	(0.525)
$LGDP_{jt}$	2.258**				1.289*	4.728*	
	(0.329)				(0.074)	(0.097)	
$LRRCP_{jt}$	−2.259*	−2.279*	−3.069*				−1.269*
	(0.522)	(0.124)	(0.978)				(0.163)
$LRSUB_{jt}$			−0.261	1.812*	1.078*		−0.208
			(0.726)	(0.080)	(0.183)		(0.103)
LT_{jt}	0.041		1.152**				0.484*
	(0.146)		(0.266)				(0.061)
DUM74		0.181					
		(0.288)					
DUM79	−0.114	−0.181	−0.615				−0.303
	(0.243)	(0.283)	(0.382)				(0.126)
DUM87	−0.010						0.063
	(0.076)						(0.091)
$\bar{R}^2$	0.958	0.910	0.958	0.937	0.978	0.984	0.944
NORM	0.960	0.314	0.876	0.146	0.339	0.702	33.262**
LMSC	17.751**	12.009**	19.307**	15.719**	15.686**	10.301**	5.062
HETRO	12.694	4.269	18.026*	8.958*	2.657	2.071	8.113
RESET	44.379**	0.885	4.352*	0.255	45.142**	2.607	5.869*

Notes: * and ** indicate that the estimates are significant at the 5% and 1% levels, respectively. Values in parentheses are standard errors. NORM is the Jarque-Bera normality test, LMSC is the Lagrange multiplier test for serial correlation, HETRO is the heteroscedasticity test and RESET is Ramsey's misspecification test.

Table 7.2 Estimates of final TVP models

	Australia	Japan	Korea	Malaysia	Singapore	UK	US
Constant	6.242*	13.823*	12.461*	9.526*	1.530	−6.423	9.841*
	(1.414)	(0.391)	(1.588)	(1.112)	(1.759)	(4.662)	(2.117)
$LGDP_{jt}$	3.490*				1.536*	2.913*	
	(0.647)				(0.248)	(0.691)	
$LRRCP_{jt}$	−0.278	0.148	−2.237*				−0.522
	(0.521)	(0.301)	(0.406)				(0.339)
$LRSUB_{jt}$			2.192*	1.325*	0.185		0.202
			(0.415)	(0.321)	(0.208)		(0.301)
LT_{jt}	−0.243		0.294				0.139
	(0.144)		(0.151)				(0.151)
Log likelihood	−12.932	1.340	−16.313	−0.529	1.283	8.604	−5.918
NORM	0.723	0.364	1.322	6.775*	5.791	0.118	9.420**
HETRO	0.233	0.534	0.674	0.161	1.122	0.315	0.316
BLQ	11.337*	15.062**	4.622	1.884	3.825	4.799	4.907

Notes: * and ** indicate that the estimates are significant at the 5% and 1% levels, respectively. Values in parentheses are standard errors. NORM refers to the normality test, HETRO refers to the heteroscedasticity test and BLQ is the Box-Ljung Q statistic for the autocorrelation test.

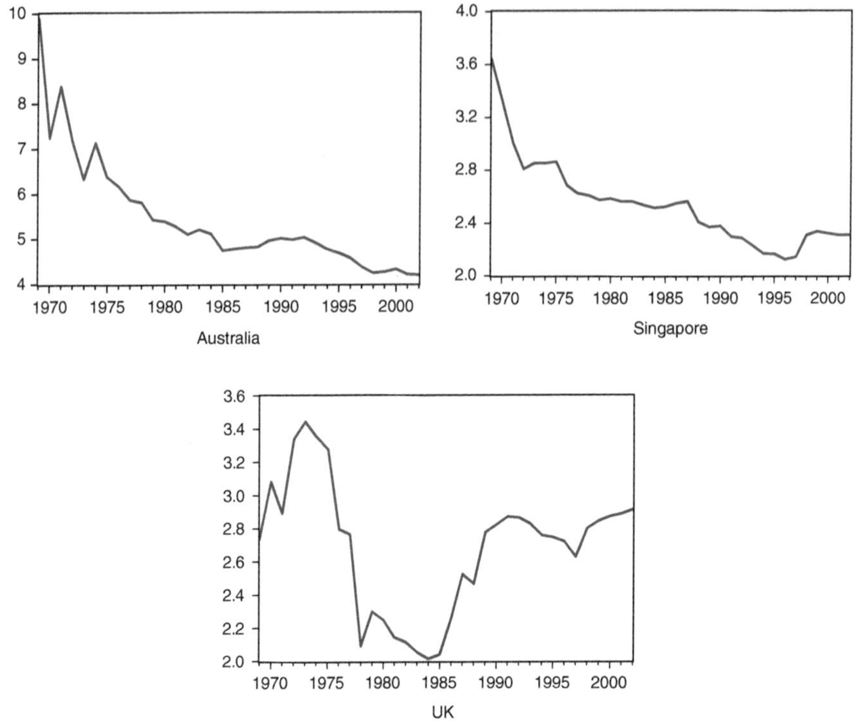

Fig. 7.1 Kalman filter estimates of income elasticities in selected TVP models

effects of the two oil crises and the economic recession during this period. However, the income elasticities in the cases of Australia and Singapore exhibit relatively smoother downward trends, probably because the economies of these countries were not affected as significantly as the economy of the UK. Because the evolution of the income elasticity is associated with changes in the economic conditions in the origin countries, the plots of the demand elasticities can provide useful information for understanding the behavioural changes of tourists. The time paths of the own-price and cross-price elasticities are also relevant for destination policymakers in terms of formulating price strategies. Because of space constraints, the plots of the price elasticities are not presented (Fig. 7.1).

7.3.2 Statistical Test Results

The one- to four-years-ahead forecasting performance of static and TVP models is examined in this study. To generate ex-post forecasts, the models are re-estimated, first using the data up to 1990, and forecasts are generated for 1991–2002. The model is then re-estimated using the data up to 1991, and forecasts are generated for 1992–2002. This estimation-forecasting procedure is repeated until all of the data up to 2001 have been exhausted. Finally, 12 one-year-ahead forecasts, 11 two-years-ahead forecasts, 10 three-years-ahead forecasts and 9 four-years-ahead forecasts are generated for a comparison of forecast accuracy.

Following previous tourism forecasting studies, forecast accuracy is measured by the MAPE and RMSPE. The results are shown in Table 7.3. The final models pass most of the diagnostic tests and do not suffer from non-normal distribution. Therefore, the MGN test is applied to the one-year-ahead forecasts of different models for each of the origin countries based on the criterion of the MSE. As the sample in this study is small, the HLN test is applied to the multiple-steps-ahead forecasts of the specific models based on the MAPE (see Table 7.4). For reasons of comparison, the HLN and MGN tests are applied to the one-year-ahead forecasts of the different models for each of the origin countries (see Table 7.5).

Table 7.3 shows that the TVP model outperforms the static model based on the error magnitude measures. This result is consistent with that of Li et al. (2006a). The HLN test results in Table 7.4 show that at different horizons, the *t*-statistics are all significant at the 1% level, which indicates the rejection of the null hypothesis that the static model and TVP model are equally accurate regarding multiple-steps-ahead forecasts. At all horizons, the TVP model outperforms the static model at the 1% level of significance. Table 7.5 reports the results of the HLN test for one-year-ahead forecasts for each of the origin countries (Column 2), along with the results of the MGN test based on the MSE (Column 3). The HLN tests show that, in the

Table 7.3 Forecast accuracy measured by the MAPE and RMSPE

Horizon	Error Measure	Static Model	TVP Model
1-year ahead	MAPE	1.904	0.845
	RSMPE	2.439	1.111
2-years-ahead	MAPE	2.299	1.274
	RSMPE	2.857	1.627
3-years-ahead	MAPE	2.612	1.660
	RSMPE	3.269	2.094
4-years-ahead	MAPE	2.848	1.986
	RSMPE	3.489	2.447
Overall	MAPE	2.416	1.441
	RSMPE	3.013	1.820

Table 7.4 Multiple-step HLN statistics

Forecast Horizon	Static vs TVP
1-year-ahead	12.589*** (TVP)
2-years-ahead	9.340*** (TVP)
3-years-ahead	7.946*** (TVP)
4-years-ahead	9.898*** (TVP)

Note: *** denotes the 1% significance level.

Table 7.5 One-year-ahead HLN and MGN statistics across countries

Origin Country	Static vs. TVP: HLN statistic	Static vs. TVP: MGN statistic
Korea	6.025*** (TVP)	5.456*** (TVP)
UK	2.055* (TVP)	1.773* (TVP)
Japan	2.731** (TVP)	3.602*** (TVP)
Malaysia	2.881** (TVP)	5.843*** (TVP)
Singapore	2.526** (TVP)	1.889* (TVP)
Australia	3.066** (TVP)	4.596*** (TVP)
US	0.231	0.211
Overall	6.915*** (TVP)	2.815** (TVP)

Note: *, ** and *** denote the 10%, 5% and 1% significance levels, respectively.

case of Korea, the TVP model outperforms the static model at the 1% level of significance, which is confirmed by the results of the MGN test. This finding indicates the rejection of the null hypothesis that the static model and TVP model are equally accurate when used to generate one-year-ahead forecasts for Korea. Similarly, in the cases of Australia, Japan, Malaysia, Singapore and the UK, the static model is outperformed by the TVP model at least at the 10% level of significance. However, in the case of the US, neither of the tests diagnosed significance differences in the one-step-ahead forecasts between the static model and TVP model. Overall, the TVP model outperforms the static model at the 1% and 5% levels of significance in the HLN and MGN tests, respectively. Table 7.5 shows that the results of the MGN and HLN tests are highly consistent in all cases. The outstanding performance of the TVP model in comparison to the static regression model is therefore confirmed by the above statistical tests.

7.4 Summary and Conclusions

This study is one of the first attempts to apply rigorous statistical tests to examine whether a significant difference exists in the forecast accuracy between alternative models in the context of tourism demand forecasting. Two econometric models have been analysed in this study: the traditional regression-based static model and the TVP model. The empirical results show that the TVP model performs well in forecasting the demand for Thai tourism by tourists from seven origin countries. The TVP model outperforms its fixed-parameter counterpart in forecasting the demand for Thai tourism by all of the origin countries at different forecasting horizons. This study provides robust empirical evidence of the superiority of the TVP model. The results suggest that by taking into account the possibility of parameter changes in the demand model, forecast accuracy can be significantly improved. This conclusion is drawn based on the current empirical study, and further examination of this issue using different datasets is recommended.

This study examines only two models, which have similar specifications. In future research, other econometric and time series forecasting models should be included in forecasting comparisons using statistical tests of equal forecast accuracy. In addition, empirical evidence has shown that forecast combinations that are based on individual forecasting models can improve forecasting accuracy. Statistical tests can also be considered when comparisons are carried out between different combination methods.

References

Andrews DWK (1991) Heteroskedasticity and autocorrelation consistent covariance matrix estiators. Econometrica 59:817–858

De Mello MM, Nell KS (2005) The forecasting ability of a cointegrated VAR system of the UK tourism demand for France, Spain and Portugal. Empir Econ 30:277–308

Dickey DA, Fuller WA (1981) Likelihood ratio statistics for autoregressive time series with a unit root. Econometrica 49:1057–1072

Diebold FX, Mariano RS (1995) Comparing predictive accuracy. J Bus Econ Stat 13: 253–263

Eadington W, Redman N (1991) Economics and tourism. Ann Tourism Res 18:41–56

Granger, CWJ, Newbold, P (1977) Forecasting economic time series. Academic Press, Orlando

Greenslade JV, Hall SG (1996) Modelling economies subject to structural change: the case of Germany. Econ Model 13:545–559

Harvey AC (1989) Forecasting structural time series models and the Kalman filter. John Wiley, New York

Harvey D, Leybourne S, Newbold P (1997) Testing the equality of prediction mean squared errors. Int J Forecast 13:281–91

Judge GG, Griffiths WE, Carter-Hill R, Lütkepohl H, Lee TC (1985) The theory and practice of econometrics, 2nd edition. Wiley, New York

Kim CJ (1993) Sources of monetary growth, uncertainty and economic activity: the time varying parameter model with heteroskedastic disturbance. Rev Econ Stat 74:483–97

Kon SC, Turner WL (2005) Neural network forecasting of tourism demand. Tourism Econ 11:301–328

Kulendran N, Witt SF (2001) Cointegration versus least squares regression. Ann Tourism Res 28:291–311

Li G, Song H, Witt SF (2005) Recent developments in econometric modeling and forecasting. J Travel Res 44:82–99

Li G, Song H, Witt SF (2006a) Forecasting tourism demand using econometric models. In: Buhalis D, Costa C (eds) Tourism management dynamics: trends, management and tools. Elsevier Butterworth-Heinemann, Oxford, pp 219–228

Li G, Wong KF, Song H, Witt SF (2006b) Time varying parameter ECM model for tourism forecasting. J Travel Res 45:175–185

Morgan WA (1939) A test for significance of the difference between the two variances in a sample from a normal bivariate population. Biometrika 31:13–19

Ocal N (2000) Nonlinear models for UK macroeconomic time series. Stud Nonlinear Dyn Econom 4:123–135

Phillips PCB, Perron P (1988) Testing for a unit root in time series regression. Biometrica 75:335–346

Riddington G (1999) Forecasting ski demand: comparing learning curve and time varying parameter approaches. J Forecast 18:205–214

Song H, Li G (2008) Tourism demand modelling and forecasting: a review of recent research. Tourism Manage 29:203–229

Song, H and Witt, SF (2000) Tourism demand modelling and forecasting: modern econometric approaches. Pergamon, Oxford

Song H, Witt SF, Jensen TC (2003a) Tourism forecasting: accuracy of alternative econometric models. Int J Forecast 19:123–141

Song H, Witt SF, Li G (2003b) Modelling and forecasting demand for Thai tourism. Tourism Econ 9:363–387

Song H, Wong KF (2003) Tourism demand modeling: a time-varying parameter approach. J Travel Research 42:57–64

Swanson NR, White H (1997) Forecasting economic time series using flexible versus fixed specification and linear versus nonlinear econometric models. Int J Forecast 13:439–461

Tucci MP (1995) Time-varying parameters: a critical introduction. Struct Change Econ Dyn 6:237–260

Witt SF, Song H, Louvieris P (2003) Statistical testing in forecasting model selection. J Travel Res 42:151–58

Wu JL (1999) A re-examination of the exchange rate-interest differential relationship: evidence from Germany and Japan. J Int Money Finance 18:319–336

Chapter 8
Estimating Tourism Impacts Using Input–Output and SAM Models in the Balearic Islands

Clemente Polo and Elisabeth Valle

8.1 Introduction

The main goal of the paper is to provide an assessment of the importance of tourism in the Balearic Islands (BI) and to estimate the impact on its economy of a fall in tourism flows in line with that observed in the last decade.[1] The BI, a rather backward region that received just a handful of curious travellers in 1950, has become a major tourism resort during the second half of the twentieth century and there seems to be little doubt that tourism has been the engine of growth that has turned the Balearic economy into one of the most prosperous Spanish regions. Recent data trends, however, seem to indicate that the sustained growth of tourism flows into the BI has come to a halt, while their economy has recorded the worst growth performance of all 17 autonomous Spanish regions since 2000.

Input–output (IO) analysis has been the traditional tool used to asses the weight of tourism in the economy and to quantify tourism impacts. (Fletcher 1994, Archer 1995, Archer and Fletcher 1996, Henry and Deane 1997, Wagner 1997 and Frechtling and Horvath 1999). Dwyer et al. (2003) and (2004), argue that the answers IO models provide are wrong because they are based on extremely unrealistic assumptions and do not take into account income feedbacks, resource limitations and price adjustments. They propose to employ extended linear (Social Accounting Matrix or SAM) models to account for income feedbacks, or, even better, applied (or computable) general equilibrium (AGE or CGE) models to account for resource constraints, market imperfections and the influence of relative prices on agents' decisions.

Despite these well known shortcomings, IO models have continued being applied to analyze impacts of tourism events on local and regional economies (Crompton

[1] Usually, tourism is understood as activities carried out by people travelling or staying out of their usual residence place.

C. Polo (✉)
Department of Economics and Economic History, Universidad Autónoma de Barcelona, Barcelona, Spain
e-mail: clemente.polo@uab.es

Á. Matias et al. (eds.), *Advances in Tourism Economics*,
DOI 10.1007/978-3-7908-2124-6_8, © Physica-Verlag Heidelberg 2009

et al. 2001, Tyrrell and Johnston 2001, Kim et al. 2003, Chhabra et al. 2003, Gelan 2003, Daniels et al. 2004, Lee and Taylor 2005, Tohmo 2005, Mules 2005 and Hodur et al. 2006) along with AGE models.[2] After all, fix prices may be an acceptable assumption in a regional context and endowments constraints may not be binding when capital and labour are highly mobile among regions. Moreover, the results of Polo and Valle 2008, indicate that AGE models can provide very unsound estimates of the effects of an external shock depending on the closure rules imposed. They also show that for some closure rules the results of AGE and IO and SAM models are highly correlated.

Following this well established tradition, the paper uses a standard IO model to estimate the weight of tourism in the Balearic economy. It may come as a surprise that, notwithstanding the importance of tourism in the region, no one has ever attempted to estimate its importance and effects on the economy. The results of the standard model are compared then with those obtained with extended IO models where residents' consumption and investment replacement demand are endogenous. As to the impact of a 10% fall in tourism flows on the Balearic economy, the paper compares IO results with those obtained with an extended SAM model.

The paper is divided into four sections. Section 8.2 provides a portrait of the Balearic economy as reflected in the regional input–output table. The IO and SAM models used to perform the simulations are outlined in Sect. 8.3. Estimates of the weight of tourism obtained with the standard IO model are presented in Sect. 8.4; then, they are compared with those calculated when consumption and investment are endogenous. Section 8.5 presents the results of simulating a 10% fall in tourism demand using both IO and SAM models. A short section with the conclusions and final remarks ends the paper.

8.2 The Role of Tourism in the Balearic Economy

The Balearic Islands, a 4,992 km^2. region with a coastal perimeter of 1,428 km., is today one of the main international tourists' resorts in Spain. In 1950, the islands were an isolated region, inhabited by 422.1 thousand people with a per capita income well below the national average, who received a handful of curious travellers (758). By the turn of the century, however, the living standard of the 878.6 thousand inhabitants of the Balearic Islands Autonomous Community (CAIB) was among the

[2]Since Adams and Parmenter (1995) modeled the impact of tourism on the Australian economy using a multiregional AGE model, the technique has been used to provide quantitative estimates of tourism impacts in Australia (Skene 1993, Madden and Thapa 2000 and Woollett et al. 2001), the USA (Blake et al. 2001), Spain (Blake 2000), the UK (Blake et al. 2003) and Indonesia (Sugiyarto et al. 2003). Zhou et al. 1997, also use a CGE model to quantify the effects of a 10% fall in tourism demand in Hawaii and Dwyer et al. 2003, analyze with a two region model the impact of an increase in tourism' flows on New South Wales, Australia's largest state.

highest in Spain and slightly above the EU-15 average.[3] In the meanwhile, the number of international visitors reached an all time peak of 10,522 thousand in 1999, amounting to 22.5% of total arrivals in Spain. Since then, the CAIB has lost considerable ground and there is great concern on the fate of an industry deemed by everybody the engine of growth in the second half of the twentieth century.[4]

The 1997 input–output table (IOT-BI97) constructed for the Economic and Treasure Department of the BI Autonomous Government provides a disaggregated picture of the islands economy.[5] Intermediate and final demand flows are distinguished by origin among domestic, rest of Spain (RES) and rest of the world (ROW). There are 54 production branches in the table: 3 in the primary sector, 18 in the manufacturing sector, the construction sector, 27 in the private services sector and 5 in the public services sector. An aggregated 5 sectors table appears in Table 8.1 to provide the reader an idea of its structure.[6]

From the viewpoint of final uses, the most remarkable aspect is the high contribution of non residents' consumption (953,179 million)[7] to final demand, somewhat lower than residents' consumption (1,285,595 million), but far greater than public consumption (200,644 million), gross capital formation (448,703 million) and exports to RES (54,483 million) and ROW (90,862 million).[8] A comparison of residents and non residents' consumption patterns reveals profound differences between them. Non residents' consumption is largely satisfied with domestic production (95.8%) and is highly concentrated in the service branches (94.2%), and, especially, in the tourism sectors of the economy. In contrast residents' consumption relies to a larger extent on imports (24.5%) and it is more balanced between manufacturing (34.8%) and service branches (59.8%).

Tourism sectors are those branches whose output is to a large extent dedicated to satisfy non residents demand and they are classified in three groups (helping us to show the results in Sect. 8.4) according to the share of domestic production

---

[3] Spain is divided in 17 Autonomous Communities plus two autonomous cities, Ceuta and Melilla, located in the northern coast of Africa. Each Community has her own Parliament and Government and is responsible for providing many public services such as public health and education. INE's recent estimates of GDP per capita corrected by price differentials place the CAIB in the third (fourth) position in 1995 (2002). The dynamism of the region is proved by the amazing 23.9% population growth registered in 1991–2001, by far the highest of all Communities

[4] The figures provided by the Institute of Tourism Studies, a research body under the Ministry of Industry, Transportation and Commerce, are 9,592 thousand international tourists for the CAIB 49,560 thousand for Spain, in 2003. The absolute loss for the CAIB is 1,052 thousand tourists since 1999 and a 3 percentage point fall in the share of the CAIB.

[5] The tables were constructed by a team of scholars from the Economics and Business Department of the Balearic Islands University led by E. Aguiló and N. Juaneda. Other members of the team were M. Payeras, F. Sastre, A. Sastre and E. Valle.

[6] A more complete analysis of the table features can be found in Polo and Valle 2002.

[7] All figures are in million pesetas (m.p.).

[8] The shares on final demand are: residents consumption, 42.4%; non residents' consumption 31.4%; public consumption 6.6%; gross formation of capital 14.8%; and exports to RES, 1.8% and exports to ROW, 3.0%.

Table 8.1 IOT-BI97 aggregated to 5 major sectors

Intermediate demand

		Agriculture	Manufacturing	Construction	Private Services	Public Services	Intermediate Uses
Agriculture	BAL	3,043.13	23,120.35	20.87	5,237.18	85.26	31,506.79
	RES	913.35	9,128.12	6.29	12,403.99	454.60	22,906.35
	ROW	126.92	810.69	0.00	1,815.42	0.00	2,753.03
	TOT	4,083.40	33,059.16	27.16	19,456.59	539.87	57,166.17
Manufacturing	BAL	4,381.50	26,112.47	41,520.07	63,547.07	6.261.98	141,823.10
	RES	8,769.28	95,119.17	40,893.08	144,759.26	14,621.87	304,162.66
	ROW	166.77	5,298.57	2,747.84	13,663.25	20.16	21,896.59
	TOT	13,317.56	126,530.20	85,161.00	221,969.59	20,903.99	467,882.34
Construction	BAL	394.00	1,828.24	274.80	45,827.84	7,961.57	56,286.45
	RES	0.00	0.00	0.00	0.00	0.00	0.00
	ROW	0.00	0.00	0.00	0.00	0.00	0.00
	TOT	394.00	1,828.24	274.80	45,827.84	7,961.57	56,286.45
Private Services	BAL	5,152.53	46,744.46	90,847.25	378,223.65	29,246.13	550,214.01
	RES	273.49	2,689.67	1,882.83	17,105.94	2,066.18	24,018.10
	ROW	9.19	298.46	802.45	3,254.91	0.00	4,365.01
	TOT	5,435.21	49,732.59	93,532.53	398,584.49	31,312.31	578,597.12
Public Services	BAL	0.00	0.00	0.00	0.00	0.00	0.00
	RES	0.00	0.00	0.00	0.00	0.00	0.00
	ROW	0.00	0.00	0.00	0.00	0.00	0.00
	TOT	0.00	0.00	0.00	0.00	0.00	0.00
Intermediate consumption	BAL	12,971.16	97,805.52	132,662.99	492,835.74	43,554.94	779,830.35
	RES	9,956.12	106,936.96	42,782.20	174,269.18	17,142.64	351,087.11
	ROW	302.88	6,407.72	3,550.29	18,733.58	20.16	29,014.63
	TOT	23,230.16	211,150.19	178,995.48	685,838.50	60,717.74	1,159,932.08

Table 8.1 (continued)

Primary matrix	Agriculture	Manufacturing	Construction	Private Services	Public Services	Total
Wages and salaries	9,293.00	63,534.53	81,194.18	500,707.70	117,229.35	772,008.76
Social contributions	1,762.20	18,958.82	22,106.30	126,450.14	25,932.46	195,209.92
Net operating surplus	19,581.10	51,165.72	85,377.36	712,790.58	0.00	868,914.76
Consumption of fixed	4,823.30	18,168.00	22,857.00	134,592.77	0.00	180,441.07
Taxes on production	241.88	1,472.14	1,235.20	13,547.45	0.00	16,496.67
Subsidies	3,986.60	4,599.70	76.00	50,937.12	0.00	59,599.42
Added value	31,714.88	148,749.50	212,694.04	1,437,151.54	143,161.81	1,973,471.76
Production value	54,945.04	359,899.69	391,689.52	2,122,990.04	203,879.55	3,133,403.84
Imports RES	52,058.16	696,994.76	0.00	39,675.41	0.00	788,728.33
Imports ROW	3,045.02	77,531.15	0.00	7,968.03	0.00	88,544.21
Total Imports	55,103.18	774,525.91	0.00	47,643.44	0.00	877,272.53
VAT	2,431.79	16,885.99	15,377.24	148,026.59	0.00	182,721.62
Total Resources	112,480.01	1,151,311.60	407,065.76	2,318,660.07	203,879.55	4,193,397.99

Table 8.1 (continued)

Final demand		Resident Consumption	Nonresident Consumption	Public Consumption	Gross Capital Formation	Exports RES	Exports ROW	Total Uses
Agriculture	BAL	12,232.43	973.77	0.00	210.63	11,140.98	121.00	56,185.59
	RES	28,276.75	1,719.55	0.00	281.67	0.00	0.00	53,184.32
	ROW	204.58	152.48	0.00	0.00	0.00	0.00	3,110.09
	TOT	40,713.76	2,845.80	0.00	492.30	11,140.98	121.00	112,480.01
Manufacturing	BAL	145,375.64	18,230.64	0.00	9,470.47	24,914.81	28,050.46	367,865.12
	RES	273,545.97	29,573.66	0.00	40,559.03	0.00	57,335.00	705,176.32
	ROW	28,087.48	3,704.68	0.00	24,581.40	0.00	0.00	78,270.15
	TOT	447,009.10	51,508.98	0.00	74,610.91	24,914.81	85,385.46	1,151,311.60
Private Services	BAL	26,395.59	891.50	0.00	323,493.22	0.00	0.00	407,066.77
	RES	0.00	0.00	0.00	0.00	0.00	0.00	0.00
	ROW	0.00	0.00	0.00	0.00	0.00	0.00	0.00
	TOT	26,395.59	891.50	0.00	323,493.22	0.00	0.00	407,066.77
Construction	BAL	751,896.27	892,372.14	0.00	49,775.76	18,427.38	5,355.14	2,268,040.71
	RES	13,207.82	4,635.08	0.00	330.32	0.00	0.00	42,191.32
	ROW	3,560.97	502.06	0.00	0.00	0.00	0.00	8,428.04
	TOT	768,665.05	897,509.28	0.00	50,106.08	18,427.38	5,355.14	2,318,660.06
Public Services	BAL	2,811.85	423.60	200,644.10	0.00	0.00	0.00	203,879.55
	RES	0.00	0.00	0.00	0.00	0.00	0.00	0.00
	ROW	0.00	0.00	0.00	0.00	0.00	0.00	0.00
	TOT	2,811.85	423.60	200,644.10	0.00	0.00	0.00	203,879.55
Intermediate consumption	BAL	938,711.78	912,891.65	200,644.10	382,950.08	54,483.17	33,526.60	3,303,037.74
	RES	315,030.54	35,928.29	0.00	41,171.02	0.00	57,335.00	800,551.96
	ROW	31,853.02	4,359.22	0.00	24,581.40	0.00	0.00	89,808.28
	TOT	1,285,595.36	953,179.16	200,644.10	448,702.51	54,483.17	90,861.60	4,193,397.99

Note: All figures are in million pesetas

absorbed by non-residents' demand, the number that appears in parenthesis after the name of each branch. The first group, High Tourism Sectors (HTS), includes 4–5 star hotels (98.09%), 1–3 star hotels (96.42%), Tourist apartments (94.48%), Other lodging (94.11%) and Car and other renting (87.33%). The second group, Tourism Sectors (TS), includes Travel agencies (58.41%), Bars and coffees shops (55.53%), Disco and other cultural services (41.94%) Restaurants (38.13%), Air Transport (37.28%) and Land Transport (31.04%). Finally, the group of Marginal Tourism Sectors (MTS), includes Other transport activities (20.58%), Real Estate (11.80%) and Sea transport (7.81%).

As to the importance of the 11 most important tourist sectors (HTS+TS), notice that they account for 32.95% of total production and 32.62% of total value added. These figures go up to 43.23% of production and 45.18% of value added when all tourism sectors are included. In the 11 tourism branches, the share of value added in domestic production is 62.34% and the share of gross surplus in value added 57.71%. The figures are somewhat higher (65.82% for value added and 66.35% for domestic production) when the MTS are added.[9]

In summary, the BI region is highly specialized in production of services, tourism services to a large extent. These service branches in general, and the 11 HTS and TS branches in particular, have a low propensity to import commodities from the rest of Spain and rest of the world, higher than average gross operating surplus on value added shares and their output is mainly satisfies non residents' demand. Clearly, the peculiar structure of the Balearic economy makes it highly sensitive to a fall in non residents' demand.

8.3 Analytical Framework

The importance of tourism branches and non residents' final consumption are a clear indication of the importance of tourism sectors in the BI economy. But this information is insufficient to calculate the share of production, value added, employment, etc., accounted for tourism activities. Fortunately, the IO model can be used to assess the weight of tourism in the BI economy.

The standard input–output model allows one to calculate the production vector y that satisfies a predetermined final demand vector d. Since the 1997 IOT distinguishes flows by origin, the equilibrium condition among production and uses by sector is set as follows

$$y = A^I y + d^I \tag{8.1}$$

[9]For Spain, these shares were 49.5 and 50.5%, respectively, in 1995. The table IOT-BI97 records a surprising negative contribution of net production taxes of –2.2% of value added. The share of wages is lowest in Agriculture (25.0%) and Cattle raising (30.6%), lies between 30 and 50% in most tourism branches and between the 45 and 65% in Construction, most manufacturing and some of services branches and takes the highest values (superior to 65%) in Fishing and Public services branches.

where A^I is the matrix of domestic intermediate input coefficients and d^I the vector of domestic final demand. An estimate of production associated with tourismy_T can be obtained solving Eq. (8.1) for the predetermined final demand vector d_T^I that stands for tourists' demand of goods and services:

$$y_T = A^I y_T + d_T^I. \tag{8.2}$$

Then, intermediate consumption, value-added, employment and imports due to tourism can be calculated for each branch multiplying the corresponding technical coefficients by the activity levels. In this way, one can calculate the share of tourism on value added or employment for the entire economy.[10]

The standard model can be modified to take into account that residents' consumption and (partially) investment may be endogenous. In the first case, the model is modified by including an additional activity that produces a consumption bundle in fixed proportions

$$\begin{pmatrix} y_T \\ C \end{pmatrix} = \begin{pmatrix} A^I & c \\ l'\bar{c} & 0 \end{pmatrix} \begin{pmatrix} y_T \\ C \end{pmatrix} + \begin{pmatrix} d_T^I \\ 0 \end{pmatrix} \tag{8.3}$$

where C stands for aggregate residents consumption, c is the vector of consumption shares, $l'$is row vector of labor coefficients, $\bar{c}$ the average consumption per unit of labor. Following Wolff (1994),[11] depreciation investment demand, K,

$$\begin{pmatrix} y_T \\ C \\ K \end{pmatrix} = \begin{pmatrix} A^I & c & i \\ l'\bar{c} & 0 & 0 \\ k' & 0 & 0 \end{pmatrix} \begin{pmatrix} y_T \\ C \\ K \end{pmatrix} + \begin{pmatrix} d_T^I \\ 0 \\ 0 \end{pmatrix} \tag{8.4}$$

k' being a row vector of fix depreciation coefficients and i the vector of technical requirements to produce one unit of the investment good.

An alternative way to make endogenous consumption and investment is to model income distribution and income expenditure decisions. Pyatt and Thorbecke (1976) and Pyatt and Round (1977) and (1979) extended the IO model beyond the productive sphere into a social accounting framework that records the entire circular income flow (production and income generation, income distribution and income utilization) at the desired level of detail. The economy is represented by a set of accounts $\{1,2,\ldots,N\}$ and economic interactions by the income flows X_{ij} from account

[10]The model can be modified to take into account that some intermediate goods used in production are tourist in nature. In order to account for that, the model can be stated as follows: $y_T \equiv A_T^I y_T + \left(d_T^I + x_T\right)$ where is the matrix of technical coefficients calculated after excluding tourism intermediate inputs in all sectors and x_T is the vector of those intermediate tourism inputs.

[11]"In order to treat capital as an endogenous input, a new (endogenous) industry is created, whose row is the capital stock replaced in each sector of the economy and whose column consists of the inputs required to produce the replacement capital stock. Final demand is valued net of replacement investment, ..." (Wolff 1994, p. 85)

i to account j. The flows are disposed in an ordered square matrix, a SAM, where each row and the corresponding column show all resources and uses of each account. Of course, total resources equal total uses for all accounts.

For any partition of the accounts into an endogenous subset $\{1,2,...,M\}$ and exogenous subset $\{M+1, M+2,...,M+N\}$, the $M \times 1$ income vector y_m of the first M endogenous accounts can be written as

$$y_m \equiv A_{mm} y_m + A_{mn} y_m, \tag{8.5}$$

where the a_{ij} element of the $M \times M$ $(M \times N)$ matrix A_{mm} (A_{mn}) is the share of the income flow from account j to account i over j's income, and y_n is the $N \times 1$ income vector of the subset of exogenous accounts. Assuming that the coefficients of the matrices A_{mm} and A_{mn} are independent on the level of income of the accounts, identity (8.5) can be used to calculate the income vector of the endogenous accounts for any given income vector y_n of the exogenous accounts

$$y_m = (I - A_{mm})^{-1} A_{mn} y_n = (I - A_{mm})^{-1} x = M_m x, \tag{8.6}$$

where $M_m = (I - A_{mm})^{-1}$ is an $M \times N$ matrix of multipliers, and $x = A_{mn} y_n$ is the vector of exogenous income directed to the endogenous accounts.

The main difference between a SAM and the standard IO model is that changes in production after a demand shock affect incomes, consumption and savings. Thus, the standard IO can be viewed as special case of a SAM model where the set of endogenous accounts is restricted to the production sectors and both resource constraints and income feedbacks are ignored. SAM models typically include as endogenous accounts at least production, factor and expenditure accounts. Their results can be compared with those of the IO model when residents' consumption is endogenous. Finally, the results IO model with depreciation capital endogenous can be compared to some extent with those of a SAM model with endogenous savings.[12]

8.4 The Weight of Tourism in the Balearic Economy

In order to assess the weight of tourism in the BI, the IO models outlined in the previous section, the matrix of domestic technical coefficients A^I has been specified using the information provided by the IOT-BI97. Unfortunately, the table only provides detailed data on consumption expenditures by non residents' consumers but no information on tourism expenditures by residents' and gross capital formation and intermediate flows due to tourism activities. Thus the reason why the estimates reported here had to be taken as lower bounds of the real weight of tourism in the

[12] In the SAM model, savings determine investment, while in the extended IO model with endogenous investment depreciation, the amount invested depends on the depreciation coefficients and the level of output of each sector.

economy. In other words, all calculations presented are carried out approximating total demand coming from tourism activities by just non residents' final demand.[13]

To assess the importance of the different components of non residents' demand, three partial simulation results are reported in the tables for each model. The simulation, HTS, shows the results obtained when the entries of the non residents' demand vector for the branches included in the HTS group (1–2 stars hotels, 3–5 stars hotels, Tourist apartments, Other lodging and Car and other renting) are set equal to their observed values and all the remaining 49 entries are equal to zero. In the simulation, HTS+TS, the entries of branches in both the HTS and TS groups (Travel agencies, Bars and coffees shops, Disco and other cultural services, Restaurants, Air Transport and Land Transport) are set equal to their observed values and the other 43 entries are zero. Finally, in the third simulation, HTS+TS+MTS, the entries of branches in the HTS, TS and MTS groups (Other transport, Real Estate and Sea Transport) are set equal to its observed values and the remaining 40 entries are equal to zero.

8.4.1 Standard Input–Output Model Estimates

Table 8.2 shows the results obtained in the four simulations with the input–output model. The rows indicate the four simulations performed and the columns the quantities of value added, employment and imports that directly or indirectly can be imputed to tourists' demand. The figures reported are in absolute terms and in percentages over the observed 1997 figures. Thus, the gross value added share required directly or indirectly to satisfy non-residents' demand is 714,900.814 million pesetas or 36.23% of gross value added in 1997. Since tourism sectors are not particularly labour or import intensive, the corresponding figures for employment, 104,148 employees that amounts to 30.12% of total employees in Balearic economy in 1997, and imports, 19.96% of imports are much lower than for value added. The result reported in the first row for HTS is striking: just 5 sectors of the economy (hotels, lodging and car renting) generate 25.89% of total value added. The conclusion of these first simulations clearly indicate that tourism sectors play a very important role in Balearic economy and that just the five highly tourism sectors (HTS), explain more than one fourth of total value added generated in 1997.

Table 8.2 Standard IO model

	Gross VA	%	Employment	%	Imports RE	%
HTS	510,941.140	25.89	67,818.714	19.61	78,020.278	9.89
HTS+TS	640,374.125	32.45	93,582.005	27.07	113,109.176	14.34
HTS+TS+MTS	676,945.495	34.30	95,699.746	27.68	116,154.256	14.73
All	714,900.814	36.23	104,148.242	30.12	157,454.770	19.96

Note: All figures are in million pesetas

[13] See Note 11.

Under the heading of total effects, Table 8.3 shows the production of the 54 sectors of the Balearic economy required to satisfy the entire vector of non-residents' demand. The direct effects figures are just the vector of non-residents' demand in the

Table 8.3 Direct and indirect effects

		Total effect	Direct effect	%	Indirect effect	%
1	Agriculture	3,629.225	285.170	7.86	3,344.055	92.14
2	Cattle raising	4,152.997	80.760	1.94	4,072.237	98.06
3	Fishing	2,497.768	607.840	24.34	1,889.928	75.66
4	Production and transformation of electrical energy	13,898.843	23.060	0.17	13,875.783	99.83
5	Water industry	4,459.390	9.700	0.22	4,449.690	99.78
6	Nonmetalic and nonenergy mineral products	1,946.855	2.400	0.12	1,944.455	99.88
7	Chemical industry	556.626	49.200	8.84	507.426	91.16
8	Metalic industry	2,364.423	830.820	35.14	1,533.603	64.86
9	Machinery	43.395	0.000	0.00	43.395	100.00
10	Naval construction	509.221	157.200	30.87	352.021	69.13
11	Food and tobacco industry	13,820.930	3,040.320	22.00	10,780.610	78.00
12	Wine and liquors industry	724.536	300.590	41.49	423.946	58.51
13	Beverage industry	6,829.333	2,616.370	38.31	4,212.963	61.69
14	Textile industry	2,120.387	1,563.410	73.73	556.977	26.27
15	Shoes industry	4,322.072	4,182.030	96.76	140.042	3.24
16	Skins and leather industry	429.745	241.410	56.18	188.335	43.82
17	Wood industry (except furniture)	927.798	0.000	0.00	927.798	100.00
18	Wood furniture industry	443.857	443.800	99.99	0.057	0.01
19	Paper industry	3,067.202	964.580	31.45	2,102.622	68.55
20	Other manufacturing industries	2,082.209	1,749.300	84.01	332.909	15.99
21	Jewellery industry	2,401.035	2,056.450	85.65	344.585	14.35
22	Construction	24,530.602	891.500	3.63	23,639.102	96.37
23	Repair services	8,397.776	0.000	0.00	8,397.776	100.00
24	Intermediate trade	3,337.554	422.360	12.65	2,915.194	87.35
25	Wholesale trade	23,087.031	4,278.990	18.53	18,808.041	81.47
26	Retail commerce	23,574.496	11,187.730	47.46	12,386.766	52.54
27	Four and five star hotels	134,173.528	134,134.895	99.97	38.633	0.03
28	One to three star hotels	368,367.016	368,179.470	99.95	187.546	0.05
29	Tourist apartments	83,907.795	83,850.531	99.93	57.264	0.07
30	Other lodging	28,594.866	28,593.842	100.00	1.024	0.00

(continued)

Table 8.3 (continued)

		Total effect	Direct effect	%	Indirect effect	%
31	Travel agencies	24,906.374	19,666.365	78.96	5,240.009	21.04
32	Bars and coffee shops	36,567.628	36,396.277	99.53	171.351	0.47
33	Restaurants	47,430.277	45,976.586	96.94	1,453.691	3.06
34	Recreational and cultural services	20,330.474	17,721.285	87.17	2,609.189	12.83
35	Car renting	24,693.263	23,264.437	94.21	1,428.826	5.79
36	Land transportation	36,630.314	27,779.505	75.84	8,850.809	24.16
37	Sea transportation	7,852.148	3,605.285	45.91	4,246.863	54.09
38	Air transportation	40,959.903	34,240.163	83.59	6,719.740	16.41
39	Related transport activities	18,165.997	8,942.824	49.23	9,223.173	50.77
40	Post office and telecommunications	12,779.269	4,930.040	38.58	7,849.229	61.42
41	Financial institutions	27,481.403	1,428.360	5.20	26,053.043	94.80
42	Social work	0.000	0.000	0.00	0.000	0.00
43	Services to corporations	29,738.006	0.000	0.00	29,738.006	100.00
44	Sport management	951.520	645.200	67.81	306.320	32.19
45	Real State	49,150.187	29,041.500	59.09	20,108.687	40.91
46	Cleaning services	9,600.467	4,577.100	47.68	5,023.367	52.32
47	Private education	164.250	124.600	75.86	39.650	24.14
48	Public education	0.000	0.000	0.00	0.000	0.00
49	Private health system	3,546.332	3,384.800	95.45	161.532	4.55
50	Public health system	423.600	423.600	100.00	0.000	0.00
51	Personal services	7,317.804	0.000	0.00	7,317.804	100.00
52	Central government	0.000	0.000	0.00	0.000	0.00
53	Autonomous government	0.000	0.000	0.00	0.000	0.00
54	Local government	0.000	0.000	0.00	0.000	0.00
		1,167,887.727	912,891.655	78.17	254,996.072	21.83

Note: All figures are in million pesetas

1997 input–output table and the indirect figures are simply the difference between the total and the direct effects figures. The percentage columns indicate the shares of direct and indirect effects over the total effect. Thus, for the entire economy the direct effect is 78.17% and the indirect production 21.83%.

For individual sectors the results vary greatly from this average. For the five highly tourism sectors, the percentage of direct effects is almost 100% for hotels, apartments and other types of lodging and a bit lower (94.21%) for Car renting. It is clear from these figures that indirect effects for HTS (and more generally for most

Table 8.4 Input–output model with endogenous residents' consumption

	Gross VA	%	Employment	%	Imports RE	%
HTS	743,681.171	37.68	111,844.152	32.35	214,317.132	27.17
HTS+TS	952,863.850	48.28	152,693.009	44.16	296,108.916	37.54
HTS+TS+MTS	997,385.587	50.54	156,314.654	45.21	303,809.883	38.52
All	1,060,855.553	53.76	169,589.537	49.05	360,052.245	45.65

Note: All figures are in million pesetas

tourism sectors) are pretty weak. In contrast, indirect effects are of great importance in most other sectors of the economy where non-residents' demand is zero or close to zero as in Agriculture, Cattle raising, Energy sectors, Water, etc. There are a few instances (Retail commerce, Post Office and telecommunications, Real Estate, Land transportation and Related transportation activities) where the percentages of both direct and indirect effects are close to 50%. Production in the tourism sector goes to satisfy tourism demand and its production is not bought from other sectors to produce. Owing to this fact, the indirect effects in the tourism sector are weak or negligible, but the indirect effects that tourism sectors generate in the rest of the sectors are very important. A way of summing up this information is by means of the tourism multiplier calculated by dividing the total effect over the direct effect. For the entire economy the figure is 1.28, for the highly tourism sectors a number pretty close to 1 and for those sectors where direct effects are nil is infinite.

8.4.2 Endogenous Residents' Consumption

In order to capture the induced effects of non-residents' consumption, the standard input–output model is expanded to endogenize residents' consumption as in Eq. (8.3). Clearly, incomes generated in the process of satisfying non-residents' demand induce residents' expenditures that in turn have direct and indirect effects on all sectors of the economy. As before, Table 8.4 sums up the effects of non-residents' demand on value added, employment and imports. First, notice that value added goes up from 36.23% in Table 8.3 to 53.76%, an increase of 17.53 percentage points due to induced effects on residents' consumption. In the case of employment and imports, the increases are even bigger, 18.93 and 25.69 percentage points, respectively. The rises are also quite similar in the other three (HTS, HTS+TS and HTS+TS+MTS) simulations. The role of the five highly tourism sectors is quite impressive: it accounts for 37.69% of total, 32.25% of employment and 27.17% of total imports.

8.4.3 Endogenous Capital Depreciation Investment

Table 8.5 shows the impact of tourism in the Balearic economy when both residents' consumption and depreciation investment are endogenous. In this case, the

Table 8.5 Input–output model with endogenous residents' consumption and depreciation investment

	Gross VA	%	Employment	%	Imports RE	%
HTS	1,010,598.979	51.21	160,246.542	46.35	327,695.392	41.55
HTS+TS	1,274,011.371	64.56	210,929.317	61.01	432,522.247	54.84
HTS+TS+MTS	1,341,415.502	67.97	218,700.414	63.25	449,942.933	57.05
All	1,422,292.256	72.07	235,131.811	68.01	513,579.150	65.11

Note: All figures are in million pesetas

value added, employment and imports required to satisfy non-residents' demand and the induced residents' consumption and investment replacement amounts to 72.07, 68.01 and 65.11%, respectively. It is quite striking that almost three fourths of total value added and employment are in one way or another generated to satisfy tourists' demands. A comparison with Table 8.4 indicates that making depreciation investment a required input rises the value added, employment and import shares almost 20 percentage points. In this scenario, it is quite remarkable that the value added imputable to the five sectors in the highly tourism sectors group, 51.21%, is more than half the total value added generated in the Balearic economy.

8.5 The Effects of a 10% Fall in Non Residents' Consumption

The recent fall of international tourism arrivals to the Balearic Islands, turns what could be an interesting academic exercise into an interesting policy issue. This section is addressed to answer the following question: How would a permanent 10% fall in tourism receipts affect value added, employment and imports from the rest of Spain? The answer depends, of course, on the model used to simulate the policy. Here, we compare the results obtained with the three versions of the IO model considered in the previous section and those obtained with two alternative SAM models.

In order to specify the SAM models, the IO table has been extended into a regional accounting matrix that provides information on income sources and uses for all agents, factors, products and other auxiliary accounts. The SAM of the Balearic economy for 1997 (SAM-BI97)[14] is a 72×72 square balanced matrix whose structure appears in Table 8.6. In addition to the 54 productive branches of the IO table, it includes two primary factors (labour and capital), a representative consumer, a business sector, two accounts for central and regional governments, the capital account, one foreign sector and one non resident consumer, and some auxiliary accounts for transfers and key taxes. A numerical aggregated SAM is provided in Table 8.7.

Table 8.8 sums up the results of simulating a 10% fall in non-residents' consumption with the standard and the extended input–output model. The fall in value

[14] A thorough analysis of social accounting matrix results can be found in Polo and Valle (2007.

Table 8.6 The structure of the SAM-BI97

	Production activities	Productive factors	Resident consumer	Business sector	Capitals account	Gov	Non resident consumer	Rest of the world		
Production activities	X_{11}	0	X_{13}	0	X_{15}	X_{16}	X_{17}	X_{18}	Y_1	
Productive factors	X_{21}	0	0	0	0	0	0	X_{28}	Y_2	
Resident consumer	0	X_{32}	0	X_{34}	0	X_{36}	0	X_{38}	Y_3	y_m
Business Sector	0	X_{42}	X_{43}	0	0	0	0	0	Y_4	
Capital account	0	0	X_{53}	X_{54}	0	X_{56}	0	0	Y_5	
Government	X_{61}	0	X_{63}	X_{64}	0	X_{66}	0	X_{68}	Y_6	
Non resident consumer	0	0	0	0	0	0	0	X_{78}	Y_7	y_n
Rest of the world	X_{81}	X_{82}	X_{83}	0	X_{85}	X_{86}	0	0	Y_8	
	Y_1	Y_2	Y_3	Y_4	Y_5	Y_6	Y_7	Y_8		
			y'_m				y'_n			

Note: All figures are in million pesetas

Table 8.7 SAM-BI97

	Agriculture	Manufacturing	Construction	Private Services	Public Services	Labor	Capital	Resident Consumer
Agriculture	4,083.400	33,059.160	27.159	19,456.585	539.869			40,713.760
Manufacturing	13,317.557	126,530.198	85,160.998	221,969.589	20,903.993			447,009.100
Construction	394.000	1,828.243	274.800	45,827.837	7,961.573			26,395.592
Private Services	5,435.207	49,732.590	93,532.527	398,584.488	31,312.307			768,665.055
Public Services								2,811.850
Labor	9,293.000	63,584.532	81,194.180	500,707.703	117,229.346			
Capital	24,404.400	69,333.717	108,234.356	847,383.354				
Resident Consumer						735,409.760	546,540.410	
Business							580,775.400	58,332.769
Nonresident Consumer								
Central Government								
Local Government								63.512
Capital Account								16,457.593
Foreign Sector	55,103.181	774,525.914		47,643.440		45,011.000	17,382.000	87,938.097
Transfers Central Gov.								
Transfers Local Gov.								
Taxes on personal income								107,521.566
Taxes on business income								
Other direct taxes								45,744.587
VAT	2,431.790	16,885.991	15,377.244	148,026.591				
Taxes on production	241.880	1,472.139	1,235.200	13,547.453				
Subsidies								
Social Contributions	1,762.200	18,958.815	22,106.300	126,450.145	25,932.461			11490.569
	116,466.614	1,155,911.300	407,142.764	2,369,597.186	203,879.548	780,420.760	1,144,697.810	1,613,144.050

Table 8.7 (continued)

	Business	Nonresident Consumer	Central Government	Local Government	Capital Account	Foreign Sector	Transfers Central Gov.	Transfers Local Gov.
Agriculture	2,845.800				492.300	11,261.976		
Manufacturing		51,508.980			74,610.910	110,300.275		
Construction		891.500			323,493.220			
Private Services		897,509.285			50,106.081	23,782.520		
Public Services		423.600	110,368.280	90,275.820				
Labor						8,412.000		
Capital						95,342.000		
Resident Consumer	113,138.490					42,977.338	169,218.000	5,860.052
Business								
Nonresident Consumer						953,179.165		
Central Government								135.278
Local Government	111.301					3,328.662	49,917.444	
Capital Account	491,980.378		119,290.250	40,980.685				
Foreign Sector					220,006.401			973.903
Transfers Central Gov.			219,135.440					
Transfers Local Gov.				6,969.233				
Taxes on personal income								
Taxes on business income	33,878.000							
Other direct taxes								
VAT								
Taxes on production								
Subsidies			46,883.235	12,716.184				
Social Contributions								
	639,108.169	953,179.165	495,677.205	150,941.922	668,708.912	1,248,583.936	219,135.444	6,969.233

Table 8.7 (continued)

	Taxes on personal income	Taxes on business income	Other direct taxes	VAT	Taxes on production	Subsidies	Social Contributions	
Agriculture						3,986.600		116,466.610
Manufacturing						4,599.700		1,155,911.300
Construction						76.000		407,142.765
Private Services						50,937.119		2,369,597.180
Public Services								203,879.550
Labor								780,420.762
Capital								1,144,697.827
Resident Consumer								1,613,144.050
Business								639,108.169
Nonresident Consumer								953,179.165
Central Government	55,745.150	33,878.000		182,721.615	16,496.672		206,700.490	495,677.205
Local Government	51,776.416		45,744.587					150,941.922
Capital Account								668,708.906
Foreign Sector								1,248,583.936
Transfers Central Gov.								219,135.440
Transfers Local Gov.								6,969.233
Taxes on personal income								107,521.566
Taxes on business income								33,878.000
Other direct taxes								45,744.587
VAT								182,721.615
Taxes on production								16,496.672
Subsidies								59,599.419
Social Contributions								206,700.490
	107,521.566	33,878.000	45,744.587	182,721.615	16,496.672	59,599.419	206,700.490	

Note: All figures are in million pesetas

added ranges from 3.62% with the standard input–output model and 7.21% when both residents' consumption and consumption of fixed capital are endogenous, and that of the employment is about half percentage point lower, but still impressive: 6.80% in simulation 3. The remaining results reported provide information of the effects when the 10% fall affects only the indicated sectors. Thus, a 10% fall in the highly tourism sectors, other things being equal, would result in a fall of value added that ranges from 2.59% with the standard input–output model and 5.12% when both residents' consumption and consumption of fixed capital are endogenous. As usual, the impacts on employment and imports are a bit lower than on value added but still remarkable.

It is also possible to simulate a 10% fall in non-residents' demand using a social accounting matrix model. In this setting, three equivalent scenarios to those reported for the input–output model can be considered: first, only productive sectors are endogenous; second, productive sectors, factor and consumption accounts are endogenous; and third, the capital account is added to the set of endogenous accounts. Table 8.9 sums up the overall effects on value added and employment in the three scenarios. Comparing the figures with those in Table 8.8, it appears that the effects of a drop in non-residents' consumption are somewhat lower than in the input–output setting. In our view, this is due to the way fixed coefficients are defined in both models: in the input–output model, they are calculated as domestic intermediate flows over domestic production, while in the social accounting matrix model they are defined as total intermediate flows over total income. The results indicate that the fall in value added and employment could be substantial and may be behind the poor performance of the Balearic economy in the last decade.

8.6 Conclusions

The growing interest in ascertaining the importance of tourism in the economy has led to establishing a suitable methodology to assess the weight of tourism and measure the impact of tourism on the economy. The BI constitute a textbook case of an economic miracle fuelled by tourism that has transformed a rather backward region in one of the main tourist resorts in the Mediterranean basin in just 50 years. It is surprising than nobody has ever attempted to measure the importance of tourism in the BI and the effects that may result from a halt or even reversal of tourism flows into the islands. This paper has provided a first assessment of the weight of tourism in the BI and estimates of a 10% fall in non residents demand.

Using a standard input–output model, we estimate that tourism generates 36.23% of the value added, 30.12 of employment and it accounts for 19.96% of total imports from the rest of Spain. When the model is extended to endogenize residents' consumption and depreciation investment, the impact of tourism rises to 72.07% in the case of value added, and 68.01 in the case of employment; moreover, it is responsible for 65.11% of all imports. In view of these figures, it is fair to say that almost three fourths of the Balearic economy is sustained by tourism when induced effects

Table 8.8 The effects of 10% fall in non residents' consumption: three input–output models

		Gross Value Added	%	Employment	%	Imports RE	%
Standard IO model	HTS	1,922,377.651	−2.59	338,972.129	−1.96	780,740.309	−1.01
	HTS+TS	1,909,434.351	−3.24	336,395.800	−2.71	777,231.419	−1.46
	HTS+TS+MTS	1,905,777.214	−3.43	336,184.026	−2.77	776,926.909	−1.50
	All	1,901,981.683	−3.62	335,339.176	−3.01	772,796.856	−2.02
Input–output model with endogenous residents' consumption	HTS	1,899,103.649	−3.77	334,569.586	−3.23	767,110.623	−2.74
	HTS+TS	1,878,185.381	−4.83	330,484.700	−4.42	758,931.442	−3.78
	HTS+TS+MTS	1,873,733.208	−5.05	330,122.536	−4.52	758,161.349	−3.88
	All	1,867,386.210	−5.38	328,795.047	−4.90	752,537.111	−4.59
Input–output model with endogenous residents' consumption and depreciation investment	HTS	1,872,411.871	−5.12	329,729.347	−4.63	755,772.798	−4.18
	HTS+TS	1,846,070.635	−6.46	324,661.071	−6.10	745,290.114	−5.51
	HTS+TS+MTS	1,839,330.219	−6.80	323,883.960	−6.33	743,548.045	5.73
	All	1,831,242.545	−7.21	322,240.821	−6.80	737,184.420	−6.54

Note: All figures are in million pesetas

Table 8.9 The effects of 10% fall in non residents' consumption in a SAM model

	SAM	SAMinv
Total value added	–5.09	–6.04
Total employment	–4.54	–5.50

are taken into account. It is clear from these results that tourism has become the leading sector of the Balearic economy. As can be seen, introducing the induced effects means a big increase in the impact of non residents' consumption in the regional economy. The impact on the value added increases 100%, the impact on employment increases 125% and finally the impact on imports from the rest of Spain increases 225%.

If the outstanding growth of tourism during the second half of the twentieth century has been the engine of the impressive economic growth of the islands, the recent fall in tourism flows since 1997 is probably the main cause of the poor performance of their economy in the last decade. The simulations we have performed with input–output and social accounting matrix models indicate that a 10% fall in non-residents' demand may reduce value added between 3.6 and 7.2% depending on the type of model (standard input–output model, extended input–output model and social accounting matrix model) used. Similar results also hold for employment. It is clear that the economic performance of the islands is tightly linked to the fate of tourism flows and that the regional government should pay a great deal of attention to analyze the causes behind its recent drop.

On the one hand, tourism has diversified, sun and sand no longer being the only option available, from rural tourism to adventure holidays and including ecotourism, all of which are related in some way to the environment. Moreover, new destinations have emerged to compete with Balearic Islands, offering similar products, not just in the Mediterranean but worldwide. Both factors, the diversification which has resulted in the environment becoming a resource and the competition posed by rival destinations with better-preserved environments, represent a threat to Balearic Islands' continued success in the tourism sector.

On the other hand, tourism is set to be one of the major beneficiaries of the changing profile of European society in the coming decades. The ageing population, improvements to health, increased life expectancy and higher income levels among retired people will all result in greater demand for tourism services. The introduction of the Euro as a common currency, the liberalisation of transport and the new technologies will all facilitate mobility and contribute to an increase in tourism.

What can be done? In the short-run, the regional government could reduce residents' taxes to counteract the external shock. It is unlikely, though, that demand oriented policies of this sort will bring significant relieve to the economy. The industry should find ways to make investments less dependable on the summer entries and the regional government should dedicate more resources to counteract the impact that tourism growth has placed on the environment. The most urgent task, however, is to find out the causes behind the recent drop of non residents' demand.

Tourism generates great economic wealth in our community, but we must also be conscious of the cost that it implies. Thus, tourism must be planned so that it grows in harmony with the economy which means trying to prevent congestion and degradation of the environment.

References

Adams PD, Parmenter BR (1995) An applied general equilibrium analysis of the economic effects of tourism in a quite small, quite open economy. Appl Econ 27:985–994

Archer B (1995) Importance of tourism for the economy of Bermuda. Ann Tourism Res 22: 918–930

Archer B, Fletcher J (1996) The economic impact of tourism in the Seychelles. Ann Tourism Res 23:32–47

Blake A (2000) The economic effects of tourism in Spain. Tourism and Travel Research Institute. Discussion Paper 2000/2

Blake A, Durbarry R, Sinclair T, Sugiyarto G (2001) Modelling tourism and travel using tourism satellite accounts and tourism policy and forecasting models. Tourism and Travel Research Institute. Discussion Paper 2001/4

Blake A, Sinclair T, Sugiyarto G (2003) Quantifying the impact of foot and mouth disease on tourism and the UK economy. Tourism Econ 9:449–465

Chhabra D, Sills E, Cubbage FW (2003) The significance of festivals to rural economies: estimating the economic impacts of Scottish highland games in North Carolina. J Travel Res 41:421–427

Conselleria d'Economia i Hisenda Govern Balear (1997) Las tablas input–output y el Sistema de Cuentas Regionales para la Comunidad Autónoma de las Islas Baleares

Crompton J, Lee S, Shuster T (2001) A guide for undertaking economic impact studies: The springfest example. J Travel Res 40:79–87

Daniels MJ, Norman WC, Henry MS (2004) Estimating income effects of a sport tourism event. Ann Tourism Res 31:180–199

Dwyer L, Forsyth P, Spurr R (2003a) Inter-industry effects of tourism growth: implications for destination managers. Tourism Econ 9:117–132

Dwyer L, Forsyth P, Spurr R (2004) Evaluating tourism's economic effects: new and old approaches. Tourism Manage 25:307–317

Dwyer L, Forsyth P, Spurr R, Vanho T (2003b) Tourism's contribution to a state economy: a multiregional general equilibrium analysis. Tourism Econ 9:431–448

Fletcher J (1994) Input–output analysis. In: Witt S, Moutinho L (eds) Tourism marketing and management handbook, 2nd edn. Prentice-Hall International, UK, pp 480–484

Frechtling D, Horvath E (1999) Estimating the multiplier effects of tourism expenditures on a local economy through a regional input–output model. J Travel Res 37:324–332

Gelan A (2003) Local economic impacts: The British Open. Ann Tourism Res 30:406–425

Henry EW, Deane B (1997) The contribution of tourism to the economy of Ireland in 1990 and 1995. Tourism Manage 18:535–553

Hodur NM, Bangsund DA, Leistritz FL, Kaatz J (2006) Estimating the contribution of a multipurpose event facility to the area economy. Tourism Econ 12:303–316

Kim SS, Chon K, Chung KY (2003) Convention industry in South Korea: an economic impact analysis. Tourism Manage 24:533–541

Lee C, Taylor T (2005) Critical reflections on the economic impact assessment of a mega-event: the case of 2002 FIFA World Cup. Tourism Manage 26:595–603

Madden J, Thapa P (2000) The contribution of tourism to the New South Wales economy. Centre for Regional Economic Analysis, University of Tasmania

Mules T (2005) Economic impacts of national park tourism on gateway communities: the case of Kosciuszko National Park. Tourism Econ 11:247–259

Polo C, Valle E (2002) Un análisis input–output de la economía balear. Estadística Española 44:393–444

Polo C, Valle E (2007) Un análisis estructural de la economía balear. Estadística Española 49: 227–257

Polo C, Valle E (2008) A general equilibrium assessment of the impact of a fall in tourism under alternative closure rules: the case of the Balearic Island. Int Reg Sci Rev 31:3–34

Pyatt G, Round JI (1977) Social Accounting matrices for development planning. Rev Income Wealth 23:339–364

Pyatt G, Round JI (1979) Accounting and fixed price multipliers in a social accounting matrix framework. Econ J 89:850–873

Pyatt G, Thorbecke E (1976) Planning techniques for a better future. ILO, Geneva

Skene J (1993) The economic impact of the growth in visitor expenditure: A quantitative assessment. Working Paper nº 92, Bureau of Industry Economics.

Sugiyarto G, Blake A, Sinclair MT (2003) Tourism and globalization: Economic Impact in Indonesia. Ann Tourism Res 30:683–701

Tohmo T (2005) Economic impacts of cultural events on local economies: an input–output analysis of the Kaustinen Folk Music Festival. Tourism Econ 11:431–451

Tyrrell T, Johnston R (2001) A framework for assessing direct economic impacts of tourist events: Distinguishing origins, destinations, and causes of expenditures. J Travel Res 40:94–100

Wagner J (1997) Estimating the economic impacts of tourism. Ann Tourism Res 24:592–608

Wolff E (1994) Productivity measurement within an input–output framework. Reg Sci Urban Econ 24:75–92

Woollett G, Townsend J, Watts G (2001) Development of QGEM-T a computable general equilibrium model of tourism. Office of Economic and Statistical Research, Queensland Government Treasury

Zhou D, Yanagida JF, Chakravorty U, Leung P (1997) Estimating economic impacts from tourism. Ann Tourism Res 24:76–89

Chapter 9
Estimating Tourism Effects on Residents: A Choice Modelling Approach to the Case of Rimini

Paolo Figini, Massimiliano Castellani, and Laura Vici

9.1 Introduction

For tourist destinations, sustainable economic development requires, together with the attainment of economic efficiency, environmental protection and social cohesion. This latter aspect implies that the local community has to be actively involved in the planning and in the management of the tourism sector, and that (the great part of) tourism earnings have to be fairly distributed among the residents.

Desires and aspirations of local residents, and their attitudes towards tourists should be carefully taken into consideration by tourism planners (Akis et al., 1996; Faulkner and Tideswell, 1997). The success of many tourism development programs depends on a local management that is sensible both to the social impact of tourism on the host population, and able to increase the benefits derived from tourism by preventing or reducing its negative aspects.

Overall, tourism has both positive and negative externalities on local populations. Previous studies corroborate these effects: Doxey (1975) finds that local residents' attitudes towards tourism may oscillate between euphoria and antagonism (see also Castellani et al., 2007). In this paper we studied how residents are affected by tourism and how they adjust their choices with respect to these effects. This approach might lead to important policy implications: policy makers are aware that tourists and residents needs are often conflicting, and they need precise tools of analysis in order to measure this trade-off and to design their policies.

In the last 15 years, the socio-economic impact of tourism and the factors affecting attitudes towards tourism in host communities have received significant attention (Alberini et al., 2005; Akis et al., 1996; Crotts and Holland, 1993; Faulkner and Tideswell, 1997; Haralambopoulos and Pizam, 1996; Lindberg and Johnson, 1997a, b; Lindberg et al., 1999; Zanatta et al., 2005). In particular, tourism impact is often disaggregated into three categories: economic, socio-cultural and environmental (Bull, 1991; Pearce, 1989; Ryan, 1991; Williams, 1979). Since tourism generally

---

P. Figini (✉)
Department of Economics, University of Bologna, Bologna, Italy
e-mail: paolo.figini@unibo.it

Á. Matias et al. (eds.), *Advances in Tourism Economics*,
DOI 10.1007/978-3-7908-2124-6_9, © Physica-Verlag Heidelberg 2009

disrupts social, cultural and environmental local systems, the non-economic impact often tends to be negative as a whole (Liu et al., 1987), whilst economic effects are perceived as positive.[1] Economic impacts are known and well measured because estimated for different purposes (Dwyer and Forsyth, 1993), whereas social and environmental effects are of difficult evaluation. Therefore, the overall benefit of tourism development is often overestimated, and might drive to sub-optimal policy decisions (Freeman, 1993). The intensity and the direction of the overall impact depends on a variety of socio-cultural and economic factors associated to the local destination, including the nature of tourism activities, tourists' personal characteristics, and the pace of tourism development (Haralambopoulos and Pizam, 1996; Wall and Mathieson, 2005).

Our study analysed residents' preferences by means of the choice modelling, a survey-based technique often used to place a value on a non-marketable or semi-public good. Its use has spread in many research fields (marketing, cultural, health, transport and environmental economics) and in recent years it has often been applied in tourism economics to analyse tourists' preferences with respect to trip attributes, recreational and heritage demand, the attractiveness of the destination and tourism policies.[2] In contrast to the main stream of the tourism literature, our paper focussed on the preferences of residents and local stake-holders regarding possible and hypothetical modifications in the urban and territorial configuration. Interviews to a representative sample of the population were conducted to estimate the willingness to pay (WTP) for (hypothetical) changes in the composition of goods.

Stated preference methods offer advantages in analysing trade-offs between tourists and residents. In particular, the possible trade-off with the local population stems from the fact that the most important resource for tourism – the environment or, more generally, the territory – is to be shared with residents. Since the "holiday" can be seen as a set of different characteristics which compose a generic good, choice experiments seem to fit data better than other stated preference methods.

The destination analysed in this paper, Rimini, is one of the major Italian seaside resorts and mass tourism destinations, with more than ten million overnight stays only in the summer months (Orsingher, 2004). Located on the Adriatic sea, Rimini is a middle-size city, with about 130,000 inhabitants and an income per capita of more than € 17,000 (higher than the Italian average). Although tourism represents

---

[1] The most important benefits include the generation of jobs and new business opportunities, the increase in the number and types of facilities, of recreational and entertainment opportunities available to residents, and the spread of new ideas into the community. On the other hand, the costs are mainly stemming from the increase in crime, noise level, pollution, degree of congestion, and to the negative impact on local culture. Pizam and Milman (1984) identified occupational, cultural, demographic impacts, mutation of consumption patterns, transformation of norms, impact on the environment. Similarly, Pearce (1989) indicated six classes of social and cultural effects, while Travis (1984) listed socio-cultural costs and benefits that may affect tourism destinations.

[2] Among the many papers that in tourism economics recently used this methodology, we mention Apostolakis and Shabbar (2005), Brau and Cao (2006), Breffle and Morey (2000), Crouch and Louviere (2004), Huybers and Bennett (2000), Huybers (2005), Morey et al. (2002) and Papatheodorou (2001).

one of the main economic sectors of the city, Rimini is now a destination in the mature stage of its development, and has been undergoing a strong diversification in the manufacturing sector and in business and cultural tourism. To summarise, different types of tourists and different types of residents[3] share the destination and ask for alternative uses of the (scarce) territory. In this paper, we focussed on residents' preferences, while we refer to Brau et al. (2008) for the analysis of tourists preferences; in the final discussion we compared our results with those of Brau et al. (2008) in order to identify synergies or trade-off in the use of the territory and to discuss some policy implications.

In particular, we aimed to detect the effects on residents preferences of changes in the intensity (levels) of six key characteristics (attributes) that identify the use of Rimini's territory.[4] Residents were interviewed in Spring 2006 and asked to indicate their preferred choices among several pairs of hypothetical alternative scenarios differing in the levels of the six attributes. Conditional logit models enabled us to estimate the relative weight of each attribute in affecting the residents' choice and allowed us to compare their preferences with those of tourists. To the best of our knowledge, this is one of the few attempts to explicitly use choice modelling to analyse residents preferences in connection with tourism. Lindberg et al. (1999); and Lindberg, (2001) used choice experiments in Åre (Sweden) to evaluate residents' willingness to accept negative impacts of tourism development (in particular in a sky resort) provided that they also receive positive effects.

The remaining of the paper is structured as follows: in Sect. 9.2 we briefly review the methodology applied and we describe the questionnaire. Section 9.3 illustrates some descriptive statistics. Section 9.4 presents the main econometric results of the choice experiments while Sect. 9.5 discusses the policy implications and sets the agenda for future research.

9.2 The Methodology and the Survey

The choice modelling is a stated-preference approach which investigates individual behaviour and estimates the value of goods (or projects) by asking people to choose among scenarios whose differences are due to systematic combinations of diverse attribute (characteristic) levels.[5] One of the advantages of choice experiments lies in their ability to model individuals' hypothetical choices for non market goods. This enables analysts to elicit individuals' willingness to pay for goods and services

[3]Preferences of residents might change accordingly to whether they work or not in the tourism sector.

[4]Recent papers on tourist preferences in Rimini are Candela et al. (2007), Figini and Troia (2006), Orsingher (2004), and Scorcu and Vici (2008).

[5]For an overview of the main differences among alternative stated preferences methodologies, particularly with respect to contingent valuation, see Brau (2007) and, more extensively, Bateman et al. (2002), Bennett and Blamey (2001), Louviere et al. (2000), and Mazzanti (2003).

that may otherwise be unattainable from observing actual behaviour. This methodology develops through three main steps (Hanley et al., 2001; Mazzanti, 2003): i) identification of the basic characteristics (attributes) of the good or project to be evaluated, which can take different values (levels); ii) each respondent has to choose among alternative hypothetical scenarios characterised by different combinations of the attribute levels; iii) the econometric analysis of their answers allows to estimate the relative importance of different attributes and, if a monetary factor or a price is included as attribute, the willingness to pay for different levels.

Consistently with the random utility theory (Thurstone, 1927; McFadden, 1974), consumers' utility is considered a latent structure that cannot be observed directly. By designing and implementing a valid preference elicitation procedure, preference orderings for a subset of choice options allows to assess a significant proportion of the unobservable consumer utility. The chosen scenario in each experiment corresponds, ceteris paribus, to the combination of attribute levels bringing the highest utility.[6]

Formally, given a sample of H respondents, with $h = 1,2,\ldots,H$, and a set of alternative choices, $j = 1,2,\ldots,J$, the random utility specification can be represented as a linear additive specification with independently and identically distributed (IID) random terms (Louviere et al., 2000)[7]:

$$U_{hj} = \beta' x_{hj} + \varepsilon_{hj}. \tag{9.1}$$

where the unobservable utility value for the choice alternative j made by consumer h is given by a deterministic and systematic component and a random term, ϵ_{hj}.

In model (2.1), the probability that an individual h picks alternative i out of J alternatives, can be represented as follows:

$$P[y_h = i] = \frac{\exp\left(\mu\beta' x_i^h\right)}{\sum_{j=1}^{J} \exp\left(\mu\beta' x_j^h\right)} \tag{9.2}$$

where y_h is a choice index, representing the choice made by individual h, and μ is a scale parameter that typically assumes value 1 (Ben-Akiva and Lerman, 1985).[8]

---

[6]Lancaster's hedonic theory (1966, 1971), which states that goods are not demanded per se, but for their elementary characteristics, can be considered the theoretical foundation of discrete choice models.

[7]The IID assumption entails the property of independence of irrelevant alternative (IIA – McFadden, 1984). Violations of the IIA assumption may arise when some alternatives are qualitatively similar to others or when there are heterogeneous preferences among respondents (Bateman et al., 2002; Morrison et al., 1996). If IIA is violated, alternative choice models should be used, such as the nested logit model (Louviere et al., 2000) or the multinomial probit model (Hausman and Wise, 1978).

[8]The scale factor μ is inversely proportional to the standard deviation of the error distribution. Assuming μ equal to 1 implies a constant error variance.

Moreover, the estimation of Eq. (9.1) with a conditional logit model, yields β coefficients allowing to evaluate the rate at which respondents are willing to trade-off one attribute to another. This rate of substitution σ is calculated as the ratio between the β coefficients of two attributes. When attributes are discrete variables, the substitute ratio σ is computed as "values of level change", as in (9.3).[9]

$$\sigma = 1 - \frac{\beta^i \Delta x_i}{\beta_S} \tag{9.3}$$

Specifically, in this paper we considered six attributes (and their levels), which are described in Table 9.1 and define the alternative scenarios.[10] The questionnaire was designed to gather information about the residents' perception of actual or hypothetical uses of Rimini territory. Direct interviews to a representative sample of Rimini population were conducted in months of February, March and April 2006.

There are several reasons why these attributes were selected. First, we had to consider important features of Rimini as regards potential interactions with tourists (trade-off and synergies) in the use of the territory and in terms of actual political debate. Since traffic congestion reduces available spaces for residents and increases time spent to commute and to reach commercial and leisure facilities, mobility risk was included as a first attribute. In order to make this attribute more concrete, we considered the project of building a coastal train connecting Rimini seaside suburbs, which is already approved and financed. The coastal train would have the effect to facilitate mobility of residents and tourists over the seaside area (therefore, reducing the traffic congestion).

The other attributes considered in the experiment were the traffic limitations on the seaside avenue (attribute n. 3) and the use of beach facilities (attribute n. 5), since in summer months the seaside area becomes, for residents as well as for tourists, the center of Rimini's cultural and recreational life.

Sustainability considerations and policies aimed at protecting and developing natural and cultural resources are common features of contemporary policy agendas. Rimini is a mass tourism destination, but also a middle-size city, and the residents' willingness to pay for a more environmental-friendly city might play a crucial role both in the policy strategy, and in terms of tourism development. This reason motivated the inclusion in the survey of the attributes of environmental protection of the

9 When the attribute is expressed in monetary terms, this trade-off σ is an "implicit price". These estimates rely on the assumption that the marginal utility of income is constant.: this holds only when small changes are considered (involving a tiny share of total individual income).

10 The identification of the six attributes and their levels was the result of frequent research meetings; a pilot test was carried out in the weeks preceding the survey and proved very useful to check the comprehension of the attributes, the clear perception of the difference in levels, and the relevance to residents of alternative scenarios. The pilot test confirmed as well that the structure of the survey was such to raise some expectation about the use of the information provided for decision making purposes. In fact, if the respondents view the process as entirely hypothetical, then their responses do not convey any economic sense (Carson, 2000).

Table 9.1 Definition of attributes and their levels

Attribute 1 – Risk of reduced mobility and traffic jams

Level 1 (*high mobility risk* – status quo): during the whole year, but particularly during summer months, roads and the transport system reach their carrying capacity, not allowing full mobility of people.

Level 2 (*low mobility risk*): the development of the coastal train allows full mobility of people and relieves the traffic system below its carrying capacity.

Attribute 2 – Environmental impact of bathing establishments and other beach services

Level 1 (*high preservation of beach environment*): The environmental impact of bathing establishments and other beach services, bars and restaurants is low (rare and small concrete buildings).

Level 2 (*medium preservation of beach environment*): there is a fair number of concrete buildings for essential services (first aid, emergency rescue, bars).

Level 3 (*low but temporary preservation of beach environment*): there is a high number of temporary buildings (e.g., in wood) for beach services, that can be removed during winter months.

Level 4 (*low preservation of beach environment* – status quo): there is a high number of permanent buildings (in concrete) for bathing establishments and other beach services.

Attribute 3 – The summer use of the seaside avenue

Level 1 (*pedestrian coastal road*): the seaside avenue is for pedestrian use, with large areas for bicycles and with decentralised parking lots.

Level 2 (*no limited traffic zone* – status quo): the seaside avenue is open to circulation, with parking lots close to the beach and no pedestrian areas.

Attribute 4 – The cultural offer

Level 1 (status quo): the city offers a few museums and a good level of heritage conservation.

Level 2 (*cultural scenario based on winter months*): Cultural investment is focussed in low-tourist season, particularly on the needs of residents.

Level 3 (*cultural scenario based on summer months*): Cultural investment is focussed in summer months, particularly on the needs of tourists.

Level 4 (*cultural scenario all year long*) Cultural investment is not focussed in any particular season, but aims to increasing the cultural heritage of the city.

Attribute 5 – Evening and night use of beach facilities

Level 1 (*beach services open during the day* – status quo): at night, limited access to the beach; bathing establishments and other beach services are closed to the public.

Level 2 (*night opening of beach services*): evening and night opening hours of bathing establishments and other beach facilities, with cultural events and shows.

Attribute 6 – Level of taxation needed to finance the projects

Level 1 (status quo) – no tax levied.

Level 2 (*low taxation*) – € 4 per month levied.

Level 3 (*medium taxation*) – € 8 per month levied.

Level 4 (*high taxation*) – € 12 per month levied.

beach (attribute n. 2) and of product differentiation through (new) cultural activities (attribute n. 4).[11]

Finally, the monetary attribute included in the survey was represented by a hypothetical local tax that residents should pay for improvements in the use of the territory (attribute n. 6).[12]

The full factorial of all the possible combinations of attribute levels would yield, in our case, 512 scenarios. A orthogonal fractional factorial design was used to reduce the number of profiles at a convenient size: 32 scenarios were identified. Pairwise comparisons were created using the shifted design strategy (Louviere et al., 2000).[13] The interviews were hence split into four groups whose respondents had to answer to different sets of 8 choice cards with different pairs of hypothetical alternative scenarios.[14] We explicitly did consider a status quo alternative, asking the respondents whether they prefer it over the two alternatives.[15]

Overall, the survey was divided into four sections[16]: the first one collected the main coordinates of the interview (date, location and length); the second part inquired into the socio-economic and demographic characteristics of the respondent and his/her household; the third section was the choice experiment and asked to choose among eight pairs of alternative scenarios, while the fourth section brought

---

[11]The attributes and their respective levels were very similar to the ones submitted to tourists in a parallel inquiry (Brau et al., 2008). Although some differences exist, particularly on the monetary and the cultural attributes, this allowed us to compare, at least partially, the elicited preferences of tourists and residents over the shared territory of Rimini.

[12]In choosing the levels of the monetary attribute, we had to balance four features: i) the levels should be in line with the projects involved, once alternative (and realistic) sources of financing (sponsorship, private co-financing, state intervention) were considered; ii) they should be expressed in an easy metric; iii) ideally they should span over the distribution of people's willingness to pay; iv) finally, we had to overcome the fact that in Italy the local administrations do not have the possibility to raise taxes dedicated to finance local projects (taxes are mainly transfers from the state).

[13]Zwerina et al. (1996) introduce four principles that a choice design should jointly satisfy in order to convey efficient estimates. Bunch et al. (1996), in evaluating generic choice designs, show that shifted designs generally have superior efficiency compared with other strategies, although for most combinations of attributes, levels, alternatives and parameters it is impossible to create a design that satisfies the four principles (Kessels et al., 2006).

[14]The pilot test showed that respondents could cope with up to eight choice pairs each. In fact, violations related to instability of preferences can arise from learning and fatigue effects (Hanley et al., 2002). In order to make clear and homogeneous the comprehension of attributes and to facilitate the individual decision process, the oral explanation of these attributes and levels was accompanied by the presentation of drawings and photos describing each scenario. In each group, the cards submitted were the same but presented every time with a different sequence, in order to avoid any question order bias.

[15]The explicit definition of the status quo allows for a more coherent evaluation of the proposed scenarios (Brau, 2007). In our case, only 7% of the stated preferences were not confirmed after the comparison with the status quo. On the use of consequentiality design in stated preference models see Boxall and Adamowicz (2002) Carson et al. (2002), Cummings and Taylor (1998), Landry and List (2007), Provencher et al. (2002), Train (1998).

[16]The questionnaire is available from the authors upon request.

together some other information about the test comprehension. In particular, the interviewer annotated the degree of comprehension, interest and facility both in answering questions and in choosing the alternatives. Problems of poor identification of alternative scenarios were not relevant: the reported level of comprehension was high (98% of the sample understood the questionnaire) and the differences in the attributes levels were clearly perceived. Interviews took on average 26 minutes.

9.3 Residents' Demographic and Social Characteristics

The questionnaire was submitted to a sample of 606 residents, stratified by gender, age, education, professional status and economic activity. This last aspect is crucial, since respondents' attitude is likely to be driven by the existence of any business connection, direct or indirect, with the tourism sector. Among active workers, 1.2% work in the primary sector, 14.4% in manufacturing, 7% in building, 22.4% in trade, 14.1% in tourism and 40.8% in other services. However, this datum is likely to underestimate the economic importance of tourism.[17] To include indirect as well as direct effects of (and links to) tourism we asked respondents to what extent their business is linked to tourism. 21.9% of the survey answered that at least 80% of their business is driven by tourism demand and another 17.2% estimated that tourism generates between 40% and 79% of their business. 9.5% of the sample estimated that tourism generates between 20% and 39% of their business while about half of the sample (51.5%) considered not to be (or very little) linked to tourism demand.

The distribution of respondents' characteristics was consistent with our sampling plan and representative of the whole population of Rimini. Table 9.2 suggests that the sample was also representative as regards income, usually the most difficult variable to investigate. The distribution of net personal income was as expected, and the percentage of non-respondent – 11.9% was quite low. With respect to educational attainment, 24.3% of the sample owns a University degree, 37% a secondary school diploma, and 38.3% a primary degree, also in line with the population characteristics. Finally, the occupational and professional status of respondents are described in Table 9.2.

As discussed in the introduction, tourism might produce positive and negative effects on residents and on the city; in fact, only 15.9% of the sample thought that tourism has no effects on general life conditions, while 66.6% perceived that life conditions improve, and only 17.5% thought that tourism brings an overall worsening. Table 9.3 summarizes the main positive and negative impacts of tourism

[17] There are two main reasons why data on economic activity are likely to underestimate the importance of tourism. First, many non-tourism activities in a city like Rimini might primarily serve tourists (let us think about a shop situated close to the beach); second, property letting might be an important source of income which does not stem from the respondent's main economic activity. In this respect, 15% of the sample declared that to have an apartment to rent, of which 2.5% rents only to tourists, 6.1% rents also to tourists while 6.4% does not rent at all to tourists.

Table 9.2 Demographic and socio-economic characteristics of the sample

Age class	%	Occupational/professional status	%
< 30	16.5	Entrepreneur	6.9
30–39	21.6	Professional	9.4
40–49	18.2	Craftsman	4.5
50–59	13.4	Manager	2.3
≥ 60	30.4	Dealer	11.9
		Employee/white collar	18.0
Income class (Euro)	%	Worker/blue collar	9.2
< 10,000	14.5	Other	3.7
10,000–14,999	18.3	House working	7.3
15,000–19,999	21.6	Student	3.8
20,000–24,999	18.6	Retired	20.5
25,000–39,999	11.1	Unemployed	2.5
≥ 40,000	4.0		
N.A.	11.9	Gender	%
		Males	52.3
		Females	47.7

Table 9.3 Perceived positive and negative effects of tourism

Type of effect	%	
No effect on general life conditions		15.9
Positive effects on general life conditions		66.6
– Economic improvement	50.7	
– Environmental and health services improvement	0.4	
– Recreational, cultural and sport activities improvement	15.5	
Negative effects on general life conditions		17.5
– Less efficiency of public services	2.0	
– Increase in the level of pollution	1.0	
– More criminality and less security	2.5	
– Worsening of traffic and mobility	10.2	
– Other	1.8	

on the city welfare. Not surprisingly, and in line with previous researches on tourism impact, economic effects (higher income levels, job opportunities, etc.) overcome social and environmental effects frequently perceived as negative (increase of noise level, crime rates, etc.): 50.7% of the sample thought that tourism has an overall positive economic impact, whilst 10.2% of the sample mainly saw the negative impact on traffic and mobility.[18]

[18] Among people whose business was related to tourism, 78.5% thought that it has a positive effect, 8.2% no effect and 13.3% a negative effect. Among people whose business was not related to tourism this distribution changed to 59.2% (positive effect), 18% (no effect) and 22.8% (negative effect).

Finally, another characteristics which is likely to interact with stated preferences is the travel mode to commute in the city: 45.7% of the sample uses the car while another 11.7% the motorcycle or the scooter. Only 23.1%, 12.7% and 6.6% of the sample use environmental-friendly travel modes: bicycle, foot and public transport respectively.

9.4 Econometric Results

Table 9.4 presents the results of a conditional logit model estimated for the whole sample and for two sub-samples based on whether residents' job activity is (at least) partially linked to tourism or not.[19] All the attribute levels, which are described in Table 9.1, were elaborated as dummy variables, with the exception of the tax levied, which took four different quantitative values corresponding to four distinct tax rates. The 0-values for the dummy variables were set up on the status quo (high mobility risk, low environmental protection of the beach, seaside avenue open to traffic, present cultural offer, beach services close at night, and no extra-tax levied). Since each hypothetical scenario was planned to "improve" the quality of the city, we were expecting positive signs for all the coefficients, except taxes.

The maximum likelihood estimates show that for the whole sample all the coefficients were statistically significant and with the expected sign, with the exception of those related to the environmental protection of the beach.[20]

In order to control for preference heterogeneity, we decided to use two main approaches.[21] Firstly, we estimated the main-effect model for different sub-samples, based on socio-demographic and economic characteristics (Tables 9.4 and 9.5). Robust results emerge: neither different aged people, nor different income classes pay attention to the preservation of the beach (Table 9.5). Even residents whose activity is based on tourism seem not to be affected in their choice by the level of beach preservation (Table 9.4). This might be due to the fact that, on the one hand, these levels are not perceived so different from the present situation, which has high permanent impact (perhaps because the seaside is mainly lived during the

[19]We inserted an alternative-specific constant (ASC) to capture those characteristics of the choice not included otherwise in the model. In our case, there might be a tendency of individuals to prefer any scenario labelled "A" (on the left of the card presented) over any other scenario labelled "B" (on the right of the card). This is a frequent finding in such models (Louviere et al., 2000), and the inclusion of the alternative-specific constant allows to effectively control for this behaviour.

[20]The temporary preservation of the beach's coefficient has a negative sign, significant at the 10% level only in the whole sample.

[21]An alternative way to include preference heterogeneity consists of using the mixed logit model (Train, 2003). However, such approach requires important assumptions on the form of distribution of the random parameters. If the distributional form is misspecified the estimates are not consistent.

Table 9.4 Estimation of conditional logit model: whole sample, tourism-based and non-tourism based local workers

Attributes and levels	Complete sample	Tourism-based job+	Non-tourism-based job++
Low mobility risk	0.305***	0.296***	0.354
	(0.033)	(0.048)	(0.078)
High preservation of beach environment	–0.052	–0.099	–0.065
	(0.058)	(0.086)	(0.135)
Medium preservation of beach environment	0.080	0.082	0.065
	(0.066)	(0.096)	(0.158)
Low (but temporary) preservation of beach environment	–0.100*	–0.112	–0.273
	(0.058)	(0.084)	(0.148)
Pedestrian coastal road	0.653***	0.713***	0.509***
	(0.034)	(0.049)	(0.079)
Cultural scenario based on winter months	0.623***	0.568***	0.659***
	(0.058)	(0.085)	(0.139)
Cultural scenario based on summer months	0.206***	0.108	0.212
	(0.065)	(0.094)	(0.156)
Cultural scenario all year long	0.447***	0.473***	0.367***
	(0.055)	(0.080)	(0.130)
Night opening of beach	0.665***	0.713***	0.762***
	(0.033)	(0.048)	(0.079)
Monthly tax levied	–0.032***	–0.023***	–0.032***
	(0.005)	(0.023)	(0.011)
Alternative specific constant	–0.056*	–0.040	–0.039
	(0.033)	(0.047)	(0.078)
Log likelihood	–2806.72	–1335.86	–497.158
Pseudo R^2	0.165	0.181	0.170
Nr. Of observations	9696	4704	1728

Note. *: significant at the 10% level; **: significant at the 5% level; ***: significant at the 1% level.
+: Sample composed by respondents who answered that at least 20% of their business is linked to tourism demand.
++: Sample composed by respondents who answered that none of their business is linked to tourism demand.

summer); on the other hand, it is probably true that the typical Rimini's skyline, shaped by huge bathing establishments and high anthropic presence in its seaside resource, is perceived as a milestone of the city landscape: a change would not be pleased.[22]

An alternative approach to deal with individual heterogeneity would be to estimate an extended model including higher order interactions between attribute levels and socio-demographic characteristics. In this way it is also possible to check

[22]Even if the pilot test confirmed that permanent and temporary preservations of the beach were perceived as different environments by residents, their choices were not significantly affected by different environmental policies.

Table 9.5 Estimation of conditional logit model: different age sub-samples; low-income and high-income sub-samples

Attributes and levels	The Young (<30)	The Adults (30–59)	The Elderly (≥60)	Low-income (≤18000)	High-income (>18000)
Low mobility risk	0.336***	0.299***	0.321***	0.326***	0.283***
	(0.082)	(0.045)	(0.061)	(0.047)	(0.047)
High preservation of beach environment	–0.197	–0.058	0.064	–0.089	–0.025
	(0.146)	(0.080)	(0.106)	(0.083)	(0.082)
Medium preservation of beach environment	–0.081	0.108	0.145	0.053	0.091
	(0.165)	(0.091)	(0.121)	(0.095)	(0.093)
Low (but temporary) preservation of beach environment	–0.256*	–0.095	0.004	–0.151*	–0.057
	(0.140)	(0.081)	(0.107)	(0.082)	(0.083)
Pedestrian coastal road	0.584***	0.635***	0.745***	0.791***	0.521***
	(0.083)	(0.046)	(0.062)	(0.049)	(0.047)
Cultural scenario based on winter months	0.864***	0.559***	0.589***	0.716***	0.554***
	(0.150)	(0.080)	(0.108)	(0.085)	(0.082)
Cultural scenario based on summer months	0.285*	0.148*	0.242**	0.264***	0.161*
	(0.162)	(0.090)	(0.119)	(0.092)	(0.092)
Cultural scenario all year long	0.699***	0.400***	0.414***	0.429***	0.462***
	(0.140)	(0.076)	(0.099)	(0.078)	(0.079)
Night opening of beach	0.678***	0.702***	0.609***	0.737***	0.601***
	(0.083)	(0.045)	(0.061)	(0.048)	(0.047)
Monthly tax levied	–0.022**	–0.031***	–0.042***	–0.037***	–0.028***
	(0.012)	(0.007)	(0.009)	(0.007)	(0.007)
Alternative specific constant	0.081	–0.044	–0.149**	–0.063	–0.049
	(0.081)	(0.045)	(0.060)	(0.046)	(0.046)
Log likelihood	–453.82	–1491.38	–848.362	–1415.14	–1381.10
Pseudo R^2	0.1816	0.1647	0.1685	0.1975	0.1352
Nr. of observations	1,600	5,152	2,944	5,088	4,608

Note:*significant at the 10% level; **significant at the 5% level; ***significant at the 1% level

whether preferences for the level of one attribute depend on other attribute levels. The vast majority of choice experiments use the main effect design only, explicitly or implicitly assuming that interactions among attributes are not significant. However, if interactions are significant, such omission leads to sub-optimal results (Hensher et al., 2005). In our experiment, the interaction coefficients were not statistically significant.[23]

[23]The only statistically significant interaction concerned residents whose business is linked to tourism, and the coefficient confirmed that they do not appreciate a pedestrianisation of the seaside

The β coefficients estimated under the conditional logit model can be used to estimate the rate at which respondents are willing to trade-off one attribute to another, as Eq. (9.3) suggests. This information provides a ranking of attribute importance that could be used by the local policy maker in designing welfare enhancing policies. The higher the ratio, the higher the relative weight of the attribute in the scenario.

Results showed that residents attach by far a great value to the possibility to stay on the beach even during the night, where shows and events could be organized, and to the pedestrian use of Rimini's esplanade. While these findings show a potential synergy with tourists in their willingness to have "a sea-side with a human face", the coefficients of the cultural attribute show a potential trade-off. In fact, residents would prefer a more lively cultural scene mainly in winter months and, only as second best, all-year long. More cultural events during summer months would be accepted only as a third best. Clearly, residents suffer a city cultural offer too biased towards summer months when, probably, cultural events are difficult to consume due to both tourists overcrowding and to the fact that many residents work (if they have tourism-based jobs) or are away for their own holidays. The importance of low mobility risk achieved by the coastal train was positively evaluated, but its importance was estimated to be half of that given to the pedestrian use of the seaside avenue.

When the attribute being sacrificed is monetary, the estimated trade-offs are "implicit prices", the amount of money respondents are willing to pay in order to receive a change in the considered attributes. The estimate of implicit prices, reported in Table 9.6, are made on a ceteris paribus hypothesis, namely for an increase in the attribute of interest given that everything else is held constant. In line with results presented in Table 9.4, a comparison of implicit prices for attributes allows to rank their relative importance for each group of respondents.[24]

Although respondents were sensitive to price differences within the experiments, the weight given to the price attribute was apparently very low and the real tax that residents were actually willing to pay for closing the seaside avenue oscillates between the high values of 15 and 32 Euro per month, depending on the group of residents (Table 9.6).

We expected that residents perceptions towards the socio-economic impact of tourism would be, ceteris paribus, a function of their direct economic dependency on the tourism industry (Haralambopoulos and Pizam, 1996). Non surprisingly, residents whose activities are based on tourism were less willing to

avenue. However, we tested the joint hypothesis that all the interactions of the extended model were not statistically significant with respect to the basic model of Table 9.4. We accepted the null hypothesis that all the coefficients of the additional interaction terms were identically equal to zero ($\chi 2(18) = 13.10$ with a p-value $= 0.7857$). Complete results are available from the authors upon requests. See also Figini et al. (2007).

[24]Note that we are dealing with discrete (and not marginal) level variations and that estimates are based on the assumption that the marginal utility of income is constant.

Table 9.6 Implicit prices (Euro per month)

Level changes	Whole sample	Non tourism based job	Tourism based job	The young	The adults	The elderly	Low income	High income
Risk of overcrowding	9.47	13.10	11.03	14.65	9.59	7.73	8.81	10.14
Variation in beach impact from high permanent to minimal impact	NSS	NSS	NSS	NSS	NSS	NSS	NSS	NSS
Variation in beach impact from high permanent to medium impact	NSS	NSS	NSS	NSS	NSS	NSS	NSS	NSS
Variation in beach impact from high permanent to high temporary impact	–3.11	–4.94	NSS	–11.14	NSS	NSS	–4.09	NSS
Promenade for pedestrians	20.29	31.50	15.86	25.44	20.38	17.93	21.39	18.61
Cultural public investment only during the winter	19.33	25.10	20.54	37.63	17.94	14.17	19.36	19.81
Cultural public investment only during the summer	6.39	NSS	NSS	12.42	4.74	5.83	7.13	5.74
Yearly cultural public investment	13.88	20.89	11.43	30.46	12.84	9.96	11.60	16.53
Beach open by night	20.66	31.49	23.74	29.53	22.54	14.65	19.92	21.49

Note: when the coefficients of Tables 9.4 or 9.5 were not statistically significant (NSS), the implicit prices were not computed.

pay for a pedestrian seaside avenue. In fact, tourism activities in Rimini are mostly located along a parallel avenue, provided with a large pavement; the opening of a larger and pedestrian area nearby, with shows and tourist attractions could threaten many firms' turnover. As discussed above, this result was robust to the inclusion in the model of second-order interactions (see Figini et al., 2007).

People aged over 60 were less willing to pay for the opening of the beach during the night, probably because they are more inclined to visit the beach during the day. On the other side, people with the highest willingness to pay for the organization of events on the beach during the night and for the pedestrianisation of the seaside avenue were residents whose activity is not linked to tourism. These people are probably direct users of tourist services, and for that reason they are more willing to pay for this sort of public investment.

Substitution rates and implicit prices provide important pieces of information to policy makers. In addition to the information on the "price" residents are willing to pay for any level of the considered attributes, policy makers learn the relative importance of each attribute in the residents' utility structure. This would allow local authorities to modify the tourist product (through multiple and simultaneous changes in the attribute levels) in order to make it consistent with residents' structure of preferences.

A different combination of levels for these attributes could improve the empathy between tourists and residents. To make this point clearer, a simulation in which policy makers could create possible alternative scenarios was built. It must be recalled that this simulation, which considered more than two alternatives at the same time, was based on the IIA assumption, which allows for creating hypothetical products by different combinations of attribute levels.

We chose four scenarios differing in the level of five attributes (the levied tax was excluded): the current situation (status quo), an environment friendly scenario, a mass-tourism scenario, and a resident friendly scenario, which attributes and levels are presented in Table 9.7. We inferred from the econometric estimates the probability that residents chose for one of these scenarios,[25] thus leading to interesting implications for the policy agenda.

Surprisingly, although choice probabilities were different among groups of residents, the ranking of these alternative scenarios was unanimously accepted: the worst scenario was the status quo, whilst the most preferred scenario was the tourist product respectful of residents' habits. Moreover, residents did not pay much attention to an environment friendly tourism product.

Analogously, by exploiting the estimates obtained in the study on tourists' preferences in Rimini (Brau et al., 2008), we built four scenarios based on four attributes in order to compare the probability that the representative tourist in Rimini chooses

[25] The probability that an individual picked each scenario out of the four alternatives was computed by inserting in Eq. (9.2) the coefficient estimated in Tables 9.4 and 9.5.

Table 9.7 Simulation of choice probabilities

Attributes	Status quo	Environment friendly scenario	Mass-tourist scenario	Resident scenario
Promenade	vehicles	pedestrians	Pedestrians	pedestrians
Overcrowding	high risk	low risk	high risk	high risk
Environment (beach) preservation	low permanent	high	low temporary	medium
Cultural supply	limited investment	yearly investment	summer investment	winter investment
Beach by night	close	close	Open	open
Choice probabilities				
Complete sample	4.37%	16.93%	33.89%	44.81%
Tourism based job	4.34%	17.32%	31.76%	46.57%
Non-tourism based job	4.73%	15.14%	30.65%	49.48%
The young	4.07%	16.86%	35.08%	43.99%
The adults	4.63%	16.57%	32.50%	46.30%
The elderly	3.89%	18.20%	34.68%	43.24%
Low income	4.37%	16.93%	33.89%	44.81%
High income	3.37%	14.48%	35.63%	46.52%

each scenario with the analogous probability for the representative resident.[26] This simulation allowed the identification of differences in the distribution of tourists' and residents' preferences among alternative scenarios, and the identification of the preferred scenarios for residents and for tourists. Moreover, it provided useful information for policy makers aiming at proposing social welfare enhancing tourism projects.

In our experiment, different rankings of alternative scenarios clearly emerged (Table 9.8): whereas the status quo was unanimously considered the worst scenario, the best alternative for tourists was the "Mass-tourism scenario", which represented the second best for residents. Vice versa, the local community preferred the "Resident scenario" which was the second choice of tourists. Neither residents nor tourists were really interested in an environmental friendly scenario, probably because it is not in the nature of a mass-tourism destination such Rimini.

[26]It must be recalled that the twin study on tourists slightly differed in the definition and in the levels of the cultural and monetary attributes. For this reason, such attributes were not considered in the simulation, and this might affect the estimated probabilities.

Table 9.8 Comparison between residents and tourists' best scenarios

Attributes	Status quo	Environment friendly scenario	Mass-tourist scenario	Resident scenario
Promenade	vehicles	pedestrians	pedestrians	Pedestrians
Overcrowding	high risk	low risk	high risk	high risk
Environment (beach) preservation	low permanent	high	low temporary	Medium
Beach by night	close	close	open	open
Choice probabilities				
Residents	8.09%	20.03%	27.39%	44.49%
Tourists	10.20%	15.96%	40.53%	33.31%

9.5 Conclusion

During their holidays, tourists produce direct and indirect effects on local residents. These tourism externalities on the local community can either be positive or negative, and in this paper we investigated how residents internalise them. Our case study was Rimini, a popular Italian seaside resort with more than ten million national and foreign overnight stays every summer. We used a stated preference approach and, in particular, a discrete choice modelling technique to test some conjectures about residents' willingness to pay for alternative scenarios regarding the use of the territory. Such approach enabled us to identify potential synergies or trade-off with tourists.

The main results are here summarized: first, residents have strong preferences over the 24-hour a day use of beach services, the pedestrianization of the seaside avenue and a cultural policy focused outside the tourism season. They are less interested in decreasing mobility risks through the project of a coastal train, while they like the present anthropic nature of Rimini's seaside. However, a deeper analysis of resident sub-samples highlights how residents whose jobs are mainly based on tourist flows are less willing to pay for the pedestrianization of the seaside avenue, since this might divert tourists attention away from their activities and tighten local competition.

Second, a comparison of our results with those of the "twin" research on tourists in Rimini (Brau et al., 2008) allowed us to highlight that there is room for potential and strong synergies in the organization of the territory. Both tourists and residents have strong preferences towards beach services open at night and towards the quality of the promenade. Both groups like the present (strong) environmental impact of bathing establishments and fairly "like" overcrowding, so the mobility risk is not at the top of their preferences.

However, there was an important dimension of potential trade-off lying in the model of cultural policy that they want for Rimini. Both groups are willing to pay for an improvement in the cultural policy, but tourists want it during the summer, while residents ask for more cultural events during winter months.

Moreover, we analysed how tourism policy and public investments in the destination might affect residents' welfare. In this respect, the forthcoming project of building a coastal train to reduce mobility risk seemed not to be a top priority in the residents' preferences. The policy implication is straightforward, since the project of transforming the seaside avenue in a pedestrian area is much more simpler and much less expensive than building a new railway.

Our exercise allowed a rough simulation of what might happen were such policies implemented. Consider the implicit prices of Table 9.6 and assume that the policy maker were able to charge all residents with an extra tax equal to their willingness to pay; for the pedestrianization of the promenade, residents are willing to pay up to € 20.47 per month; if taxpayers in Rimini are around 100,000, these numbers would lead to an extra revenue of up to € 24 million that could be used both to finance the project and to compensate losers from its implementation. However, residents might easily decide to pass the extra tax burden on tourists, since they are also willing to pay for the pedestrianization of the promenade (see Brau et al., 2008).

To the best of our knowledge, ours was one of the first attempts to check for any synergy and trade-off between tourists and residents' preferences in a mass tourism destination, by applying the choice experiment technique on the local population. In the case of a mature destination such as Rimini, which recently made a great effort to diversify mainly towards business and cultural tourism, further research calls for other choice experiments, this time aimed to uncover preferences of "out of season" (business and cultural) tourists.

References

Akis S, Peristianis N, Warner J (1996) Residents' attitudes to tourism development: the case of Cyprus. Tourism Management 17:481–494

Alberini A, Rosato P, Zanatta V (2005) Combining actual and contingent behaviour to estimate the value of sport fishing in the lagoon of Venice. Ecol Econ 61(2–3):530–41.

Apostolakis A, Shabbar J (2005) Stated preferences for two Cretan heritage attractions. Ann Tourism Res 32(4):985–1005

Bateman IJ, Carson RT, Day B, Hanemann M, Hanley N, Hett T, Jones-Lee M, Loomes G, Mourato S, Ozdemiroglu E, Pearce DW, Sugden R, Swanson J (2002) Economic valuation with stated preference techniques. Edward Elgar, Cheltenham, UK

Ben-Akiva M, Lerman S (1985) Discrete choice analysis: theory and application to travel demand. MIT Press, Cambridge MA

Bennett J, Blamey R (eds.) (2001) The choice modelling approach to environmental valuation. Edward Elgar, Cheltenham

Boxall PC, Adamowicz WL (2002) Understanding heterogeneous preferences in random utility models: A latent class approach. Environ Resour Econ 23:421–446

Brau R, Cao D (2006) Uncovering the macrostructure of tourists' preferences. A choice experiment analysis of tourism demand to Sardinia, FEEM Working Paper 33/2006

Brau R (2007) Il choice modelling nell'analisi del turismo sostenibile. In: Punzo L, Usai S (eds.) L'estate al mare. McGraw-Hill, Milan

Brau R, Scorcu AE, Vici L (2008) Assessing visitor satisfaction with tourism rejuvenation policies: the case of Rimini, Italy. J Environ Plann Manage (Forthcoming)

Breffle W, Morey E (2000) Investigating preference heterogeneity in a repeated discrete-choice recreation demand model of Atlantic salmon fishing. Mar Resour Econ 15:1–20

Bull A (1991) The economics of travel and tourism. Longman Cheshire, Melbourne
Bunch DS, Louviere JJ, Anderson DA (1996) A comparison of experimental design strategies for multinomial Logit models: The Case of Generic Attributes. Working Paper, Graduate School of Management, University of California, Davis
Candela G, Giannerini S, Scorcu AE (2007) Le caratteristiche strutturali di una destinazione matura. Il caso di Rimini. Economia dei Servizi 1:123–46
Carson RT (2000) Contingent valuation: a user's guide. Environ Sci Technol 34:1413–1418
Carson RT, Groves T, List JA, Machina M (2002) Probabilistic Influence and Supplemental Benefits: A field test of the two key assumptions underlying stated preferences. Working Paper, University of California
Castellani M, Candela G, Dieci R (2007) Il turismo responsabile: un'opportunità per le destinazioni turistiche e per i turisti. Polit Econ 23(1):83–102
Crotts JC, Holland SM (1993) Objective indicators of the impact of rural tourism development in the state of Florida. J Sustainable Tourism 1: 112–120
Crouch GI, Louviere JJ (2004) The determinants of convention site selection: a logistic choice model from experimental data. J Travel Res 43(2): 118–130
Cummings RG, Taylor LO (1998) Does realism matter in contingent valuation surveys? Land Econ 74: 203–15
Doxey GV (1975) A causation theory of visitor-resident irritants: methodology and research inferences. Proceedings of the Travel Research Association, 6th annual conference, San Diego, California, pp. 195–198
Dwyer L, Forsyth P (1993) Assessing the benefits and costs of inbound tourism. Ann Tourism Res 20: 751–768
Faulkner HW, Tideswell C (1997) A framework for monitoring community impacts of tourism. J Sustainable Tourism 5(1):3–28
Figini P, Troia T (2006) Le caratteristiche dei turisti a Rimini: un confronto tra due recenti indagini. Sistemaeconomico 11(3):5–20
Figini P, Castellani M, Vici L (2007) Estimating tourist external effects on residents: a choice modelling application to Rimini. FEEM working paper 76.07
Freeman AM (1993) The measurement of environmental and resource values. Resources for the Future, Washington DC 332–341
Hanley N, Wright R, Koop G (2002) Modelling recreation demand using choice experiments: climbing in Scotland. Environ Resour Econ 22:449–466
Hanley N, Mourato S, Wright R (2001) Choice modelling: a superior alternative for environmental valuation. J Econ Surv 15:435–462
Haralambopoulos N, Pizam A (1996) Perceived impacts of tourism: the case of samos. Ann Tourism Res 23:503–526
Hausman J, McFadden D (1984) Specification tests for the multinomial logit model. Econometrica 52:1219–1240
Hausman J, Wise D (1978) A conditional probit model for qualitative choice: discrete decisions recognizing interdependence and heterogeneous preferences. Econometrica 46:403–426
Hensher D, Rose J, Greene W (2005) Applied choice analysis: a primer. Cambridge University Press, Cambridge
Huybers T (2005) Destination choice modelling: what's in a name?. Tourism Econ 11(3): 329–350
Huybers T, Bennett J (2000) Impact of the environment on holiday destination choices of prospective UK tourists: implications for Tropical North Queensland. Tourism Econ 6:21–46
Kessels R, Goos P, Vanderbroek M (2006) A comparison of criteria to sesign efficient choice experiments. J Mark Res 43:409–419
Lancaster K (1966) A new approach to consumer theory. J Polit Econ 74(2):132–157
Lancaster K (1971) Consumer demand – a new approach. Columbia University Press, New York
Landry CE, List JA (2007) Using ex ante approaches to obtain credible signals of value in contingent markets: evidence from the field. Am J Agric Econ 89(2):420–32

Lindberg, K., Andersson TD, Dellaert BGC (2001) Tourism development: assessing social gains and losses. Ann Tourism Res 28(4):1010–1030
Lindberg K, Dellaert BGC, Rassing CR (1999) Resident trade-offs: a choice modeling approach. Ann Tourism Res 26(3):554–69
Lindberg K, Johnson R.L. (1997a) The economic values of tourism's social impacts. Ann Tourism Res 24:90–116
Lindberg K, Johnson RL (1997b) Modelling resident attitudes toward tourism. Ann Tourism Res 24:402–424
Liu J, Sheldon P, Var T (1987) A cross-national approach to determining resident perceptions of the impact of tourism on the environment. Ann Tourism Res 14:17–37
Louviere JJ, Hensher DA, Swait JD (2000) Stated choice methods. Cambridge University Press, Cambridge
Mazzanti M (2003) Discrete choice models and valuation experiments. J Econ Stud 30:584–604
McFadden D (1974) Conditional logit analysis of qualitative choice behaviour. In: Zarembka P (ed) Frontiers in econometrics. Academic Press, New York
McFadden D (1984) Econometric analysis of qualitative response models. In: Griliches Z, Intriligator MD (eds.) Handbook of econometrics II. Elsevier Science, Amsterdam, pp 1395–1457
Morey E, Rossmann KG, Chestnut LG, Ragland S (2002) Valuing reduced acid deposition injuries to cultural resources: marble monuments in Washington DC. In: Navrud S, Ready RC (eds) Applying environmental valuation techniques to historic buildings, monuments and artifacts. Edward Elgar, Cheltenham, UK
Morrison MD, Bennett JW, Blamey RK, Louviere JJ (1996) A comparison of stated preference techniques for estimating environmental values. Choice Modelling Research Report 1, University College, The University of New South Wales, Canberra
Orsingher C (ed) (2004) Comprendere il turismo nella Provincia di Rimini. Mimeo, Comune di Rimini
Papatheodorou A (2001) Why people travel to different places. Ann Tourism Res 28(1):164–179
Pearce DG (1989) Social impacts of tourism. In: Social cultural and environmental impacts of tourism, NSW Tourism Commission, Sydney, pp 1–39
Pizam A, Milman A (1984) The social impacts of tourism. UNEP Ind Environ 7(1):11–14
Provencher B, Baerenklau KA, Bishop RC (2002) A finite mixture logit model of recreational angling with serially correlated random utility. Am J Agric Econ 84:1066–1075
Ryan C (1991) Recreational tourism: a social science perspective. Routledge, London
Scorcu AE, Vici L (2008) Il turismo balneare a Rimini: scenario attuale e possibili evoluzioni nelle preferenze dei turisti. Sistemaeconomico, forthcoming
Thurstone LL (1927) A Law of comparative judgement. Psychol Rev 34: 273–286
Train KE (1998) Recreation demand models with taste differences over people. Land Econ 74(2):230–9
Train, K.,2003. Discrete choice methods with simulation. Cambridge University Press, Cambridge
Travis AS (1984) Social and cultural aspects of tourism. UNEP Ind Environ 7(1):22–24
Wall G, Mathieson A (2005) Tourism: change, impacts and opportunities. Pearson Prentice Hall, Essex, UK
Williams TA (1979) Impact of domestic tourism in host population: the evolution of a model. Tourist Recreation Res 4(1):15–21
Zanatta V, Rosato P, Alberini A, Reppas D (2005) The impact of speed limits on recreational boating in the lagoon of Venice. FEEM Working Paper 135/05
Zwerina K, Huber J, Kuhfeld WF (1996) A general method for constructing efficient choice designs. Working Paper, Fuqua School of Business, Duke University

Chapter 10
Willingness to Pay for Airline Services: A Stated Choice Experiment

Pedro Telhado Pereira, António Almeida,
António Gomes de Menezes, and José Cabral Vieira

10.1 Introduction

It is widely recognized that airlines are increasingly exposed to fierce levels of competition across all market segments, especially in the tourism segment (Gilbert and Wong 2003). Hence, it comes as no surprise that airlines have been devoting increasing attention to service differentiation strategies that seek to cater to the heterogeneous preferences of passengers (Rose et al. 2005). As a result, there is a growing body of research on stated preferences (SP) discrete choice models that are used to elicit passengers' preferences.

As Hensher et al. (2001) argue, revealed preferences (RP) data are limited in that they are applicable in explaining current passenger choices, but are a risky domain within which to assess the potential gains from changes in fares and service levels well outside the combinations observed. Stated choice (SC) experiments have become a very popular workhorse to extend the domain of choice as defined by the attributes of alternatives through offering individuals combinations of levels of attributes that are not necessarily available in real markets. Through a systematic varying in these combinations we are able to construct the preference functions of individuals and use this information to predict gains associated with new offerings. In addition, Hess et al. (2006) argue that RP data may provide misleading information if auxiliary data are poor or absent. For instance, consider a fare-sensitive passenger who due to the lack of availability accepts a high fare. From RP data without auxiliary data on availability one may wrongly infer that such passenger is fare-insensitive. SC methods, however, circumvent such problems by construction.

Recent empirical research on SC methods and airline choice has focused, quite naturally, on large hubs (Hess et al. 2006). Recent examples of such studies include Pels et al. (2001, 2003), Basar and Bhat (2004), Cao and Mokhtarian (2005a, b),

P.T. Pereira (✉)
Department of Management and Economics, University of Madeira and CEEAplA, Funchal, Portugal
e-mail: ppereira@uma.pt

DOI 10.1007/978-3-7908-2124-6_10, © Physica-Verlag Heidelberg 2009

and Hess and Polak (2005a, b) – who all use data collected in the San Francisco Bay Area, and Hess and Polak (2005c) – who use data from the Greater London Area. These hubs are dominated by passengers who travel for non-tourism related reasons and, quite importantly, have remarkably different expectations regarding airline services from passengers who travel for tourism related reasons (Gilbert and Wong 2003).

Our paper contributes to the literature by focusing on the tourism segment. In particular, our paper analyzes the route from Funchal (to Madeira, Portugal) to Las Palmas (to Canary Islands, Spain): a route that connects two well-known touristic destinations and that is mainly used by tourists. We argue that SC methods are well suited to elicit travelling tourists' preferences and, thus, to inform airlines about the potential gains from alternative service differentiation strategies in the competitive tourism segment.[1]

We implement a stated preferences choice game which, and to be brief, asks airline passengers to choose between two competing airlines that differ, in a trade-off sense, in several attributes, such as ticket cost, penalties for changing tickets, punctuality warranties and daily flight frequencies. Hence, our SC experiment is based on a quite realistic task that airline passengers perform every day. We follow, among others, Cao and Mokhtarian (2005a, b) who argue that individuals adapt their travel-related strategies according to a number of objective and subjective influences, and, hence, we control for individual characteristics. We find systematic variations in the willingness to pay measures for improvements in service levels, such as punctuality warranties, between passengers who travel for tourism related reasons and passengers who travel for work related reasons and, concomitantly, we uncover a potential gain for airlines from exploring such heterogeneous preferences.

The paper is organized as follows. Section 10.2 describes the data. Section 10.3 presents the econometric model. Section 10.4 discusses the results. Section 10.5 concludes.

10.2 Data

10.2.1 The Stated Preferences Choice Game

Our SC game was implemented through questionnaires ministered at Funchal's Airport, near the boarding gate, after security checkpoint. A total of 242 questionnaires were asked between May 19th and July 23rd 2005. Only passengers who were about to take a flight from Funchal to Las Palmas were interviewed, to make sure that they were familiar with the questions asked.

---

[1] We also note that SC methods have been recently applied to a variety of tourism economic problems aside airline choice. Recent examples of such applications include Kelly et al. (2006), Dutta et al. (2007) and Kim et al. (2007).

The questionnaires had 3 sections. In the first section, a number of questions were asked about the trip, such as: airline; connection at destination; connecting airline; fare class (business, economy); departure time; trip cost; trip motive; trip frequency; who pays for the trip; number of people flying with the interviewee; advance of purchasing the ticket; mode of purchasing the ticket; and frequent flyer program.

In the second section, the individuals were confronted with a stated preferences choice game. In particular, with the aid of a laptop computer, the individuals were asked to choose one of two virtual airlines that differed in the following dimensions, as shown in Table 10.1 below (see Street et al. 2005) on the construction of choice sets):

The virtual airlines were described in terms of attributes related to cost, penalties for changes in the tickets, daily flight frequencies and punctuality warranties. These attributes were defined ex ante as being important airline choice determinants for passengers and within the influence of airline operators. To enhance the interviewee's understanding of the game, some attributes which we may care about were left out of our SC experiment. In particular, due to the short-haul nature of the flight (slightly less than one hour) travel time, leg room and food service were not considered in our SC experiment. As usual in the literature, the levels of the attributes considered in our SC experiment encompass the status quo and non-marginal changes (Hess et al. 2006). We also note that our SC experiment considers the actual cost paid by the interviewee and, in this sense, our exercise uses RP data combined with SP data, as Adler et al. (2005) suggest.

Figure 10.1, below, is a "Print Screen" of WinMint v. 2.1 (in Portuguese, but also understood by Spaniards), the software used in our SC experiment.

The SC game presented the passengers with a choice between two virtual airlines, none of which dominated the other in all dimensions, in the sense that all games

Table 10.1 Levels of attributes

Variable	Levels	Definition
Cost (C)	1	C+20%
	2	C
	3	C–20%
Penalty for changes in a ticket (P)	First Class 0	30%
	First Class 1	10%
	First Class 2	0%
	Economy 0	100%
	Economy 1	50%
	Economy 2	30%
Frequency	0	2 flights per day
	1	4 flights per day
	2	6 flights per day
Punctuality Warranties	0	No compensation for delay
	1	Free ticket for the same trip
	2	Full reimbursement

Fig. 10.1 Print screen of SC experiment

considered had trade-offs built-in. Each of the 242 individuals interviewed played the game 10 times. Hence, our econometric model described in the next section uses 2420 observations.

In the third and last section, the individuals were asked about their socioeconomic status, such as: residence county; number of people living in the household; number of workers in the household; household income; age; gender; educational attainment; sector of occupation; type of job; weekly working hours and net monthly individual income.

10.2.2 Descriptive Statistics

While we did collect extensive information about individual characteristics, we preserve on space and describe our sample in a succinct manner below. Table 10.2 below summarizes some of the continuous variables in the data set.

Table 10.2 Descriptive statistics

Variable	Obs.	Mean	S. Dev.	Median
Cost (€)	242	120	43	100
Monthly Gross Household Income (€)	242	2617	2431	2001
Monthly Net Personal Income (€)	242	1351		1003
Age (years)	242	41	13	39

Mean reported one-way ticket cost is € 120. Most interviewees flew with Binter (61%). A vast majority, 90%, of the interviewees travelled as tourists while only 9% of the interviewees travelled for work related reasons. Most interviewees flew with an economy ticket (78%) or a super-economy ticket (20%) while very few interviewees flew first class (2%). 96% of the interviewees bought their tickets in an agency. A slight majority, 51%, of the interviewees were females.

10.3 Model

10.3.1 Benchmark Model

Our econometric work is based on the random utility theory (see McFadden (1974) or Greene (2003)), succinctly described in this section. Assume that the random utility of alternative j for an individual q, U_{jq} is given by:

$$U_{jq} = V_{jq} + \varepsilon_{jq} \tag{10.1}$$

where V_{jq} is the systematic or representative utility (conditional indirect utility) and ε_{jq} is a random term. Individual q chooses alternative$j$if and only if $U_{jq} \geq U_{iq} \neq j$. In such a case, and given (10.1):

$$U_{jq} \geq U_{iq} \Leftrightarrow$$

$$V_{jq} + \varepsilon_{jq} \geq V_{iq} + \varepsilon_{iq} \Leftrightarrow$$

$$\varepsilon_{iq} - \varepsilon_{jq} \leq V_{jq} - V_{iq} \forall i \neq j$$

As utilities are random variables, the probability that individual q chooses alternative j is:

$$P_{jq} = P\left(\varepsilon_{iq} - \varepsilon_{jq} \leq V_{jq} - V_{iq}\right), \forall i \neq j \tag{10.2}$$

When the random term ε_{jq} follows a Gumbel distribution, then P_{jq} reads:

$$P_{jq} = \frac{e^{V_{jq}}}{\sum_{i=1}^{N} e^{V_{jq}}} \tag{10.3}$$

where N is the number of alternatives. The expression for P_{jq} given by (10.3) is the essence of the well-known multinomial logit model.

10.3.2 Microeconometric Model

We estimate a conditional logit model, since we have ten observations (games) per individual, and, hence, we control for individual fixed effects. The estimation was carried out with STATA Intercooled 8. As usual in the literature (Fowkes and Wardman (1988) and Louviere et al. (2000)), we estimate two alternative specifications of the conditional indirect utility. In Model 1 we do not consider interactions between attributes and the conditional indirect utility reads:

$$V_j = \theta_C C + \theta_P P + \theta_{Fr} Fr + \theta_{R_1} R_1 + \theta_{R_2} R_2, j = 1{,}2 \qquad (10.4)$$

In Model 2 we consider interactions between attributes:

$$\begin{aligned} V_j = \theta_C C + (\theta_P + \theta_{PW} W)\, P + \theta_{Fr} Fr + \left(\theta_{R_1} + \theta_{R_1 W} W\right) R_1 \\ + \left(\theta_{R_2} + \theta_{R_2 W} W\right) R_2, j = 1{,}2 \end{aligned} \qquad (10.5)$$

Table 10.3 defines the variables used in our econometric work.

After estimation of the models above, it is possible to compute willingness to pay (WTP) measures for improvements. For continuous variables the subjective value of attribute q_{kj} reads:

$$WTP^{j}_{q_{kj}} = \frac{dI}{dq_{kj}} = \frac{\frac{\partial v_j}{\partial q_{kj}}}{\frac{\partial v_j}{\partial I}} = \frac{\frac{\partial v_j}{\partial q_{kj}}}{\frac{\partial v_j}{\partial c_j}} = -\frac{dc_j}{dq_{kj}}$$

where I stands for income and $\frac{\partial v_j}{\partial I} = -\frac{\partial v_j}{\partial c_j}$. For binary variables the relevant expression is as follows:

$$WTP^{j}_{q_{kj}} = \frac{V_j^1 - V_j^0}{\frac{\partial v_j}{\partial I}}$$

where V_j^i is the conditional indirect utility of alternative j when the level of the attribute equals $i = 0{,}1$.

Table 10.3 Variables' definitions

Variable	Meaning
C	cost of one-way ticket
P	penalty for changes in the ticket
Fr	daily flight frequency
R_1	binary variable equal to 1 if punctuality warranty level equals 1 (see Table 10.1)
R_2	binary variable equal to 1 if punctuality warranty level equals 2 (see Table 10.1)
W	binary variable equal to 1 if trip motive is work

10.4 Results

Table 10.4 summarizes the results for Models 1 and 2, were we display the determinants of airline choice (t-statistics in parentheses) for both models.

The signs are as expected from utility theory and the estimates are statistically significant, with some notable exceptions discussed below. We first discuss the results of Model 1. As expected, the likelihood of choosing an airline decreases with travel cost and increases with flight frequency and punctuality warranties. However, penalties to change tickets seem not to matter as an airline choice determinant, as the associated coefficient is not statistically significant. We now turn our attention to Model 2. To be brief, adding the interaction terms does not change the results obtained under Model 1 both at a qualitative and at a quantitative level. It is interesting to note that passengers who travel for work related reasons assign a negative and statistically significant value to higher penalties to change the tickets. In order to obtain a feel of the economic importance of these results we compute the willingness to pay measures for improvements in the service levels, presented in Tables 10.5 and 10.6.

Given that the sample mean cost of a one way ticket is about € 120, we find that willingness to pay measures are quite high. In particular, willingness to pay to enjoy punctuality warranties, from level 0 – of no compensation for flight delays – to 1 – free ticket for the same trip if flight delayed – is about € 79 or 66% of the sample mean of the reported one way ticket cost. Similarly, willingness to pay to improve

Table 10.4 Results for Model 1 and Model 2

Variable	Model 1	Model 2
Cost (θ_C)	–0.0139***	–0.0139***
	(–8.21)	(–8.16)
Penalty (θ_P)	0.0000	–0.0002
	(0.30)	(1.15)
Frequency (θ_{Fr})	0.0590***	0.0580***
	(2.73)	(2.67)
Punctuality Warranty 1	1.1122***	1.1724***
(θ_{R_1})	(13.47)	(13.52)
Punctuality Warranty 2	0.8586***	0.8796***
(θ_{R_2})	(9.91)	(9.82)
Penalty*Work (θ_{PW})		–0.0177***
		(–3.53)
Punctuality Warranty		–0.6838***
1*Work (θ_{R_1W})		(–2.55)
Punctuality Warranty		–0.2949
2*Work (θ_{R_2W})		(–1.19)
Log – L(θ)	-3700	-3696
Log – L(θ)	-3890	-3889
Number of observations	2420	2420

***1%; **5%; *10% (significance level)

Table 10.5 Willingness to pay measures for Model 1

Event	WTP (euros)
Penalty for changes in ticket	0.004
Daily Flight Frequency	4.23
Punctuality Warranty: level 0 to level 1	79.66
Punctuality Warranty: level 0 to level 2	61.49

Table 10.6 Willingness to pay measures for Model 2

Event	WTP (euros)
Penalty for changes in the ticket:	1.11
Trip motive: work/business	0.17
Trip motive: tourism	
Daily Flight Frequency	4.17
Punctuality Warranty: level 0 to level 1	
Trip motive: work/business	35.12
Trip motive: tourism	84.28
Punctuality Warranty: level 0 to level 2	
Trip motive: work/business	42.03
Trip motive: tourism	63.23

punctuality warranties from level 0 to level 2 – money refund if flight delayed – is also quite high: about € 61. Interestingly, having the ticket refunded is worth less than having a ticket to the same journey at a different date. This may be explained by a desire to undertake the trip even at a different date, avoid the hassle of buying a new ticket and save on the ticket cost. Table 10.6 below displays willingness to pay measures when we consider interactions between trip attributes (Model 2):

We note that willingness to pay measures for improvements in punctuality warranties are quite high. We also note that tourists are more willing to pay for punctuality warranties than passengers who travel for work related reasons. The potential gain from patronizing such punctuality warranty is, thus, quite large.

10.5 Conclusions

In this paper, we conducted a SC experiment to elicit passengers' preferences for airline services attributes in a touristic route. The main results were as expected from utility theory and are of high statistical quality. Among the several results found, we note that willingness to pay measures for improvements in punctuality warranties are quite high – in some cases, above half of the sample mean of the cost of a one-way ticket – especially for passengers travelling for tourism related reasons.

Hence, the potential gains from patronizing such non-marginal changes in service levels are large, and, concomitantly, SC experiments along the lines of ours are effective tools for airlines to devise service differentiation strategies to cater to passengers' heterogeneous preferences.

AcknowledgmentsWe thank support from Interreg III-B, MOVIECAM Project.

References

Adler T, Falzarano C, Spitz G (2005) Modelling service trade-offs in air itinerary choices. Transport Res Rec 1915:20–26

Basar, G., Bhat C. (2004) A Parameterized Consideration Set model for airport choice: an application to the San Francisco bay area. Transport Res B: Methodol 38(10):889–904

Cao X, Mokhtarian P (2005a) How do individuals adapt their personal travel? A conceptual exploration of the consideration of travel-related strategies. Transp Policy 12(3):199–206

Cao X, Mokhtarian P (2005b) How do individuals adapt their personal travel? Objective and subjective influences on the consideration of travel-related strategies for San Francisco Bay Area commuters. Transp Policy 12(4):291–302

Dutta M, Banerjee S, Husain Z (2007) Untapped demand for heritage: A contingent valuation study of Prinsep Ghat, Calcutta. Tourism Manage 28(1): 83–95

Fowkes A, Wardman M (1988) The design of stated preference travel choice experiments with special reference to interpersonal taste variations. J Transp Econ Policy 22(1):27–44

Gilbert D, Wong R (2003) Passenger expectations and airline services: a Hong Kong based study. Tourism Manage 24(5):519–532

Greene W (2003) Econometric analysis. Prenctice Hall, New Jersey

Hensher D, Stopher P, Louviere J (2001) An exploratory analysis of the effect of numbers of choice sets in designed choice experiments: An airline choice application. J Air Transp Manage 7(6):373–379

Hess S, Adler T, Polak J (2006) Modelling airport and airline choice behaviour with the use of stated preferences survey data. Mimeo, Imperial College London

Hess S, Polak J (2005a) Accounting for random taste heterogeneity in airport-choice modelling. Transport Res Rec 1915:36–43

Hess S, Polak J (2005b) Mixed logit modelling of airport choice in multi-airport regions. J Air Transp Manage 11(2):59–68

Hess S, Polak J (2005c) Exploring the potential for cross-nesting structures in airport- choice analysis: a case study of the Greater London area. Transport Res E: Log 42(2):63–81

Kelly J, Haider W, Williams P, Englund K (2006) Stated preferences of tourists for eco-efficient destination planning options. Tourism Manage (in press)

Kim S, Wong K, Cho M (2007) Assessing the economic value of a world heritage site and willingness-to-pay determinants: a case of Changdeok Palace. Tourism Manage 28(1):317–322

Louviere J, Hensher D, Swait J (2000) Stated choice methods: analysis and applications. Cambridge University Press, Cambridge

McFadden D (1974) The measurement of urban travel demand. J Public Econ 3(4):303–328

Pels E, Nijkamp P, Rietveld P (2001) Airport and airline choice in a multi-airport region: an empirical analysis for the San Francisco bay area. Reg Stud 35(1):1–9

Pels E, Nijkamp P, Rietveld P (2003) Access to and competition between airports: a case study for the San Francisco bay area. Trans Res A: Policy Pract 37(1):71–83

Rose J, Hensher D, Greene W (2005) Recovering costs through price and service differentiation: accounting for exogenous information on attribute processing strategies in airline choice. J Air Transp Manage 11(6):400–407

Street D, Burgess L, Louviere L (2005) Quick and easy choice sets: constructing optimal and near optimal stated choice experiments. Int J Res Mark 22(4):459–470

Chapter 11
Forecasting Hotel Overnights in the Autonomous Region of the Azores

Carlos Santos, Gualter Couto, and Pedro Miguel Pimentel

11.1 Introduction

In the last eleven years the number of overnights in the Portuguese Autonomous Region of the Azores has increased five times. The impact of this increase in employment, in the balance of payments and in the economy in general as been very significant. Tourism planning is essential since the tourism industry has contributed to a significant share of the gross national product (8%).

Forecasting assumes a fundamental role in tourism planning, according to Archer (1987). Taking into consideration the above, this paper concentrates on the application of various time series methods in order to forecasting monthly overnights in hotels located in the same region between January 2002 and December 2004. Forecasts are based on monthly data covering January 1993 to December 2001.

The objective is to find the degree to which the forecasts of overnights segmented by country of origin, present smaller errors when compared with the forecasts of the total overnights in the Region. Each forecasting method selected according to the tourist's country of origin is also analyzed in order to find potential optimal combinations of different forecasting methods that could improve the accuracy of total overnights forecasts in the Azores.

This paper is divided as follows. Section 11.2 presents a literature review regarding tourism demand forecasting. Sections 11.3 and 11.4 define the methodology applied and describe the used data. Section 5 presents the results analysis. Section 11.6 contains the conclusions and future research recommendations.

11.2 Brief Literature Review

According to Chu (1998a) there are various forecasting techniques available that can be chosen based on the following criteria: the precision of the forecasts results,

C. Santos (✉)
Business and Economics Department, University of the Azores, CEEAplA,
Ponta Delgada, Azores, Portugal
e-mail: csantos@notes.uac.pt

Á. Matias et al. (eds.), *Advances in Tourism Economics*,
DOI 10.1007/978-3-7908-2124-6_11,

whether the technique is easy to use or not, the cost involved and whether the forecasting results can be rapidly obtained. Precision is the most important forecasting characteristic, according to the following: "*The accuracy of the forecasts will affect the quality of the management decision ... In the tourism industry, in common with the most other service sectors, the need to forecasting accurately is especially acute because of the perishable nature of the product. Unfilled airline seats and unused hotel rooms cannot be stockpiled*" (Archer 1987).

Makridakis et al. (1998) divide forecasting methods into the following two categories: quantitative and qualitative methods. Quantitative methods are more precise than qualitative ones (Makridakis and Hibon 1979). Quantitative techniques can be divided into causal and time series models. While causal models use functional relations between variables, time series modeling uses past information about the variable in order to estimate its future values. According to the literature, when the objective is to perform short term forecasts, methods based on time series should be used. On the other hand, when the objective is forecasting, or explore the impact of independent variables on the forecasted variable, causal methods should be used (Chu 1998a).

Even though the newest research is orientated for the robustness of more sophisticated forecasting methods, in some past empirical studies the *naïve* prediction models tend to produce more robust results in comparison to the more sophisticated models (Martin and Witt 1989; Sheldon 1993; and Song and Witt 2000). According to Kulendran and King (1997) and Kulendran and Witt (2001), even the prediction models that incorporate the most recent, at that time, techniques developed in econometric models still present less robust results then the naive methods.

Regarding econometric forecasting accuracy, Song et al. (2003) have analysed the precision of 6 alternative econometric models in tourism prediction. Their conclusions reveal that the results are only slightly more precise in the short-run predictions of sophisticated models than those of simpler time series univariate models.

According to Witt and Witt (1995), when the goal is to compare the forecasting results from different methods in tourism, time series models fit this aim. According to these authors, most studies calculate the degree of accuracy using the same sample that was used for the basis estimations.

In Chu (1998b) six techniques were applied (time series approaches: *Naïve* I, *Naïve* II, *Linear Trend*, *Sine Wave*, *Holt-Winters* and ARIMA) in order to forecasting tourism demand in ten countries (Japan, Taiwan, South Korea, Hong-Kong, Philippines, Indonesia, Singapore, Thailand, Australia and New Zealand). The research concludes that the ARIMA method was the most accurate for nine of the ten countries in the study, using MAPE (*Mean Absolute Percentage Error*) as the criterion for accuracy.

As far as the causal methods are concerned the models' complexity has increased with time (Witt and Witt 1995). Amongst tourism demand causal forecasting methods, we emphasize the Gravitational and Neural Networks models. As Sheldon and Var (1985) state, gravitational models are based on gravitational law principles, where the degree of interaction between two geographical areas varies directly with the concentration of people and inversely with distance. These models have been successfully applied in order to forecasting the international tourism flows. The objective of those applications is to reduce the shortcoming of time series models given that these cannot anticipate variations besides the ones given on past data. On the other hand, time series models do not have the limitations of traditional causal models such as multicolinearity between independent variables (Law 2000).

11.3 Methodology

Given the study's objective, various time series techniques were used in order to forecasting the number of overnights in the Azores, namely: *Naïve* I (NI), *Naïve* II (NII), Classic Decomposition (CD), Exponential Smoothing of *Holt-Winters* with seasonality (HW) and SARIMA.

The forecasts based on *naïve* techniques are obtained through the following formulas:
$\hat{F}^{NI}_{t+1} = Y_t$ and $\hat{F}^{NII}_{t+1} = Y_t\left[1 + \frac{Y_t - Y_{t-1}}{Y_{t-1}}\right]$, where: $\hat{F}^{NI}_{t+1}$ is the forecast for period *t+1* using *Naïve* I technique; $\hat{F}^{NII}_{t+1}$ is the forecast for period *t+1*, using *Naïve* II technique and; Y_t is the observation of period *t*.

These two techniques are frequently mentioned in the tourism industry forecasts as stated by Witt and Witt (1995) and Chu (1998b), amongst others. These techniques are used mostly when the objective is to compare their performance with more sophisticated forecasting techniques. In the *Naïve* methods, the forecast for the next period is based on the real observation of the previous period.

The classic decomposition technique, $Y_t = S_t + T_t + E_t$, uses logarithmic[1] data. The trend variable (T_t) was computed using centered moving average with order 12, based on 13 observations. The first and thirteenth observations get half the weight of the remaining observations. Seasonality (S_t) corresponds to the difference between observed overnights (Y_t) and the trend (T_t) in each month. The error component (E_t) is the difference between Y_t and the sum of $\hat{T}_t$ and $\hat{S}_t$.

The exponential smoothing *Holt-Winters* technique with seasonality was applied using *software ITSM: Forecast 6.0 (PEST)*. In order to make the series' variance stationary we used the *Box-Cox*[2] transformation with *lambda* equal to zero.

The SARIMA models for each case were initially identified through correlation chart analysis of the series (ACF – *Autocorrelation Function* and PACF – *Partial Autocorrelation Function*).

After identifying the potential models, the best model was selected considering the *AICc* measure *(Akaikes Information Criterion corrected)*, the significance

[1] In order to achieve stationarity in sample's variance.

[2] *Box-Cox* transformation: $X_t = \begin{cases} \frac{Y_t^{\lambda}-1}{\lambda}, \lambda \neq 0 \\ \ln(Y_t), \lambda = 0 \end{cases}$

of the estimated coefficients (test t)[3] and the characteristics of white noise models (trough visualization of ACF and PACF of the residuals and Ljung-Box Q*[4] statistic). The SARIMA model estimation was done through the maximum likelihood method using *ITSM software: Forecast 6.0 (PEST)*. Before estimating the coefficients a *Box-Cox* transformation with *lambda* equal zero was done, in order to remove non stationarity of the sample's variance, and the first difference[5] and the seasonal difference[6] were performed (we found a significant correlation between the observations lagged by one interval multiple of twelve), in order to make the process static in the mean.

The five techniques were applied to the total overnights and to overnights segmented by country of origin. In the last case, each forecasting method was applied to each segmented overnights by tourist's country of origin. Afterwards, the forecasted overnights according to the same method were all added up in order to evaluate the accuracy of the total overnights forecasting method.

The quality of forecasting methods accuracy was evaluated using MSE and MAPE. Once various scales influence the MSE indicator, and as stated by Makridakis et al. (1998), more emphasis is placed on the mean absolute percentage error assuming no contradicting evidence.

11.4 Data

This paper uses monthly data of the overnights in the Azores segmented by tourist's country of origin. The total number of overnights in the Azores is subdivided in seven countries of origin: Portugal (PT); Germany (G); Spain (SP); United States of America (USA); France (FR); United Kingdom (UK); Northern European Countries (NC) and; Other Countries (OC) – The data can be seen in Figs. 11.1 and 11.2.

The Northern European Countries include Denmark, Finland, Norway and Sweden. Other Countries include countries that do not represent a significant share of total overnights in the Azores.

The total sample is composed of 139 monthly observations, between January 1993 and March 2004, published by the Regional Office of Azorean Statistics (ROAS).

According to ROAS, of total overnights sample, 60,87% are tourists from Portugal's mainland, 9,92% are from Germany, 8,17% are from Northern Europe, 2,89%, 2,61%, 1,50% and 1,12% are from America, England, France and Spain, respectively. The remaining tourists (12,93%) come from other countries.

[3] H_0: Coefficient $= 0$ e H_1: Coefficient $\neq 0$

[4] H_0: $\rho_1 = \rho_2 = \ldots = \rho_n = 0$ e H_1: There is at least one $\rho_i \neq 0$

[5] $\nabla X_t = X_t - X_{t-1} = (1 - B)X_t$

[6] $\nabla_{12} X_t = X_t - X_{t-12} = (1 - B^{12})X_t$

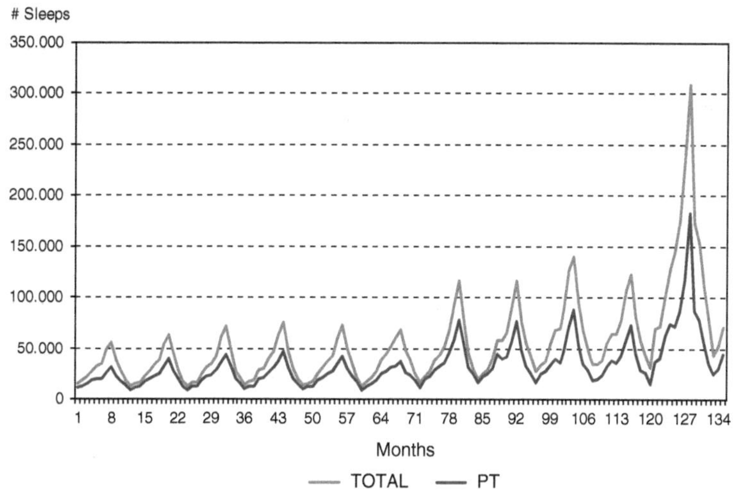

Fig. 11.1 Overnights in the Azores between January 1993 and March 2004 – Total overnights of Portuguese tourists

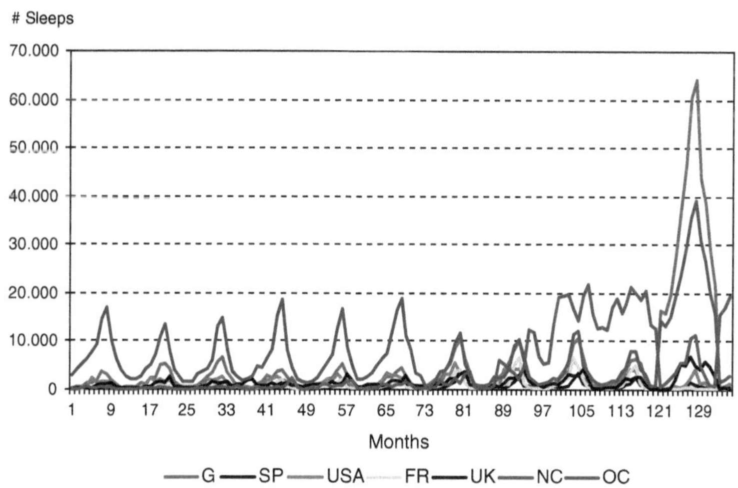

Fig. 11.2 Overnights in the Azores between January 1993 and March 2004 – Overnights by tourist's country of origin

The total data as well as the segmented data sample reveal a strong seasonal pattern, but do not present seasonal characteristics as far as the average and the variance are concerned.

Given that one of the objectives is to test the accuracy among all five forecasting techniques, the sample was subdivided into two sub-samples: January 1993 to December 2001; and January 2002 to March 2004. The forecasting error measurement of each method was based on the interval between January 2002 and March 2004. The period between January 1993 and December 2001 was the base period used for the estimation of the forecasting models parameters.

11.5 Results and Analysis

The following charts show the comparison between the monthly overnights forecasts in the Azores based on five different methods and the real overnights between January 2002 and March 2004. Figure 11.3 uses total data sample and Fig. 11.4 uses segmented data sample.

Table 11.1 presents the ex-post forecasting errors in both cases, namely: the total overnights in the Azores based on total data sample (Fig. 11.3); and overnights (Fig. 11.4) segmented by tourist's country of origin. In this table, the total overnights forecasts based on the segmented data set is computed using the same method for all eight countries of origin, separately.

According to the MAPE error measurement criterion it can be seen that, except with the *Naïve* and SARIMA methods, forecasting total overnights in the Azores using the data segmented by country of origin is more precise than forecasting using

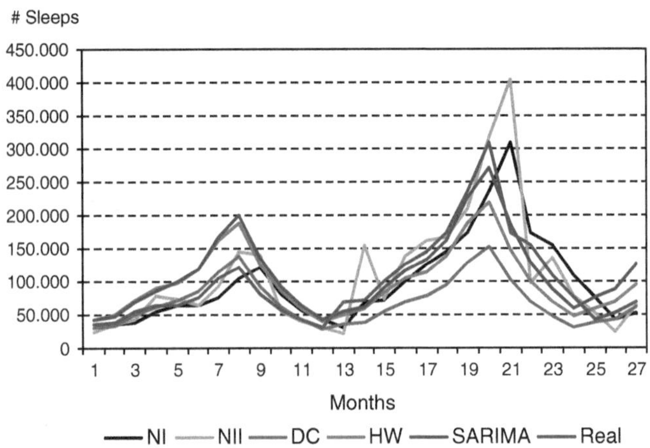

Fig. 11.3 Real and forecasted monthly overnights in the Azores of total data between January 2002 and March 2004

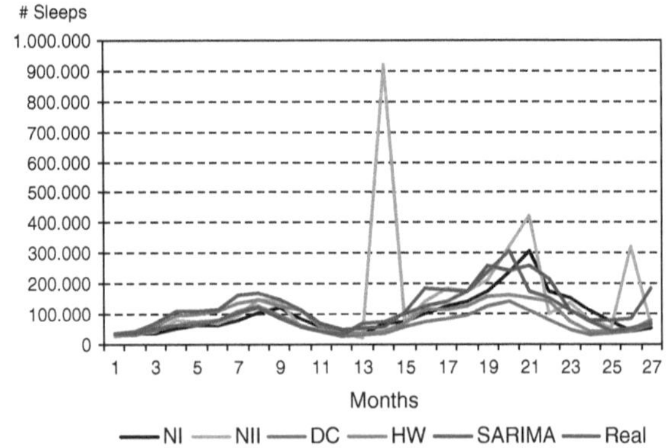

Fig. 11.4 Real and forecasted monthly overnights in the Azores of subdivided data between January 2002 and March 2004

Table 11.1 Forecasting error measurement for total overnights in the Azores, considering ex-post forecasting with total data and segmented data, between January 2002 and March 2004

Error measure	MSE		MAPE	
Technique	Aggregate	Disaggregate	Aggregate (%)	Disaggregate (%)
Naïve I	1,509,395,151	1,509,395,151	28.16	28.16
Naïve II	2,757,875,523	32,211,003,132	28.4	85.85
Holt-Winters	1,322,705,238	1,746,299,908	33.7	29.53
Classic decomposition	2,722,541,255	2,666,284,504	27.4	26.48
* $(1,1,1)\ (0,1,1)_{12}$	1,024,544,190	2,118,816,522	34.3	44.38

* The ARIMA parameters are applied only to aggregate estimate

the total data. We can also see that among all methods used, the Classic Decomposition is the one that seems the most accurate for both the total and the segmented data sample.

If we analyze the data using the MSE criterion the conclusions are different. In this case the SARIMA method is the one that presents the most accurate results for the total data sample. For the segmented data sample, the *Naïve* I method is the best. As opposed to other methods, only the Classic Decomposition method presents the biggest accuracy when applied to the segmented data sample.

In short, considering all forecasting methods, the one with the lowest MSE is the SARIMA, when using the total data sample. In the case of the segmented data sample the lowest MAPE is obtained using the Classic Decomposition.

According to Table 11.2 and considering the MSE criterion, the *Naïve I* method gives the best ex-post forecasts for all countries except Portugal where the best model is SARIMA. Note that this exception is important in the total overnights forecasts for the Azores since tourists from Portugal's mainland represent over 60% of total overnights.

Under MAPE criterion, the Classic Decomposition method is the best method to forecasting Portuguese tourists' overnights as well as to forecasting overnights of tourists from other countries. The SARIMA model is the most appropriate to forecasting overnights for tourists coming from Germany and United Kingdom. In all other cases, the best method was the *Naïve I* which seems to be the most accurate.

Based on the previous table and trying to achieve the most accurate forecasts for total overnights by country of origin, the most accurate forecasting method for each country of origin were selected, taking into account the MSE and MAPE error measures.

The results presented in Table 11.3 indicate that when the selection criteria of the forecasting methods by country of origin is the MSE criterion, there are significant improvements in the total overnights forecasts for the Azores, using the segmented data sample (this forecasting method show smaller error measures compared to all other forecasting methods used). On the other hand, when the selection criteria is

Table 11.2 Forecasting error measurement for overnights by country of origin in the Azores between January 2002 and March 2004

Technique					SARIMA	
Origin Country	Naïve I	Naïve II	Classic decomposition	Holt-Winters	Model	Error
MSE						
Portugal (PT)	709,558,350	1,843,351,419	595,798,787	727,466,122	$(1,1,2)(0,1,1)_{12}$	396,815,102
Germany (G)	66,310,863	12,852,062,743	595,798,787	444,405,707	$(0,1,1)(0,1,1)_{12}$	547,057,629
Spain (SP)	286,321	1,397,397	345,304	563,673	$(4,1,0)(0,1,1)_{12}$	1,226,272
United States of America (USA)	926,902	2,471,339	3,412,727	3,177,182	$(0,1,1)(1,1,0)_{12}$	4,102,824
France (FR)	770,461	1,423,731	3,649,512	4,092,225	$(3,1,1)(0,1,1)_{12}$	3,410,122
United Kingdom (UK)	1,515,076	25,851,991	2,970,991	3,278,553	$(0,1,1)(1,1,0)_{12}$	7,469,403
Nordic Countries (NC)	21,007,923	3,042,615,732	98,171,021	1,125,542,987	$(0,1,2)(1,1,1)_{12}$	4,727,153,590
Other Countries (OC)	25,997,577	1,716,913,976	196,316,099	233,070,255	$(3,1,0)(10,1,1)_{12}$	142,632,736
MAP						
Portugal (PT)	31.89%	38.97%	25.54%	28.22%	$(0,1,2)(0,1,1)_{12}$	28.62%
Germany (G)	351.48%	410.17%	73.36%	99.97%	$(0,1,1)(0,1,1)_{12}$	62.09%
Spain (SP)	49.01%	82.59%	73.91%	92.29%	$(4,1,0)(0,1,1)_{12}$	139.23%
United States of America (USA)	54.94%	63.06%	139.14%	127.85%	$(0,1,1)(1,1,0)_{12}$	128.86%
France (FR)	56.10%	73.03%	342.76%	331.69%	$(3,1,1)(0,1,1)_{12}$	308.43%
United Kingdom (UK)	104.48%	123.24%	248.17%	140.29%	$(0,1,1)(1,1,0)_{12}$	62.43%
Nordic Countries (NC)	110.56%	171.11%	172.36%	680.77%	$(0,1,2)(1,1,1)_{12}$	1410.89%
Other Countries (OC)	66.54%	122.55%	53.05%	57.74%	$(3,1,0)(0,1,1)_{12}$	59.90%

Table 11.3 Forecasting error measurement for total overnights in the Azores between January 2002 and March 2004, considering the best method for each country of origin.[7]

Selection Criteria	MSE			MAPE		
Origin Country	*Naïve* I	Classic Decomp.	SARIMA	*Naïve* I	Classic Decomp.	SARIMA
Portugal (PT)			x		x	
Germany (G)	x					x
Spain (SP)	x			x		
United States of America (USA)	x			x		
France (FR)	x			x		
United Kingdom (UK)	x					x
Nordic Countries (NC)	x			x		
Other Countries (OC)	x				x	
MAPE of Total Overnights	715,234,677			3,949,211,377		
MAPE of Total Overnights	20.80%			32.53%		

the MAPE criterion, the accuracy measure in forecasting total overnights based on the segmented data sample, is not superior to all other forecasting methods used.

The forecasts, computed according to the results presented on Tables 11.2 and 11.3 using the selection criterion MSE, and the real values are compared in Fig. 11.5.

In the case of ex-ante forecasting it is worthwhile noticing that the *Naïve I* method produces a flat forecasting. Therefore, its use could potentially give a worst accuracy measure for this particular time series, when the ex-ante temporal forecasting horizon is greater than one period. Similarly, the *Naïve* II method considers a constant growth rate for ex-ante forecasting covering more than one period. Therefore, this last method may also be inadequate for heavily seasonal series. Thus, if the goal is to conduct an ex-ante forecasting, covering more than one period based on the segmented data sample (Table 11.2), then the lowest MSE is reached when the following methods are used: Classic Decomposition for forecasting overnights of Spanish, English and Scandinavian tourists; *Holt-Winters* for

[7]Total overnights forecasts based on segmented data sample given by he sum of the forecasts using the most accurate forecasting method for each one of the tourists' eight countries of origin.

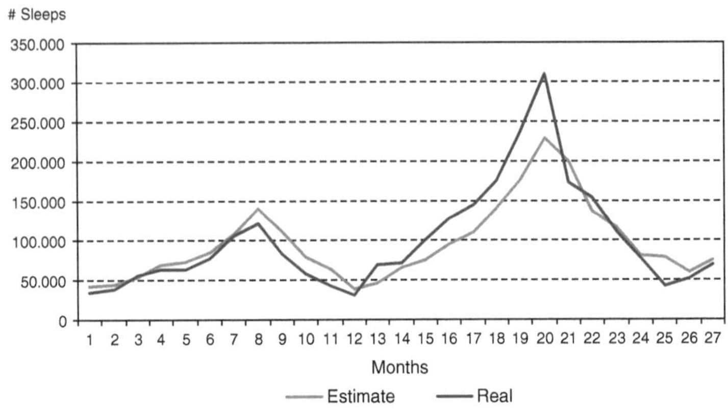

Fig. 11.5 Forecasted and actual monthly overnights in the Azores based on the subdivided data sample for tourist's country of origin, using the best method, from January 2002 to March 2004

forecasting overnights of German and American tourists; SARIMA for forecasting overnights of Portuguese and French tourists, as well as of tourists from Other Countries.

In this sense, it's possible to point out that for ex-ante forecasting, covering more than one period, the total overnights using segmented data sample should be forecasted according to the combination of the best method (selected by MSE), for each country of origin (not including the *Naive* methods) given that the error measurement is more accurate according to MAPE. This can be verified in Tables 11.1 and 11.4.

Tables 11.3 and 11.4 show that the MSE and MAPE accuracy measure in forecasting the total overnights, considering the best method by tourist's country of origin, is consistent, contrary to other previous cases.

The high values for the different error measurements are probably due to the fact that between January 2002 and March 2004, the overnight pattern is atypical when compared to the standard overnights registered until December 2001 (there was a steady growth along the years). In 2002 there was a slight decrease when compared to 2001, while in 2003 there was a strong growth (more than 100% when compared to 2001).

11.6 Conclusions

The results obtained with our data sample for the Azores do not totally support the SARIMA models superiority in tourism forecasting.

This paper also shows that there is not always a consistency between the error measurement given by the MSE and the MAPE criteria. This may be due to the existence of different scales in the number of overnights, regarding each tourist's country of origin. Further research on this issue should be undertaken in future.

Table 11.4 Forecasting error measurement for total overnight in the Azores between January 2002 and March 2002, considering the best method (excluding the *Naïve* methods) for each country of origin

Selection Criteria	*MSE*			*MAPE*		
Origin Country	Classic Decomp.	Holt – Winters	SARIMA	Classic Decomp.	Holt – Winters	SARIMA
Portugal (PT)			x	x		
Germany (G)		x				x
Spain (SP)	x			x		
United States of America (USA)		x			x	
France (FR)			x			x
United Kingdom (UK)	x					x
Nordic Countries (NC)	x			x		
Other Countries (OC)			x	x		
MAPE of Total Overnights	1,793,824,437			2,936,023,315		
MAPE of Total Overnights	23.97%			28.19%		

The MSE accuracy measure is the best criterion to select the most accurate method by tourist's country of origin when the objective is forecasting ex-post and ex-ante total overnights based on the segmented data sample. The forecasting method using the best method selected for each country of origin was the one that achieved the best results for all forecasting methods.

In order to forecasting total overnights in the Azores for the next period based on the segmented data sample, the most accurate method is the SARIMA method for the overnights of Portuguese tourists and the *Naïve* I method for each one of the remaining countries of origin.

When the goal is forecasting total overnights in the Azores for a time horizon of more than one period, the following methods should be applied using segmented data set: Classic Decomposition for forecasting overnights of tourists from Spain, United Kingdom and Nordic Countries; *Holt-Winters* for forecasting overnights of tourists from Germany and United States of America; SARIMA for forecasting overnights of tourists from Portugal, France and Other Countries.

Regarding future research on this subject, it would be helpful to test ex-ante forecasting accuracy based on structural time series models and causal models, particularly the gravitational and the neural network models. More sophisticated forecasting models, like the ones used in Smeral and Witt (1996), Smeral (2004), and Witt, Song and Wanhill (2004), may reinforce the accuracy gains regarding the use of segmented data by country of origin.

References

Archer B (1987) Demand forecasting and estimation. In: Ritchie JRB, Goeldner CR (Eds) Travel tourism and hospitality research. Wiley, New York, pp. 77–85

Chu F (1998a) Forecasting tourism: a combined approach. Tourism Manage 19(6):515–520

Chu F (1998b) Forecasting tourism demand in asian-pacific countries. Ann Tourism Res 25(3):597–615

Kulendran N King M (1997) Forecasting international quarterly tourism flows using error correction and time séries models. Int J Forecast 13:319–327

Kulendran N Witt S (2001) Cointegration versus least squares regression. Ann Tourism Res 28:291–311

Law R (2000) Back-propagation learning in improving the accuracy of neural network-based tourism demand forecasting. Tourism Manage 21: 331–340

Makridakis S Hibon M (1979) Accuracy of forecasting: an empirical investigation. J R Stat Soc A 142 (2):97–125

Makridakis S, Wheelwrigth S, Hyndman R (1998) Forecasting: methods and applications. Wiley, New York

Martin C, Witt S (1989) Forecasting tourism demand: a comparison of the accuracy of several quantitative methods. Int J Forecast 5:5–15

Murteira B, Müller D, Turkman K (1993) Análise de Sucessões Cronológicas. McGraw-Hill, Columbus, OH

Sheldon P (1993) Forecasting tourism: expenditures versus arrivals. J Travel Res 32 (1):13–20

Sheldon P, Var T (1985) Tourism forecasting: a review of empirical research. J Forecast 4:183–195

Smeral E (2004) Long-term forecasts for international tourism. Tourism Econ 10(2):145–166

Smeral E Witt S (1996) Econometric forecast of tourism demand to 2005. Ann Tourism Res 23(4):891–907

Song H Witt S (2000) Tourism demand modelling and forecasting: modern econometric approaches. Pergamon, Oxford

Song H, Witt S, Jensen T (2003) Tourism forecasting: accuracy of alternative econometric models. Int J Forecast 19:123–141

Witt S Witt C (1995) Forecasting tourism demand: a review of empirical research. Int J Forecast 11:447–475

Witt S, Song H, Wanhill S (2004) Forecasting tourism-generated employment: the case of Denmark. Tourism Econ 10(2):167–176

Part III
Trends in the Tourist Market

Chapter 12
The International Competitiveness of Trade in Tourism Services: Evidence from Romania

Ana Bobirca and Cristiana Cristureanu

12.1 Introduction

Tourism is the only service activity that can potentially provide trading opportunities for all nations, regardless of their level of development. However, it is also a sector where there is clearly an uneven distribution of benefits that is largely dependant on countries' ability to strengthen their performance in the global economy, which in turn requires improving their competitiveness.

Since the beginning of the 1990s, Romania has experienced major changes in its tourism exports volume, growth rate and structure. These disparate fluctuations have all influenced the relative competitive position of Romania on the international tourism market and have been associated with changes in its tourism trade balance. In the same time, the new and more heterogeneous European architecture has induced significant changes in Romania's regional tourism competitiveness.

Against this background, the paper attempts to suggest a framework for assessing the international competitiveness of Romania's tourism services trade, by focusing on the relationship between competitiveness and tourism trade performance.

To this end, the first part starts by introducing the concept of international competitiveness and by presenting, evaluating and systematizing key issues of the complex analysis on international competitiveness. The paper subsequently considers the relationship between export performance and international competitiveness, as well as its relevance for international tourism. The second part includes a macro overview of the tourism sector, focusing specifically on its importance to the economy. The third part of the paper sets out in detail the framework for calculating the proposed measures of competitiveness and shows the importance of the methodological approach in interpreting the information provided by these indicators. It also illustrates the recent performance of Romanian tourism, based on an integrated

A. Bobirca (✉)
Faculty of International Business and Economics, Academy of Economic Studies, Bucharest, Romania
e-mail: Ana.Bobirca@rei.ase.ro

Á. Matias et al. (eds.), *Advances in Tourism Economics*,
DOI 10.1007/978-3-7908-2124-6_12,

measure of international trade competitiveness. The paper concludes by explaining the competitive position of Romania on the European tourism market and by identifying research issues that require further study.

12.2 Perspectives on International Competitiveness – The Relationship Between Export Performance and International Competitiveness and its Relevance for International Tourism

The concept of international competitiveness, although controversial and elusive, has gained acceptance and continues to attract the attention of both academics and policymakers worldwide.

Most measures of international competitiveness that have so far been considered were undertaken at the economy-wide level (Garelli 2003) and generally refer to the ability of a country to produce goods and services that meet the test of international markets, while simultaneously maintaining and expanding the real income of its citizens (European Commission 2007).

Because competitiveness ultimately depends upon firms in a country competing successfully on the domestic and international markets, attention has focused on competitiveness at the firm level (Porter 1990), where it is generally understood to refer to "... the ability of the firm to retain and, better still, enlarge its global market share, increase its profits and expand" (Clark and Guy 1998, OECD 1993).

According to traditional economic theory, a firm can gain competitive advantage through comparative cost of production by, for example, reducing labor cost. However, recent research suggests that non-price factors are equally important determinants of competitiveness. The range of non-price factors is diverse and includes human resource endowment, such as skills; technical factors, such as research and development capabilities and the ability to innovate; managerial and organizational factors, both internal to the firm and externally organized through relationships with other bodies, customers, suppliers, public and private research institutes, and other firms (Clark and Guy 1998, Fagerberg 1986). Together, these factors determine the ability of the firm to compete successfully in international markets, on the background of changing technological, economic, and social environments. Export performance and the ability of the firm to maintain its market share remain the ultimate indicators of international competitiveness.

Consequently, although widely proclaimed, the *theoretical bases* of international competitiveness as it relates to national economies and their international trade have been less analyzed in academic literature. Thus, the nature, benefits and constraints on a nation of being internationally competitive remain ambiguous (Coldwell 2000, Krugman 1994, 1996).

International competitiveness, within the context of trade in goods and services, refers to *a nation securing and maintaining a trade advantage vis-à-vis the rest of the world.*

International competitiveness is advanced whenever the economic welfare of a nation is enhanced through an increase in the flow of trade or through an alteration in the conditions of trade starting from a presumed initial equilibrium (Coldwell 2000).

Trade theory asserts that economic welfare is dependent on the production of goods and services that a country has comparative advantage in. This, in effect, means that international competitiveness is secured when production is in line with a country's comparative advantage situation. If countries perform well internationally and compete successfully for export markets, this could be a sign of their sound international competitiveness.

Therefore, at the international level, competitiveness can be defined as the ability of an economy to attract the demand for its exports and the investment to supply that demand, all within social norms that result in an improved standard of living for its citizens. This, in turn, depends on the macro and microeconomic policies, regulations and institutions that affect the productivity of the economy's factors of production and the costs of doing business.

A review of available literature and empirical evidences supports the notion that international competitiveness can be explained, to some extent, by a country's ability to export (Dollar and Wolff 1993, Fagerberg et al. 2004). There is, in fact, a self-recurring relationship between export performance and international competitiveness. Exports are the *first level of international competitiveness affirmation.* The improvement in export performance leads to an increase in a country's competitiveness. This effect is a result of enterprises' skills, knowledge, propensity to innovate and use new technology, ability to exploit technological opportunities in a successfully commercial way, etc.

On the other hand, in striving to achieve successful exports in highly competitive global markets, a country is forced to improve its competitiveness. The more competitive a country is, the more economically powerful it is. Consequently, it is more capable to compete on the global market, to attract people with higher level of knowledge, skills, to buy new technologies, etc., and to improve its export performance, as well as to achieve better export results. This can, in turn, favor additional innovations and trigger an improvement in its competitiveness.

Consequently, export performance and competitiveness should not be considered in isolation, since they are mutually interdependent.

However, competitiveness should not be equated only with a country's ability to export. The evolution of export market shares is also an important element of trade competitiveness, while the latter is just a component of a nation's competitiveness defined by the European Declaration of Lisbon as the capacity to improve and raise the standard of living of its habitants by providing more and higher quality employment, and a greater social cohesion. The gains or losses of world market shares by individual countries are often considered as an index of their trade competitiveness. However, market share growth depends also on structural factors. Due to changes in demand, a country's geographical and sectoral specialization at the beginning of a period is an important factor shaping future market share growth. Similarly, the country's ability to adapt its exports to such changes will also affect the final outcome.

Furthermore, the concept of international competitiveness in tourism services also encompasses *qualitative factors*, that are difficult to quantify; the quality of services involved, the degree of specialization, the capacity for technological innovation, the quality of human resources (Rubalcaba and Cuadrado 2001) are factors that may influence a country's tourism trade performance favorably. Likewise, high rates of productivity growth are often sought as a way of strengthening competitiveness. But it is not necessarily the case that favorable structural factors of this sort will give rise to increased sales on foreign markets. They may, instead, show up as improving terms of trade brought about through exchange-rate appreciation, while leaving export performance broadly unchanged. It is for this reason, as well as because these factors are hard to measure in quantitative terms, that consideration here is confined to a more specific and integrated method for determining Romania's relative competitive position in international tourism.

12.3 An Overview of Romania's International Trade in Tourism Services

12.3.1 Key Facts

Romania's Travel and Tourism Economy[1] currently shows a return to positive territory, following negative results posted during the early years of economic transition, with an optimistic outlook for growth over the next ten years, much stronger than that of the EU.

With a 4.8% contribution of tourism to GDP, Romania ranks the 162nd among 174 countries, being currently among the lower-tier, tourism-intensive countries of the region and the world. However, Romania's prospects for tourism sector growth are better than for most of its neighbours and competitors within the regional and world ranking, i.e. 6.7% contribution to GDP over the next 10 years and 12th position, respectively (World Travel and Tourism Council 2007).

Romania's Travel and Tourism Industry[2] contributed 1.9% to GDP in 2006, rising to 2.5% of total GDP by 2016, while in the European Union, the Travel and Tourism Industry posted a GDP contribution of 3.9% in 2006 (World Travel and Tourism Council 2007).

While the Travel and Tourism Economy accounts for 8.7% of global employment, Romania's Travel and Tourism Economy employment was estimated at 485,000 jobs in 2006, representing 5.8% of total employment, or one in every 17.4 jobs. The current 265,000 Travel and Tourism Industry jobs account for 3.1% of total employment, as compared with 4.2% of total employment in the European Union (8.6 million jobs) (World Travel and Tourism Council 2007).

---

[1] Broad concept developed by the World Tourism and Travel Council and used in Tourism Satellite Accounting, referring to both the direct and indirect economic impacts of tourism.

[2] Narrower concept developed by the World Tourism and Travel Council and used in Tourism Satellite Accounting, referring only to the direct economic impact of tourism.

Travel and Tourism represented, in the European Union, 13.0% of total exports in 2006. In Romania, exports make up a very important share of Travel and Tourism's contribution to GDP. Out of the total Romanian exports, Travel and Tourism represented 5.2% (1.2 billion Euros) in 2004, with a prospect to increase, in nominal terms, to 1.8 billion Euros (4.6% of total) by 2016 (World Travel and Tourism Council 2007).

The vast majority of international arrivals in Romania are from Europe. Since 2000, some 95% of visitors every year have been intra-regional. Out of these, a growing number – 75% according to 2004 figures – represent arrivals from the five countries with which Romania shares a border: Ukraine, Moldavia, Bulgaria, Hungary, Serbia and Montenegro.

12.3.2 Major Findings

The analysis shows that, while still lagging behind the developed economies, the trend towards a service-oriented society is observable for Romania. This is also reflected by the increasing proportion of GDP attributable to tourism services and the growing share of employment in the tourism services sector.

Although the overall tourism balance of Romania is positive, EU represents a net exporter of tourism services to Romania (the tourism balance is negative, with a worsening deficit from 2005 to 2006); still, the propensity to trade with EU partners is stronger in this field, reflecting a higher degree of integration into the EU tourism services market (EUROSTAT 2003, 2004, 2005, 2006).

- While Romania's Travel and Tourism is growing in terms of international visitors, the country's tourism receipts have been lagging considerably behind neighboring countries. In 2004, Romania registered some 38% of those registered by Bulgaria, approximately 12% of those registered by Hungary and the Czech Republic and a mere 7% of Croatia's receipts. This reflects the fact that many of Romania's visitors do not stay overnight or spend anything while they are in the country, an important weakness to address for any tourism plan going forward (EUROSTAT 2003, 2004, 20058, 2006).
- Within EU-15 countries, Romania's largest markets are Germany, Italy, France, Austria and the UK. Worryingly, arrivals from all of the EU-15 countries showed negative growth in 2004. This can be attributed in part to the accession of ten new countries to the EU and related incentives for visitors to these countries, such as low-cost airlines.
- Growth in 2004 was driven by Hungary, which showed a 69% increase in arrivals in Romania. Outside Europe, Romania's main international markets are the USA, which has shown steady growth since 2000, to 111,000 arrivals in 2004, as American tourists have started to be aware of the fact that Romania is more than a "Dracula" destination; and Israel, although the Israeli market has remained stagnant in recent years. Tourists from China are also expected to increase in the future, as Romania received approved destination status in June 2004 (EUROSTAT 2003, 2004, 2005, 2006).

- Analysis of accommodation figures shows that a large number of these visitors do not stay in registered facilities and either reside with friends or relatives, or do not overnight in Romania. Thus, it is difficult to quantify their impact on the economy.
- The majority of international arrivals to Romania are by road, again mirroring the large proportion of the country's visitors from bordering countries. However, arrivals by air have also seen a healthy rise over the past five years, with increased frequency of scheduled services and some charters operating in regional airports. As Romania is forced to liberalize its aviation industry as a consequence of EU accession, air transport is set to rise dramatically in the near future. Arrivals by rail are decreasing at almost the same rate that air arrivals are increasing, as air travel becomes cheaper and more accessible.

12.4 Methods for Assessing the International Competitiveness of Trade in Tourism Services

12.4.1 The Research Method

For the specific assessment of the international competitiveness of trade in tourism services, the underlying methodological approach undertaken in this study is based on the idea that *the economy with an improving degree of competitiveness in tourism services is the one able to enhance the size of its tourism services exports to a certain market*. Similarly, the economy with a declining degree of competitiveness is the one that increases the size of its tourism services imports coming from other countries. The greater or smaller degree of competitiveness a country (or sector) has shows the nature and degree of participation it has – through its exports – in the imports carried out by the analyzed market, i.e., a country improves its competitiveness in the way that the other country increases its imports coming from the former one (Mandeng 1991).

In addition, the process of inserting a country in the international economy is *related not only to its exporting progresses, but also to the behavior and actions of other competitors*. The model is adapted from De la Guardia, Molero, and Valadez (De la Guardia et al. 2004) that introduced the aspect of the dynamic nature of markets and implemented through their work an ex—post assessment of services competitiveness, by providing a descriptive reference on the changes produced in the competitiveness level and specialization degree, in international trade.

The *commercial advantage* is *revealed* through the evolution of tourism exports – which reflects improvements in competitiveness, and through the evolution of tourism imports that reflects a worsening of the commercial advantage.

Based on the aforesaid, the changes in the international tourism services trade competitiveness are measured through the analysis of different variables:

1. the first variable is the *market share* or participation in the market, and measures the portion of the market that is supplied by a certain country or the tourism sector of this country;

2. the second variable used is the *export structure* of the analyzed country. This variable reflects the relative weight of the tourism sector in the total exports of that country;
3. finally, by means of the *import structure* of the market, the degree of dynamism that the tourism sector has in the analyzed import market can be determined.

Through the combination of the aforementioned variables, three "tourism competitiveness matrices" (see Table 12.1) are constructed, that allow for the description of Romania's international tourism trade development profile.

The Market Share Competitiveness Matrix illustrates the fact that a country's tourism exports can be classified according to their international competitiveness starting from the behavior of the country's market share in tourism exports and the evolution of the world tourism services imports over time.

In effect, the world market share held by each country in tourism services exports can increase or diminish throughout time; such modifications take place in the same time with the increase or decline that tourism imports register in international trade.

This allows for the classification of a country's tourism exports as *performing*, *missed opportunities*, *declining* and *retreating*.

Tourism services are *performing* when a country enhances its market share in tourism, in circumstances in which this activity has an increasing importance in world wide trade.

Tourism services are *missed opportunities* when a country is losing market share, while international trade in the sector is enhancing.

Declining are those tourism services in which the exporting country increases its market share, while the international market is shrinking.

Finally, we define the situation of tourism services as *retreating* when this economic activity, besides losing market share, registers a decline of dynamism in international trade.

The *competitiveness matrix of the export structure* is obtained relating the behavior of a country's tourism services export structure with the tourism services import dynamism of the international market.

This matrix shows how the adjustments of the export structure can take place in the same direction or in the opposite direction with respect to the changes in world imports structure.

Table 12.1 The tourism competitiveness matrix

Market share Export structure Specialization index	Declining Retreating	Performing Missed opportunity
Import market structure		

Source: adapted from De la Guardia et al., 2004

The different segments of services exports, including tourism, can be classified, from the point of view of their international competitiveness, through the changes that take place in the services export structure of the country and the world services imports structure throughout time.

Combining these two variables, tourism, as a services exporting sector can be classified as *performing, missed opportunity*, *declining* and *retreating,* with the equivalent meaning mentioned before.

Finally, tourism exports can also be classified from the point of view of their international competitiveness throughout time, when the degree of *trade specialization* of each country and the evolution of the world imports are simultaneously analyzed.

The specialization index is defined as the relative participation that an exporting sector of a country has in world trade.[3]

Similarly, tourism, as an exporting sector can be classified as *performing, missed opportunity*, *declining* and *retreating,* with an identical interpretation to the ones previously indicated.

Our aim here is to adapt and apply the model developed by De la Guardia, Molero, and Valadez in order to assess the international competitiveness of tourism services, using information related to the current situation of the EU-25 countries and to that of Romania, based on the statistical information available.

Balance of payments transactions for tourism services are less easy to link to actual tourism services provision than is the case for goods; some tourism activities may be difficult to disentangle from goods or capital transactions. Countries have developed unique national methods for assembling the data: some have tended to rely more on statistical surveys and others have relied more on central banks' administrative systems. Even so, there has been and still remains considerable variation in data collection methods. To compound the picture, methods of collection have changed considerably over time.

Despite these troubles, we believe that the forthcoming descriptive analysis could bring some highlights on international competitiveness and the factors determining the commercial position in tourism services trade.

The sample data is drawn from UNCTAD-IMF-BOP Statistics on Trade in Services by sector and country (OECD 2003, 2004, 2005, 2006, UNCTAD 2003, 2004, 2005, 2006), a data-set which covers exports (credits) and imports (debits) of three main services categories: transportation, tourism and travel and other commercial services, according to the concepts and definitions of the IMF Balance of Payments Manual with a focus on tourism services. Data-set comprises the 25 EU countries, Romania and the world (178 countries) and covers a yearly time period comprising 2003, 2004, 2005 and 2006.

[3]The specialization index is defined as the ratio of a services category exports to total services exports of a country with respect to the same ratio to the world economy. The index measures the country's revealed comparative advantage in exports according to the Balassa formula. Values above 1 indicate that the country is specialized in the sector under review.

12.4.2 The Research Results

12.4.2.1 The Indicators

The evolution of the market share shows the penetration ability of tourism as a services exporting sector of each country in the international economy.

The data reveal that, for the analyzed period, the EU-25 economies were among the main world suppliers of tourism services, since they maintained an overall participation next to 45% of the world supply in tourism exports.

Altogether, the group constituted by these countries slightly diminished the held proportions of the world quota in tourism services (–0.68% growth rate).

From the perspective of individual countries, the economies that registered an increase of their quotas in the world market of tourism services were, in order, those of Poland, Estonia, Lithuania, UK and Luxemburg.

By contrast, especially significant are the results registered by countries like Hungary, Finland and Spain, which decreased their market share in tourism.

Romania's market share in tourism services exports declined at both world level (*Romania – world*) and in relation to EU-25 countries (*Romania – EU-25*), but the decrease in the latter case was more severe (20.85%, as opposed to 4.65%). Also, the reduction in Romania's market share on the EU-25 market was much higher then the overall European market retreat.

Through the analysis of the *export structure* we can appreciate the importance that export of services has as currency provider for the EU-25 economies and Romania.

Data show that, in relation to the examined services sectors, the exports of tourism services represent about 27% of the overall services exports in the EU-25 countries and about 28% at world level, meaning that, compared to the world export structure, the EU-25 countries exhibit a similar pattern, with a slight negative deviation for tourism services.

In the analyzed period, most of the countries registered minor decreases in their currency entry through exports of tourism services. The countries that opposed this trend were Poland, Estonia, Malta, Germany, UK.

In Romania, tourism services represent about 14% of the overall services exports, which is below the world and European average (27–28%).The evolution is similar with that signaled above, meaning that the structure of Romania's exports is altered in the detriment of tourism services, that are decreasing both in relation to the world and to the EU-25 countries, but with a much higher amplitude in the latter case (27.85%, as compared to 6.14%).

Finally, through the analysis of the *import structure*, we can illustrate the changes that have taken place in the world imports of tourism services.

The first relevant fact reflected by the data is that EU-25 tourism import activities evolved in the same direction as compared to the world, but with a different growth rate (0.98% increase in tourism imports for EU-25 countries, as compared to 2.31% at world level). With respect to the services import structure itself, it is similar at EU-25 level and world level, with tourism services representing about 26–28% of services imports.

The highest increase in the contribution of tourism imports to the overall imports was felt in Poland, Lithuania, Spain and The Nederland's.

The structure is different in Romania, with tourism services accounting for only 16% of the overall services imports. In relation to the EU-25 countries, the percentage is slightly higher, i.e. 18.2%.

While at the world level and the EU-25 countries level the greater relative weight of the imports increase corresponded to the activity of tourism, these services are decreasing their contribution to services imports in Romania; the corresponding rate is much higher at world level (14.19%) than in relation to EU-25 countries (4.95%).

12.4.2.2 The Tourism Competitiveness Matrices

As it has already been indicated, a first assessment procedure of a country's competitiveness in tourism services consists of analyzing simultaneously the market share that an economy holds with respect to tourism services exports and the changes that are taking place in the world tourism trade (imports) throughout time.

The results of the analysis are reflected in Table 12.2, where countries examined in accordance with these criteria have been ordered.

A second tourism competitiveness assessment procedure consists of simultaneously analyzing the behavior that the export structure of the economy has throughout time, and the changes that take place in the structure of world trade, with emphasis on tourism services (see Table 12.3).

A third and most complex tourism competitiveness assessment procedure consists of analyzing, simultaneously, the behavior that the economy has with regard to its commercial specialization and the path shown by international trade throughout the time (see Table 12.4).

In its turn, the degree of commercial specialization of a country can evolve in the same direction in which international trade operates or the opposite. Thus, tourism as an exporting sector of a country can be winning or losing weight in specialization terms, at the same time that the size of the international trade in tourism services expands or declines.

Table 12.2 The market share competitiveness matrix for tourism services

Declining: -	Performing: Estonia, Germany, Latvia, Lithuania, Luxembourg, Poland, Portugal, Slovenia, UK
Retreating: -	Missed opportunities: Austria, Belgium, Cyprus, Czech Republic, Finland, France, Hungary, Ireland, Italy, Malta, Netherlands, Spain, *Romania – world,* *Romania – EU-25,* *EU-25*

Source: own calculations

Table 12.3 The export structure competitiveness matrix for tourism services

Declining:	Performing:
-	Estonia, Germany, Latvia, Malta, Poland, UK
Retreating:	Missed opportunities:
-	Austria, Belgium, Cyprus, Czech Republic, Finland, France, Hungary, Ireland, Italy, Lithuania, Luxembourg, Netherlands, Portugal, Slovenia, Spain, *Romania – world,* *Romania – EU-25,* *EU-25*

Source: own calculations

Table 12.4 The specialization index competitiveness matrix for tourism services

Declining:	Performing:
-	Estonia, Germany, Malta, Netherlands, Poland, Spain, UK
Retreating:	Missed opportunities:
-	Austria, Belgium, Cyprus, Czech Republic, Finland, France, Hungary, Ireland, Italy, Latvia, Lithuania, Luxembourg, Portugal, Slovenia, *Romania – world,* *Romania – EU-25,* *EU-25*

Source: own calculations

Such behaviors allow for the classification of the EU-25 and Romanian tourism services sectors from the perspective of their greater or smaller competitiveness level.

12.5 The Competitive Position of Romania on the European Tourism Market. Concluding Remarks

1. While world tourism imports are growing (20%), EU-25 countries are loosing market share (–0.68% market share growth rate) and so is Romania (–4.65% market share growth rate). The severe decrease of Romania's market share on the EU-25 market (–20.86% market share growth rate) as compared to the world illustrates the fact that Romania is loosing market share much faster on the European market, even though European tourism imports are growing. It is worth mentioning that this growth is slower than world tourism imports growth (6.12%, as compared to 20%). This might mean that, although the number of tourists from

EU-25 countries is higher than from the rest of the world, the revenues have a different structure.

The fact that tourism services in Romania are losing market share, while international tourism trade is enhancing allows for its classification as *missed opportunity.*

2. While the contribution of tourism to world services imports is increasing (2.31%), its participation to EU-25 countries services exports is decreasing (0.38%). In Romania, the contribution of tourism to exports is diminishing even more (6.14%). In relation to EU-25 countries, while tourism services contribution to imports growth rate is of 0.98% (lower than at world level), the decrease in the tourism services contribution to exports in Romania is much more severe (27.85%). This shows that Romania is downgrading its revenues coming from tourism exports to the EU-25 more than towards the world, in a context in which the market of tourism services is enhancing.

   The result of that comparison is outstanding, because the consequences that derive for Romania are not the same if a significant part of its currency income comes from an international activity in expansion or contraction.

   The losses of the tourism sector, within the export structure of Romania reflect smaller currency entries through these exports, which affects the external balances of the economy and, consequently, its future possibilities of economic growth.

   Relating these circumstances to the changes in the structure of international tourism trade, it was possible to classify the tourism exporting sector of Romania as *missed opportunity.* This classification is confirmed by the worsening tourism balance deficit in relation to EU-25 countries, while being evident a tendency to cover the deficit at world level in 2005 (positive tourism balance in 2005).

3. The tourism specialization index of EU-25 countries is 0.96 and decreasing, suggesting that EU-25 countries' comparative advantage in tourism services is slightly diminishing.

   Because the percentage of tourism exports by Romania to the EU-25 countries in the total exports of services by Romania to the EU-25 is higher than with respect to the world, Romania's specialization index for tourism services is also higher with respect to EU-25 countries (0.73 as compared to 0.52), but with a tendency towards closing this gap in time.

   The evolution of Romania's degree of commercial specialization in tourism in the opposite direction in which international trade with tourism services operates, representing a loss of weight in specialization terms in Romania's tourism sector, at the same time that international tourism trade expands, allows for the classification of tourism services trade as *missed opportunity.*

4. Consequently, this integrated approach induces the conclusion that Romania's international trade in tourism services, both in relation to EU-25 countries (to a larger extent) and to the world in general is experiencing a decrease in market share, contribution to exports and specialization degree, on the background of an expanding world trade in tourism services.

5. The macroeconomic effects derived from the fact that a country decreases the quota that it maintains on the world market, or that its export structure is modified or that it reduces its specialization degree are different depending on the own behavior of the international economy and the sectors in which such changes take place.
6. In macroeconomic terms, the forward linkages and backward linkages derived from the export of tourism services are different depending on their structure and quality. In other words, the implications for the economy are very different depending on the structure of tourism services exports. The method applied in this paper for the study of the international competitiveness of tourism services avoids one approach to competitiveness that, at least from a statistical standpoint, seems to be not specific enough or not operative enough, i.e. *quality and structure of services*. This factor is extremely important when analyzing competitiveness, but the statistical approach is quite complex. For this reason, a statistical calculation of competitiveness in terms of quality has not been performed here and can constitute the subject of further research.
7. In spite of the efforts undertaken by the international institutions in order to progress in the knowledge of the tourism services sector, it is necessary to have more extended series and precise statistics than the ones normally provided. The lack of information is especially severe with respect to travel services. That deficiency makes difficult any research, since this sub-sector has a very important weight in the behavior of the services sector. For that reason, in the present paper it has been avoided to enter into more details with respect to this sector.
8. This paper constitutes a first and necessary step towards a deeper and more complex assessment of the Romanian tourism sector and also towards designing a policy map aimed at enhancing the competitiveness of the sector.
9. Becoming a full-member of the European Union might have positive effects on the process of overcoming the existing weaknesses in the tourism services trade competitiveness of Romania. Repeating the above analysis in a couple of years could bring results that would better reveal the consequences of becoming a European Union member in terms of tourism services trade competitiveness.

References

Clark J, Guy K (1998) Innovation and competitiveness: a review. Technol Anal Strat Manage 10(3):363–395.

Coldwell D (2000) The question of international competitiveness. Int Adv Econ Res 6(3):February

De la Guardia C, Molero J, Valadez P (2004) International competitiveness in services in some European countries: basic facts and a preliminary attempt of interpretation, paper presented at the SETI Workshop, Bruges

Dollar D, Wolff EN (1993) Competitiveness, Convergence, and International Specialization. MIT Press, Cambridge, MA

European Commission (1997) The competitiveness of European Industry, Luxembourg

EUROSTAT (2003, 2004, 2005, 2006), Statistics on trade in services

Fagerberg J(1986) Technology, Growth and International Competitiveness, Norsk Utenrikpolitisk Institut, VUPI rapport, No 95, March

Fagerberg J, Knell M, Srholec M (2004) Competitiveness of Nations: Economic Growth in the ECE Region, January.
Garelli S (2003) Competitiveness of Nations: The Fundamentals, IMD World Competitiveness Report
IMF (2003, 2004, 2005, 2006) Balance of Payments and International Investment Position Statistics.
Krugman P (1994) Competitiveness: a dangerous obsession, Foreign Affairs, March/April.
Krugman P (1996) Pop internationalism. MIT Press, Cambridge MA
Mandeng O (1991) International competitiveness and international specialization. Eclac Rev 45, December
OECD (1993) STI Review 13: Special Issue on Globalization, Paris: Organisation for Economic Cooperation and Development.
Porter M (1990) The competitive advantage of nations. Macmillan, New York
Rubalcaba L, Cuadrado J (2001) Internationalisation of service industries: A comparative approach, Working paper 4/2001, SERVILAB
UNCTAD (2003, 2004, 2005, 2006), UNCTAD Handbook of Statistics.
World Travel and Tourism Council (2007), Romanian Tourism Satellite Account

Chapter 13
Travellers' Intentions to Purchase Travel Products Online: The Role of Shopping Orientation

Jan Møller Jensen

13.1 Introduction

Usage of the Internet and subsequent Internet retail sales have increased dramatically over the last years. According to Statistics Denmark, for 2007, 76% of the Danish population uses the Internet at least once a week. 69% of the Internet users have purchased products or services on the Internet. Statistics further reveal that travel products are the most popular category to be purchased on the Internet. 49% of the Internet users have bought travel products online and this figure seems to be steadily rising. No doubt, with more and more travellers perceiving the Internet as an alternative to more traditional visits to travel agent offices, the integration of the Internet into the travel and tourism industry becomes an important challenge to the traditional role of travel agencies. Airlines and wholesale travel operators are beginning to market their products directly to the traveller through their websites, and virtual travel agencies are selling travel products directly via the Internet. Yet, although purchasing travel products online obviously has many advantages to the potential travellers, this paper suggests that there will probably always be a segment of travellers who prefer to use the traditional channels for purchasing their travel products. As such, it is important to detect and understand influencing variables of travellers' intentions to purchase travel products online.

This paper tries to increase our understanding of travellers' adoption (or rejection) of Internet shopping for travel products. More specifically, the paper suggests a number of potential motivating factors and barriers as perceived by travellers, when deciding to purchase travel products online or offline. The author discusses how these aspects may either enhance or reduce travellers' intentions to purchase travel products online. Of special concern is the importance of travellers' shopping orientation. The author draws on literature on shopping orientation and argues that for many purchasers of travel products, the act of visiting a travel agency is seen as an important part of the travel experience itself. Indeed, many purchasers may

J. Møller Jensen (✉)
Department of Marketing, University of Southern Denmark, Denmark
e-mail: jmj@sam.sdu.dk

Á. Matias et al. (eds.), *Advances in Tourism Economics*,
DOI 10.1007/978-3-7908-2124-6_13, © Physica-Verlag Heidelberg 2009

experience visits to travel agencies more as fun than as work (see Holbrook and Hirschman, 1982) and resist giving up these benefits by shifting their purchase from offline to online channels. A conceptual model of travellers' intentions to purchase travel products online is presented along with a number of hypotheses.

13.2 Model Development and Research Hypotheses

An extensive review of the research on consumers' intentions to purchase online, suggests various factors inducing or inhibiting consumers' adoption of this new way of purchasing. These antecedents include a number of variables related to the consumer, the product and the new purchasing medium itself (Vijayasarathy, 2001, 2003).

13.2.1 Consumers' Prior Experience with Internet Usage and Internet Purchases

Previous studies have reported that the more consumers gain experience with Internet use, the more likely they will adopt Internet shopping (Weber and Roehl, 1999). Experienced Internet users may perceive online purchases as easier and less risky. Furthermore, we expect the perceived risk and/or trouble with Internet purchasing to decrease even more as the consumer becomes more familiar with Internet purchases. It is therefore hypothesized that:

H_1: A traveller's experience with Internet usage influences experience with Internet shopping positively

H_2: A traveller's experience with Internet usage will have a direct effect on that traveller's intention to purchase travel products online

H_3: A traveller's experience with Internet shopping will have a direct effect on that traveller's intention to purchase travel products online

13.2.2 Motivators and Barriers to Internet purchasing

Consumers' risk concerns are among the most frequently-mentioned barriers to purchasing online (Hoffman et al., 1999; Jarvenpaa and Tractinsky, 1999; Pavlou, 2001). Although the perceived risk of online transactions is expected to decline with more Internet usage and Internet purchasing, it is proposed that perceived risk will still have a negative influence on travellers' willingness to purchase travel products on the Internet. Therefore, it is hypothesized that:

H_4: A traveller's experience with Internet usage influences the perceived risk of Internet purchasing negatively

H_5: A traveller's experience with Internet purchasing influences the perceived risk of Internet purchasing negatively

H_6: A traveller's perceived risk of Internet purchasing will have a negative effect on that traveller's intention to purchase travel products online

Along with cost savings, access to greater product variety and convenience matters are recurrently pointed out as important factors motivating consumers' adoption of online purchasing (Fenech and O'Cass, 2001). A wider selection of agencies and travel products has been shown to motivate travellers to purchase online. Therefore, it is hypothesized that:

H_7: A traveller's preference for greater product variety has a positive influence on that travellers' intentions to purchase travel products online.

The issue of convenience has been associated with trial and adoption of non-store shopping environments (Darian, 1987; Eastlick and Lotz, 1999; Fenech and O'Cass, 2001). Darian (1987) suggests five dimensions of convenience for in-home shoppers, including reducing time spent on shopping, providing flexibility in the timing of shopping, saving physical efforts of visiting traditional stores, reducing aggravation and the possibility of impulse shopping in response to advertisements received while at home. Therefore, it is proposed that:

H_8: A traveller seeking convenience when shopping travel products will be more likely to purchase travel products online

While much research on shopping motivation has often focused on the utilitarian aspects of the shopping process (e.g. saving time and/or money) other researchers have emphasized the role of hedonic motives (e.g. store atmosphere, shopping for fun) for retail channel preferences (Babin et al., 1994; Childers et al., 2001). In this view, the visit to travel agencies is seen more as fun than as work to be done, and therefore the traveller will have to 'sacrifice' this benefit if adopting the Internet as a purchasing medium for travel products. However, the traveller's preference for convenience may be negatively related to that traveller's perceived loss of hedonic aspects when shopping online. Therefore, it is hypothesized that:

H_9: If a traveller thinks that he/she has to give up hedonic aspects by not visiting a travel agency, that traveller will be less likely to purchase travel products online.

H_{10}: If a traveller seeks convenience when shopping travel products, that traveller will be less likely to perceive a loss of hedonic aspects by not visiting a travel agency

13.2.3 The Traveller's Shopping Orientation

Since Stone's (1954) seminal work, several researchers have documented that consumers' shopping orientation has an impact on their patronage behaviour, including also their store choice (Bellinger and Korgaonkar, 1980; Korgaonkar et al., 1985). Research in shopping orientation typically distinguishes between economic (or conventional) shoppers and recreational shoppers. Economic shoppers act as 'problem solvers', they often dislike shopping, and therefore approach retail stores from a time- and money-saving point of view. In contrast, recreational shoppers enjoy the act of shopping, and therefore approach retail environments emphasizing the emotional aspects of shopping (Bellinger and Korgaonkar, 1980; Hirschman and

Holbrook, 1982). Recently, researchers have investigated the role of shopping orientation on consumers' intentions to purchase online. Donthu and Garcia (1999) and Rohm and Swaminathan (2004) found that online shoppers were likely to be convenience seekers. Likewise, it is suggested here, that convenience-oriented travel purchasers (here named as 'quick shoppers') will be more likely to purchase travel products online as opposed to recreational shoppers with a more experience-oriented approach to visiting travel agencies. From this point of view, it is hypothesised that:

H_{11}: 'Quick shoppers' will be more likely to place importance on convenience matters, when shopping travel products online.

H_{12}: Travellers oriented towards quick shopping will be more likely to purchase travel products online.

H_{13}: Travellers viewing visits to travel agencies as a positive experience in itself, will be less concerned about convenience when purchasing travel products

H_{14}: Travellers viewing visits to travel agencies as a positive experience in itself, will be more likely to think they will have to sacrifice hedonic aspects if purchasing travel products online

H_{15}: Travellers viewing visits to travel agencies as a positive experience in itself, will be less likely to purchase travel products online

All hypotheses are summarized in the conceptual model displayed in Fig. 13.1.

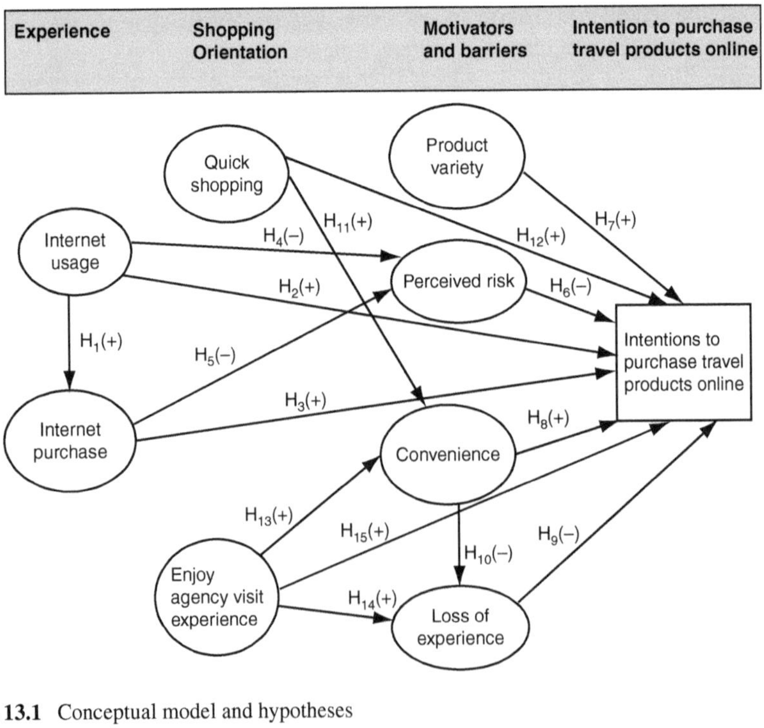

Fig. 13.1 Conceptual model and hypotheses

13.3 Methods

In Fig. 13.1, most constructs are more or less latent unobservable variables. In order to obtain reasonably accurate measures of such constructs, the literature (e.g. Hair et al., 1988) recommends developing multi-item scales with a least two items, preferable three or more items This goal was achieved for all but the construct of *Intentions to purchase travel products online*, which unfortunately is only measured by a single question. Accordingly, the latter construct is represented in Fig. 13.1 as a square, whereas the multi-item measured constructs are illustrated as ovals. Each construct and its corresponding items and response scales are displayed in the Appendix.

13.3.1 Data Collection

The data used in the study were collected in October 2006 with a questionnaire constructed for an e-survey. This data collection method excludes non-users of the internet from the sample. Yet, since access to the Internet obviously is a requirement in order to purchase travel products online, an e-survey was seen as a purposeful way of data collection. The sampling method used in the research was non-probabilistic, based on convenience. Students in two marketing classes at the University of Southern Denmark distributed an e-mail with a link to the questionnaire to potential respondents, sampled in order to meet variations with respect to demographic variables, as for example gender and age. The sample used in this study is 287 respondents who purchase travel products at least once a year.

13.3.2 Sample Profile

The respondents usable for this study were relatively evenly distributed in terms of gender: male (42%) and female (58%). Approximately 65% of the respondents were between 20 and 29 years of age, 11% between 30 and 39 years of age, 4% were between 40 and 49 year of age, and 20 were above 50 years of age. This over representation of respondents between 20 and 29 of age clearly reflects the sampling procedure with students contacting friends and relatives. 47% were students and 53% were either taking or had finished a higher degree of education. 60% were married or living with another person. 20% had children at home.

13.4 Results

The model in Fig. 13.1 was translated into a LISREL model consisting of a measurement part (confirmatory factor analysis) and a structural equation part (simultaneous linear regression). The relationship between variables was estimated by maximum likelihood estimation. A two-stage approach (cf. Anderson and Gerbing, 1988; Gerbing and Anderson, 1992) tested the proposed model. First, confirmatory factor analysis was conducted on the applied multi-item scales in order to ensure that the measures of the constructs are reliable and valid before attempting to draw conclusions about relations between constructs. Next, the measurement model and the structural equation paths were estimated simultaneously to test the proposed model (overall model).

Table 13.1 shows the results of the confirmatory factor analysis (CFA). The aim of CFA is to verify the factor structure as proposed. Prior to examining results from

Table 13.1 Confirmatory factor analyses results (n = 287)

Construct/ indicator	Standardized factor loading[a]	Standard error	t–value	Construct reliability[b]	Extracted variance[c]
H1 Enjoy agency visit experience				0.838	0.636
EAV1	0.697	–	–		
EAV2	0.893	0.102	12.403		
EAV3	0.790	0.091	11.873		
H2 Quick shopping				0.773	0.543
QS1	0.739	–	–		
QS2	0.898	0.151	8.915		
QS3	0.526	0.094	8.200		
H3 Loss of Experience				0.847	0.650
LoE1	0.882	–	–		
LoE2	0.787	0.864	14.600		
LoE3	0.743	0.789	13.681		
H4 Convenience				0.743	0.549
C1	0.839	–	–		
C2	0.734	0.085	10.775		
C3	0.636	0.100	9.732		
H5 Product variety				0.793	0.658
PV1	0.762	–	–		
PV2	0.857	0.178	6.680		
H6 Perceived risk				0.784	0.552
PR1	0.867	–	–		
PR2	0.697	0.081	10.798		
PR3	0.646	0.062	10.135		
H7 Experience with Internet usage				0.585	0.416
EIU1	0.711	–	–		
EIU2	0.571	0.317	5.895		
H8 Experience with Internet purchase				0.724	0.568
EIP1	0.717	–	–		
EIP2	0.788	0.110	8.614		

$\chi^2 = 170.982$ P = 0.280 χ^2/DF = 1.062 RMSEA= 0.015 HI 90 0.031
GFI = 0.948; AGFI = 0.925; CFI = 0.995; NFI = 0.925; TLI = 0.994

[a] The first item for each construct was set to 1.

[b] Calculated as $\frac{\sum(\text{Std. Loadings})^2}{\sum(\text{Std. Loadings})^2+\sum \xi \gamma j}$

[c] Calculated as $\frac{\sum \text{Std. Loadings}^2}{\sum \text{Std. Loadings}^2+\sum \xi \gamma j}$

elaborating on the figures in Table 13.1 we call attention to the fact that we χ^2 (161) = 170.98 is insignificant (p>0.05) indicating that the model fit the data in an absolute sense.

The GFI value (0.948) is well above the recommended 0.90 threshold level. RMSEA, which is less dependent on sample size, stands for root mean square error of approximation and refers to lack of fit between the proposed model and the population covariance matrix. RMSEA for the measurement model is well below the threshold of 0.05 with the 90% confidence interval between 0.01 and 0.03, indicating a very good fit (Brown and Cudeck, 1993; Hair et al., 1998). To conclude, the results indicate a good overall fit between the model and the observed data.

From the high figures on t-values (all well above the 0.01 level of 2.64), it can be concluded that all factor loadings statistically are highly significant. Furthermore, all loadings show values higher than the recommended 0.40 level (Hair et al., 1998). For each latent variable, construct reliability and extracted variance were computed using indicator standardized loadings and measurement errors (Hair et al., 1998). With the exception of *Experience with Internet Usage* (η7), all latent variables have construct reliabilities above the generally-agreed threshold of 0.70, and the extracted variances for the constructs well above the recommended level of 0.40 (Hair et al., 2006). Although, the reliability coefficient (= 0.585) of *Experience with Internet usage* is slightly below the accepted lower limit of 0.60, the results generally support an acceptable level of unidimensionality and convergent validity in the measurement model.

Discriminant validity of the latent variables was tested by applying the approach proposed by Fornell and Lacker (1981). In Table 13.2, the diagonals represent average amount of extracted variance for each construct as reported in Table 13.1. The other entries represent the squares of correlations among constructs (i.e. the shared variance among constructs). An examination of the matrix displayed in Table 13.1 shows a very good level of discriminant validity of all constructs, except for *Experience with internet usage* sharing a relative high amount of variance with experience

Table 13.2 Discriminant validity of constructs

	η1	η2	η3	η4	η5	η6	η7	η8
η1 Enjoy agency visit experience	**0.64**	–	–	–	–	–	–	–
η2 Quick shopping	0.03	**0.54**	–	–	–	–	–	–
η3 Loss of experience	0.36	0.00	**0.65**	–	–	–	–	–
η4 Convenience	0.07	0.00	0.19	**0.55**	–	–	–	–
η5 Product variety	0.01	0.00	0.03	0.16	**0.66**	–	–	–
η6 Perceived risk	0.02	0.00	0.08	0.00	0.01	**0.55**	–	–
η7 Experience with Internet usage	0.01	0.00	0.02	0.01	0.21	0.21	**0.41**	–
η8 Experience with Internet purchase	0.01	0.00	0.02	0.00	0.34	0.34	0.42	**0.57**

Note: Diagonals represent average amount of extracted variance for each construct; non-diagionals represent the shared variance between constructs (calculated as the squares of correlations between constructs

with internet purchase. Yet, considering the hypothesized path between those two constructs, this relative high correlation is not surprising.

For all other constructs, extracted variance (displayed as diagonal entries) is well above the shared variance with other constructs (displayed as non diagonals).

13.4.1 Overall Model Fit

Tables 13.3 and 13.4 display the results of testing the proposed theoretical model. In the lower part of Table 13.3, the results of the structural equation modelling reveal that the χ^2 for the estimated model was 246.52 (df 196; $p<0.008$). This result

Table 13.3 Hypothesis testing (n = 287)

H_x	Construct relationships	Estimates	Std. error	t-value
H_1	Experience with Internet usage → Experience with Internet purchase	0.644	0.470	5.10**
H_2	Experience with Internet usage → Intention to purchase travel prod. Online	−0.013	0.151	−0.13
H_3	Experience with Internet purchase→ Intention to purchase travel prod. Online	0.142	0.042	1.34
H_4	Experience with Internet usage → Perceived risk	−0.147	0.183	−1.21
H_5	Experience with Internet Purchase → Perceived risk	−0.491	0.048	−4.14**
H_6	Perceived risk→ Intention to purchase travel prod. Online	−0.143	0.080	−1.86
H_7	Product variety → Intention to purchase travel prod. Online	0.110	0.070	2.15*
H_8	Convenience→ Intention to purchase travel prod. Online	0.137	0.159	2.15*
H_9	Loss of experience→ Intention to purchase travel prod. Online	−0.384	0.090	−4.71**
H_{10}	Convenience → Loss of experience	−0.304	0.066	−4.82**
H_{11}	Quick shopping → Convenience	0.033	0.076	0.49
H_{12}	Quick shopping → Intention to purchase travel prod. Online	−0.018	0.068	−0.34
H_{13}	Enjoy agency visit experience → Convenience	−0.258	0.068	−3.66**
H_{14}	Enjoy agency visit experience → Loss of experience	0.522	0.068	7.61**
H_{15}	Enjoy agency visit experience → Intention to purchase travel prod. online	−0.074	0.079	−1.03

Note: χ^2 (196) = 246,52, P = 0.008; χ^2/DF = 1,258; CFI = 0.977; NFI = 0.901; GFI = 0.930; AGFI = 0,901; TLI = 0.972; RMSEA = 0.03; HI(90) = 0.04; HOELTER(.05) = 267; HOELTER(.01) = 285

* Significant at the p< 0.05 level

** Significant at the p< 0.01 level

Table 13.4 Explained propotion of variance (n = 287)

Construct	Squared multiple correlations (R^2)
Intentions to purchase travel products online	0.33
Loss of experience	0.45
Convenience	0.07
Experience with Internet purchase	0.42
Perceived risk	0.36

Note: χ^2 (196) = 246,52, $P = 0.008$; χ^2/DF = 1,258; CFI =0.977; NFI = 0.901;
GFI = 0.930; AGFI=0,901; TLI = 0.972; RMSEA=0.03; HI(90)=0.04;
HOELTER(0.05) = 267; HOELTER(.01) = 285

indicates that the model fails to fit in an absolute sense. However, for samples with n>200, most researchers recommend that the χ^2-measure should be complemented with other goodness-of-fit measures (Hair et al., 1998). As shown, the results of the full model (structural and measurement models) indicate a good fit (GFI: 0.930; AGFI: 0.901; NFI = 0.901; CFI = 0.977 and RMSEA 0.03) providing acceptable support for the model as proposed.

13.4.2 Hypothesis Testing

To begin with the influences of travellers' prior experience with Internet usage and Internet purchasing, structural equation results support that a traveller's familiarity with Internet usage has a strong influence on that traveller's Internet purchasing (H_1: $r = 0.644$; $t = 5.10$; $p < 0.01$). Indeed, 42% of *Internet purchasing* is explained by *Internet usage* (refer to the R^2 figure in Table 13.4). Interestingly, travellers' Internet usage and prior Internet purchasing have no direct effect on their intentions to purchase travel products online (H_2: $r = -0.013$; $t = -0.13$; and H_3: $r = 0.142$; $t = 1.34$). In order to investigate whether the two constructs have an indirect effect through reducing the perceived risk of Internet purchasing, we first inspect their respective influence on *Perceived risk.* The results support that travellers' perceived risk decreases along with their experience with Internet purchasing (H_5: $r = -0.491$; $t = -4.14$; $p < 0.01$), but not with their Internet usage in general (H_4: $r = -0.147$; $t = -0.121$). However, considering that the influence from *Perceived risk* on *Intentions to purchase travel products online* is only close significance at the 0.05 level (H_6: $r = -0.143$; $t = -1.86$; $0.05 < p < 0.10$) we are not able to conclude any indirect effect from experience with Internet purchasing.

Turning to the motivators and barriers to purchasing travel products online, the results reveal that about one-third (33%) of the variance in intentions to purchase travel products online can be explained by the proposed model (refer to the R^2 figure in Table 13.4). Most of the explained variance in intentions to purchase travel products online is produced by travellers' perceived *loss of experience* from not visiting an agency (H_9: $r = -0.384$; $t = -4.71$; $p < 0.01$), but also *convenience*

(H_8: $r = 0.137$; $t = 2.15$; $p < 0.05$) and preference for better *product variety* (H_7: $r = 0.110$; $t = 2.15$; $p < 0.05$) are influencing the travellers' intentions to purchase travel products online. In addition to the direct effect, convenience also has an indirect effect, produced through its significant relationship with the travellers' perceived loss of experience (H_{10}: $r = -0.304$; $t = -4.82$; $p < 0.01$). As concluded above, *perceived risk* has no significant influence.

Finally, the results show that travellers' intention to purchase travel products online cannot be explained directly by their shopping orientation alone (H_{12}: $r = -0.018$; $t = -0.34$; and H_{15}: $r = -0.074$; $t = -1.03$), but indirectly through the effect of shopping orientation on the importance of motivators and barriers for purchasing travel products online. Travellers who enjoy the experience of visiting travel agencies are significantly less likely to prefer convenience (H_{13}: $r = -0.258$; $t = -3{,}66$; $p < 0.01$) and significantly more likely to perceive purchasing travel products online as a loss of experience (H_{14}: $r = 0.522$; $t = 7.66$; $p < 0.01$).

13.5 Summary and Managerial Implications

This study provides travel and tourism marketers with important insights on travellers' tendency to purchase travel products online. First, and contrary to our expectations, travellers' prior experience with Internet usage and online purchasing in general has no direct influence on their intentions to purchase travel products online. Yet, the results did support that travellers' perceived risk associated with purchasing travel products online decreases along with their experience with online purchasing in general. Although, only close to significant at a 0.05 level, the results further suggest that a reduction in risk perception increases travellers' intentions to purchase travel products online. In this light travel marketers may expect a larger proportion of travellers to purchase their travel products online in the future

Yet, the results also support that travellers' shopping orientation affect their perceived motivators and barriers to purchase travel products online and that such barriers – in turn – may affect their willingness to purchase travel products online. Travellers who enjoy the experience of visiting travel agencies are significantly less likely to prefer convenience and significantly more likely to perceive purchasing travel products online as a loss of experience. 'Quick shoppers' tend to strive more for convenience, and therefore, are more likely to choose the Internet as a purchase channel. The findings have implications for both travel e-tailers and retailers. The results suggest that there exist two separate segments, one more suitable for e-tailing and another segment more prone to purchase their travel products in traditional stores. On the one side, this finding suggests that e-tailers might consider that they cannot compete solely on convenience and product variety. If they want to attract the entire travel market to e-tailing they need to create web-stores matching the recreational shoppers experience oriented motives. On the other side, travel marketers selling through traditional stores may prevent travellers from purchasing online by focusing even more on experience-related aspects in the selling process.

Finally, the results support that convenience and better product variety are important motivators for travellers to purchase their travel products online. This finding suggests in the first place that travel e-tailers may offer easy-to-use travel sites and provide wide product variety in order to attain competitive advantages compared to traditional travel stores and other travel e-tailers as well. On the other hand, traditional travel retailers may also strive for convenience and broad product variety in order to prevent their customers from purchasing travel products online.

13.6 Limitations and Suggestions for Further Research

The data used in this study were based on a convenience sample comprising an over representation of younger travellers. Generalisation of the results is therefore questionable. However, it seems plausible to expect that a sample including a larger proportion of elderly travellers may reveal a larger proportion of travellers enjoying visits to travel agencies, and therefore, provide an even stronger support for the role of shopping orientation. Yet, future research may investigate the role of shopping orientation on a sample comprising a more balanced proportion of age groups in order to verify this.

In this study the role of shopping orientation was analysed using structural equation modelling on the total sample. Future investigations may use multi-group analyses to detect differences across various types of travellers. Research on shopping orientation with respect to other product categories (e.g. clothing and groceries) has found gender-related differences. It may also be interesting to investigate if shopping orientation and tendency to online purchasing vary between individual travellers and group travellers.

The dependent variable in this study was online purchasing of travel products. Further studies may also investigate the role of shopping orientation on travellers' intentions to seek information online.

The paper used a quantitative approach to investigate the role of shopping orientation. Although the study provides evidence for the role of shopping orientation we need more research using qualitative approaches in order to fully understand what kind of losses the recreational shopper expects to experience when purchasing online.

Appendix

Construct/indicator *If not otherwise mentioned, a 5-point Likert scale anchored at 1 = totally disagree and 5 = totally agree has been used*
η1 Enjoy agency visit experience
AVE1 I associate visiting a travel agency with a positive and interesting experience
AVE2 For me, visiting one or more travel agencies is an important part of the overall travel experience itself

AVE3 I like the ambiance when visiting a travel agency
η2 Quick shopping
QS1 I'm rarely in a hurry, when purchasing my travel products (reversed)
QS2 I usually have plenty of time, when purchasing my travel products (reversed)
QS3 When planning the holiday, I usually want to get it over with as quickly as possible
η3 Loss of experience
LoE1 I would not like purchasing travel products without the ambiance and atmosphere of visiting a travel agency
LoE2 I would lose too much of the positive experience in planning my travel, if I had to book/purchase my holiday/travel products on the Internet
LoE3 I would miss the atmosphere of visiting the travel agency if I were to purchase my travel products online.
η4 Convenience
If I should purchase my travel products online it would mainly be...
C1 because it is less stressful to purchase travel products online
C2 because you can carry out the purchase without too much trouble
C3 because you can purchase outside normal opening hours
η5 Product variety
If I should purchase my travel products online it would mainly be...
PV1 because there is a larger choice of products when purchasing online
PV2 because you can find more individual/special holidays/travel products online
η6 Perceived risk
PR1 I am reluctant to use my credit card on the internet
PR2 It is too risky to purchase products online
PR3 I feel insecure about revealing my personal information on the internet
η7 Experience with Internet Usage
EIU1 How often do you go on the Internet including at work, at study institution or private home? 1 = Less/never; 2 = 2–3 times a month; 3 = 1–2 times a week; 4 = 3–4 times a week; 5 = 5–6 times a week; 6 = several times daily
EIU2 How will you characterize yourself as an Internet user? 1 = I am an absolute novice; 2 = I know what is most important to know; 3 = I am an average standard user; 4 = I am an experienced user; 5 = I am a super user
η8 Experience with Internet purchase
EIP1 How many times have you bought product/services online, within the last 12 months?
EIP2 Number of products from a list of 16 products/services bought online by the respondent?
Intentions to purchase travel products online
How likely would you be to purchase at least one of your next three purchases of travel products on the Internet? 5-point scale with anchors from 1 = 'very unlikely' to 5 = 'very likely'

References

Babin JB, Darden WR, Griffin M (1994) Work and/or fun: measuring hedonic and utilitarian shopping value. J Consum Res 20:644–656
Bellinger DN, Korgaonkar PK (1980) Profiling the recreational shopper. J Retailing 56:77–92
Brown MW, Cudeck R (1993) Alternative ways of assessing model fit. In: Bollen KA, Long JS (eds) Testing structural equation models. Sage, Thousand Oaks, CA, pp136–162
Card JA, Chen CY, Cole ST (2003) Online travel products shopping: differences between shoppers and nonshoppers. J Travel Res 42:133–139
Childers TL, Carr CL, Carson S (2001) Hedonic and utilitarian motivations for online retail shopping behavior. J Retailing 177(4):511–535

Darian JC (1987) In-home shopping: are there consumer segments? J Retailing 63(2):163–186
Donthu N, Garcia A (1999) The internet shopper. J Adv Res 39(3): 52–58
Eastlick MA, Lotz S (1999) Profiling potential adopters and non-adopters of an interactive electronic shopping medium. Int J Retail Distrib Manage 27(6):209–223
Fenech T, O'Cass A (2001) Internet users' adoption of Web retailing: user and product dimensions. J Prod Brand Manage 10(6):361–381
Fornell C, Lacker DF (1981) Evaluating structural equation models with unobservable variables and measurement error. J Mark Res 18:39–50
Hair JF, Anderson RE, Tatham RL and Black WC (1998, 2006) Multivariate data analysis. Prentice-Hall International, Englewood Cliffs, NJ
Hirschman EC, Holbrook MB (1982) Hedonic consumption: emerging concepts, methods and propositions. J Mark 46:92–101
Holbrook MB, Hirschman EC (1982) The experiential aspects of consumption: Consumer fantasies, feelings and fun. J Consum Res 9:132–140
Korgaonkar PK, Lund D, Price B (1985) A structural equations approach toward examination of store attitude and store patronage behaviour. J Retailing 61(2):39–60
Rohm AJ, Swaminathan V (2004) A typology of online shoppers based on shopping motivations. J Bus Res 57: 748–757
Stone GP (1954) City and urban identification: observations on the social psychology of city life. Am J Sociol 60:36–45
Vijayasarathy LR (2001) Beyond beliefs: the impact of shopping orientations, product types, and shopping aids on attitude and intention to use online shopping. Q J Electron Comm 2(2):99–113
Vijayasarathy LR (2003) Shopping orientations, product types and internet shopping intentions. Electron Mark: Int J Electron Comm Bus Media 1(1):67–79
Statistic Denmark: http://www.dst.dk/upload/bef2007e_001.pdf
Weber K, Roehl WS (1999) Profiling people searching for and purchasing travel products on the world wide web. J Travel Res 37(3):291–298

Chapter 14
Coopetition in Infomediation: General Analysis and Application to e-Tourism

Paul Belleflamme and Nicolas Neysen

14.1 Introduction

The integration of the Internet within human organizations and, in particular, in the mechanisms of business administration has already caused multiple organizational changes. Some economic actors disappeared while other actors appeared because of the opportunities created by the Internet and, in a more general way, by the revolution associated with the information and communication technologies (ICT). Among these new actors of the virtual economic field, we find electronic platforms which enable buyers and sellers on a particular market to exchange information on the products, to compare the characteristics of various products and, if necessary, to carry out online transactions (Lin 2006). Such platforms are perceived at the same time as means of treating and diffusing information, and as new resources enabling firms to increase their competitiveness (Baile and Trahand 1999). In this article, we propose to distinguish between two types of platforms: the *electronic marketplace* (EMP) and the *online information platform* (OIP). Whereas the first type allows buyers and sellers to operate and to conclude online transactions, the second type focuses more specifically on the informational exchange without playing a role in the transaction.

These two types of virtual platforms often coexist within the same sector. For instance, in the tourism sector, online directories, web portals, classified ads, etc. are examples of OIPs (Buhalis and Licata 2002). Their business is defined by the gathering of the whole existing and recognized supply of holiday services (flights, accommodations, leisure parks, restaurants, etc). This information is then available at a single place in order to propose an aggregate offer to the attention of potential buyers (tourists seeking places for their next holiday time). On the other hand, online booking centers or electronic travel agencies are examples of EMPs; these ones

P. Belleflamme (✉)
CORE and Louvain School of Management, Université catholique de Louvain, 34 Voie du Roman Pays, 1348 Louvain-la-Neuve, Belgium
e-mail: paul.belleflamme@uclouvain.be

Á. Matias et al. (eds.), *Advances in Tourism Economics*,
DOI 10.1007/978-3-7908-2124-6_14, © Physica-Verlag Heidelberg 2009

allow users to choose a product, to carry out the reservation, and even to secure the payment of the stay by electronic payment (González 2004).

Going beyond the mere terminological distinction between EMP and OIP, we aim to analyze the main similarities and differences between these two types of electronic platforms. On the one hand, the two types are both characterized by the paradox of any participation in a marketplace: by offering similar goods and services, all the suppliers present on an EMP or an OIP are competitors, but at the same time they collaborate in making this virtual marketplace successful. On the other hand, EMPs and OIPs differ in the services they offer to their participants, but compete for the participation of the same sets of users (basically, sellers and buyers). Moreover, the competition between EMPs and OIPs takes place within an intricate web of externalities: (i) within a platforms, there are indirect network externalities (buyers favor the participation of more sellers and sellers favor the participation of more buyers); also, because sellers compete with one another, there are negative externalities among them; (ii) across different platforms, the benefits offered to users by platform A are likely to spill over to platform B (because users can " multi-home" , i.e., they can register with several intermediaries as explained in foodnote 1) and free-riding may then occur. Our objective in this article is to propose a rigorous framework in order to disentangle these various effects and, thereby, to highlight the main management issues surrounding competition and cooperation within EMPs or OIPs. Indeed, we already know that the digitalization of all the processes in the tourism industry enables organizations to enhance their efficiency (Buhalis and Licata 2002). Throughout the paper, we illustrate our general analysis through the case of e-tourism, with suppliers (accommodation owners) and buyers (tourists buying online). In this article, electronic platforms are tourism organizations that have to face new realities of strategic relationships with all their stakeholders.

The remainder of the article is organized as follows. In Sect. 14.2, we replace the concept of electronic platforms in its context, namely the context of market intermediation. We contrast the hypotheses of *disintermediation* and *re-intermediation*; we describe how *infomediation* is a concept that rises directly from the re-intermediation concept and, thereby, we explain why it is necessary to distinguish between EMPs and OIPs. In Sect. 14.3, we study the collaboration paradox on a platform by referring to the concept of coopetition, which combines competition and cooperation. In Sect. 14.4, we formalize the intuitions drawn from the previous sections by developing an industrial organization model. Finally, we conclude by a discussion of our paper and we state a number of important issues for future research.

14.2 Intermediation and ICT

In order to understand the implications of the distinction between an EMP and an OIP, it is necessary to refer to the intermediation theory. Actually, these virtual entities are intermediaries whose roles rise directly from the evolution of the intermediation in parallel with the evolution of ICTs over the last decades (Curchod 2006).

An intermediary is an economic agent who helps a supplier/seller and a buyer/consumer to meet and to carry out a particular transaction, either by buying to the supplier in order to resell to the purchaser, or by simply helping these two protagonists to find each other (Spulber 2003). Let us notice that in both cases, the intermediary does not derive any utility from the consumption of the exchanged goods (Biglaiser 1993). His profit either comes from the margin of its buy and resell operations or is represented by the wage for his intermediation role. The work of an intermediary generally leads to a centralized offer by minimizing search costs for the two parts of the transaction (Rubinstein and Wolinsky 1987).

14.2.1 The Disintermediation Hypothesis

With the development of ICT and more specifically the Internet, the traditional intermediary enters reluctantly in direct competition with decentralized electronic exchanges where consumers and producers meet in order to negotiate directly the final prices and the transaction terms. The Internet is thus perceived as a virtual tool that establishes direct relations between suppliers and consumers. Hence, the disintermediation hypothesis supposing a gradual elimination of the various actors of the value chain (Malone et al. 1987).

However, there are several reasons for which this hypothesis cannot be validated in its extreme version (disappearance of any economic actor acting as an intermediary). Firstly, it is difficult to believe in a completely digitalized market because of technological barriers. Undeniably, the current state of technology does not make it possible to find satisfactory electronic equivalent for all types of transactions. Secondly, the concerned actors may not always find it beneficial to make the transactions become entirely electronic, be it for strategic reasons or even to ensure that information remains private (Brousseau 2002). Finally, the producer is not always able to ensure a routing of his products towards the purchaser. Indeed, even if negotiations, contractual agreement and invoicing (electronic payment) can be made digital, the routing of the product remains a material problem. As reminded by Brousseau (2002), the space proximity and the physical meeting between protagonists thus remain significant.

Consequently, the disintermediation hypothesis is not entirely justified since it is stated only in terms of cost reduction (transaction costs theory), without tackling the question of the added value of intermediation (Benda 2004) and the role of the intermediary as an economic agent (Tran 2004).

14.2.2 From Electronic Intermediation to Infomediation

The previous analysis leads us to conclude the following: while it is clear that the existence of the intermediaries is not threatened, it is also clear that their role has to change considerably (Baile and Trahand 1999). Consequently, one can expect an adaptation of the traditional intermediaries to the new needs generated by the information society, but also the emergence of new virtual actors with a tendency to exploit specific niches (Biglaiser 1993).

The so-called re-intermediation hypothesis finds its roots in the latter observation. It comes as a reaction to the preceding disintermediation theory, which is considered as too peremptory and not realistic enough. Behind the re-intermediation term thus hides the electronic intermediation which, as we mentioned earlier, is inherent in various electronic platforms (Brynjolfsson and Seidmann 1997). Electronic intermediaries turn out to be essential from a strategic point of view because information on the Internet reaches an extreme level of complexity (in quantitative as well as qualitative terms). The latter finding casts serious doubts on the earlier argument according to which the Internet minimizes search costs (Giaglis 2002). In addition, electronic intermediaries represent a significant medium for firms confronted with an increasingly uncertain environment, as it allows sharing information in a very short period of time (Baumard and Benvenuti 1998). An EMP is defined as an interorganizational information system that allows and facilitates Internet-based commercial relationships among multiple buyers and sellers (Akoka and Lang 2002). So, EMPs might be considered as virtual shopping malls and in the existing literature it is usual to find EMPs and OIPs used as synonyms (Benda 2004). However, we wish here to establish a distinction between these two virtual entities.

At first glance, OIPs and EMPs seem to be relatively similar since both are electronic places that provide higher market-exposure to the seller and attract a great number of buyers. Nevertheless, their roles are quite different. On the one hand, EMPs act as traditional intermediaries, which means that they do not just play a role of matching both sides of the market. They also provide a complete service from the beginning to the finalization of the transaction, so that both sides never enter directly in contact. For providing this service, EMPs generally charge a com mission, which represents transaction costs and a profit margin. On the other hand, OIPs only play an information role. They do not care whether the transaction works successfully out, but they improve coordination between the two sides of the market, allowing buyers and sellers to manage the whole transaction by themselves. In this latter case, it is not longer possible for the infomediary to control transactions, so that they prefer to charge one or both sides of the market with a fixed fee (wright 2004).

So, while an EMP clearly allows participants to trade directly, the OIP only aims at providing information (Spulber 2003).

In the present article, we refer to an OIP as any system whose objective is to collect the information available on particular products and services in order to present it in a comprehensive, organized, synthetic and easily accessible form, to the attention of the buyer. Consequently, it represents an information tool and not a transaction tool, as is the case for an EMP. An OIP can thus be considered as a type of innovating intermediary thanks to which information gains in credibility (Oxley and Yeung 2001). To support this terminological differentiation, the literature has coined the term of *infomediary* (Ordanini and Pal 2001), which usefully characterizes an OIP. An infomediary is traditionally defined as a merchant of information. This information concerns either the buyer or the supplier of goods and services.

In the first case, the infomediary collects data concerning a particular population of buyers, it analyses and structures this data to obtain useful information that it then sells to a supplier, which is directly concerned with the population and the corresponding market. Hence, the infomediary in contact with the market follows the evolution and the tendency of this market and contributes to a certain extent to the development of the offer (Giaglis 2002). In the second case, the infomediary collects data about multiple producers and suppliers of the same good or service in order to propose this information to the potential buyers present on this market segment and requesting a high degree of transparency and comparability of information.

Figure 14.1 presents the most outstanding differences between an EMP and an OIP as we conceive them here. This shows that these two different platforms do not respond to identical needs. Actually, an EMP is more specifically addressed to a supplier who wants to outsource his sale function, whereas an OIP responds to a promotion need. Hence, while a supplier who is not able -or does not want- to ensure transactions tends to join an EMP, a supplier who is not able -or does not want- to ensure its promotion function tends to join an OIP.[1]

For infomediation to exist, it is necessary that the activity add some value, exactly as for traditional intermediation. If information relates to the buyer side, there is room for an infomediary only if the supplier is not able to observe, to collect and to treat the data itself. If information relates to the seller side, the infomediation activity is useful if it is difficult for a buyer to observe the whole supply of goods and services. The latter situation can be attributed to various reasons: very fragmented market, difficult access to information, lack of time, consumer not very inclined to support the search costs, etc.

EMP	OIP
Ensures a restrictive promotion (without informational transparency)	Ensures a wide promotion (with informational transparency)
Becomes actor of the transaction	Remains outside the transaction
Endorse responsibilities as for the realization of the transaction	Endorses responsibilities as for the veracity of information
The intermediation cost is generally supported by the buyer	The infomediation cost is generally supported by the supplier

Fig. 14.1 Differences between EMP and OIP

[1]Clearly, reality is a bit more complex than that as an EMP also achieves a promotional role, and as sellers have the opportunity to simultaneously register with and EMP an an OIP (for instance, a supplier may go to an OIP because this gives him a larger promotion scope, and simultaneously adhere to an EMP in order to increase his sales). The latter phenomenon is usually referred to as "multihoming". Considering the complexities resulting from multihoming (which can also exist on the buyers' side) goes beyond the scope of the present analysis.

Fig. 14.2 Organization of concepts

General	Interorganizational Information Systems on the Internet	
Category	Electronic Marketplaces (EMP)	Online Information Platforms (OIP)
Tourism	eTravel Agencies	eTravel Databases
Activity	Intermediation	Infomediation

In the e-Tourism sector, lots of websites are OIPs.[2] Information concerns the supply of tourism services as noted above and is proposed to people organizing a city trip or any other kind of holiday. It is useful to recall that the tourism sector benefits considerably from the possibilities offered by the Internet (Rayman and Molina 2001, Buhalis 2001). Indeed, a large range of transactions related to the tourism sector is nowadays very common (buying plane tickets on the web; participating to holidays online auctions; searching sunny destinations on the web instead of using paper catalogues; etc). In such a context, the presence of an OIP can therefore prove to be necessary and justified (Doolin et al. 2002).

EMPs can also be identified in the tourism sector as electronic travel agencies on which it is possible to choose a product, to carry out the reservation, and even to secure the payment of the stay by electronic payment.[3] As for the case of traditional agencies, they are remunerated on the basis of a commission, which is generally directly integrated by marking up the basic price of the product established by the supplier. Contrary to the information platform, the booking platform does not support informational transparency. Firstly, regarding product information, we note that EMPs do not post the real prices of the products or services: prices include an additional fee (the commission) that is meant to compensate the EMP for its services. Secondly, regarding information about suppliers, travel agencies maintain it secret in order to prevent buyers from directly contacting suppliers and thereby, bypassing the EMP's intermediation process. Indeed, an increasing number of suppliers are equipped in computer systems, which allows them to manage themselves the requests and services related to the booking. Figure 14.2 summarizes our comparison between EMP and OIP. We now turn to the analysis of the relationships between participants in the same platform.

14.3 Coopetition on an Electronic Platform

Before analyzing the links existing between platform participants, we will first see why these different actors join an OIP or an EMP. As for a buyer, the benefit of joining an electronic platform is twofold. Firstly, the buyer has access to a large number

[2]Here are a few examples of tourism oriented OIPs: calagtour.org, egypthotelsdb.com, ruralindex.net, ruraltrip.com.

[3]Some examples of tourism oriented EMPs are: booking.com, nouvelles-frontieres.com, travelonline.com, govoyages.com.

of suppliers in a single place, which clearly reduces his search costs. Indeed, as we mentioned before, the profusion of information currently available on the Internet does not make it possible any more to consider this medium of communication as a low search cost tool. Let us notice that if the monetary cost has strongly dropped (because telecommunication tariffs have been in constant fall over the last years and also because of the emergence of free online communication tools), the search cost due to the constant growth of the mass of information on the Internet appreciably increased.[4] Secondly, the buyer is confronted with information coming straight from the supplier, which guarantees prices that are not skewed by a commissioning mechanism and also a direct bond with the supplier to start a transaction.

Concerning the supplier, his interest is economic as well as strategic. The economic advantage stems from the fact that by joining a platform the supplier partly externalizes his promotion function to an agent, which carries it out at a lower cost (economies of scale) and facilitates coordination between the two sides of the market. Participating in an electronic platform also yields strategic benefits as it allows the supplier to access new markets and thus to gain new market shares at the expense of suppliers who remain outside the network (Benda 2004). However, the supplier who joins an EMP or an OIP is forced to share these competitive advantages with the rival suppliers who already joined the platform.

In her work about EMPs, Benda identifies three types of suppliers on the basis of their perception of the stakes they have in the collaboration: *refractories*, *non refractories* and *proactives* (Benda 2004). Instead of giving a formal definition for each category, we adapt it hereafter to our e-Tourism framework.

Refractory suppliers are not present on a platform because they consider that their own online promotion methods or their other advertising campaigns are largely sufficient. In the majority of the cases, these suppliers ensure an effective presence on the Internet by using their advanced competences in computer science. By doing this and despite lower means than those implemented by the intermediary, they attract enough visitors to be satisfied.

Non refractory suppliers are participating in the platform as long as their participation in it gets them a higher turnover. Moreover, they require that the profits be higher than the cost of participation. If the intermediary is in its development stage, such suppliers minimize their participation (for example by subscribing to a free trial promotion) while waiting to see whether the platform's development will be beneficial for them or not.

Proactive suppliers are also on the platform. They consider that it can help them at various levels. Firstly, they are convinced that as an actor of the tourism sector, a successful presence on the Internet is essential. Secondly, they find the intermediary useful to benefit from a virtual quality window, which will give a positive image of their services. Thirdly, they note an increase of their sales, even if it is difficult to quantify these repercussions.

[4] As Varian et Lyman (2002) document it, 550 billion new documents and more than 7,5 million Web pages are created every day.

Whether they are non-refractory or proactive, suppliers collaborate in the construction and the development of the electronic platform simply through their participation in it. From this point of view, it seems correct to say that they act like partners pursuing a common goal: the mutualisation of means in order to conquer a larger share of the market. However, from the fact that these suppliers propose services and products relating to the same sector, there exists a possibility of comparability. They remain thus also competitors. We wish to underline the paradoxical character of an ambivalent relationship between several suppliers active on the same market, which can be established conceptually in two steps: initially, cooperation between economic agents to achieve a satisfactory common goal for all (in the present case, an increase in the market size); then, competition between the same agents in order to enjoy individually the benefits of the cooperation (here, the largest possible share of the market).

Such a competing collaboration is usually justified by three goals: the research of a critical size, the mutualization of costs and the introduction of barriers for new entrants (Tran 2004). For the tourism sector facing globalization, the research of a critical size is fundamental. In a context of global competition, it is easy to understand that cost mutualization appears as a natural way to a widened and effective action. Lastly, given that the sector under review remains largely open (the leisure and accommodation supply increases significantly every year), the participation to an electronic platform can, from a strategic point of view, be used to minimize strong competition by establishing barriers to entry.

The main characteristic of the coopetition phenomenon (Koenig 1996) is to combine simultaneously a collective strategy (cooperation, i.e. participation to the same platform and contribution of each supplier to the development of this platform) and several individual strategies (competition as the participants to the same platform remain competitors with one another) (Nalebuff and Brandenburger 1996, Bengtsson and Kock 2002). Coopetition is a helpful theory to analyze tourism economics and strategy. Moreover, the concept has been recently used in the case of tourism firms (Pesämaa and Eriksson 2006, Della Corte and Sciarelli 2006).

Figure 14.3 illustrates this concept starting from two competing suppliers active on the same market and potentially on the same platform. If the two agents stay out of the platform, they play the traditional game of competition. If only one of the suppliers joins the platform, then he has a competitive advantage over the other, insofar as he benefits alone from the entire common infrastructure created. However, it is obvious that for this participation to be transformed into a durable competitive advantage, it is necessary that the intermediary gives itself the means of being known on the buyers' side. Lastly, as we already described it, if both suppliers join the platform, they play the ambivalent game of coopetition: competition is

		Does S1 join the platform?	
		Yes	**No**
Does S2 join the platform?	**Yes**	Coopetition	Advantage for S2
	No	Advantage for S1	Competition

Fig. 14.3 Coopetition vs. competition

strong because suppliers are on an equal foot, but joint participation makes the platform more attractive for buyers, which increases expected profits for both suppliers. In the next section, we develop an industrial organization model to formalize this situation.

14.4 A Formal Model of Coopetition on a Platform

To analyze the strategic interaction between an intermediary holding a virtual platform and its potential adherents, we consider the following three-stage game: in the first stage, the intermediary sets a registration fee F that suppliers must pay to use its services; in the second stage, the suppliers observe F and simultaneously decide whether or not to register with the intermediary; in the third stage, the suppliers simultaneously choose the quantity of services they provide. We solve the game backwards for its subgame-perfect Nash equilibria.

To get the main insights from the modelization, we start with a simplified situation with only two suppliers of accommodation. Next, we generalize our results assuming an arbitrary number of suppliers.

14.4.1 A Model with 2 Suppliers

Suppose there are two suppliers of accommodation, noted 1 and 2 , and a single intermediary. The inverse demand function for the service provided by supplier i is given by $p_i = 1 + m_i - q_i - dq_j$ $(i \neq j \in \{1,2\})$ where

- p_i is the price for one unit of service (say, e.g., one night per person in the accommodation),
- q_i and q_j are the quantities of service provided respectively by suppliers i and j (these quantities can be thought of as the accommodation capacity, e.g., the number of rooms or of beds),
- $d \in (0,1)$ is an inverse measure of product differentiation between the services of the two suppliers (the lower d, the more services are differentiated; for $d = 0$, the two services are totally differentiated and the two demands are independent; at the other extreme, for $d = 1$, the two services are seen as perfectly substitutable), and
- m_i indicates the "market-exposure" (or *brand recognition*) of service i (the larger m_i, the higher the willingness to pay of each consumer whatever the quantities q_i and q_j produced by the firms).

Before competing *à la Cournot* on the product market (i.e., suppliers simultaneously set their quantity, taking the quantity of the rival as given), suppliers observe the registration fee F charged by the intermediary and decide whether or not to register. Being listed on the intermediary's website has the effect of increasing the supplier's market exposure (with respect to self-promotion via other means). Moreover, infomediation generates network effects insofar as each supplier's exposure further increases when the other supplier also registers with the intermediary. As explained above, such network effects can be justified by scale and scope economies in promotional activities enjoyed by the intermediary, and because consumers are willing to pay more for both services when they are given the opportunity to compare them more easily. We translate this idea by assuming that $m_i = 0$ when supplier i does not adhere to the intermediary, $m_i = m$ when supplier i is the only supplier who adheres to the intermediary, and $m_i = M$ when both suppliers adhere to the intermediary, with $0 < m < M$.

The registration with the intermediary also lowers the cost of supplying accommodation. The supplier indeed outsources a share of its transaction costs to the intermediary. When an accommodation is on the intermediary's website for instance, the supplier does not have to promote its services anymore since it is already done by the intermediary. Let us remind that we assume here that the supplier does not have the opportunity to multihome since there exists only one intermediating platform. Accordingly, we denote the constant marginal cost of accommodation services by c for a supplier who does not register with the intermediary, and by γ for a supplier who does, and we assume $\gamma < c < 1$.

14.4.1.1 Production Decisions

We start by solving the Cournot game suppliers play at stage 3. Supplier i's profit function can be written as $\pi_i = (1 + m_i - q_i - dq_j)q_i - c_i q_i$. Setting to zero the derivative of profit with respect to q_i, we derive supplier i's reaction function: $q_i(q_j) = \frac{1}{2}(1 + m_i - c_i - dq_j)$. We proceed in the same way for the other supplier. Solving for the system of equations in two unknowns given by the two reaction functions, we find the Nash equilibrium quantities and profits:

$$q_i^* = \frac{2 - d + 2(m_i - c_i) - d\left(m_j - c_j\right)}{4 - d^2}, \pi_i^* = (q_i^*)^2, i \neq j \in \{1, 2\}. \qquad (14.1)$$

In the above expression, the exact values of (m_i, c_i) and $\left(m_j, c_j\right)$ depend on the adhesion decisions made by the suppliers at stage 2 (we note A for 'adhesion' and N for 'non adhesion'). There are three situations to consider.

- If no supplier adheres to the platform, then $(m_i, c_i) = \left(m_j, c_j\right) = (0, c)$. Substituting these values into expression (1.1), we obtain the equilibrium profits, which are the same for the two suppliers:

$$\pi_i = \pi_j = \pi^{NN} = \left(\frac{1-c}{2+d}\right)^2.$$

- If supplier i adheres while supplier j does not, then $(m_i, c_i) = (m,\gamma)$ and $\left(m_j, c_j\right) = (0, c)$. In that case, the suppliers' equilibrium profits differ and are respectively given by[5]

$$\pi_i = \pi^{AN} = \left(\frac{2-d+2(m-\gamma)+dc}{4-d^2}\right)^2 - F,$$

$$\pi_j = \pi^{NA} = \left(\frac{2-d-2c-d(m-\gamma)}{4-d^2}\right)^2.$$

- Finally, if both suppliers adhere to the platform, then $(m_i, c_i) = (m_j, c_j) = (M, \gamma)$. We use again expression (1.1) to find the equilibrium profits for the two suppliers as

$$\pi_i = \pi_j = \pi^{AA} = \left(\frac{1+M-\gamma}{2+d}\right)^2 - F.$$

14.4.1.2 Coopetition

Before looking for the equilibrium adhesion decisions at stage 2, we want to illustrate what coopetition means in the present setting. As explained in the previous section, *coopetition* mixes some form of *cooperation* (which is translated here by the assumption that $M > m$, i.e. market exposure is larger when both suppliers register with the intermediary) and of *competition* (adhesion decisions are strategic, i.e. they are carried out with a view to affecting the environment in which product market competition is played). To assess how these two opposite forces balance each other, we compute how equilibrium profit changes when the other supplier also registers with the intermediary. That is, we compare π^{AN} with π^{AA}. Simple computations establish that:

$$\pi^{AA} > \pi^{AN} \Leftrightarrow 2(M-m) > dM + d(c-\gamma). \tag{14.2}$$

Condition (14.2) says that each supplier welcomes the adhesion of the other supplier to the platform as long as this adhesion generates more benefits (on the left-hand side) than costs (on the right-hand side). The benefits (or the *cooperation effect*) stem from the increased exposure, $(M-m)$, that affects the Cournot equilibrium quantity by a factor 2. The costs (or the *competition effect*) are due to the improved competitive position of the rival supplier: by adhering, the rival supplier boosts its exposure (from 0 to M) and reduces its marginal cost (from c to γ); the impact of these two effects on the Cournot equilibrium quantity are proportional to d. We thus see that the cooperation effect is more likely to dominate the competition effect (i) the larger the network effects (measured by the increased exposure, $M-m$) and (ii) the lower the intensity of competition between the two suppliers (measured by the degree of product substitutability, d).

[5] We restrict the attention to parameter configurations such that $2-d-2c-d(m-\gamma) > 0$.

14.4.1.3 Registration Decisions

We now turn to stage 2 of the game and analyze the suppliers' decision to register with the intermediary. Supposing that supplier j does not register, supplier i prefers to register provided that

$$\pi^{AN} \geq \pi^{NN} \Leftrightarrow F \leq \left(\frac{2-d+2(m-\gamma)+dc}{4-d^2}\right)^2 - \left(\frac{1-c}{2+d}\right)^2 \equiv F_1. \qquad (14.3)$$

It is clear that each supplier is willing to pay a positive amount, i.e. $F_1 > 0$, to be the sole adherent to the intermediary, as it increases exposure (from 0 to m) and reduces marginal cost (from c to γ), without improving the rival firm's situation.

Similarly, supposing now that supplier j does register, supplier i prefers to register as well provided that

$$\pi^{AA} \geq \pi^{NA} \Leftrightarrow F \leq \left(\frac{1+M-\gamma}{2+d}\right)^2 - \left(\frac{2-d-2c-d(m-\gamma)}{4-d^2}\right)^2 \equiv F_2. \qquad (14.4)$$

As in the previous case, adhesion reduces marginal cost from c to γ . In terms of exposure, the effect is mixed. Compared to the previous case, the increase in exposure is larger (from 0 to M) but the rival supplier also benefits (its exposure increases from m to M). Yet, the former effect clearly dominates the latter, meaning that each supplier is also willing to pay a positive amount, i.e. $F_2 > 0$, to join the other supplier on the intermediary's platform.[6]

The ranking of the two thresholds, F_1 and F_2, depends on the parameter values. We need thus to distinguish between two cases.

Case A: $F_2 > F_1$. In that case, a supplier is willing to pay more for the intermediary's services when the two suppliers use them. This means that the cooperation effect dominates the competition effect. The Nash equilibrium of the second stage is then characterized as follows:

$$\begin{cases} \text{for } F \leq F_1, & \text{2 registrations,} \\ \text{for } F_1 < F \leq F_2, & \text{0 or 2 registrations,} \\ \text{for } F > F_2, & \text{no registration.} \end{cases}$$

We observe that an intermediate fee ($F_1 < F \leq F_2$) generates multiple equilibria (0 or 2 registrations). We are then in a typical coordination game: each supplier finds it optimal to mimic the choice of the other supplier because registration is worthwhile if it increases market exposure from m to M, but not from 0 to m.

[6]However, as we discussed above, a supplier might not want *to be joined* if the competition effect dominates the cooperation effect (that is, it is possible to have $\pi^{AN} > \pi^{AA} > \pi^{NA}$).

Case B: $F_2 < F_1$. Here, a supplier is willing to pay more for the intermediary's services when it is the only one to use them. For that case to be observed, the competition effect must be sufficiently stronger than the cooperation effect (i.e., d must be large and $(M - m)$ small). The Nash equilibrium of the second stage is then characterized as follows:

$$\begin{cases} \text{for } F \leq F_2, & \text{2 registrations,} \\ \text{for } F_2 < F \leq F_1, & \text{1 registration,} \\ \text{for } F > F_1, & \text{no registration.} \end{cases}$$

In contrast with Case A, we observe here that any fee set by the intermediary generates a unique equilibrium.

14.4.1.4 Intermediary's Pricing Decision

We are now in a position to derive the intermediary's optimal conduct in stage 1. We distinguish again between two cases. In Case A, the intermediary attracts either the two suppliers or none of them. He is sure to attract them if he sets $F \leq F_1$. If he raises the fee up to F_2, he still has a chance of attracting the two suppliers, but this depends on the suppliers coordinating on this equilibrium. However, the suppliers might as well coordinate on the other equilibrium and refrain both from registering. If the intermediary is unable to coordinate the choices of the suppliers, it seems reasonable to predict that he will prefer to play it safe by setting $F = F_1$.

In Case B, the intermediary knows that to attract the two suppliers, it has to lower the registration fee from F_1 to F_2 (as each supplier is willing to pay less when the other supplier also joins). The intermediary finds it profitable to do so as long as $2F_2 > F_1$. Whether this inequality is satisfied or not depends on the parameter values.

Collecting the previous results, we can characterize the subgame-perfect equilibrium of the game as follows:

- if $F_1 \leq F_2$, the intermediary sets $F = F_1$ and the two suppliers register;
- if $F_2 \leq F_1 \leq 2F_2$, the intermediary sets $F = F_2$ and the two suppliers register;
- if $F_1 \geq 2F_2$, the intermediary sets $F = F_1$ and only one supplier registers.

14.4.1.5 EMP vs OIP

The previous analysis can easily be enriched by considering that the intermediary can either be an EMP or an OIP. As argued in the previous sections, an EMP has both a transactional and informational role, while an OIP only has the latter. It seems thus reasonable to assume that an EMP generates a larger reduction in transaction costs for its adherents than an OIP. In the present model, we could write $\gamma^e < \gamma^o$, where the superscrits e and o refer respectively to an EMP and an OIP. A quick look at expressions (14.3) and (14.4) reveals that both F_1 and F_2 decrease with γ. Hence, we have $F_1^e > F_1^o$ and $F_2^e > F_2^o$. This implies, not surprisingly, that an EMP is able to charge higher fees than an OIP. Alternatively, if an EMP charges the same fee as an OIP, it is able to capture a share of its members' profits by charging variable fees (i.e. a commission, up to the difference $\gamma^o - \gamma^e$), without loosing adherents.

14.4.2 Extension to Several Suppliers

The previous model can be generalized to an arbitrary number of suppliers, $N > 2$, by letting the exposure parameter m_i be equal to αn when supplier i adheres to the intermediary along with $(n-1)$ other suppliers (with $\alpha > 0$) and, as before, equal to zero when supplier i does not adhere. Naturally, this increases the complexity of the model. So, to gain some insight, we compensate by simplifying the cost structure. In what follows, we assume that registration with the intermediary does not reduce the marginal cost of supplying accommodation; in particular, we pose $c = \gamma = 0$.

Under these assumptions, we can again solve for the subgame-perfect equilibria of the three-stage game. Supposing that n (with $0 < n < N$) suppliers have joined the intermediary at stage 2 of the game, we denote by $\pi^{in}(n)$ the equilibrium profit at stage 3 of a typical supplier who joined the intermediary (and who is thus is among the n " in" suppliers); similarly, let $\pi^{out}(n)$ denote the equilibrium profit of a typical supplier who did not join the intermediary (and who is thus among the $N-n$ " out" suppliers).[7]

Let us first give a more precise assessment of the coopetition phenomenon. As above, we want to assess how a member's equilibrium profit changes when an additional supplier joins the intermediary. We therefore compute the difference $\pi^{in}(n+1)-\pi^{in}(n)$. Focusing here on the case of homogeneous products (i.e., $d = 1$), we can readily establish that *the change in profit is positive if and only if the intermediary comprises less than half of the population of suppliers* (i.e., if $n < N/2$). The corollary of this result is that, as the intermediary grows larger than this critical size, the equilibrium profit of each member decreases when an additional firm joins the intermediary. The intuition for this result is akin to the one we described in the case with two suppliers. In such a setting, the enlargement of the intermediary's member base induces two simultaneous contrasting effects on the members' profits: on the one hand, the members benefit from the increase in the demand they face (a positive "cooperation effect"), but on the other hand, they suffer from increased competition due to the increased demand that their competitors enjoy as well (a negative "competition effect"). As a result, there is a critical size after which the admission of new members on an electronic pltaform has an adverse effect on the initial members' profit.

Now, turning to stage 1 of the game, we would like to measure how much a supplier is willing to pay in order to become the nth member of the intermediary. This supplier would be willing to pay up to its change in profits: $f(n) \equiv \pi^{in}(n) -$

[7]A technical appendix containing the detailed computations can be obtained from the authors upon request.

$\pi^{out}(n-1)$, i.e., the difference between the profit after joining the intermediary (when n suppliers are with the intermediary) and the profit before joining (when only $n-1$ were with the intermediary).[8] The function $f(n)$ can be interpreted as a demand function for the intermediary's services: for a given quantity of service (i.e., for a given number n of members), $f(n)$ indicates the highest membership fee at which the service can be sold. The optimal level of the membership fee can thus be indirectly obtained by letting the intermediary select the optimal number of members, i.e., the number n^* that maximizes the intermediary's profit, $\Pi(n) = nf(n)$. Some line of computations establish that the first derivative of $\Pi(n)$ with respect to n is negative at $n = N$. This implies that *the intermediary never finds it profitable to induce full membership: the intermediary's optimum is to attract a strict subset of the existing pool of suppliers*. The intuition for this result is again to be found in the coopetition phenomenon.

14.5 Discussion and Research Questions

In this paper, we introduce various business issues related to intermediation and electronic markets. First, even if intermediaries will continue to play a role in the digital economy, we note that they will be increasingly confronted to infomediation. Indeed, infomediaries emerge nowadays as a new category of intermediaries in a business context where buyers and sellers interact more easily with one another but still need to process a lot of information. Second, whether they are buyers or sellers, participants in the same electronic platform are in a particular position since they cooperate to the collective success of the platform while they remain competitors. We refer to the strategic concept of *coopetition* to describe this ambivalent reality. Third, we develop an economic model of an electronic platform built on industrial organization theory. The main analytical results drawn from this simple model are that (i) suppliers might suffer from the participation of other suppliers in the same platform (because the competition effect might be stronger than the cooperation effect), and (ii) the platform owner never finds it optimal to attract all suppliers.

To conclude our analysis, we propose several directions for future research. First, several empirical studies show the importance of the competing advantages related to the participation in an electronic platform (Brousseau 2002) and of the integration of the Internet –and the ICT in general– to the strategy of the firm. However, if one considers the same market or common branch of industry, it is possible to meet several platforms that enter in competition (Tran 2004). This latter phenomenon can be seen as a move of competition from an individual dimension (agent against agent) to a collective dimension (platform against platform). In order to shed some light on

[8] It can be shown that $f(n)$ first increases with n, then reaches a maximum and then starts to decrease with n; the reason for the decrease is to be found in the competition effect which makes $\pi^{in}(n)$ decrease with n for $n > N/2$.

this platform competition, we can rely on the industrial organization theory and its concept of *two-sided market* (Jullien 2005, Rochet and Tirole 2003, Amstrong and Wright 2007). Indeed, with electronic platforms we are in the presence of positive indirect network effects since the more agents there are on one side of the platform (e.g., suppliers), the higher the agents' utility on the other side (e.g., buyers).

With respect to the model we developed in the previous section (with a single intermediary and several suppliers), the literature on two-sided markets offers two useful extensions. First, the buyers' side is explicitly modelled. That is, buyers also choose whether or not to register with a platform and their willingness to do so increases with the (expected) number of sellers present on the platform.[9] Second, several platforms compete to get both the suppliers and the buyers on board.

Concerning the latter issue, existing models examine the competition between two symmetric, possibily horizontally differentiated, platforms. However, this approach is not completely satisfactory for the tourism sector, as we observe two important additional complexities. First, the competition is between vertically differentiated platforms. That is, EMPs and OIPs target the same two groups (suppliers of accommodation and tourists) but offer different intermediation services, and may use different pricing modes. Second, buyers and sellers keep the opportunity to transact directly, i.e. without using the intermediation services provided by the platforms.

To the best of our knowledge, such issues have not been tackled so far in the literature (either in industrial organization or in strategy). We see thus there a promising area for future research. In particular, we identify a number of questions that should be investigated, both on theoretical and on empirical grounds:

- What are the best pricing strategies in the competition between vertically differentiated platforms? Is the high-quality platform able to charge higher prices on both sides of the market? Is the low-quality platform forced to pursue a niche strategy?
- Since buyers and suppliers facing several platforms may decide to multihome, what does it imply for the competitive game among platforms?
- Beyond competition between various types of platforms, there exist positive externalities between their activities, which are advantageous for each of them. What is the exact nature of such externalities and how do they affect competition?

References

Akoka J, Lang D (2002) Les places de marché électroniques et reconfiguration des processus interorganisationnels. Actes du 7`eme colloque de l'AIM, Tunisie

Armstrong M, Wright J (2007) Two-sided markets, competitive bottlenecks and exclusive contracts. Econ Theo, 32(2):353–380

[9]In our model, the indirect network effects on the buyers' side are implicitly taken into account through the demand expansion resulting from increased suppliers' participation.

Baile S, Trahand J (1999) Les systèmes d'information interorganisationnels, contributions et cadre des recherches. Systèmes d'Information et Management 4(2):3–17

Bailey J, Bakos Y (1997) An exploratory study of the emerging role of electronic intermediaries. Int J Electron Comm 1(3):7–20

Baumard P, Benvenuti JA (1998) Compétitivité et systémes d'information: de l'outil d'analyse au management stratégique. Inter Editions, Paris, 249p

Benda J (2004) L'utilisation d'une place de marché électronique : une stratégie collective contre des stratégies individuelles ? – une étude exploratoire de trois cas. Actes de la 13`eme conférence de l'AIMS

Bengtsson M, Kock S (2000) Coopetition in business networks – to cooperate and compete simultaneously. Ind Mark Manage 29(5):411–426

Biglaiser G (1993) Middlemen as experts. RAND J Econ 24(2):212–223

Brousseau E (2002) The governance of transactions by commercial intermediaries: an analysis of the re-engineering of intermediation by electronic commerce. Int J Econ Bus 9(3):353–374

Brynjolfsson E, Seidmann A (1997) A call for exploration: introduction to special issue on frontier research on information systems and economics. Manage Sci 43(12):1605–1607

Buhalis D, Licata MC (2002) The future eTourism intermediaries. Tourism Manage 23(3):207–220

Buhalis D (2001) Tourism and cyberspace. Ann Tourism Res 28(1):232–235

Caillaud B, Jullien B (2003) Competing cybermediaries. Eur Econ Rev 45:797–808

Curchod C (2006) Stratégies d'intermédiation et dynamiques des marchés: une relecture du phénomène Internet. Actes de la 15ème conférence de l'AIMS. Genève, 13–16 juin

Della Corte V, Sciarelli M (2006) Coopetition among tourist destinations: a resource based theory perspective. 2nd Workshop on Coopetition Strategy, Milan

Doolin B, Burgess L, Cooper J (2002) Evaluating the use of theWeb for tourism marketing: a case study from New Zealand. Tourism Manage 23(5):557–561

Edgell DL, Haenisch RT (1995) Coopetition: global tourism beyond the millennium. International Policy Publishing, Kansas City, 148p

Evans DJ, Hagiu A, Schmalensee R (2005) A surbey of the economic role of software platforms in computer-based industries. CES Econ Stud 51:189–224

Giaglis MG (2002) Towards a predictive model for electronic marketplaces intermediation opportunities. Working paper, University of the Aegean, Chios, Greece. 18 Paul Belleflamme and Nicolas Neysen

González AG (2004) PayPal: the legal status of C2C payment systems. Comput Law Security Report 20(4):293–299

Jullien B (2005) Two-sided markets and electronic intermediaries. CES Econ Stud 51:235–262

Koenig G (1996) Management stratégique: paradoxes, interactions et apprentissages: construction et gestion des activités. Management d'exigences contradictoires, Nathan, Paris, 543p

Lin A (2006) The acceptance and use of a business-to-business information system. Int J Inform Manage 26(5):386–400

Malone TW, Yates J, Benjamin R (1987) Electronic markets and electronic hierarchies. Commun ACM 30(6):484–497

Nalebuff BJ, Brandenburger AM (1996) Co-opetition. Profile books, London, 289p

Ordanini A, Pol A (2001) Infomediation and competitive advantage in b2b digital marketplaces. Eur Manage J 19(3):276–285

Oxley JE, Yeung B (2001) E-commerce readiness: institutional environment and international competitiveness. J Int Bus Stud 32(4):705–723

Pesämaa O, Eriksson E (2006) Coopetition among nature-based tourism firms: competition at a local level and cooperation at a destination level. 2nd Workshop on coopetition strategy, Milan

Rayman L, Molina A (2001) Internet-based tourism services: business issues and trends. Futures 33(7):589–605

Rochet J-C, Tirole J (2003) Platform competition in two-sided markets. J Eur Econ Assoc n_1: 990–1029

Rubinstein A, Wolinsky A (1987) Middelmen. Q J Econ 102::581–593

Spulber DF (2003) The intermediation theory of the firm: integrating economic and management approaches to strategy. Manage Decis Econ 24:253–266

Spulber DF (1996) Market microstructure and intermediation. J Econ Perspect 10(3):135–152

Tran S (2004) Systèmes d'information inter-organisationnels et processus concurrentiels: le cas des places de marché électroniques. Document de travail, Université Paris IX Dauphine, Paris

Varian H, Lyman P (2002) How much information? University of California in Berkeley, Berkeley, California

Wright J (2004) The determinants of optimal interchange fees in payment systems. J Ind Econ 52:1–26

Chapter 15
Do Tourism Firms Have Economic Incentives to Undertake Voluntary Environmental Initiatives?

Esther Blanco, Javier Lozano, and Javier Rey-Maquieira

15.1 Introduction

Sustainable development of tourism destinations is one of the growing topics in tourism literature. Initially, research on this respect focused only on the negative ecological impacts derived from tourism growth (see Hunter and Green 1995; OECD 1980 among others). Later, the discussion gained more balance between the positive and negative environmental impacts and the inclusion of the economic and social arenas in the analysis (Farrell and Twining-Ward 2004; Garrod and Fyall 1998; Hunter-Jones 1997; Hunter 1997; Rege 2000; Ritchie and Crouch 2003; WTO 1999, 2004a, b). Still, the governance arena has only tangentially been addressed, and environmental policy-making has relied on traditional policy prescriptions where public administrations are assumed to play a crucial role as central planners.

Literature on institutional analysis demonstrates that, in addition to command-and-and control initiatives, there is a wide range of alternative institutional designs for the governance of natural assets (Ostrom 1990). Among them, voluntary actions by users of natural resources are particularly relevant for tourism. Either best practices (as the tour operators initiatives for sustainable tourism), environmental management systems (as ISO 14001 and EMAS) or tourism collaborations and partnerships for sustainability (see some examples in Bramwell and Lane 2000; WTO 2001) are emerging in many tourism destinations, thus demonstrating their viability. Considering these voluntary initiatives for policy-making requires information on the economic incentives behind their emergence and stability. Research in the area has been mainly descriptive and lacks analytical and theoretical richness. This analytical vigor would be necessary to allow researchers to deeply understand current situations and to use previous experiences towards future improvements in policy design.

The objective of the present chapter is to analyze empirical evidence on voluntary environmental action at tourism destinations. This is done in order to extract

E. Blanco (✉)
University of the Balearic Islands, Edifici Jovellanos, Balears, Spain
e-mail: ester.blanco@uib.es

Á. Matias et al. (eds.), *Advances in Tourism Economics*,
DOI 10.1007/978-3-7908-2124-6_15, © Physica-Verlag Heidelberg 2009

evidence explaining economic incentives leading to the creation of voluntary initiatives for sustainability. Empirical studies show that results do not seem to support classic mainstream economic theory (which proposes free-riding as the dominate strategy for operating agents), on open access natural resources. Therefore, environmental policy-making should consider this evidence and reformulate the underlying assumptions on agents' behavior. The remainder of the paper is organized as follows: Section 15.2 presents the debate on "pays to be green". It reviews both the mainstream literature on the relationship between the environmental and economic performance of firms and the sub-branch of literature addressing tourism firms. Section 15.3 conceptualizes the evidence of Sect. 15.2 under a very simple game theory approach. This is done in order to analyze the strategic incentives of agents to undertake voluntary initiatives. This is a new conceptualization that has not previously been considered. Section 15.4 includes considerations to be made on the governance of natural assets. Finally, Sect. 15.5 serves as the conclusion.

15.2 Environmental and Economic Performance of Firms

The literature on the relationship between environmental and economic performance of tourism firms is very recent and scarce. The mainstream literature on the economic consequences from voluntary environmental action focuses on US manufacturing firms. The original motivation of this research is based on complaints by executive managers, during the 1960s and 70s, about more stringent environmental laws being passed by the US government. Increased environmental requirements were said to decrease firms' capacity to make profits, creating the wisdom of a trade-off between green and competitive firms. Since then, there has been an ongoing debate on the validity of this wisdom. Empirical research addressing this issue has not yet reached a consensus. This section starts by clarifying previous results regarding manufacturing firms by matching the results to specific research questions. Much of the debate on the relationship between environmental and economic performance for tourism firms is highly influenced by research on the manufacturing sector. Based on empirical similarities, it has been suggested that service firms can greatly benefit from the research, models and frameworks that have been developed to guide the environmental policies of manufacturers (Foster et al. 2000). Empirical results on the relationship between environmental and economic performance of tourism firms is presented in the second part of this section, along with the relationships with respect to research on the manufacturing industry.

15.2.1 The Mainstream Debate

Initial studies addressing the debate on the trade-off between being green or competitive approach the "pays to be green" question with an all-or-nothing ultimatum. These first studies mainly report a weak positive correlation between the environmental and economic performance of manufacturing firms, the significance of which varies for different time periods under consideration (Bragdon and Marlin 1972; Chen and Metcalf 1980; Jaggi and Freedman 1992; Mahapatra 1984; Spicer 1978). However, due to the small number of observations, these results are not representative of a reference population. In addition, it has been recognized that the question of whether or not it pays to be green cannot have an unconditional answer (Reinhardt 1999).

In order to disentangle the determinants within this debate, we have pursued a review of the research in this area, organizing it in the following specific research questions:

First, what green initiatives pay? Authors addressing this question show that there are no common economic consequences across all types of environmental management alternatives (Hart and Ahuja 1996; Judge and Douglas 1998; King and Lenox 2002; Klassen and Whybark 1999; Russo and Fouts 1997). In general, preventive strategies have been shown to generate increased economic results, while reactive approaches result in either insignificant or negative impacts on the bottom line.

Second, when does it pay to be green? In this case, the focus moves to the underlying attributes and bundles of capabilities that enable firms to obtain positive results from environmental actions. Some findings have been made in this area, showing that different combinations of resources and managerial decisions are relevant to determine economic consequences of environmental initiatives (Christmann 2000; King and Lenox 2002; Klassen and Whybark 1999).

Third, until when does it pay to be green? The background motivation of this research comes from the recognition that each firm has its optimum abatement level, where the marginal private cost of abatement equals the marginal private benefit of the last abated unit. Whenever environmental actions generate an economic gain, the initial abatement level is below its private optimum. However, after subsequent abatement efforts all firms will eventually reach their optimum, after which, economic loses will appear. Although the final conclusions of this research are still tentative, there is evidence to support the claim that the average threshold is situated well below the requirements established by current environmental regulations in the US. Therefore, firms are capable of generating economic gains by over-complying with environmental standards (Dowell et al. 2000; Konar and Cohen 2001).

Fourth, do stock-holders reward green firms? In fact, this question refers to whether there is a significant difference in the market returns for environmental responsible firms with respect to the general market. Results show a positive market reaction to environmental performance (Derwall et al. 2005; Guenster et al. 2006; Yamahita et al. 1999). However, it is still not clear whether this result comes from an actual positive stable valuation by the capital markets or from a temporary miss-pricing situation.

In sum, results show that different environmental strategies, for different types of firms, undertaken with different intensities, lead to both differences in significance and sign of the relation between environmental and economic performance variables. Therefore, current research is advanced enough to empirically demonstrate that in *some* occasions it actually pays to be green for the manufacturing industry while in others (as initially expected) it does not. Thus, it is important for executive managers to identify their particular situation before designing their preferred environmental strategy, if they chose a strategy at all.

15.2.2 The Debate for Tourism Firms

The literature on tourism firms lacks a well-defined structure. This is because this literature is recent and scarce, and therefore the richer research on the manufacturing industry might be useful in guiding future research and on conceptualizing theoretical backgrounds. Nevertheless, this recommendation should be taken with caution. There are special peculiarities of tourism firms that should be considered for the study of the relationship between environmental and economic performance in the tourism industry.

First of all, there are some important aspects that characterize the tourism industry, and that influence the innovative environmental-technological behavior of firms (Orfila-Sintes et al. 2005). These specificities are relevant to this study since environmental-technological innovations are an important source of enhanced environmental behavior. Some of these characteristics are presented below:

- Coterminality: Two contradicting effects have been proposed to derive from the close interaction between production and consumption. On the one hand, it is argued that customers' pressure on firms to improve their environmental behavior is higher when there is close contact (Ayuso 2006; Stoeckl 2004). On the other hand, it is argued that it can generate a situation of conflicting interests between environmental management and satisfaction (Foster et al. 2000; Grove et al. 1996; Kassinis and Soteriou 2005; Stoeckl 2004) or safety (Foster et al. 2000), concerns that are typically solved in a manner detrimental to environmental efforts.
- Time-perishability: It is argued that idle capacity implies wasted resources, with associated environmental pressures (Foster et al. 2000). Particularly referring to fixed environmental impacts (as an airplane trip), the higher the occupancy of the facilities, the lesser the unitary impact.
- Heterogeneity: The tourism industry is heterogeneous both on the type of firms being part of it and on the production within a given firm. This determines that, as shown by the literature on manufacturing, a proper analysis requires the question "when does it pay to be green?" That is, what specific characteristics of a firm rule the relationship between environmental performance and economic results (Grove et al. 1996). As shown below, empirical applications undertaken refer only to upper level accommodation establishments, and therefore results might be restricted to this dataset.
- Market factors and competition: Market structure is one of the important contextual factors determining the sign and strength of the relationship between economic and environmental performance of firms. Thus, complex structures in the tourism industry, where both suppliers (Orfila-Sintes et al. 2005) and tour

operators (Ayuso 2006; Orfila-Sintes et al. 2005) are present should be considered in empirical analyses. These are major stakeholders that influence the innovative environmental behavior of tourism firms.

In addition to innovativeness differences, empirical analyses for tourism firms should take into consideration other differential characteristics of tourism:

- The soft nature of tourism firms' environmental pressures: Studies on manufacturing firms measure firms' environmental behavior by means of emissions of toxic pollutants. If the environmental behavior of tourism firms were evaluated with these measures, the result would be a useless classification of all firms as non-polluting (or very low-polluting). Rather, empirical applications for tourism firms have evaluated their environmental behavior by means of management variables. Therefore, empirical studies are evaluating the relationship between economic performance and efforts developed by firms to reduce their environmental impacts.
- Increased complexity of lagged effects: Depending on the degree of seasonality at the destination and on sales of the tourism product, different temporal gaps might appear between firms' environmental activity and its economic repercussion on the balance sheet.
- Scarce information: The availability of information at the relevant level for tourism firms is more limited than for the manufacturing industry. This is true both for environmental and economic performance variables, making empirical research in this area extremely difficult. Due to this data scarcity, empirical applications for the tourism industry, based on statistical methodologies, make use of questionnaires to obtain both dependent and independent variables. As a result, common method-bias problems arise that can only be partially corrected. Therefore, efforts should be conducted in the future to measure more objectively the performance of firms, in both their environmental and economic dimensions. The tourism industry is an opaque economic activity for which few indicators are currently available, though efforts are underway to correct this situation (WTO 2004a). The publication of the environmental statements for EMAS implementation could be an interesting source of relevant information. However, comparability (among firms and for firms along time) might be conditioned by differences in indicators used for presenting the information in different reports.

The convergence of all these particularities determines that research on the economic impacts of voluntary environmental initiatives by tourism firms has only recently emerged. This has been the case despite efforts undertaken to bring attention to the potential benefits gained by a broader and deeper commitment to the environment by service organizations (Davis 1991; Foster et al. 2000; Grove et al. 1996). Table 15.1 summarizes past research undertaken within this literature.

Research in this field starts with case studies. These case studies analyze particular firms' situations, lacking any statistical generalization. The study by Enz and Siguaw (1999) is a good example of these initial research efforts. They examine

Table 15.1 Main literature on environmental-economic performance tourism firms

Study	Sample	Environmental variables	Economic variables	Methodology	Results
Enz and Siguaw 1998	4 Hotel US	–	–	Case Study	+
Goodman, 2000	Hotels Sweden	–	–	Case Study	+
Álvarez et al., 2001	296 Hotels Spain	Environmental cost and savings, training, ecological purchasing, ecological marketing campaigns, customer environmental cooperation, and energy, water and waste savings	Occupancy rate, current-year profitability and profitability over the last three years. Self-reported.	Cluster analysis and ANOVA	+
Rivera, 2002	164 Hotels Costa Rica	Management of the physical and biological environment and of hotel facilities, guest environmental education, and cooperation with local communities.	Prices and sales.	ANOVA Regression	+/no sign
Carmona-Moreno et al., 2004	268 Hotels Spain	Environmental management (technological and organisational practices on pollution prevention and control), recognition of environmental issues as a strategic capability and previous experience.	Subjective profitability.	Cluster analysis and ANOVA	+/no sign
Kassinis and Soteriou, 2005	104 Hotels Europe	Use of energy saving measures, recycling practices and water saving measures.	Growth in profits, growth in revenues and market share. Self-reported.	Regression	+
Claver-Cortés et al. 2007	114 Hotels Spain (Alicante)	Environmental certificates, environmental cost and savings, training, ecological purchasing, ecological marketing campaigns, energy and water savings.	Occupancy rates, total gross operative profit, gross operating profits and subjective evaluations. Self-reported.	Mann-Whitney's U-test	+/no sign

hotels that were named as US environmental best-practice champions by the Cornell University School of Hotel Administration. Enz and Siguaw find that all hotels argue that cost savings, operating efficiencies, and marketing opportunities derive from their environmental initiatives and provide several examples of each. Another similar contribution is by Goodman (2000), analyzing the case of Scandic Hotels, the largest hotel chain of Northern Europe. This company was on the verge of collapse in the early 1990s. The author explains how a change in management permitted the firm to turn corporate performance around. Two major strategic principles were implemented: employee empowerment and environmental responsibility. Partnerships with suppliers proved crucial for Scandic's sustainability program. With its volume of purchases, Scandic was able to impose very restrictive environmental conditions on their suppliers, forcing them to create innovations in both product and process. Goodman presents these partnerships as win-win situations: Scandic obtained its environmental objectives and related economic improvements while suppliers gained market differentiation and competitive advantage from these innovations. Scandic's accounting results increased around two hundred percent in six years, moving from losses to profitability. The main conclusion of the paper is that strategies for environmental sustainability are not solely the domain of financially secure companies, but that such efforts can also support a turnaround. This idea is also supported by Reinhardt (1999), who states that "dramatic cost savings are often found when a company is under tremendous pressure" (Reinhardt 1999 p. 154), referring to examples similar to the one of Goodman (2000).

More recent studies progress to the use of statistical methodologies. The studies by Álvarez et al. (2001), Carmona-Moreno et al. (2004) and Claver-Cortés et al. (2007) analyze whether significant differences exist in economic results for hotels with different environmental positions. Empirical examinations by Álvarez et al. (2001) and Carmona-Moreno et al. (2004) are remarkably similar: In both cases they first conduct a cluster analysis for identifying groups of hotels with similar environmental strategies. The cluster analysis is then followed by an ANOVA test to determine differences in occupancy and profitability between the groups. Their reference population is in both cases 3-, 4- and 5-star Spanish hotels, from which samples are obtained from a surveying process with a similar number of observations (296 for Álvarez et al. 2001; and 268 for Carmona-Moreno et al. 2004) and for a similar time period (late 1998 – beginning 1999). However, environmental strategies have been measured differently in the two studies.

The study by Álvarez et al. (2001) considers seven variables to capture hotel environmental management, including qualification of environmental costs and savings, environmental training programs, deployment of green purchasing policies, use of green arguments in marketing, demand for customer cooperation in environmental protection programs and energy, water and waste saving actions. The authors compare the economic performance of three different groups classified according to identified environmental strategies. The ANOVA test shows that there is an increase in profitability as more proactive behaviors are adopted. Occupancy rates are significantly different between each of the groups, and lagged profitability is only significantly higher for the proactive group with respect to the other groups.

In addition to evaluating economic results from different environmental strategies, the authors undertake a hierarchical regression analysis to evaluate determinants of the environmental performance of hotels, including facility age, size, chain affiliation, stakeholder environmental pressure and other control variables such as hotels' legal category and predominant clientele.

Claver-Cortés et al. (2007) replicate the former part of the study by Álvarez et al. (2001) using a sample of hotels in a particular Spanish region, Alicante. Econometrically, they undertake a Mann-Whitney's U-test for two independent samples using Bonferroni's correction. Their estimates are weaker, and only occupancy rate per bed is significantly higher for more proactive hotels with respect to the reactive group. Total gross operative profit and gross operating profit were also included in the analysis but no significant relation with firms' environmental strategy was found. The authors partially attribute these results to the fact that the application of environmental strategies was very recent in the region analyzed. They defend that environmental strategies may positively affect the bottom line after a longer time period.

Also considering the potential influence of time on the estimates, Álvarez et al. (2001) suggest evaluating long-term effects of environmental management on financial performance as a line of future research. The objective would be to test whether the effects obtained by them are only temporal or are stable for longer time periods. This concern should lead researchers to be cautious in how they extrapolate results, since findings might be determined by the environmental practices currently in place, and would not hold for different scenarios of environmental activities. It could be the case that the present positive results derive from gathering "low-hanging fruits" in the sense of Hart and Ahuja (1996), which would be currently available due to the weak environmental regulation of the tourism industry, but that will be depleted sooner or latter after subsequent abatement efforts.

Carmona-Moreno et al. (2004), extends the concept of environmental strategy, with respect to that of Álvarez et al. (2001), to include not only environmental management variables but also previous experience in environmental management and its recognition as a strategic capability of the firm. Carmona-Moreno et al. consider, when defining environmental strategy, the perception of managers on the relevancy of whether or not environmental protection activities can provide a sustainable competitive advantage. This might be related to the voluntary nature of its implementation, since managers who see environmental initiatives as a means to obtaining competitive advantage might be more ready to introduce them voluntarily. In addition, Carmona-Moreno et al. argue that experience is relevant in a hotel's environmental strategy due to time requirements for effective customer involvement and pollution prevention inclusion in organizational routines. Based on this extended view of environmental sustainability the authors identify four groups of firms by means of a cluster analysis: experienced, hopeful, indifferent and incipient. When comparing economic performance between the groups, the results are not conclusive. It has been found that hotels with the lowest values for all environmental variables obtain on average a significantly lower profitability than the rest, and no significant difference in profitability is found between the other three groups Occupancy results show certain significant differences between some of the groups, though no ordering can be established. The authors recommend using more formalized procedures in the future for the identification of the direction of causality between the variables.

This formalization is the objective of Rivera (2002). The author empirically analyzes the relationship between enrollment in voluntary environmental programs and economic results. He considers a sample of Costa Rican hotels, which includes several establishments participating in the Costa Rican Certification for Sustainable Tourism. Rivera first undertakes correlation and mean comparisons, which are consistent with the above results. In addition, the analysis is extended to include a recursive two-stage estimation method that corrects for self-selection bias and provides consistent estimates of participation benefits. His results show that participation in the program without showing a superior level of environmental performance does not result in price premiums. Most importantly, Rivera demonstrates that hotels with higher levels of environmental performance are significantly related to higher room prices (about $30 per night higher than the room prices of hotels not enrolled in voluntary programs). As in the case of Álvarez et al. (2001), results for occupancy are less clear.

Kassinis and Soteriou (2005) provide further research on the use of more formal ized procedures within this literature. Highlighting the distinctive characteristics of services vis-à-vis goods, the authors argue that the profit chain framework could be used to examine the relationship between the implementation of environmental practices and performance for service firms. Building on Heskett et al.'s (1994) service profit chain, the authors defend that the environmental practices are arguably built into the service design and, as such, might impact upon customer satisfaction and loyalty, and through them upon the performance of firms. In order to test this hypothesis, the authors develop a structural equation model. The model is empirically tested for hotels with rankings ranging from superior deluxe to first class at European top tourist destinations receiving more than ten million visitors per year. Their empirical estimates show a significant and positive impact of environmental management practices on satisfaction, of satisfaction on loyalty and lastly, of loyalty on economic performance. It is a highly interesting fact that no additional significant direct effect of environmental management practices on economic performance is found. Consequently, the relationship between environmental management practices and economic results is channeled through customer satisfaction and not through other direct cost impacts.

Kassinis and Soteriou's (2005) conclusions are consistent with Rivera's (2002) findings, and are supported by complementary research by other authors. Parra et al. (2004) estimate that perception of the importance of environmental resource management by hotel executives is significantly greater as the firm's control over pricing increases. Moreover, Kirk (1998) shows that hotels that have already initiated environmental improvements are more likely to associate environmental management with increased profitability and marketing advances. And lastly, González and

León (2001) conclude that accommodation establishments where adoptive behavior is predominantly driven by the demand side undertake more environmental innovations.

Overall, despite the partial nature of the research, consistent evidence for the pays to be green hypothesis for the hotel sector – to which studies have been restricted until the present – can be observed. Nevertheless, it must be taken into consideration that these findings (showing that a demand effect determines increased economic results from environmental performance by firms), may be influenced by the dataset considered. Results might be conditional on the upper level accommodation establishments under analysis, the type of environmental management practices considered, the intensity of the environmental practices in place, or the nature based character of the tourism destinations. Even with this limitation, evidence reviewed in this section shows that at least for *a certain proportion* of firms in the tourism industry, it pays to undertake voluntary environmental action.

15.3 Strategic Incentives of Tourism Firms

In the literature reviewed in the previous section, no strategic interaction among firms was considered. Firms are assumed to undertake environmental decisions in a manner of decisions by one firm being independent of decisions of others and vice versa. However, in real life it is difficult to assume that a firm's environmental behavior has no strategic component. When considering strategic interaction among users of natural resources, economic theory often argues that social dilemmas necessarily emerge due to free-riding incentives. This situation has often been formalized as a prisoner's dilemma game (Ostrom 1990), where each player has the dominant strategy to not contribute to environmental quality no matter what the other player chooses. Free-riding expectations are mostly driven by concerns on management of open access resources presented by Hardin (Hardin 1968) in *the tragedy of the commons*. According to Hardin, rational users seek to maximize their private gain, demanding additional units of the resource until his or her individual benefits equal the expected costs, which are shared by all users. Thus, users are trapped in a situation leading inevitably to overuse and degradation of the resource. As Hardin puts it, "ruin is the destination toward which all men rush, each pursuing his own best interest in a society that believes in the freedom of the commons." (Hardin 1968 p. 1244).

According to this standard view of management of natural resources, no voluntary contribution is expected to be undertaken by firms. Therefore, best practices, environmental management systems or tourism collaborations, and partnerships for sustainability already commented on in the introduction are not anticipated to emerge. In addition, the previous section shows that, at least for a certain proportion of firms in the tourism industry, it pays to be green. In this section we analyze the implications of this evidence under a strategic setting by means of a very simple game-theory conceptualization. This is a first step to understand the economic incentives of tourism firms to undertake voluntary action. The literature presented

Fig. 15.1 Game structure for voluntary environmental action by tourism firms

		Player2	
		Voluntary action	No action
Player1	Voluntary action	a_1, a_2	b_1, c_2
	No action	c_1, b_2	d_1, d_2

in the previous section might seem rather limited to build a game on but, despite the scarce studies undertaken, its results are consistent for upper class hotels and in line with findings for the manufacturing industry.

To present the tourism firms' environmental management a two player game such as that presented in Fig. 15.1 can be used. Let us assume for the sake of a realistic description that representative players are asymmetric. Players undertake single decisions simultaneously and independently of the other player on their preferred strategies. Available strategies for each player are either to undertake, or not, voluntary environmental actions by the means and intensity more adequate to them. In a prisoner's dilemma the game has the following structure of payoffs, as referred to in Fig. 15.1: $a_1 > d_1$, $a_2 > d_2$, $a_1 < c_1$, $a_2 < c_2$, $b_1 < d_1$, and $b_2 < d_2$. This structure determines that the resulting Nash equilibrium is the one in the cell where none of the players undertakes voluntary action.

Making use of Fig. 15.1, an alternative structure of payoffs can be argued under the light of evidence in the previous section. Evidence shows that in real life some firms at tourism destinations undertake voluntary environmental initiatives, whereas others do not. Let us assume, without any loss of generality, that player 1 is a representative player of firms undertaking voluntary environmental initiatives and player 2 is a representative player of firms not doing so. Therefore, it could be argued that in reality, we might be in a situation such as that of the shadowed cell in Fig. 15.1.

Evidence in the previous section supports the idea that firms that undertake voluntary environmental initiatives outperform those which do not do so (Álvarez et al. 2001; Carmona-Moreno et al. 2004; Claver-Cortés et al. 2007; Kassinis and Soteriou 2005; Rivera 2002). In our game setting, this is consistent with b_1 being higher than c_2 $(b_1 > c_2)$, which contradicts generalized free-riding expectations. Free-riders (type 2 firms) obtain lower payoffs than firms undertaking environmental efforts (type 1 firms).

In addition, further relations between the payoffs can be explored. The relationships between b_1 and d_1, and a_2 and c_2 can be analyzed by assuming that players are rational and have sufficient information, and that the situation in the shadowed cell in Fig. 15.1 is the result of the free decision by each agent on its preferred strategy.

- Given that player 2 does not undertake environmental action, player 1's available strategies are to undertake voluntary action (obtaining b_1 as a result) or not undertaking environmental action (obtaining d_1). Since player 1 undertakes voluntary actions, then player 1 prefers b_1 to d_1. As a result it can de argued that $b_1 > d_1$.

- Given that player 1 undertakes environmental action, player 2's available strategies are to undertake voluntary action (obtaining a_2) or not doing so (obtaining c_2). As player 2 prefers not to undertake voluntary actions, player 2 prefers c_2 to a_2. Therefore, $c_2 > a_2$.

To explore other relationships between parameter values in the game, it is necessary to extract further insights from empirical evidence. Let us make some comments that might shed some light on the relationship between c_1 and a_1:

- Results by Rivera (2002) and Kassinis and Soteriou (2005) show that the actual factor behind the empirical observation that firms which undertake voluntary environmental initiatives outperform those not doing so comes from a demand effect that results in increased prices. That is to say, player 1 can charge a price premium, p_1, with respect to the other firms at the destination when undertaking voluntary environmental initiatives that entail a green differentiation recognized by consumers. This p_1 premium diminishes as other firms at the destination undertake environmental actions, since player 1 loses differential attributes. The sensibility of p_1 to environmental strategies of other firms depends on the background theory explaining why $b_1 > c_2$. Taking advantage of the rich theoretical developments for the manufacturing sector, some discussion can be made in this respect. Some authors argue that the relevant theory explaining competitive advantages of green firms is the resource-based view of firms (Christmann 2000; Judge and Douglas 1998; King and Lenox 2002; Klassen and Whybark 1999; Russo and Fouts 1997). This theory claims that competitive advantage is built around internal competencies of firms, arising from assets that are inimitable and valuable. Environmental management is argued to generate certain tangible, intangible or personnel-based resources that can induce competitive advantage for firms (Russo and Fouts 1997). Under this theory the sensitivity of p_1 to the environmental action of other firms would be lower than when the relevant theory is the first-mover advantage, as supported by other authors (Nehrt 1996; Russo and Fouts 1997). In the latter case the benefits derived from environmental initiatives for type 1 firms will be more rapidly dissipated as other firms at the destination follow the same strategy. In both cases, the size of p_1 premiums depends on the population of "green" and "dirty" firms at the destination.
- In addition, it can be hypothesized that a second price premium, p_2, may be in place due to the positive externalities generated by environmental initiatives. When player 1 undertakes voluntary environmental actions he does so because he expects to obtain an economic gain from these actions. But at the same time, when making voluntary environmental contributions player 1 improves the environmental quality at the entire tourism destination, of which all firms can benefit. Then, all tourism firms are able to charge an extra price p_2 for their products (with respect to the tourism products at other destinations), as a result of player 1's environmental efforts. This p_2 premium is related to the number of "green"

firms at the destination in an opposite respect to p_1. It can be expected that p_2 increases as long as the number of firms in the tourism destination undertaking voluntary actions boosts.

Overall, when the combined effects of p_1 and p_2 determine that a_1 is higher than c_1, developing environmental initiatives would be player 1's dominant strategy. However, the state of empirical research is such that the interrelation between p_1 and p_2 price premiums and the influence of the proportion of "green" firms at the destination cannot be ascertained.

Nevertheless, given the empirical findings in the literature presented in the previous section, it can be argued that the strategic behavior of a certain segment of tourism firms seems to not support a prisoners' dilemma game structure. Consistently, while there are examples of tourism destinations that have overexploited their natural resources, thereby losing their appeal and stagnating, it is also true that others have been able to overturn *tragedy* expectations. There is a growing literature analyzing individual voluntary initiatives by tourism firms and collaborations, and for sustainability partnerships all around the world (Bramwell and Lane 2000; WTO 2001). In sum, it seems that free-riding is not the only possible result of the use of natural resources by tourism firms.

15.4 Some Reflection on the Governance of Tourism Natural Assets

Tourism expansion has been generally described to entail congestion, degradation of natural assets, weak management of waste effluents and other negative impacts that have become the basis for the extensive literature on the ecological impacts of tourism (for some examples see Knowles and Curtis 1999; Morgan 1991; Tisdell 2001). This has been combined with a long economic tradition, which considers that users of natural resources are trapped in a social dilemma leading to inevitable overuse and degradation of environmental quality. As already mentioned, these expectations are based on the tragedy of the commons (Hardin 1968). This considers that some natural resources are subtractable and nonexcludabile assets. The former refers to goods for which appropriation by one user deters appropriation by others, and the latter, that exclusion of potential users is not possible at an acceptable cost. According to Hardin (1968) the resulting outcome is overexploitation and degradation of resources. Much research in the natural and social sciences has explored the management implications of subtractability and nonexcludabiliby (Hardin 1998). In this line, the tourism literature has postulated the existence of a tragedy of the *tourism* commons, which leads to the tragedy of the *tourism product* (Briassoulis 2002). According to this view, the tourism commons would be subject to the characteristic problems of overuse, lack of incentive for investment and general mismanagement (Briassoulis 2002; Healy 1994; Sinclair and Stabler 1997, pp. 155–181). Overall, the existence of a coordination problem for the management of tourism natural assets is anticipated. Agents are expected to systematically free-ride on others, and therefore no voluntary action for environmental protection or cooperation to preserve the commons is predicted. As a result, public intervention has been considered necessary to preserve natural assets. The tourism literature has supported, in a certain way, this view of environmental management when describing the inexorable environmental impoverishment of the destinations as they grow (for some examples see Knowles and Curtis 1999; Morgan 1991).

In recent times, this pessimistic view has been broadened by the appearance of tourism collaborations and partnerships for sustainability, stakeholder management, and community involvement. The emergence of voluntary initiatives to preserve natural resources at tourism destinations is fostering a governance change for natural assets. Environmental policy to preserve the basis of a tourism attraction is increasingly emphasizing the role of voluntary initiatives in a regulatory context mostly driven by command and control mandates. Corporate environmental performance is gaining prominence among business leaders, academics, investors, and governments across many economic sectors (Andrews 1998). In OECD countries, this comes from criticism of the effectiveness of command and control regulations as well as an increasing belief in potential cost-efficiency improvements when industries are given flexibility to select their methods of pollution control (Khanna 2001).

Testing the validity of this perspective to environmental management should question its viability as a policy approach and not only as anecdotal evidence. There are authors who argue that given their non-mandatory nature, voluntary initiatives must generate for firms short-term net economic gains to promote "greener" behavior (Andrews 1998; Rivera 2002). The literature review presented in this chapter seems to support that, at least for a certain proportion of firms in the tourism industry; it actually pays to be green. However, even though empirical applications included in this review refer to initiatives voluntarily undertaken by firms that are not legally mandated, it is not possible to completely disentangle economic results that stem from these voluntary initiatives from those stemming from institutional arrangements Institutions might include informal norms of behavior among users or of regulatory pressures by the government, among others.

Norms of behavior are relevant insofar as these might determine informal social benefits derived for those users who follow agreements. It can be hypothesized that users of natural resources at tourism destinations might hold information about each other and information about the context in which the social interaction happens. These pieces of information can transform material payoffs of an externally-defined strategic setting into an internal decision-making process (Cardenas and Ostrom 2004). This internal game, represented by utility measures, might include informal social benefits derived from following norms of behavior or shared strategies between users. According to Osés and Viladrich (2007), users of natural resources can receive the following from a community when adhering to agreed-upon strategies: social inclusion and public consideration, everyday favors and signs of approval that make life easier and more pleasant, moral support in difficult circumstances, and certain bestowals and positions.

In addition to norms of behavior, regulatory pressures might influence firms' environmental behavior. Its influence is determined by the fact that the system of governance is an intervening variable that affects the way in which firms respond to their external pressures. It is unlikely that firms will acquiesce to pressures from environmental groups and other social interests when business interests dominate the policy-making process. They may change, however, their responses and pacify external pressures when they fear a threat of increased regulation or a change in governance environment. This can happen, for example, when social interests increase and sustain an issue in the media and the awareness of the general public (Cashore and Vertinsky 2000). The mismanagement of natural resources by the tourism industry can generate social conflict and residents' mobilization against tourism activities (Kousis 2000) due to their concerns about the environmental impacts of tourism (see Bujosa and Rosselló 2007; Kuvan and Akan 2005; Liu et al. 1987 among others).

In sum, as Marshall (2005) states, in no way does this increased support for self-regulation by the industry deny a vital role for the state. Self-regulation may correct some private inefficiencies and may support efficient regimes to manage externalities and common pool resources, but it is not a viable substitute for environmental governance (Andrews 1998). Therefore, the government should reinvent itself such that it complements rather than displaces or absorbs self-organizing capacities at smaller levels of social interaction (Marshall 2005). For example, empirical examinations in Costa Rica suggest that in addition to market incentives, adequate institutional pressures may also be necessary conditions for adherence to environmental management systems by hotels in order to promote compliance above and beyond regulated environmental behavior (Rivera 2004).

In sum, there is scope for further research and more rigorous analyses of the modification of incentives by environmental regulations in order to better re-design policies to complement voluntary action. Outcomes resulting from environmental policies are crucially dependent on the incentive structure of agents. In fact, wrong or incomplete information about agents' incentives can be an important source of policy failure. If policymakers do not understand how particular combinations of rules affect actions and outcomes in particular situations, policy changes may produce unexpected and, at times, disastrous outcomes (Ostrom 2005).

15.5 Conclusion

The present study evaluates the current state of knowledge on the analysis of the economic incentives of tourism firms to undertake voluntary environmental action. From this analysis it has been first observed that the mainstream literature on the voluntary action of firms for environmental protection focuses on the US manufacturing industry. This literature is well structured in the type of questions posed and is based on relevant background theory. A certain part of this information can be useful (though cautiously) for the analysis of tourism firms, which are the interest of the present contribution. For tourism firms, literature on the economic incentives for voluntary environmental management is still recent and scarce. Even so, it has rapidly evolved towards sophisticated statistical methodologies that enable researchers to start understanding the relevant economic forces behind voluntary action. The current state of knowledge provides a consistent – though partial – evidence for the pays to be green hypothesis for tourism firms. Therefore, certain firms are better off than others when undertaking voluntary environmental initiatives at the present situation. Assuming that firms are rational and are well informed, it can be argued that at least a proportion of firms in the tourism literature have economic incentives to undertake voluntary environmental initiatives.

This is a result not expected a priori. Under the traditional view of the tragedy of the commons, users of the natural resources are trapped in a situation inevitably leading to the overuse and depletion of the resources. Policy-making derived from this view is designed by only considering the existence of free-riding firms. Then, public intervention is supported in order to avoid depletion of resources. Outcomes resulting from environmental policies are crucially dependent on the incentive structure of agents. Consequently, environmental policies that are inspired by free-riding expectations and not on actual evaluations of potential voluntary actions at the destination might have unpredicted results. It could be the case that policies crafted for free-riding firms change the contextual factors on which firms that actually undertake voluntary action are embedded. Under this circumstance, a firm's preferred strategy can change from an initial proactive perspective to a latter, compliant position, thus modifying its derived economic payoffs and environmental contributions. The evidence presented in this chapter, the emergence of tourism collaborations and partnerships for sustainability all around the world (Bramwell and Lane 2000; WTO 2001), and the extensive research existing for the better management of natural assets (Calveras and Vera-Hernández 2005; Huybers and Bennett 2002; Ostrom 1990, 2005; WTO 2001) should urge environmental policy-makers at tourism destinations to overcome simple traditional policy approaches. There is a wide range of alternative mechanisms for the governance of natural assets, and tourism destinations should explore those that are the most adequate for them.

The use of the correct background theoretical framework by policy-makers can be a useful tool for increasing the probability of selecting rules for better outcomes. The more informed the decision-making process for environmental policy, the higher the probability of obtaining desirable results. Achieving this objective requires further information on the economic and institutional factors that determine the adoption of voluntary initiatives for environmental policy-making at tourism destinations. Efforts should be made in this direction in order to reach better governance of natural assets at tourism destinations.

References

Álvarez MJ, Burgos J, Céspedes JJ (2001) An analysis of environmental management, organizational context and performance of Spanish hotels. Omega 29(6):457–471

Andrews R (1998) Environmental regulation and business 'self-regulation'. Policy Sci 31:177–197

Ayuso S (2006) Adoption of voluntary environmental tools for sustainable tourism: analysing the experience of Spanish hotels. Corp Soc Responsib Environ Manage 13(4):207–220

Bragdon HH, Marlin J (1972) Is pollution profitable? Risk management April:9–18
Bramwell B, Lane B (2000) Collaborations and partnerships in tourism planning. In: Bramwell B, Lane B (eds) Tourism collaborations and partnerships: Politics, practice and sustainability. Clevedon: Channel View Publications, pp 1–19
Briassoulis H (2002) Sustainable tourism and the question of the commons. Ann Tourism Res 29(4):1065–1085
Bujosa A, Rosselló J (2007) Modeling environmental attitudes toward tourism. Tourism Manage 28(3):688–695
Calveras A, Vera-Hernández M (2005) Quality externalities among hotel establishments: what is the impact of tour operators? Tourism Econ 11(4):571–593
Cardenas J, Ostrom E (2004) What do people bring into the game? Experiments in the field about cooperation in the commons. Agr Sys 82:307–326
Carmona-Moreno E, Céspedes-Lorente J, de Burgos-Jimenez J (2004) Environmental strategies in Spanish Hotels: Contextual factors and performance. Serv Ind J 24(3):101–130
Cashore B, Vertinsky I (2000) Policy networks and firm behaviours: Governance systems and firms reponses to external demands for sustainable forest management. Policy Sci 33:1–20
Claver-Cortés E, Molina-Azoín JF, Pereira-Moliner J, López-Gamero MD (2007) Environmental strategies and their impact on hotel performance. J Sus Tourism 15(6):663–679
Chen KH, Metcalf RW (1980) The relationship between pollution control record and financial indicators revisited. Account Rev 55(1):168–177
Christmann P (2000) Effects of "Best Practices" of environmental management on cost advantage: the role of complementary assets. Acad Manage J 43(4):663–680
Davis JJ (1991) A blueprint for green marketing. J Bus Strateg 12(4):14–17
Derwall J, Guenster N, Bauer R, Koedijk K (2005) The eco-efficiency premium puzzle. Financ Anal J 61(2):51–63
Dowell G, Hart S, Yeung B (2000) Do corporate global environmental standards create or destroy market value? Manage Sci 46(8):1059–1074
Enz CA, Siguaw JA (1999) Best hotel environmental practices. Cornell Hotel Restaur Adm Q 40(5):72–77
Farrell BH, Twining-Ward L (2004) Reconceptualizing tourism. Ann Tourism Res 31(2):274–295
Foster TSJ, Sampson SE, Dunn SC (2000) The impact of customer contact on environmental initiatives for service firms. Int J Oper Prod Manage 20(2):197–203
Garrod B, Fyall A (1998) Beyond the rhetoric of sustainable tourism? Tourism Manage 19: 199–212
González M, León CJ (2001) The adoption of environmental innovations in the hotel industry of Gran Canaria. Tourism Econ 7(2):117–190
Goodman A (2000) Implementing sustainability in service operations at Scandic hotels. Interfaces 30(3):202–214
Grove SJ, Fisk RP, Pickett GM, Kangun N (1996) Going green in the service sector: Social responsibility issues, implications and implementation. Eur J Mark 30(5):56–66
Guenster N, Derwall J, Bauer R, Koedijk K. (2006). The economic value of corporate eco-efficiency [Electronic Version]. Retrieved 26 January 2007 from http://ssrn.com/abstract = 675628
Hardin G (1968) The tragedy of the commons. Science 163(13):1243–1248
Hardin G (1998) Extensions of "The Tragedy of the Commons". Science 280(5364):682–683
Hart SL, Ahuja G (1996) Does it pay to be green? An empirical examination of the relationship between emission reduction and firm performance. Bus Strateg Environ 5(1):30–37
Healy RG (1994) The "common pool" problem in tourism landscapes. Ann Tourism Res 21(3): 596–611
Heskett JL, Jones TO, Loveman GW, Sasser WE, Schlesinger LA (1994) Putting the service-profit chain to work. Harv Bus Rev 72(2):164–175.
Hunter-Jones P (1997) Sustainable Tourism. Ann Tourism Res 24(2):477–478
Hunter C (1997) Sustainable tourism as an adaptive paradigm. Ann Tourism Res 24:850–867

Hunter C, Green H (1995) Tourism and the environment, London
Huybers T, Bennett F (2002) Environmental management and the competitiveness of nature-based tourism destinations. Edward Elgar Publishing, Cheltenham
Jaggi B, Freedman M (1992) An examination of the impact of pollution performance on economic and market performance: Pulp and paper firms. J Bus Finance Account 19(5):697–713
Judge W, Douglas TJ (1998) Performance implications of incorporating natural environmental issues into the strategic planning process: An empirical assessment. J Manage Stud 35(2): 241–262
Kassinis GI, Soteriou AC (2005) Greening service organizations: environmental management practices and performance. In: Sharma S, Aragón-Correa JA (eds) Corporate environmental strategy and competitive advantage. Edward Elgar, Cheltenham, pp 115–138
Khanna M (2001) Non-mandatory approaches to environmental protection. J Econ Surv 15(3): 291–324
King AA, Lenox MJ (2002) Exploring the locus of profitable pollution reduction. Manage Sci 48(2):289–299
Kirk D (1998) Attitudes to environmental management held by a group of hotel managers in Edinburg. Hospitality Manage 17:33–47
Klassen RD, Whybark CD (1999) The impact of environmental technologies on manufacturing performance. Acad Manage J 42(6):599–615
Knowles T, Curtis S (1999) The market viability of European mass tourist destinations: a post-stagnation life-cycle analysis. Int J Tourism Res 1(2):87–96
Konar S, Cohen MA (2001) Does the market value environmental performance? Rev Econ Stat 83(2):281–289
Kousis M (2000) Tourism and the environment: A social movement perspective. Ann Tourism Res 27(2):468–489
Kuvan Y, Akan P (2005) Residents' attitudes toward general and forest-related impacts of tourism: the case of Belek, Antaya. Tourism Manage 26(5):691–706
Liu JC, Sheldon PJ, Var T (1987) Resident perceptions of the environmental impacts of tourism. Ann Tourism Res 14(1):17–37
Mahapatra S (1984) Investor reaction to a corporate social accounting. J Bus Financ Account 11(1):29–40
Marshall GR (2005) Economics for collaborative environmental management: renegotiating the commons. Earthscan, Sterling
Morgan M (1991) Dressing up to survive: marketing majorca anew. Tourism Manage 12(1):15–20
Nehrt C (1996) Timing and intensity effects of environmental investments. Strateg Manage J 17(7):535–547
OECD (1980) The impact of tourism on the environment. OECD, Paris
Orfila-Sintes F, Crespí-Cladera R, Martínez-Ros E (2005) Innovation activity in the hotel industry: Evidence from Balearic Islands. Tourism Manage 26(6):851–865
Osés N, Viladrich M (2007) On the sustainability of common property resources. J Environ Econ Manage 53:393–410
Ostrom E (1990) Governing the commons: The evolution of institutions for collective action. Cambridge University Press, New York
Ostrom E (2005) Understanding institutional diversity. Woodstock. Princeton University Press, Princeton, NJ
Parra E, García FJ, Guitiérrez D (2004) Importance of environmental resources and capabilities for firm's competitiveness. The case of the hotel industry in the Canary Islands. Anatolia 15(2): 183–199
Rege M (2000) Strategic policy and environmental quality. Environ Res Econ 15(3):279–296
Reinhardt FL (1999) Bringing the environment down to earth. Harv Bus Rev 77(4):149–157
Ritchie B, Crouch G (2003) The competitive destination: a sustainable tourism perspective. CABI Publishing, Wallingford
Rivera J (2002) Assessing a voluntary environmental initiative in the developing world: the costa rican certification for sustainable tourism. Policy Sci 35:333–360

Rivera J (2004) Institutional pressures and voluntary environmental behavior in developing countries: evidence from the Costa Rican hotel industry. Soc Nat Resour 17:779–797

Russo MV, Fouts PA (1997) A resource-based perspective on corporate environmental performance and profitability. Acad Manage J 40(3):534–559

Sinclair TM, Stabler M (1997) The economics of tourism. Routledge, London

Spicer BH (1978) Investors, corporate social performance and information disclosure: an empirical study. Account Rev 53(1):94–111

Stoeckl N (2004) The private costs and benefits of environmental self-regulation: which firms have most to gain? Bus Strateg Environ 13(3):135–155

Tisdell C (2001) National gains from international tourism in the light of environmental factors: Further considerations. In: Tisdell C (ed) Tourism economics, the environment and development: analysis and policy. Edward Elgar, Cheltenham, UK

WTO (1999) Sustainable development of tourism: an annotated bibliography. World Tourism Organization, Madrid

WTO (2001) Public-private sector cooperation: enhancing tourism competitiveness. World Tourism Organization, Madrid

WTO (2004a) Indicators of sustainable development for tourism destinations: a guidebook. World Tourism Organization, Madrid

WTO (2004b) Sustainable tourism resource management. World Tourism Organization, Madrid

Yamahita M, Sen S, Roberts MC (1999) The rewards for environmental conscientiousness in the US capital markets. J Financ Strateg Decis 12(1):73–8

Chapter 16
Tourism and Strategic Competition in the Air Transport Industry

Susana Teles, Manuela Sarmento, and Álvaro Matias

16.1 Introduction

Many industries have realised that fostering continuous face-to-face competition battles leads companies to financial exhaustion, intellectual emptiness and general worse preparedness to new stages of competition and innovation. Also, this type of competition does not secure the company the lowest cost, the best products or the highest profits.

In fact, many multinational companies have found that the best way to compete in the long run is through collaboration, hence leaving destructive competition aside as a structural option. Companies may then generate value added for customers and stakeholders, by selectively sharing and negotiating control, costs, capital, market access, information and technology with competitors and suppliers. However, this does not mean that competition ceases to exist; it is quite the opposite, as evidenced by computer and commercial aircraft markets.

Yet, competition in the airline industry is a relatively recent phenomenon, since one has to consider that the aviation sector has moved over the last quarter of the twentieth century from a patchwork of individual and state protected companies to a liberalized system of globally interconnected corporate organizations (see Martin and Voltes-Dorta 2008 and Nijkamp 2008). The increasing liberalization of the skies both in Europe and in the US over the last few years has in turn impacted positively in the price-competitiveness of the traditional tourism packages and therefore deserves to be carefully assessed through a comprehensive approach.

In this paper, we start by briefly referring to the everlasting symbiotic relationship between the evolution of aviation and the development of the tourism phenomenon. The concept of strategy and strategic alliances is then considered by addressing possible types of partnership, management and key factors in benefit sharing. In particular, analysis will focus on strategic alliances in the air transport sector, with emphasis on the benefits and contributions of an airline to an alliance and the types

S. Teles (✉)
Department of Management and Economics, Universidade da Madeira, Funchal, Portugal,
e-mail: s_teles@sapo.pt

Á. Matias et al. (eds.), *Advances in Tourism Economics*,
DOI 10.1007/978-3-7908-2124-6_16, © Physica-Verlag Heidelberg 2009

of agreement in place between air carriers. Finally, the trends envisaged for the sector are also taken into consideration.

16.2 Tourism and Aviation: A Symbiotic Interaction Since Ever

Tourism has only become a global phenomenon when the benefits of aviation have evolved from a privilege of a few to a market service available to all. In fact, air transport and tourism have always been interlinked; with tourism being a driving factor for and often a catalyst of change in air transport; most notably throughout the development of new business models such as charter airlines or low-cost carriers (Biegera and Wittmerb 2006). At the same time, the evolution of air transport opened new destinations and tourism potential by allowing customers to perform long-haul excursions, on one hand, and significantly expanding demand, on the other hand, once that deregulation occurred and free market competition has set in.

As Reggiani et al. (2009) clearly summarize, the aviation sector has traditionally been a publicly controlled industry, with a high degree of government intervention, for both strategic and economic reasons. This process started back in 1919, with the Paris Convention stipulating that states have sovereign rights in the airspace above their territories, which lead to the necessity of establishing a series of bilateral agreements between countries willing to be flied over by international airlines. The subsequent Chicago Convention (1944) introduced a distinction between various forms of freedom for using the airspace, ranging from the 1st freedom (the right to fly over the territory of a contracting state without landing) to the 8th freedom (the right to transport passengers and cargo within another state between the airports in that state).

Consequently, the airline sector ultimately became overregulated an inefficient. More recently, however, the inevitable deregulation process started to materialize. In fact, as it became increasingly evident that the liberalization of air services between countries generates significant additional opportunities for consumers, shippers, and the numerous direct and indirect entities and individuals affected by such liberalization, a collective consciousness started to evolve and gain advantage among both market agents and regulators. Conversely, it became also evident that restrictive bilateral air services agreements between countries was stifling air travel, tourism and business, and, consequently, economic growth and job creation.

Under this background, in the USA, the Airline Deregulation Act (1978) set the tone for a clear market orientation of the aviation sector, and around a decade later in Europe a series of gradual steps (so-called packages) have been introduced – under the political guidance of the European Commission – to ensure a full deregulation of the European airline sector by the end of the twentieth century, based on an integrated airline market ruled by fair competition and sound economic growth.

The latest and decisive step in this deregulation process was the Open Skies Agreement signed in Washington between the USA and Europe on the 30th of April

2007. This agreement entered in force on the 30th of March 2008 and has since then played a decisive role in the opening of more opportunities for air companies on both sides of the Atlantic to increase their financial viability and market shares in a free competition for the skies across the Atlantic.

This changing trend in regulatory regimes in the European airline sector has increased competition in the marketplace and prompted various new actions and strategies of European carriers in the past decade, such as mergers, take-overs and alliances. Yet, fierce competition has also led to the financial exhaustion of several existing carriers (as was the case with Swissair and Sabena). More competition in a free market in Europe has largely had the same effects as in the USA in the past, notwithstanding the fact that flag carriers managed to keep a large share of the European air transport market.

As a result of the above, the European aviation market is now a place of increased competition, leading, on one hand, to gains in economic efficiency and lower prices and, on the other hand, also stimulating companies to engage into strategic alliances to reinforce their competition strengths. The tourism market benefits directly from this process both through lower prices and market expansion (new destinations and routes).

16.3 The Concept of Strategy

The term strategy derives from the Greek word *strategia*, comprised by the noun *stratos*, which means army, and the suffix *ag*, which means to lead. It literally refers to the mission of a military commander. Prior to the word is the concept of strategy itself, addressed in 500 BC by Sun Tzu in the treatise "The Art of War". Reflections and in-depth considerations about military strategy were subsequently used by companies, given the common ground found between the two realities. An army requires direction and purpose, adequate resource management and the coordination of decisions made or planned by different individuals, just as a company to achieve its goals. There are also similarities in other options taken in both circumstances, namely when it matters to retreat in order to assess the opponents' strength, force the opponent to take a stand, concentrate resources, strike clear exposures, target a specific segment, regroup and expand.

The essence of a company's strategy is to attain higher financial performance, distinguishing from competitors and paving the way to ensure survival and prosperity. However, the company does not intend to put forward a strategy that cannot be submitted to changes. The drawn-up plan must be dynamic and tailored to market transformations as regards the various consumer needs and preferences, competitor strategies, the company's own experience, the emergence of new opportunities and threats, unforeseen circumstances and even new strategic thinking.

Often the strategy is construed with the formulation of a plan incorporating the company's objectives, policies and initiatives, with the purpose of creating a competitive advantage in the industry served. This is the scope of a formal strategy.

However, companies may only have clusters of philosophies and programmes, lacking cohesion, flexibility and sense of industry positioning.

Grant (2005) highlights the two contrary approaches in strategy formulation followed by McGill University, led by Mintzberg, and by the Boston Consulting Group (BCG). The first maintains that experience, intuition and interaction between thought and action are of the essence to the formulation of a strategy, whereas the second points out an intentional, rational and analytical process of a plan devised by senior administrators or managers.

Clearly, the two approaches are not antagonist; rather, they supplement each other in the formulation of a strategy, insofar as they are key elements, despite having a different degree of relevance depending on the company's level. The company must be concerned with developing its own strategies for each organisational level, which will originate and materialise in general strategies. The strategy must embrace all critical activities of a company, providing it with a sense of unit, direction and purpose.

The successful implementation of a strategy is a challenge posed to every corporate manager. It is a delicate task, for it implies motivating all company members towards the proposed guidance, and this may not be easily accepted. However, only with effective implementation will it be possible for the company to close in on its maximum potential.

The economic literature on this theme puts forward distinct definitions of strategy, notwithstanding the absence of a universally accepted definition. Definitions are generally built up from the respective observations. Yet, among the various authors the choice is often a broadly based topic, and so is the selection of where and how to compete. Porter (1996) summarises this matter by saying that "the essence of strategy is to choose to perform different activities than rivals".

Thompson and Strickland (1995, p. 6) claim that strategy is the pattern of actions employed by managers to reach strategic and financial performance targets. In addition, the challenge lies also in coherently adjusting business decisions and competitive action taken at all company levels. Also, the company may choose to have a pro-active or reactive and defensive attitude, giving rise to intentional or adaptation strategies, depending on the adopted stance.

According to Hax and Majluf (1996), strategy may be seen as a multidimensional concept that embraces all critical activities of a company, providing it with a sense of unity, direction and purpose, and serving as a vehicle to facilitate the necessary changes induced by its environment, in an effort to achieve a long-term sustainable advantage. These authors separate the concept of strategy from the process of strategic formation, stating that the first comprises content and substance, while the second is the element determining the key players in charge of formulating and implementing the strategy and the tasks assigned to each one.

Freire (1997) refers that strategy may be described as the series of corporate decisions and actions which are consistently targeted at providing customers with more value than that offered by competitors, at the level of price, performance, speed or service. Given that strategy is the means to achieve goals, and ultimately entrepreneurial success, the author feels a need to clarify that this concept is substantiated by long-term survival, sustained growth, adequate profitability and innovation capacity.

Quinn (1998) defines strategy as the pattern or plan that integrates an organisation's major goals, policies, and action sequences into a cohesive whole. The author stresses the importance of its helping to marshal and allocate the organisation's resources and recognising its internal competencies, in order to anticipate changes in the environment and moves by its opponents.

Although not putting forward a definition, Grant (2005) refers that it is the consistency of direction based on a clear understanding of the "game" being played and a keen awareness of how to manoeuvre into a position of advantage, ensuring therefore the survival and prosperity of the company. For this author, the evolution of strategy has been more driven by the practical needs of business than by the development of theory.

Bruce Henderson (quoted by Grant 2005) – the founder of the BCG matrix approach – observed that a strategy is mostly a deliberate search for a plan of action that develops a business's competitive advantage and compounds it.

16.4 Strategic Alliances in Global Market Places

The business world is usually portrayed as strongly competitive: to survive, a company needs to achieve a better effective performance than competitors and be ready to annihilate its opponents.

This climate of permanent conflict is not, however, necessarily the most effective and common way of competing. Based on their own experience, companies have found that they need to know when and how to compete. In fact, to know when and how to cooperate is of the essence.

In historical terms, export companies from industrialised nations sought to form alliances with companies from less developed countries, where they would be able to place and trade their products. These agreements were often conducted to gain access to markets in less developed countries, whose governments impose restrictions and local requirements to the entry of foreign companies.

As of the 1990s, leading companies from several parts of the world entered into strategic alliances, in order to strengthen their mutual capacity to serve total geographical areas and move towards global market participation. However, the projections of a few, that by 2000 there would only be a dozen major competitor networks in each sector, did not materialise.

According to Freire (1997), a strategic alliance is translated into a collaboration agreement between two or more companies, with the purpose of complementing their competences, by pursuing a common project, over a given period of time.

The formulation of strategic alliances builds on three basic elements: the maintenance of the independence of each partner; the sharing of strategic resources; and the establishment of a validity period.

Not all strategic alliances will cover the same objectives. These are determined by allied companies and may comprehend the expansion of the trade position; the acquisition of technology, commodities and components; cost-cutting efforts, the sharing of scale economies; response to local government pressure (e.g. in China and India foreign companies are required to have local partners); the filling of gaps in terms of technical expertise or manufacture; and the creation of standards. In technology-based industries, such as aerospace, the rapidly growing international collaboration mirrors the companies' wish to have access to the various technological competences. This notwithstanding, there is certainly a common purpose to any alliance, which is to create better conditions for all partners involved.

Depending on the pursued goal, alliances take the form of joint research and development, joint acquisitions, production and marketing arrangements, vertical partnerships, licensing, joint ventures and shareholding. Alliances do not always involve formal agreements; they can often be entirely informal, although this is not always explicit.

The impact of alliances on the industry's competitive nature can be considered at two levels. Firstly, there are the relationships between different groups of strategic alliances and, secondly, the relationships within the alliance itself have to be considered.

The first level focuses on the fact that the various alliance groups are competing among themselves and/or with individual companies, and it is important that, when making decisions, a member company takes into consideration the competitiveness of allied companies as well as the relative strength of firms integrating competitor groups. By channelling their competitive energies towards the common rivals of allied companies, alliances are affecting competition. Also, it is also worth stressing that alliances may offset corporate competitive disadvantages, influencing an industry's competitive strength/structure.

The second level shows the different degrees of influence that companies exert within the membership alliance, with existing dominant and non-dominant partners. The latter obviously intend to reach the leaders' state of competence, while the former seek to expand their influence on the industry.

16.5 Strategic Alliances in the Air Transport Sector

A strategic alliance is an opportunity for an airline carrier that comprises a management challenge requiring a set of resources, mostly in terms of human talent and updated information, but also involving control and distribution systems.

It is clear-cut that alliances pursue different objectives and do not develop the same competences as airlines. Jaan Albrecht (Beting 2006), who has been appointed President of Star Alliance clearly states that "we are not and we will never be an airline. We will not pasteurise our product, nor standardise our images. That is a responsibility of airlines, which we definitely are not". Strategic alliances are built on the premise of creating more value for each air carrier, originating in the extended network coverage and in operation coordination. They are assumed to perform sales leveraging, allowing cost cutting and restricting competition. Alliance partners are contractually bound to sell their partners' seats and services, often through preference in the reservation systems of travel agents, ensuring better access to the market.

Cost-cutting can be attained through a better deployment of resources, scale economies and investment maximisation. Airports from different geographical areas, such as London, Paris, Warsaw, Bangkok or Tokyo, tend to have a separate area assigned to alliances. This is the case of the new Los Angeles airport terminal, which has 15 boarding gates for the exclusive use of Star Alliance members. Another way of cutting costs is to increment codesharing services, as proven by Austrian airlines, which decided to interrupt flights from Wien to Chicago, redirecting passengers to New York, from where they would depart served by United Airlines, but maintaining the flight code of Austrian airlines. The company continued to serve that market with no need to use its Airbus A330 in the mentioned route, which resulted in a huge resource saving.

Allied airlines seek to offer the same type of ground service in the various countries, with a certain degree of standardisation, so that passengers do not feel uncomfortable or odd in an airport served by a partner.

Figure 16.1 lays out the tasks expected of a member company and, on the other hand, which benefits it is expected to eventually reap.

According to a paper by Iatrou and Alamdari (2005), in 2002 companies believed that belonging to an alliance brought about an increased occupancy rate, and higher revenue and profits. If they had chosen to continue not to be part of an alliance this could have meant a loss of traffic for allied companies, which would place them in a situation of competitive disadvantage. This is confirmed by Kleymann (2005), who concludes that airlines, by seeking to form alliances, are making a necessary defensive move.

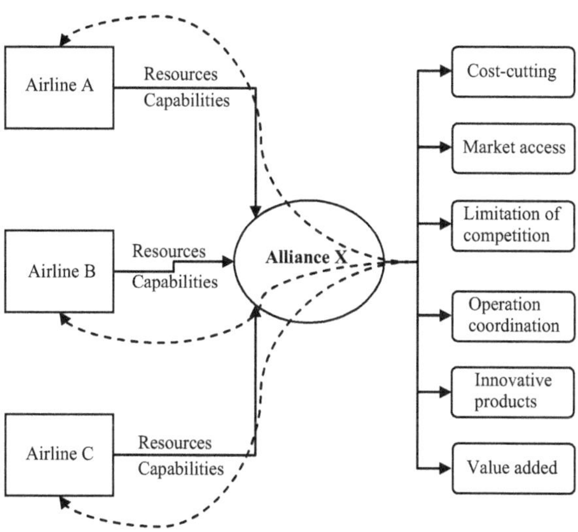

Fig. 16.1 Contributions and benefits of an airline integrating an alliance

Alliances may allow for the specialisation of a company, enabling it to concentrate on forecast products without wasting resources. However, this creates a certain degree of dependence vis-à-vis the alliance itself. Should it fail, the company will be in a situation of competitive disadvantage, e.g. in relation to a market it may have abandoned. Companies have therefore to understand this independence/dependence duality and be guided by an approach that does not excessively depend on the alliance of which they are members.

The positioning of airlines vis-à-vis strategic alliances has evolved, given that in the 1980s they were only considered for simple immediate growth, access to new markets and the possibility of circumventing bilateral restrictions. The air transport industry up until then was not liberalised, and this hindered the development of air carriers along the same lines as other industries. The sector saw high losses in the early 1990s, due to the decline in air transport demand, and again early this decade (in the wake of the terrorist attacks on 11 September, unfavourable economic conditions and the SARS epidemic). This boosted the potential for strategic alliances, given that it allowed partner companies to gain access to their partners' customers without having to create new services or purchase more aircraft, giving rise to increased revenue and profits for airlines.

A number of companies attempted to strengthen their market position through the merger or acquisition of rival air carriers, consolidating operations under a brand name. SAS – Scandinavian Airlines (SAS) acquired its Norwegian competitor Braathens, and American Airlines acquired the distressed airline TWA – TransWorld Airlines (TWA).

By endeavouring to protect national interests, legislation has not allowed for an unlimited growth of airlines in foreign countries, which has also fostered the emergence of strategic alliances. Iatrou and Alamdari (2004) illustrate the example of non-European air carriers, which may only acquire up to 49% of a European company, with no chance of gaining a dominant position. The same holds for the United States, although the limit in this country is much stricter, i.e. a share of only 25%.

An air carrier gains a strong position in an alliance if it dominates an attractive, highly profitable market, entry into which is, however, difficult, due to its being geographically remote or to cultural barriers. This occurs even in case of a deregulation situation. The Japanese airline ANA – All Nipon Airlines is a partner of Star Alliance, having opened access to that important market. In turn, ANA – All Nipon Airlines cut down the number of its intercontinental flights and started offering them through partner airlines.

Airlines may also reach a strong position in an alliance if they offer a series of different connections to specific markets. This is the case of British Airways, Air France or KLM – Royal Dutch Airlines (KLM).

16.5.1 Types of Agreement Between Airlines

IATA defines an airline alliance as the participation of three or more companies in a commercial relationship or joint venture, where an identified product is promoted under a single trade name or brand, by airlines or their agents. The use of a common brand or name causes alliance services to be recognised in airports and other locations with enforced bilateral agreements.

French (1997) considers that collaboration agreements between airlines may include one or every accomplishable possibility of partnership, partly depending on the size of the strategic alliance. For an alliance to be considered strategic one must assess its degree of cooperation and worldwide coverage. Airlines are willing to share their resources with one or more companies, with benefits for all partners, rendering their capacity supply more efficient and making it reach far into the market. Alliances vary in their degree of commitment and distinguish from each other in terms of codesharing, joint services, block reservations, marketing agreements or joint marketing, joint fares, franchising arrangements, schedule coordination, wet lease, frequent flyer benefits, cooperation and reciprocity, inter alia.

The most common type of agreement between airlines is, in fact, codesharing, accounting for almost two thirds of contracts signed between companies. It applies to the whole allied company network, to some members, or even to single routes within alliances. Besides the additional services offered, the great advantage of codesharing is that it makes it possible to highlight the flight in the computer reservation system's lists, thereby obtaining a more favourable display position.

16.5.2 Current Strategic Alliances

Strategic alliances share common goals, such as distinctive features that imply exclusiveness, in contrast to simple networks of partners with no formal integration.

Airlines integrating a given alliance restructure the flight connections they serve, especially intercontinental flights, guiding their operations towards hub airports, granting partner companies flight connections to secondary cities. For 20 years SAS airlines has been serving 36 intercontinental locations from Copenhagen, although a few only once or twice a week and with a several stops; in 2004 it served only eight, but almost all on a daily basis, totalling more flights than before.

It is instrumental for alliances to have partners in every major geographical area in the world, so as to be able to easily access any area. In the Oneworld alliance Finnair and Iberia cover the far north and south of Europe, with Iberia also reaching the Latin American market. Local partners define key hubs par excellence. In Europe, however, there is duplication in coverage by each alliance, given that in historical terms each country had its flag carrier with one or more hub airports.

16.5.2.1 Star Alliance

Air Canada, Lufthansa, SAS, Thai Airways International and United Airlines launched Star Alliance on 14 May 1997, thus creating the first global airline alliance, as a result of several previous successful agreements between some of these companies. As of October 1992, when Air Canada and United Airlines signed an alliance agreement, there was a succession of partnership contracts at various levels between a number of companies, namely at the level of joint marketing, code sharing flights and schedule coordination.

The launch of Star Alliance was targeted at facilitating global air transport, focusing on the coordination of flight connections, making them simpler, with no delays for customers, and extending frequent flyer benefits to the whole network, including lounge access for executive classes at the airport.

The alliance is currently composed of the founding airlines, in association with Asiana Airlines, US Airways, Air New Zealand, Austrian Airlines, Singapore Airlines, Varig, ANA – All Nipon Airways, bmi – British Midland, Spanair, LOT – Polish Airlines, TAP (whose application for membership was approved in June 2004), South African Airways, Swiss, and the regional companies Adria, Blue 1 and Croatia Airlines. Adherence by this type of airline allowed for the expansion to other regions and other types of customer, thereby improving the competitive positioning of members.

16.5.2.2 Skyteam

On 22 June 1999 Air France and Delta Airlines signed a long-term strategic agreement, which laid the foundations for a great global alliance. In August that year they launched the SkyTeam Europe Pass, with the purpose of offering simplicity and speed, low prices and the possibility for customers who visited multiple destinations in the European continent to earn additional frequent flyer points.

Precisely a year after the signing of a strategic agreement between Air France and Delta Airlines, the setting-up of a new consumer-based global alliance was announced. At the time SkyTeam counted on the participation of Aeromexico, Air France, Delta Airlines and Korean Air. In this period, the alliance offered 6,402 daily flights to 451 destinations in 98 countries. Its major concern was to provide a consistent level of performance, quality and detailed attention, customer service wise. Hence the slogan "Caring More About You".

However, the alliance was not limited to passenger traffic agreements. In September 2000 partners decided to widen the scope of the cargo handling contract.

SkyTeam is composed of Aeroflot, Aeromexico, Air France, Alitalia, China Southern, CSA – Czech Airlines, KLM, Continental Airlines, Delta Airlines, Korean Air, NWA – Northwest Airlines, Air Europe, Copa Airlines and Kenya Airways. The 11 companies offer 16,409 daily flights to 841 destinations in 162 countries, positioning as leaders in the number of daily flights offered, which is an advantage to business class passengers, who have a greater supply available.

16.5.2.3 Oneworld

On 21 September 1998 five world market leader airlines announced the setting-up of a new customer-oriented global alliance. American Airlines, British Airways, Canadian Airlines, Cathay Pacific Airways and Qantas Airways intended to raise the standard of air travel worldwide. With this purpose in view, they would use the name and logo of the *Oneworld* alliance in addition to the airline's identification in airports and in other information signs, schedules and printed materials. Companies committed to carry out joint advertising campaigns in key markets around the world, to help implement the alliance's slogan "Oneworld revolves around you".

Approximately eight years after, the alliance currently comprises Cathay Pacific Airways, Qantas, Finnair, Aer Lingus, Iberia, Japan Airlines (JAL), Malév, LAN and Royal Jordanian, in addition to American Airlines and British Airways with their 20 affiliated companies.

Allied companies recognise that being part of an alliance enables them to provide their customers with more services and benefits, which they would not be able to provide on an individual basis. This includes a widened network of routes and the opportunity to earn and redeem frequent flyer miles and points throughout the whole network. In addition, they consider that the existing relationships between allied airlines are intensifying.

Figures 16.2 and 16.3 illustrate developments in airline alliances from 2002 to 2004 at the level of served countries and airports respectively. Although SkyTeam

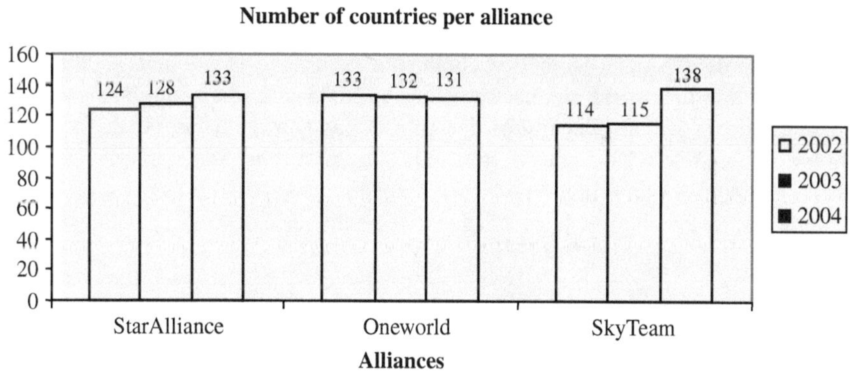

Fig. 16.2 Number of countries per alliance (Sources: Oneworld/SkyTeam/StarAlliance)

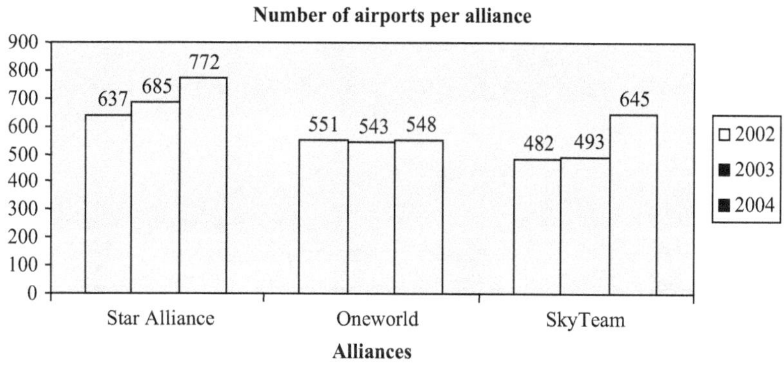

Fig. 16.3 Number of airports per alliance (Sources: Oneworld/SkyTeam/StarAlliance)

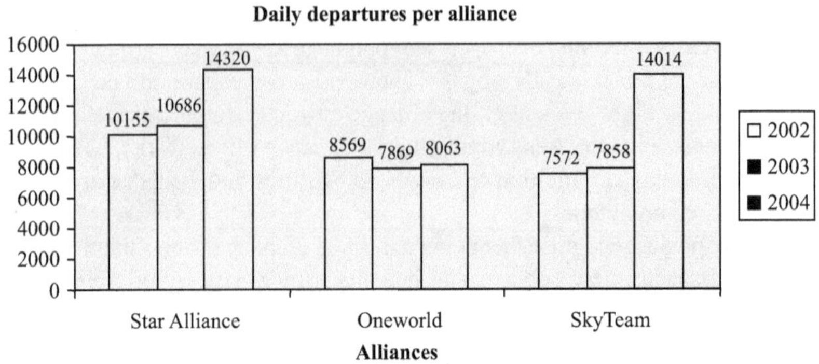

Fig. 16.4 Daily departures per alliance (Sources: Oneworld/SkyTeam/StarAlliance)

records the most significant increase (in the reference years 21% and 33.8% growth for countries and airports served) and operates in a greater number of countries, Star Alliance continues to have the highest presence at airports.

As regards daily departures, developments are similar to previously illustrated data, with the Oneworld alliance declining in 2003 and recovering somewhat in 2004 in terms of daily departures per alliance, as shown in Fig. 16.4. SkyTeam saw a remarkable 85% increase from 2002 to 2004, and Star Alliance grew by 41%, although continuing to experience a positive change. The fact that SkyTeam recorded such a high growth level is due to the adherence of KLM, Continental and Northwest in September 2004.

Figure 16.5 shows daily code sharing flights per alliance, stress being laid on an increase by around 325% in Skyteam, while the daily code sharing flights of Star Alliance and Oneworld increased by 74% and 31% respectively from 2002 to 2004.

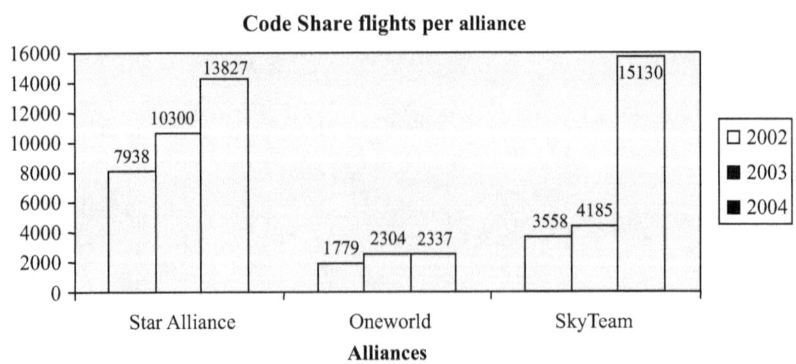

Fig. 16.5 Daily code sharing flights per alliance (Sources: Oneworld/SkyTeam/StarAlliance)

16.5.3 Trends of Strategic Alliances in the Air Transport Sector

Developments in strategic alliances have been ongoing and seem to have reached the first development stage, given that there are still numerous aspects worthy of review, as a result of errors identified in the past, which the industry is now seeking to refine and improve.

Brueckner and Pels (2005) argues that European air transport industry observers are of the opinion that the flag carrier system has introduced too many air carriers into a relatively small geographical area. A viable option is the consolidation of the European industry, with recourse to crossborder mergers, a possibility brought about by deregulation in the European Union.

If this option materialises and given that air carriers belong to different global alliance groups, new realignments will occur at corporate level, similarly to KLM and Northwest, founding members of the Wings alliance. With the merger in 2004 of Air France and KLM, partners in distinct strategic alliances, KLM and its partner Northwest joined the Air France alliance, SkyTeam. The global alliance was thus consolidated by the presence of four of the major world airlines.

Dennis (2005) advocates that mergers between major companies belonging to distinct alliance groups may contribute to reduce competition or monopolies in specific locations, where a few airlines hold a dominant position. The author stresses that if alliances do merge (as a consequence of the merger of companies integrating it) there may be a return to an industry where all air carriers cooperate with each other (similarly to the IATA agreement). Hence, smaller companies are more protected in terms of market access and smaller hub airports are favoured.

Average-sized cities are expected to be less served by flag carriers, given that these cannot offer the synergies of the main hubs and are exposed to competition from low-cost airlines, which in 2003 held 15% of the intra-European market. This will not occur in cities where flag carriers have a strong competitive position.

It follows that the consequences of airline alliance group strategies will have a bearing at the level of airports and local economies. The attractiveness of a city as a location to implement and carry on business depends directly on its accessibility. If regular transportation is not ensured, this may lead companies to transfer to more accessible cities in terms of air transport, thereby contributing to a rise in the region's unemployment. The commercial aircraft manufacturer Boeing relocated its head office from Seattle to Chicago, given that the latter supplied direct air transport services.

In fact, the geographical patterns of demand no longer determine the design of alliance networks; instead, the strategies developed are an increasingly decisive influence to locations for industrial development and economic activity.

Airlines have also abandoned a number of routes and are expected to continue redefining their flights according to the stance of the alliance to which they belong, so as to jointly create competitive advantages. The SAS airline operated to Hong Kong from Copenhagen. However, it changed its service in favour of Star Alliance flight connections via Bangkok with Thai Airways or via Frankfurt am Main with Lufthansa.

Dennis (2005) claims that up until now strategic alliance groups continue to seek more efficient ways of organising, given that the level of integration within alliances is far from being perfect and it is likely that airlines within the same alliance continue to compete, neglecting their partners' strategies.

According to the World Tourism Organisation (WTO), most flights will be served by one of the three alliances groups – mega-alliances – by 2010, if major companies achieve their goals, thus implying a decline in competition. This may entail a serious risk for passengers, if these groups decide to divide world regions among themselves, creating spheres of major influence, contributing to the weakening of non-allied competitors, and causing a rise in the value of fares.

Albers et al. (2005) defends that in the future there should be alliances between airlines and airports, as a way of responding to increased competition, for it will allow both parties to develop competitive advantages. The alliance between Lufthansa and the Munich airport guaranteed the preference in slots for the airline and a reduction in costs and risks for the airport, given that part of the investment was ensured by Lufthansa.

16.5.4 On the Low-Cost Revolution

Another important trend to be considered for the future ahead on what concerns airline transport is the one of low-cost airlines. In fact, these companies comprise a somewhat new concept of strategic management which has shown successful and is intrinsically different in the way they approach cost (see Page 2005, p. 298, for example).

The low-cost companies have benefited significantly from the liberalization of the air transport occurred in the early 90s in Europe, seizing the opportunity through substantial innovation mainly on the side of operational and administrative costs – part of this is indeed web-innovation, but there are also other aspects of strategic nature that should be decoupled from the web-revolution, such as the use of secondary airports (charging lower rates) and the placement of their headquarters in less central places. Other important aspects of the business model of low cost airlines are its focus in point-to-point networks, highly average daily aircraft utilization rates, one aircraft type, fast turnarounds, no commissions to travel agents and also no-frills provided to passengers.

According to Almeida (2008), in 2007 there were about 60 low-cost airlines operating in Europe, with Easyjet and Ryanair ranking first, both in terms of overall number of passengers and financial performance. These two low-cost airlines carried altogether around 74 million passengers in 2006 and are still in an expanding trend, both in terms of routes and fleet expansion. As a result, the market share of low-cost carriers in Europe has soared over the last years, reaching around 17% of all flights by end 2006 (EUROCONTROL data). Increasing petrol costs, however, when considered together with additional efficiency strains stemming from increasing competition should conduct the low-cost market to a stabilization path.

Overall, the low-cost airline business equals innovative use of economics, marketing, geography and management (Page 2005), and in spite of its success being highly based on the overall combination of these factors, there is strong competition ahead on this field as traditional air carriers adapt to the new competitive conditions and gradually strike back. So far consumers have benefited substantially from this increasing competition in the air transport market, either in terms of prices and the diversity of supply.

The benefits of the air service liberalization for tourism and, in particular, the ones stemming from the so-called "low-cost revolution" are huge. As referred in Sect. 16.2, when the benefits of aviation have evolved from a privilege of a few to a market service available to all, tourism become a global phenomenon. Low-cost airlines have not only provided access to air travel to the common citizen, but have also made available destinations previously unreachable, therefore quickly becoming an important instrument of mass tourism and market expansion. This structural change corresponds to a supply shock analytically expressed by an expanding shift in the supply curve, leading to a new dynamic market equilibrium with increased quantities and lower prices. At the end of the adjustment process the consumer (most times tourist) is the ultimate beneficiary of wider choices at better prices.

Notwithstanding the obvious benefits of the "low-cost revolution" to the development of tourism, it should be also considered that the effects of low-cost carrier operations go beyond the strict context of the tourism sector itself by affecting land-use and infrastructure planning policies (Rebollo and Baidal 2008), gradually shaping a new scenario in certain destinations covered by well established low-cost routes, as is the case for the increasing specialization trend of tourism in real estate along the Spanish and Portuguese Mediterranean coasts, for example. These spatial effects in economics systems and territories are materializing as the renovated air transport market evolves and constitute fertile matter for future research.

In fact, the emergence of low-cost carriers, following air travel deregulation in Europe and abroad, prompts major implications for individual firms and regional economies (Williams and Baláž, 2008). The activities of low-cost carriers have had also substantial impacts on flows of migrant labour force, knowledge, business connectivity and investment, and other markets, especially on what concerns tourism. The resulting implications to institutions and regional externalities contribute to net changes in the transaction costs of individual firms, regional competitiveness, and the unfolding and increasingly interconnected map of uneven regional development in Europe. This is, however, an extension of the current subject, being – again – one possible path for future research.

16.6 Conclusions

Tourism is today a global phenomenon with a substantial and factual economic importance in an increasing number of states around the world. The role of air transport in the wide spreading of the tourism phenomenon is sometimes so obvious and common sensed that it tends to blend in the history of aviation itself.

However, the increased competition in the air transport market stemming from the deregulation process started in Europe in the late eighties prompted a series of new actions and competitive strategies from European carriers in the past decade, such as mergers, take-overs and alliances. As a result of this process (supply shock), a new dynamic market equilibrium occurred, with increased quantities and lower prices, benefiting tourism and travel.

The air transport market is characterized by having a limited number of supply agents. This somewhat oligopolistic nature of the market implies that competitors often tend to regard certain forms of strategic cooperation as a more efficient way of competing. The increasing number of alliances established among air transport companies in the recent past is a trend reflecting this tendency to enrol into cooperative games in an increasingly competitive industry.

The conditions for the occurrence of mega-alliances between major air companies – as well as the eventual merging of existing alliances – exist therefore in the market and will eventually reinforce over time. Airports will most probably engage also into cooperative agreements with airlines, evolving to global alliances in order to ease the competition effort and keep pace with the competitive advantages acquired.

Small market niches will probably remain to be explored by low-cost airlines, which are flexible enough (namely in terms of the cost structure) to continue to benefit from the residual demand from official carriers, apart from their own competitiveness for well established destinations. In this sense, the most efficient low-cost airlines will continue to face important sources of competitive pressure from the most consolidated airline strategic alliances, namely on what regards domestic and short distance flights.

References

Albers S, Koch B, Ruff C (2005) Strategic alliances between airlines and airports: theoretical assessment and practical evidence. J Air Transp Manage 11:49–58

Almeida CR (2008) A Operação das Companhias Aéreas de Baixo Custo no Aeroporto de Faro (1996–2006). In: Matias A, Sardinha R (eds) Avanços em Economia e Gestão do Turismo: Novas Tendências, Sustentabilidade e Desenvolvimento Regional. Editora Piaget, Lisboa, Portugal

Beting G (2006) Star alliance – A estrela mais brilhante. www.jetsite.com.br/mostra_mkt.asp?codi=27. Accessed 15 February 2006.

Biegera T, Wittmerb A. (2006) Air transport and tourism – Perspectives and challenges for destinations, airlines and governments. J Air Transp Manage 12(1):40–46

Bleeke J, Ernst D (1994) Collaborating to compete. In: Mintzberg H, Lampel JB, Quinn JB, Ghoshal S (eds) The strategy process. Prentice Hall, Hempstead

Brueckner JK, Pels E (2005) European airline mergers, alliance consolidation, and consumer welfare. J Air Transp Manage 11:27–41

Dennis N (2005) Industry consolidation and future airline network structures in Europe. J Air Transp Manage 11:175–183

Freire A (1997) Estratégia: sucesso em Portugal. Editorial Verbo, Lisboa, Portugal

French T (1997) Global trends in Airline Alliances. Travel Tourism Anal 4:81–101

French T (1998) Europe's regional airlines. Travel Tourism Anal 5:1–18

Grant RM (2005) Contemporary strategy analysis. Blackwell, Oxford

Hax AC, Majluf NS (1996) The strategy concept and process: a pragmatic approach. Prentice Hall, New Jersey

Iatrou K, Alamdari F (2005) The empirical analysis of the impact of alliances on airline operations. J Air Transp Manage 11:127–134

Kleymann B (2005) The dynamics of multilateral allying: a process perspective on airline alliances. J Air Transp Manage 11:135–147

Martin JC, Voltes-Dorta A (2008) Theoretical evidence of exciting pitfalls in measuring hubbing practices in airline networks. Netw Spat Econ 9:161–182

Nijkamp P (2008) Policy developments in the airline industry. In: de Jong D, Kaashoek B, Zondag WJ (eds) Blue skies or storm clouds. Airlines Magazine Foundation, pp 20–25

Quinn JB (1998) Strategy for change. In: Mintzberg H, Lampel JB, Quinn JB, Ghoshal S (eds) The strategy process. Prentice Hall, Hempstead, UK, pp 5–13

Page SJ (2005) Transport and tourism: global perspectives (second edition). Prentice Hall, Hempstead, UK

Porter ME (1996) What is strategy. Harv Bus Rev 96608:61–78

Vera Rebollo JF, Ivars Baidal JA (2008) Spread of low-cost carriers: tourism and regional policy effects in Spain. Reg Stud (in press)

Reggiani A, Nijkamp P, Cento A (2009) Connectivity and competition in airline networks: a study of Lufthansa's network. In: Vervest PHM, Zheng L, Liere DW van (eds) The network experience. Springer, Berlin

Thompson AA, Strickland AJ (1995) Strategic management: concepts and cases. Richard Irwin, Chicago

Williams AM, Baláž V (2008) Low-cost carriers, economies of flows and regional externalities. Reg Stud (in press)

Chapter 17
An Estimation of Tourism Dependence in French Rural Areas

Jean-Christophe Dissart, Francis Aubert, and Stéphanie Truchet

17.1 Introduction

Tourism activity is characterized by trips with an associated set of goods and services including lodging, transportation, food and beverage delivery, personal and recreation services. This economic sector is difficult to define precisely because some of the related activities are not used exclusively for tourism consumption (e.g., restaurants), and thus depend on the permanent vs. temporary population ratio. Though isolating tourism jobs is not easy, it is acknowledged that this "quasi-sector" plays an increasingly important role in the national economy, and is becoming strategic to the development of some areas. Such is the case of many rural areas where a shift away from traditional extractive and manufacturing activities has enhanced the role of hosting functions in general, tourism functions in particular, in local economic growth.

On the demand side of rural tourism, there is an interest in nature and landscape attributes, which are associated with healthy and quiet living conditions. For instance, including environmental variables in hedonic pricing models shows an impact of site characteristics on the rental prices of rural lodging (Mollard et al. 2006). On the supply side, two models of the tourism firm are usually found in rural areas. One model uses significant low-skilled labour but little capital and technology, while adding value to fixed "natural" assets (Eadington and Redman 1991). This model matches rural entrepreneurship relatively well because it is based on family capital and labour and creates activities that suit farm diversification and household pluriactivity. A second, capital intensive, high-skilled labour model may be observed in "specialized" tourism resorts. Often found in mountain or seaside areas, this second model is relatively nonexistent in "ordinary" rural areas (except in leisure parks).

Thus, the type of tourism developing in rural areas is mainly extensive and based on local natural features. From a regional development perspective, the analysis

---

J-C. Dissart (✉)
Cemagref, UR DTM, Grenoble, France
e-mail: stophe.dissart@cemagref.fr

Á. Matias et al. (eds.), *Advances in Tourism Economics*,
DOI 10.1007/978-3-7908-2124-6_17, © Physica-Verlag Heidelberg 2009

of this type of tourism involves three complementary dimensions: (i) conditional factors associated with public goods, (ii) setting up a consistent tourism offer, and (iii) domino effects on the local economy.

First, rural tourism adds value to fixed assets that often have a local public good status. Nature goods are strictly localized; their development and protection management associates rights and uses for which the public sphere plays a major role. Moreover, tourism activity increases consumption of local public services and may require additional utility capacity to meet the needs of the permanent plus temporary population. These are not strict preconditions for the existence of tourism[1] because a given level of under-development or isolation may attract pioneering activities. However, the development of a significant tourism activity requires that public services and local amenities be available and maintained.

The second dimension pertains to how fragmented smaller projects add up to a consistent local offer. Contrary to resorts, which are planned and built in an integrated manner, rural tourism is made up of aggregated individual initiatives that more or less refer to a common context –a *pays d'accueil touristique*[2] for instance. Indeed, the issue is to provide a full and consistent array of tourism activities. The supply of primary goods and services (such as lodging and recreation activities) may adjust through competition, but nothing guarantees the implementation of secondary functions (e.g., fairs) over a reasonable time range. Moreover, territorial cohesion implies that user conflicts over access to fixed assets have been solved. Consequently, there is a need for an overall regulation of the local tourism offer, and it is critical to define an appropriate scale for coordinating tourism initiatives.

Third is the question of regional economic impacts of tourism activities. In addition to direct tourism jobs, indirect (in activities that have business relations with tourism activities per se) as well as induced (in sectors that benefit from increased demand due to higher local income in tourism activities) jobs must be taken into account. The analysis of indirect jobs requires input–output models to estimate intersectoral relation coefficients for every economic sector in contact with the tourism sector. The analysis of induced effects is based on the estimation of a multiplier that calculates demand changes in the residentiary sector after an exogenous shock changes income flows in the regional system.[3] These two methods are sensitive to the size of the study region and to the degree of integration of the given economy (Vollet 1998).

The objectives of the paper focus on identifying the importance of tourism activities in rural areas. First, tourism-related jobs have to be identified, then the level of tourism activity is analyzed with respect to both the role of natural resources and local growth. In order to take regional effects into account, the analysis is conducted at Functional Economic Area (FEA, *bassin de vie*) level. The rest of the

[1] Assuming elementary conditions of accessibility.

[2] An area with a multimunicipal organization (e.g., an association) that brings together all stakeholders in order to implement a tourism development project.

[3] Additional income due to tourist spending is considered exogenous.

paper is organized as follows. Section 17.2 presents efforts to define rural tourism in the French and North American literatures. Section 17.3 presents data and methods. The results regarding FEA classification, tourism dependence and regional economic indicators are presented and discussed in Section 17.4. The conclusion outlines study limits and further research topics.

17.2 Literature Review

The most frequent definition of tourism refers to tourist consumption (i.e., induced by at least one overnight stay for leisure and other purposes). An alternative definition may also be suggested on the basis of the set of goods and services supplied by the tourism branch: "Tourism is the aggregate of all businesses that directly provide goods or services to facilitate business, pleasure, and leisure activities away from the home environment" (Smith 1988, 1983). This supply-side approach is more appropriate for regional analyses that differentiate between areas in terms of tourism activity (and employment in particular).

The distinction between rural tourism and other kinds of tourism is vague because the usual rural-urban distinction (e.g., urban area zoning) is not sufficient. It must be extended by a second classification that considers the nature of tourist destinations. Major tourism-related organizations thus make a distinction between city, seaside, mountain, and countryside tourism, the latter comprising leftovers from the first three. According to this typology and data from the Ministry of Tourism regarding trips for personal purposes (Direction du Tourisme 2006), "countryside" tourism is equivalent, in terms of number of nights, to "city" tourism (around 30%), before "mountain" tourism (20%), but after "seaside" tourism (40%).[4] In terms of full-time equivalent jobs, however, the situation is different (Baccaïni et al. 2006): urban tourism accounts for over 48% of total tourism jobs, followed by seaside (23%), then rural (19%), then mountains (9.5%, including ski resorts). If the share of local employment in tourism is considered, then rural tourism is at the same level as urban tourism: around 3% (Baccaïni et al. 2006). However, in the countryside, tourism tends to be characterized by relatively shorter stays and the importance of family contacts and friends.

More generally, focusing on tourism leads to refine the notion of residentiary (i.e., population-dependent, in an export base theoretical framework) economy. In defining FEAs, INSEE (2003) took the classic primary-secondary-tertiary typology a step further by distinguishing agrifood (agriculture and agrifood processing), manufacturing and residentiary specializations, where the latter (i.e., in which at least 50% of the jobs are in population-dependent activities) is differentiated according to tourism. Using a lodging capacity criterion relative to the resident population (ratio > 1.5), about 10% of FEAs exhibit a residentiary-touristic specialization. Analyzing the situation of rural areas on a municipality basis, Aubert et al. (2006)

[4] As several destinations may be reached taking only one single trip, the total is greater than 100%.

differentiated between three types of communes for which tourism is significant: "non performing soft tourism", "attractive tourist sites", and "tourism economies with uncertain performance". The differences were related to the spatial organization of tourism activities (spread vs. polarized), and to their economic performance in terms of employment base (i.e., sometimes weak and often precarious). These results match those of other studies that tend to question the impact of tourism activities on rural economic development (Dissart 2005). In this perspective, a comparison of the French vs. American situation is interesting.

Indeed, in order to provide relevant information to policymakers, researchers and public officials, the Economic Research Service of the US Department of Agriculture has created a specific typology.[5] It includes recreation activity among seven overlapping categories of policy-relevant themes: (1) housing stress, (2) low-education, (3) low-employment, (4) persistent poverty, (5) population loss, (6) nonmetro recreation, and (7) retirement destination. The nonmetro recreation category comprises 334 counties, i.e., 16% of rural counties (USDA-ERS 2005). This designation is based on a combination of factors including the share of employment or share of earnings in recreation-related industries in 1999, the share of seasonally or occasionally used housing units in 2000, and per capita receipts from motels and hotels in 1997.

The "nonmetro recreation" type is actually an update and an extension of the pioneering work of Beale and Johnson (1998) who identified 285 recreational counties using two types of criteria. On the one hand, empirical criteria: (1) share of employment and income in recreation services (lodging for the most part), share of seasonal or occasional or recreation housing, with a value for two of these three variables greater than two-thirds of a standard deviation above the national mean, or (2) lodging revenues per capita greater than US$100. On the other hand, a context criterion – presence of recreation activity- was used to remove observations with a significant trip activity but without a recreation objective: using guidebooks or maps, Beale and Johnson (1998) removed clusters of motels and restaurants located along major East-West highways where travellers do not stay for recreational activities.

Following Beale and Johnson (1998), but also Leatherman and Marcouiller (1996), English et al. (2000) analyzed tourism dependence and estimated its effects on US rural counties. In order to take account of structural differences in resources, cluster analysis was used to group similar counties with respect to population density, distance from metropolitan areas, and the proportion of county area in cropland, forests, range/pasture, and mountains. Within each cluster, they estimated the share of export employment, distinguishing between tourism stays (based on resources) and other stays (business or family related), by using data on four economic sectors: lodging, eating and drinking, recreation services and retail trade. In particular, the

[5]The typology (USDA-ERS 2005) classifies all US counties according to six non-overlapping categories of economic dependence, primarily established on the basis of the share of annual labor and proprietors' earnings from a given sector over the 1998–2000 period. Thus are distinguished the following dependence categories: farming, mining, manufacturing, government (Federal/State), services, and nonspecialized.

share of export employment in tourism-sensitive sectors was estimated by regression analysis, taking account of recreation resources grouped into four categories (urban, land, water and winter resources) by principal components analysis. Last, they defined tourism-dependent counties as those with more than double the national percentage for tourism jobs and income, and compared them to other rural counties with respect to several indicators (income, population, economic structure and housing). Tourism-dependent counties experienced greater increases in population growth and housing construction than other rural counties.

17.3 Data and Methods

17.3.1 Data

Data were collected at Functional Economic Area level (FEA, *bassin de vie*). An FEA is an aggregate of communes and defined as the smallest area over which its population has access to both services and employment (INSEE 2003). Among the 1,916 FEAs defined over the French metropolitan territory, 1,745 correspond to small town FEAs, i.e., rural FEAs (Julien 2007). FEAs were chosen because they correspond more to economic reality than purely administrative boundaries, and they offer a satisfactory amount of data at a relatively fine scale.

The analysis is based on two major categories of data. First, natural resource data were mainly collected from the European database Corine Land Cover. The CLC2000 database provides a biophysical inventory of land cover that is based on satellite images for the year 2000. Land covers are stratified according to a hierarchical nomenclature arranged in three levels and 44 classes, with 5 major land cover types: artificial surfaces, agricultural areas, forests and semi-natural areas, wetlands, and water bodies. Land cover attributes were overlayed with a commune grid, which yielded area values per commune for every land cover class. These values were aggregated at FEA level, then divided by total FEA area in order to obtain relative values of land cover for all CLC classes.

As topographic variation is a source of attractiveness (see, e.g., McGranahan 1999), a corresponding variable was created using IGN data: the difference between the altitude of the town hall in the FEA's main commune and the maximum altitude in the FEA.

On the other hand, socioeconomic data, including tourism indicators, were collected from several sources. Tourism indicators are of two types: the commune's tourism lodging capacity, and tourism employment. The former was operationalized with three variables: number of hotel rooms and campground spaces (INSEE website) and second-homes (*Direction Générale des Collectivités Locales*); to obtain a relative measure, these variables were divided by total FEA area. Data on tourism employment were collected from the Unedic website. Data on paid employment are available from the year 1993 on, for several geographic scales (from commune to district) and several levels of economic sector nomenclature (from NES 16 to NAF 700). Commune data on total employment and tourism sector employment (see Box 17.1) were downloaded at the NAF 700 level for the year 2003.

Box 17.1 Tourism-sensitive activities

INSEE and the Ministry of Tourism have identified 15 tourism sensitive activities that satisfy tourist needs. In the French Activity Nomenclature (NAF rev. 1, 2003), these activities are classified as follows:

- Lodging: tourism hotels with a restaurant (551A); tourism hotels without a restaurant (551C); other hotels (551E); youth hostels (552A); campgrounds (552C); other tourism lodging (552E)
- Restaurants and cafés: traditional restaurants (553A); fast-food restaurants (553B); *cafés tabacs*[6] (554A); bars (554B)
- Other activities: cable cars, ski lifts (602C); travel agencies (633Z); beauty salons (930E); spa and thalassotherapy activities (930 K); other body care (930L)

Employment in these sectors was aggregated at FEA level, then divided by total area employment in order to obtain a proportion of tourism employment for every FEA. To account for structural differences between FEAs, these values were refined using the minimum requirements method (see next section).

To model the influence of tourism dependence on regional indicators, other socioeconomic variables were retained for the analysis:

- Dependent variables: population, employment, income. Regarding the latter, there was no information for 1,550 communes (included in the 1,745 rural FEAs) with fewer than 10 (taxable or non-taxable) households.
- Control variables: demographic composition (share of population aged under 20 or over 60); proportion of employment in the three major economic sectors (agriculture and agrifood processing, manufacturing, residentiary); access time to the closest urban core; and a global score that reflects the presence of jobs and services (see INSEE 2003). Indeed, five weighted components (with a 0-4 value range) make up a global score for each FEA: (1) score on competing services (e.g., supermarkets), (2) on non competing services (e.g., police force), (3) on education services (e.g., high schools), (4) on health services (e.g., physicians), and (5) on job offers. The latter, which is critical to define the boundaries of the FEA, is given a weight of 8 (out of 20) in the calculation of the global score.

Overall, the analysis used data for the years 1999 (population census), 2000 (Corine Land Cover) or 2003 (tourism indicators), unless otherwise indicated.

[6]Cafés in which tobacco is sold.

17.3.2 Methods

The analysis was carried out in several steps: (1) clustering of FEAs according to resources; (2) estimation of tourism employment in clusters (using the minimum requirements technique); (3) identification of formed clusters' key features; (4) definition of tourism-dependent FEAs; (5) estimation of the impact of resources on tourism indicators; and (6) estimation of the impact of tourism dependence on regional development indicators.

First, in order to work with similar FEAs from the perspective of landscape features, a cluster analysis of resources was performed. To obtain a distribution of FEAs over major types of resources and to account for the sensitivity of cluster analysis to variable correlation (implicit weight), CLC classes were grouped. First, an analysis done with the 5 major land covers showed that, in rural FEAs, the vast majority of land is covered by agricultural areas (63.8%) and forests and semi-natural areas (29.9%); the remainder is split between artificial surfaces (5%), water bodies (0.8%) and wetlands (0.5%). To get a finer distribution, a more detailed land cover nomenclature was considered: (1) within agricultural areas, arable land (31%) and other agricultural uses of the land (permanent crops, pastures, heterogeneous agricultural areas: 33%), and (2) within forests and semi-natural areas, forests (24%) and semi-natural areas (scrub, herbaceous, little or no vegetation: 6%). As the analysis showed a high level of correlation between semi-natural areas and topographic variation, the former was dropped, but category 3.3.1 (beaches, dunes, sands) was added to the wetlands category because of a high level of correlation between the two.

To account for the weight of the residentiary economy, and because the minimum requirements technique assumes similar economic structures, population was added to the set of clustering criterion variables.[7] As variables were measured in different units, they were standardized to a mean of 0 and a standard deviation of 1.

Cluster analysis used the fastclus procedure in SAS®, which yields disjoint clusters from a large number of observations over quantitative variables. This method, often called k-means, uses Euclidean distances, with a least squares estimation of cluster centres. Each iteration of the algorithm reduces the least squares criterion until convergence is achieved; cluster centres are then the means of the observations that are assigned to each cluster.

The final number of clusters was decided on the basis of several empirical criteria, including pseudo F and cubic clustering criterion values (local or global maximum value, or a significant change in the values of these statistics), value (and change in value, in particular when the gain becomes less than 5%) of the R^2.

Final clusters were distinguished using the values taken by clustering criterion variables on the coefficient of variation statistic (standard deviation/mean * 100). A low value of this coefficient indicates relative non dispersion of the values of a clustering variable, hence a salient feature of the considered cluster.

---

[7]Note that area is correlated with population, and population density is proxied by the share of artificial surfaces within a given FEA.

The second step of the analysis consisted in estimating the share of tourism jobs within clusters. Those are relatively easy to identify whenever corresponding activities depend exclusively on tourism demand (e.g., hotels or ski lifts); but tourism jobs are more difficult to count when activities satisfy the demand of both tourists and the local population (e.g., retail stores or restaurants). Several techniques exist to estimate the level of employment that satisfies tourism demand; it is defined as the surplus of jobs which results from the regular or seasonal presence of tourists (Terrier et al. 2005). One such technique is the location quotient which uses, as a benchmark, a geographic (also economic) scale that is greater than the unit of analysis; for example, the administrative region or the nation, relatively to the FEA.

Another technique is the minimum requirements, which uses as a reference a scale that is identical to the unit of analysis (Ullman 1968). The assumption is that similar regions exhibit similar consumption patterns and export propensities. Within a given cluster, the FEA that presents the minimum employment value in tourism-sensitive activities is assumed to satisfy local demand only, i.e., the value of tourism export employment is considered nil. In other FEAs, the share of export employment is equal to the difference between the share of employment in tourism-sensitive activities and the minimum value observed for the cluster: in other words, all FEAs (except for the minimum) are exporters in order to satisfy non resident demand (Leatherman and Marcouiller 1996).

Consequently, the formula to estimate the share of tourism export employment for FEA i in cluster j is the following:

$$\mathrm{EX}_{ij} = (\mathrm{et}_{ij}/\mathrm{eT}_{ij}) - \min(\mathrm{et}_{ij}/\mathrm{eT}_{ij})$$

Where EX_{ij} is the share of tourism export employment for FEA i in cluster j; et_{ij} is the level of tourism employment for FEA i in cluster j; eT_{ij} is the level of total employment for FEA i in cluster j; and min (.) is the minimum function that identifies the minimum value of the $\mathrm{et}_{ij}/\mathrm{eT}_{ij}$ ratio for all FEAs i in cluster j.

Cluster key features were identified on the basis of both cluster analysis and the estimation of tourism employment, i.e., values taken by clustering variables and tourism indicators in the formed clusters, including tests for differences between means to assess the statistical significance of observed differences.

Fourth step: the identification of FEAs specialized in "tourism". Following English et al. (2000), we used a value that is greater than twice the national average as an indicator of dependence. Lodging and employment variables were combined with the following decision rule: a rural FEA is identified as tourism-specialized (or -dependent) if it exhibits a value for the proportion of tourism export employment that is greater than twice the national average AND a value for the density of hotel rooms OR campground spaces OR second-homes that is greater than twice the national average. A related dummy variable for tourism dependence (DEPTRSM) was created so that each rural FEA may be considered as specialized in tourism activity or not.

Table 17.1 Variables retained for the analysis

Name	Description	Source
	Dependent variables	
PSDC99[a]	Population (1999)	INSEE[b]
TOT_EMPL	Number of jobs (1999)	INSEE[b]
ERNET99BV	Sum of net taxable income (€, 1999)	b.o.d.f. DGI
DHTCH03	Density of hotel rooms (#/km^2, 2003)	b.o.d.f. INSEE[c]
DCPGE03	Density of campground spaces (#/km^2, 2003)	b.o.d.f. INSEE[c]
DRSCND03	Density of second homes (#/km^2, 2003)	b.o.d.f. DGCL
MRTRSM03	Share of tourism export employment (%, 2003)	b.o.d.f. UNEDIC[d]
	Resource (clustering and explanatory) variables	
VARTOPOG	Topographic variation (m, 2000)	b.o.d.f. IGN
PCTARTIF	Share of artificial surfaces (%, 2000)	b.o.d.f. CLC[e]
PCTARABL	Share of arable land (%, 2000)	b.o.d.f. CLC[e]
PCTOTHAG	Share of other agriculture: permanent crops, pastures, heterogeneous agric. areas (%, 2000)	b.o.d.f. CLC[e]
PCTFORET	Share of forests (%, 2000)	b.o.d.f. CLC[e]
PCTHUMO2	Share of wetlands and water bodies (%, 2000)	b.o.d.f. CLC[e]
	Other control (explanatory) variables	
POPAGE	Share of population aged 60 or over (%, 1999)	b.o.d.f. INSEE[b]
PCTRES	Share of jobs in residentiary services (%, 1999)	b.o.d.f. INSEE[b]
PCTAA	Share of jobs in agriculture and agrifood (%, 1999)	b.o.d.f. INSEE[b]
TT_PU99	Average access time to closest urban core (min, 1999)	INSEE[b]
SCORE20	Score on jobs and services potential (over 20, 1999)	INSEE[b]
DEPTRSM	Dummy for tourism dependence	Authors

b.o.d.f.: based on data from
[a] also a clustering variable.
[b] ruralbv1 file (http://www.insee.fr/fr/ffc/docs_ffc/bassins_vie/bassins_vie.htm).
[c] Commune capacity in tourism lodging (http://www.insee.fr/fr/ffc/docs_ffc/tourisme.htm).
[d] Annual statistics by geographic area (http://info.assedic.fr/unistatis/index.php).
[e] Corine Land Cover (http://www.ifen.fr/donIndic/Donnees/corine/presentation.htm).

Last steps: regression analysis was used to estimate impacts. On the one hand, in order to assess the relationship between resources and tourism indicators, each indicator (employment, hotel room, campground space, second-home) was regressed on clustering variables. On the other hand, to assess the impact of tourism dependence on regional development indicators, classic indicators (population, employment, income) were regressed on the tourism dependence dummy and a set of control variables[8] (demographic composition of the FEA, its economic structure, its dis-

[8]Due to a high level of correlation level between the proportion of senior and young populations ($\rho > 0.91$), the latter was dropped from the specification (priority was given to the variable that could reflect the importance of amenity-driven retiree migration). Likewise, the level of correlation between the share of manufacturing employment and the two other sectors (residentiary services in particular, with $\rho > 0.68$) led us to drop this variable from model specification.

tance to the closest urban core, and its score in terms of access to jobs and services). For the last two steps, the chosen estimator was Ordinary Least Squares (OLS).

As a conclusion, Table 17.1 summarizes variables and their respective sources.

17.4 Results and Discussion

17.4.1 Cluster Analysis

Choosing clusters formed by cluster analysis necessarily implies a tradeoff between depicting the diversity of situations and observing patterns across observations. The final number of clusters is 4; it was determined from values taken by the selection criteria (pseudo F, CCC, R^2) for several runs (choice of the number of clusters formed) of the k-means procedure. This solution presents an R^2 value of 0.44. Results are detailed in Table 17.2 (standardized variables).

Iterations confirmed that a combination of wetlands and water bodies yielded a better solution from a statistical viewpoint. Relatively recurrent outliers were detected, all located in the *département* of Hérault (especially Marseillan and Palavas-les-Flots, but also Aigues-Mortes, Villeneuve-les-Maguelone, and Le Grau-du-Roi). As these observations are major tourism destinations and did not appear immediately (at least not before the number of clusters was greater than or equal to the number of clustering variables), it was decided to keep them.

Based on coefficient of variation values that are less than 100 (highlighted in Table 17.2), the clusters formed may be interpreted as follows:

- Cluster 1 comprises 606 rural FEAs. It is mainly characterized by the absence of topographic variation and other agriculture (permanent crops, pastures), but the presence of arable land (field crops).
- Cluster 2 comprises 28 FEAs. Like cluster 1, it is mostly characterized by the absence of topographic variation. Contrary to cluster 1, though, there is a relative absence of field crops and forests, but presence of water resources (wetlands and water bodies). In a less salient way, cluster 2 also comprises FEAs where the proportion of artificial surfaces is relatively high.
- Cluster 3, with 428 observations, features a deficit of arable land that is counterbalanced by the presence of forests, and to a lesser extent by topographic variation.
- Last, cluster 4 comprises the greatest number of observations (683 FEAs). A greater-than-average presence of pastures and permanent crops, and to a lesser extent a marked absence of topographic variation, field crops and forests, are the salient features of this cluster.

In conclusion and generally speaking, there are four clusters of resources: (1) field crop plains, (2) water, (3) forests and topographic variation, and (4) pastures and permanent crops. Population turns out not to be a discriminant variable in the definition of these resource-like FEAs. In contrast, natural resource and landscape

Table 17.2 Cluster analysis results

Variable		Cluster 1	Cluster 2	Cluster 3	Cluster 4
	N=	606	28	428	683
Population	Mean	0.0842	−0.1054	−0.0777	−0.0217
	Stand. deviat.	1.0159	0.5244	0.9869	1.0050
	Coeff. var.	1,207	−497	−1,271	−4,629
Topogr. var. (m)	Mean	−0.4368	−0.5292	1.1234	−0.2947
	Stand. deviat.	0.1754	0.1673	1.4710	0.3376
	Coeff. var.	−40	−32	131	−115
Artif. surf. (%)	Mean	0.2178	1.8846	−0.3095	−0.0766
	Stand. deviat.	1.1997	2.0225	0.6598	0.7694
	Coeff. var.	551	107	−213	−1005
Arable land (%)	Mean	1.1012	−0.8300	−0.9230	−0.3646
	Stand. deviat.	0.6478	0.5536	0.3673	0.5610
	Coeff. var.	59	−67	−40	−154
Other agric. land (%)	Mean	−0.7621	−0.1375	−0.4591	0.9696
	Stand. deviat.	0.5224	0.9454	0.6604	0.6450
	Coeff. var.	−69	−688	−144	67
Forests (%)	Mean	−0.4088	−0.9842	1.3065	−0.4156
	Stand. deviat.	0.6178	0.6057	0.7858	0.6204
	Coeff. var.	−151	−62	60	−149
Water area (%)	Mean	−0.1186	6.3893	−0.1047	−0.0911
	Stand. deviat.	0.3642	3.3974	0.3920	0.4274
	Coeff. var.	−307	53	−374	−469

Coefficient of variation < 100.

feature variables do enable a statistical differentiation of FEAs and corresponding clusters. Water resources seem to be particularly discriminant: they are the key feature of one of the clusters, though it is the smallest one (28 FEAs).

17.4.2 Key Features

Tests for differences between means as well as regression analysis were used to analyze the differences between cluster resources and whether they have a differentiated impact on tourism. Results for the means tests regarding clustering and tourism variables are presented in Table 17.3.

Formed clusters present values that, in general, are statistically different (even with a conservative test, see Table 17.3). This result is indeed expected for clustering criterion variables because cluster analysis aims at creating groups of observations

Table 17.3 Comparing cluster means of criterion and tourism variables

Variables	Cluster 1 (N = 606)	Cluster 2 (N = 28)	Cluster 3 (N = 428)	Cluster 4 (N = 683)	Differences[a] between cluster means?
Clustering variables					
Population	12,967	11,150	11,416	11,952	None (except 1–3)
Topographic variation (m)	99.65	52.43	896.91	172.26	All
Artificial surfaces (%)	6.19	15.43	3.27	4.56	All
Arable land (%)	58.49	9.04	6.65	20.95	All (except 2–3)
Other agric. land (%)	17.25	30.62	23.74	54.31	All (except 2–3)
Forests (%)	16.12	5.26	48.49	15.99	All (except 1–4)
Water area (%)	0.84	30.40	0.90	0.96	All (except 1–3/1–4/3–4)
Tourism variables					
Hotel room density (#/km^2)	0.54	9.56	1.35	0.79	All (except 1–4/2–3)
Campground space density (#/km^2)	2.48	79.71	2.85	3.00	All (except 1–3/1–4/3–4)
Second home density (#/km^2)	5.36	164.28	8.95	7.01	All (except 1–4/3–4)
Tourism employ. (%)	3.45	10.88	9.76	4.00	All, except 2–3

[a] Statistically significant difference between 2 means (p-value ≤ 0.05; sample variances assumed unequal).

such that inter-cluster differences are maximized while minimizing intra-cluster differences. However, means tests on tourism indicators also show statistically significant differences between clusters. Except for campground spaces, which are spatially concentrated in cluster 2 (water resources), hotel room and second-home density and the local share of tourism employment are generally different from one cluster to another. That is to say, differences in natural resources do match differences in tourism intensity.

17.4.3 Tourism Dependence

Using the criterion of twice the rural national average on the four tourism indicators (share of tourism employment, density of hotel rooms, density of campground spaces, density of second-homes), several groups of FEAs were identified:

Table 17.4 Characteristics of tourism-dependent FEAs (N = 102)

Variable	Mean	Stand. deviat.	Minimum	Maximum
Tourism employment (%)	25.25	15.57	10.82	71.59
Density of hotel rooms (#/km^2)	8.97	16.40	0	110.83
Density of campground spaces (#/km^2)	38.55	99.34	0	871.67
Density of second homes (#/km^2)	88.46	204.00	1.28	1,940.83

- Specialization in hotel rooms (DHTCH03 > 2*0.98): 143 FEAs with an average of 9 hotel rooms per km2 (8.76).
- Specialization in campground spaces (DCPGE03 > 2*4.01): 111 FEAs with an average of 48 campground spaces per km2 (47.83);
- Specialization in second-homes (DRSCND03 > 2*9.44): 118 FEAs with an average of 97 second homes per km2 (96.64);
- Specialization in tourism employment (MRTRSM03 > 2*5.33): 173 FEAs with an average share of 23% of tourism export employment (23.21).

When employment and lodging criteria are combined, 102 FEAs are identified as tourism-dependent or -specialized, with the following values on tourism indicators (Table 17.4): On average, tourism-dependent FEAs present a share of tourism export employment of 25%, and 9 hotel rooms, 39 campground spaces and 88 second-homes per km^2. These FEAs are heterogeneously distributed both from a cluster and a location perspective (Appendix 2).

From a cluster perspective, most tourism-dependent FEAs are located in cluster 3 (53 FEAs, that is, over half of tourism-dependent FEAs), then in cluster 4 (24 FEAs), then in cluster 1 (15 FEAs), last in cluster 2 (10 FEAs). Therefore, in cluster 3 (forests, topographic variation) the highest count of tourism-specialized FEAs is found, and cluster 2 (water resources) presents the lowest count of such FEAs.

As the number of observations per cluster shows high variation, these results should also be considered in a relative perspective. Then, cluster 2 (water resources) comes first, since a cluster 2 FEA has a probability over 33% (10/28 = 0.36) to be specialized in tourism. In contrast, with 15 tourism-specialized FEAs out of a total of 606, cluster 1 (field crop plains) FEAs present the lowest probability of being tourism-dependent (0.02). By ascending order, cluster 4 (pastures, permanent crops: 0.03) then cluster 3 (forests, topographic variation: 0.12) are found. In this perspective, water resources and topographic variation (correlated with the absence of field crops) seem to condition, to a significant extent, tourism dependence.

The distribution of tourism-dependent FEAs (Appendix 3) from a *département* perspective depicts that Pyrénées-Orientales has the highest number of tourism-dependent FEAs (9), followed by Haute-Savoie (8), then Savoie (7), then Hérault and Morbihan (6 FEAs each), then Var (5). Those 6 *départements* (out of 96 in metropolitan France, i.e., 6%) comprise 40% of tourism-dependent FEAs. By descending order, there are 5 *départements* with 4 dependent FEAs each (Calvados, Gironde, Isère, Haut-Rhin, Vendée), and then 4 *départements* with 3 FEAs each (Charente-Maritime, Finistère, Landes, Puy-de-Dôme). In conclusion, 72% of tourism-specialized FEAs are located in 15 *départements* (that is, 16%).

17.4.4 Regression Analysis

Regression analysis was used to identify the contribution of various factors to the variation of two groups of variables: tourism indicators and classic indicators of regional growth (population, employment, income).

First, the share of tourism employment, hotel room density, campground space density and second-home density were regressed on clustering criterion variables, except population: topographic variation, share of total FEA area in artificial surfaces, arable land, pastures and permanent crops, forests, and wetlands and water bodies. Population was not included in the final specifications[9] for two reasons: (1) it was not a discriminant variable in cluster analysis; and (2) we chose to focus on the resource-tourism relationship.

As PCTARABL was correlated with VARTOPOG, PCTOTHAG and PCTFORET ($.46 < |\rho| < .52$), and its inclusion in the models resulted in a condition index close to 30, it was removed from model specification. Moreover, to some extent, the presence of field crops is an indicator of the "banality" of the landscape (especially in plains). Therefore, the absence of PCTARABL in model specification may be interpreted as a "background" against which less commonplace resources are highlighted. After dropping PCTARABL, no correlation coefficient value was greater than 0.40, and the condition index dropped to less than 8. The results (corrected for heteroskedasticity) are presented in Table 17.5.

Table 17.5 shows that all models display strong overall significance (Fisher test). The value of the coefficient of determination is greater than 31%, except for the hotel room model (19%). Tourism employment and lodging density can probably be related to additional explanatory variables, but collectively resource variables account for about twenty percent (employment) to one third (lodging) of the variation in the dependent variables.

In terms of variable significance, the employment model is different from the three others in the sense that every independent variable is strongly statistically significant (t value > 2.576). In other models, VARTOPOG and PCTARTIF are significant at 1% in the lodging models; water resources range from non significance (hotel room density model) to 10% significance; last, other agricultural land and forests are not significant in the lodging models. In terms of signs, results are consistent across the four models. Thus, artificial surfaces, topographic variation and water resources are systematically positive. PCTOTHAG and PCTFORET are statistically significant in the employment model only, where they are negative.

[9]Previous model specifications included population; results turned out to be very similar.

Table 17.5 Regression analysis: Tourism indicators

Independent variables	Tourism employment (%)	Hotel room density (#/km^2)	Campground space density (#/km^2)	Second home density (#/km^2)
Intercept	[a]***3,8449	***–1.3225	***–8.1333	***–12.1128
	[b](7.457)	(–3.337)	(–3.044)	(–4.199)
Topogr. var. (m)	***0.0088	***0.0014	***0.0025	***0.0098
	(11.223)	(5.989)	(3.931)	(7.644)
Artif. surf. (%)	***0.1342	***0.2594	***1.0985	***1.8304
	(2.668)	(4.308)	(2.657)	(3.728)
Other agric. land (%)	***–0.0369	0.0032	0.0395	0.0326
	(–4.972)	(0.685)	(1.427)	(0.594)
Forests (%)	***–0.0457	0.0043	0.0342	–0.0082
	(–3.631)	(0.718)	(1.621)	(–0.263)
Water area (%)	***0.2150	0.2656	*2.7159	*6.0811
	(5.909)	(1.384)	(1.864)	(1.868)
N	1,745	1,745	1,745	1,745
F	***173.52	***81.22	***162.58	***176.17
R^2	0.3328	0.1893	0.3185	0.3362
Adjust.-R^2	0.3309	0.1870	0.3166	0.3343

[a] parameter estimate; [b] (t value corrected for heteroskedasticity).
***1% significance; **5% significance; *10% significance.
t critical values: 2.576 (1%), 1.960 (5%), 1.645 (10%).

In conclusion, these results seem consistent and contradictory at the same time. Indeed, water resources and topographic variation variables stand out as positively associated with tourism indicators, which is consistent with what is known of the attractiveness of these resources. In addition, and perhaps this result is less intuitive regarding rural areas, the proportion of artificial surfaces has a positive impact. As this variable proxies density (be that population or infrastructure), the result seems to indicate that tourism activity is associated with high infrastructure density, which is consistent with mass tourism features (be that seaside or mountains).

A second series of models was used to analyze the relationship between regional growth indicators and several explanatory factors, including demographic and economic composition, accessibility, service level, and tourism dependence.

The highest correlation coefficient value was 0.44, between the POPAGE (share of population aged 60 or more) and PCTAA (share of employment in the farming and agrifood processing sectors) variables; all other values were less than 0.40. Results for this series of models (all with a condition index value under 18) are detailed in Table 17.6.

All regional growth models exhibit strong overall statistical significance (Fisher test, 1% significance level). The value of the coefficient of determination ranges from 0.45 (income model) to 0.56 (employment model).

All variables are strongly statistically significant (1%), except PCTRES in the employment model (5%). Parameter signs are consistent across the three models. They show a negative association between, on the one hand, the proportion of the

Table 17.6 Regression analysis: Regional indicators

Independent variables	Population	Employment	Income
Intercept	[a]***9,160.5717 [b](8.833)	***3,319.8012 (8.861)	***12,267,586 (10.196)
Population aged 60 or over (%)	***–396.6190 (–12.995)	***–140.4796 (–12.740)	***–509,091 (–14.377)
Jobs in residentiary services (%)	***105.2510 (6.775)	**11.4713 (2.044)	***113,556 (6.301)
Jobs in agriculture and agrifood (%)	***–61.9683 (–3.140)	***–25.5760 (–3.587)	***–99,662 (–4.353)
Access time to closest urban core (min)	***–129.4271 (–12.406)	***–50.6177 (–13.430)	***–126,029 (–10.412)
Jobs and services score (/20)	***1,139.7585 (33.179)	***499.6619 (40.261)	***1,184,694 (29.726)
Tourism dependence dummy	***–6,530.5014 (–8.513)	***–1,510.7290 (–5.451)	***–5,155,377 (–5.792)
N	1,745	1,745	1,745
F	***276.05	***364.35	***237.58
R^2	0.4880	0.5571	0.4506
Adjusted–R^2	0.4862	0.5556	0.4487

[a] parameter estimate; [b] (t value).
***1% significance; **5% significance; *10% significance.
t critical values: 2.576 (1%), 1.960 (5%), 1.645 (10%).

elderly population, importance of the agrifood sector (both farming and food manufacturing) and tourism dependence, and on the other hand, population, employment and income level. In contrast, the statistical relationship is positive when considering the weight of the residentiary sector, accessibility (the negative sign of TT_PU99 indicates that the more access time to the urban core is reduced, the more positive the impact on population, employment, and income) and the level of access to job offers and services.

Overall, these results are in line with previous results regarding regional growth factors, such as accessibility. The negative impact of the proportion of the elderly population is also expected: this population has usually reached the age of retirement, hence the negative impact on total employment, with a level of income that is indeed stable but lower than that of the labour force, hence the negative impact on income. The negative association between the level of population and the proportion of elderly people shows that retiree migration is not happening across all rural areas but is probably limited to amenity-rich areas.

The negative results for the agrifood sector may be explained by the fact that, in rural areas, farming certainly predominates over food processing; given the reduction in farm population and farming activity, it is not surprising that PCTAA parameters are negative. Also, this result is consistent with the positive sign of PCTRES in the three models: for several years, the rural economy has been shifting from extractive to service activities. Last, the level of services (and especially when it takes job offers into account) is a factor of attractiveness, hence the positive sign for the parameter of SCORE20, as expected.

The systematically negative sign of DEPTRSM (the tourism dependence dummy variable) still needs to be explained. This result is a priori surprising because tourism is often touted as a local development strategy. In this analysis, dependence (or specialization) is based on an employment variable and a lodging variable (be that hotel room, campground space or second-home). Consequently, tourism specialization, i.e., a large share of tourism employment and a high value of lodging capacity, does not seem to lead to higher levels of regional growth indicators. The list of tourism-dependent FEAs tends to highlight traditional locations (seaside and mountains, including resorts). Do observed impacts show negative, induced effects related to mass tourism?

17.5 Conclusions

17.5.1 Summary and Result Implications

Results demonstrate the possibility of identifying resource-consistent regions with a cluster analysis mostly based on land cover and altitude. In such regions, which are endowed with different resources, tourism indicators also exhibit different values. Topographic variation, artificial surfaces and, to a lesser extent, water resources seem to be most correlated with tourism indicators.

Using tourism employment and lodging capacity, tourism-specialized FEAs can also be identified. We identified 102 such FEAs (out of a total of 1,745 rural FEAs) that are very unequally distributed across the metropolitan territory. Contrary to accessibility and services, tourism dependence does not lead to higher regional growth levels.

These results question the territorialization of tourism public policy as a function of available resources. Moreover, given the negative impact of tourism specialization, and the location of the corresponding FEAs, it seems appropriate to question the induced effects of mass tourism. In this perspective, tourism policy could address the next two issues more precisely.

First, improve the promotion of regions that tend to be underused today in order to deconcentrate tourism activity and distribute it better across the territory. This strategy could rely on promotion campaigns that would highlight the difference and the specificity of an "alternative" type of tourism, even by promoting adjacent FEAs that are not as highly tourism-specialized today and may satisfy different tourist expectations.

Second, make better use of the concentration of tourism in order to stimulate local economic activity and create more jobs and income. This would include several components: (1) attract population and firms on the basis of existing natural amenities; (2) actively convert some second-homes (or hotels) into main residences, which would imply rehabilitation efforts of existing housing (e.g., surface increase) and would stimulate the local housing industry as well as improve the quality of housing supply; (3) offer a range of services so that yearlong residency becomes easier and more pleasant –in a way, deseasonalize community life.

For implementation to be achieved, such policies must involve a minimum amount of political will, multimunicipal planning, and land control. Deconcentrated state services and local governments should help local decision-makers in their pursuit of tourism activities with larger positive impacts on the local economy.

17.5.2 Study Limits and Further Research Topics

A number of limits of the analysis suggest further research topics.

First, given the exploratory nature of this paper, tourism-sensitive activities were grouped as a single "tourism employment" set. However, all these activities are not directly dependent on tourism: such is the case of hotels without a restaurant, but not of beauty salons that depend, to a major extent, on the residentiary economy. Other sectors (e.g., retailing) are impacted by tourism but are not included in tourism-sensitive activities. Consequently, a further research topic could consist in providing a more refined estimation of tourism employment, by differentiating sectors and taking into account activities that are not considered tourism-sensitive but nonetheless impacted by tourists, and by better separating the tourism vs. residentiary share of local employment.

Next, although the variables used for cluster analysis reflect landscape features, they do not account for all tourism resources in a given area. For example, a landscape diversity index could be added (assuming that the more diversified the landscape, the more attractive the area) as well as climatic condition variables (e.g., to account for warm summers) or information regarding cultural resources (such as built heritage) or sports facilities. Also, information regarding the quality of the environment or biodiversity (e.g., protected areas) could be added. In conclusion, cluster analysis could include a larger set of variables, possibly reduced via principal components analysis.

Two categories were used to define dependence: tourism employment and lodging capacity. Yet, the impacts induced by second-homes are not necessarily the same as those induced by hotels and campgrounds. Therefore, a supplementary analysis could focus on the differential impacts of the type of lodging.

Last, the employment equation features some endogeneity because SCORE20 depends to a significant extent on the employment score, which itself is a function of job offers and the level of labour force employed. Further modelling efforts could use a global score based on all components (competing, non competing, education, and health services) except employment. However, it can be noticed that the estimated parameter of SCORE20 displays similar properties (significant and positive) across the three models.

Acknowledgments We would like to thank Frédéric Bray, Jean-Jacques Collicard and André Torre (UR DTM, Cemagref Grenoble) for Corine Land Cover data preparation, as well as Denis Lépicier (UMR Cesaer, Dijon) for his help in preparing FEA data.

Appendix 1: Descriptive Statistics of Variables (N = 1,745)

Variable	Mean	Stand. deviat.	Minimum	Maximum
Topographic variation (m)	322.86	511.02	0.00	3760.00
Artificial surfaces (%)	4.99	5.54	0.00	65.00
Arable land (%)	30.29	25.61	0.00	97.89
Other agric. land (%)	33.56	21.40	0.00	90.14
Forests (%)	23.83	18.87	0.00	88.86
Water area (%)	1.38	4.54	0.00	77.80
Population	12,160.22	9582.09	270.00	60,700.00
FEA area (km^2)	245.83	231.28	0.40	1,887.00
Jobs and services score (/20)	11.36	5.04	0.00	20.00
Access time to closest urban core (mn)	30.10	16.37	0.00	126.20
Number of jobs	3,962.38	3,722.25	285.00	25,588.00
Sum of net taxable income (€)	12,883,618.10	10,732,241.80	228,165.97	67,032,732.02
Density of hotel rooms (#/km^2)	0.98	4.76	0.00	110.83
Density of campground spaces (#/km^2)	4.01	26.32	0.00	871.67
Density of second homes (#/km^2)	9.44	54.33	0.28	1,940.83
Tourism employment (%)	5.33	7.75	0.00	71.59
Tourism dependence dummy	0.06	0.23	0.00	1.00
Population aged 60 or over (%)	25.56	6.55	5.36	48.21
Jobs in residentiary services (%)	52.38	12.46	16.32	96.25
Jobs in agriculture and agrifood (%)	16.91	10.22	0.46	63.67

Appendix 2: List of Tourism-Dependent FEAs

FEA code	FEA label	Cluster	FEA code	FEA label	Cluster
01143	Divonne-les-Bains	3	56240	Sarzeau	4
01173	Gex	3	60482	Orry-la-Ville	3
04006	Allos	3	61483	Tessé-la-Madeleine	4
04094	Gréoux-les-Bains	3	62318	Etaples	1
07330	Vallon-Pont-d'Arc	3	62604	Neufchâtel-Hardelot	1
11202	Leucate	2	63047	La Bourboule	4
13022	Cassis	3	63103	Châtelguyon	4
13104	Carry-le-Rouet	1	63236	Mont-Dore	3
14191	Courseulles-sur-Mer	1	64495	Saint-Pée-sur-Nivelle	3

FEA code	FEA label	Cluster	FEA code	FEA label	Cluster
14333	Honfleur	4	65362	Pierrefitte-Nestalas	3
14488	Ouistreham	1	65388	Saint-Lary-Soulan	3
14715	Trouville-sur-Mer	4	66003	Amélie-les-Bains-Palalda	3
17093	Le Château-d'Oléron	2	66008	Argelès-sur-Mer	4
17161	La Flotte	2	66016	Banyuls-sur-Mer	4
17452	La Tremblade	3	66024	Le Boulou	3
22194	Plestin-les-Grèves	4	66037	Canet-en-Roussillon	2
29040	Le Conquet	4	66117	Mont-Louis	1
29058	Fouesnant	4	66124	Font-Romeu-Odeillo-Via	3
29217	Pont-Aven	4	66148	Port-Vendres	4
2A041	Bonifacio	4	66222	Vernet-les-Bains	3
2A065	Cargèse	3	68162	Kaysersberg	3
2B134	L'Ile-Rousse	3	68226	Munster	3
31042	Bagnères-de-Luchon	3	68249	Orbey	3
32096	Cazaubon	4	68269	Ribeauvillé	3
33203	Hourtin	3	73006	Aime	3
33214	Lacanau	3	73054	Bourg-Saint-Maurice	3
33394	Saint-Emilion	4	73181	Moûtiers	3
33514	Soulac-sur-Mer	4	73227	Saint-Bon-Tarentaise	3
34003	Agde	4	73257	Saint-Martin-de-Belleville	3
34126	Lamalou-les-Bains	3	73296	Tignes	3
34150	Marseillan	2	73304	Val-d'Isère	3
34192	Palavas-les-Flots	2	74001	Abondance	3
34299	Sérignan	2	74056	Chamonix-Mont-Blanc	3
34344	Le Grau-du-Roi	2	74080	La Clusaz	3
35049	Cancale	1	74191	Morzine	3
38006	Allevard	3	74238	Saint-Jean-d'Aulps	3
38052	Le Bourg-d'Oisans	3	74258	Samoëns	3
38253	Mont-de-Lans	3	74276	Taninges	3
38548	Villard-de-Lans	3	74280	Thônes	3
39470	Les Rousses	3	80688	Rue	1
40046	Biscarrosse	2	80721	Saint-Valery-sur-Somme	1
40065	Capbreton	3	83019	Le Lavandou	3
40310	Soustons	3	83036	Cavalaire-sur-Mer	1
44211	La Turballe	1	83107	Roquebrune-sur-Argens	3
50031	Barneville-Carteret	4	83115	Sainte-Maxime	3
50410	Pontorson	1	83119	Saint-Tropez	3
56034	Carnac	4	85113	L'Ile-d'Yeu	1
56054	Etel	1	85234	Saint-Jean-de-Monts	4
56069	Groix	1	85288	Talmont-Saint-Hilaire	4
56152	Le Palais	4	85294	La Tranche-sur-Mer	4
56186	Quiberon	2	88196	Gérardmer	3

Appendix 3: Location of Tourism-Dependent FEAs

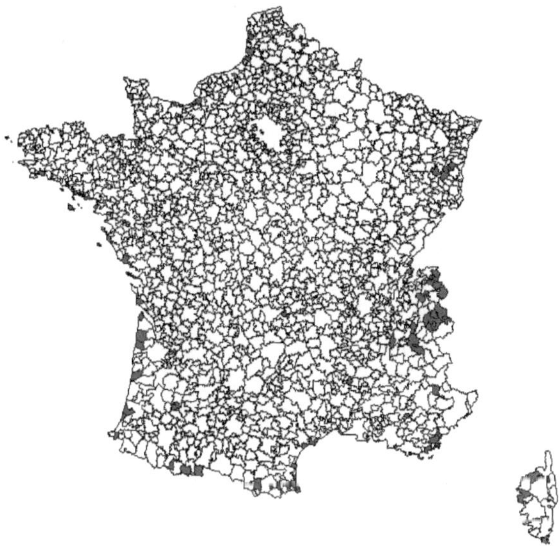

References

Aubert F, Lépicier D, Schaeffer Y (2006) Diagnostic des espaces ruraux français: proposition de méthode sur données communales et résultats à l'échelle du territoire national. Notes et Etudes Econ 26

Baccaïni B, Thomas G, Khiati A (2006) L'emploi salarié dans le tourisme: une nouvelle estimation. INSEE Prem 1099

Beale CL, Johnson KM (1998) The identification of recreational counties in nonmetropolitan areas of the USA. Popul Res Policy Rev 17(1):37–53

Direction du Tourisme (2006) Mémento du tourisme 2006. Ministère délégué au Tourisme, Paris

Dissart J-C (2005) Installations récréatives extérieures et développement économique régional: Le cas des zones rurales isolées aux Etats-Unis. Rev d'Econ Rég et Urbaine 2:217–248

Eadington WR, Redman M (1991) Economics and tourism. Ann Tour Res 18:41–56

English DBK, Marcouiller DW, Cordell HK (2000) Tourism dependence in rural America: estimates and effects. Soc Nat Resour 13(3):185–202

INSEE (2003) Structuration de l'espace rural: Une approche par les bassins de vie. Rapp pour la DATAR, avec la participation de IFEN/INRA/SCESS, Paris

Julien P (2007) Des bassins de vie, au service de l'aménagement du territoire. Econ et Stat 402: 25–39

Leatherman JC, Marcouiller DW (1996) Estimating tourism's share of local income from secondary data sources. Rev Reg Stud 26(3):317–339

McGranahan DA (1999) Natural amenities drive rural population change. Agric Econ Rep no 781, Washington, USDA-ERS

Mollard A, Rambonilaza M, Vollet D (2006) Aménités environnementales et rente territoriale sur un marché de services différenciés: Le cas du marché des gîtes ruraux labellisés en France. Rev d'Econ Politique 116(2): 251–276

Smith SLJ (1988) Defining tourism: a supply-side view. Ann Tour Res 15: 179–90

Terrier C, Sylvander M, Khiati A, Moncéré V (2005) Population présente: Méthodes de détermination à partir des enquêtes sur les touristes. Commun aux Journ de Méthodol Stat de l'INSEE, 15 mars

Ullman EL (1968) Minimum requirements after a decade: a critique and an appraisal. Econ Geogr 44(4):364–369

USDA-ERS (2005) Measuring rurality: 2004 county typology codes. http://www.ers.usda.gov/Briefing/Rurality/Typology/. Accessed 20 February 2007

Vollet D (1998) Estimating the direct and indirect impact of residential and recreational functions on rural areas: an application to five small areas of France. Eur Rev Agric Econ 25(4):528–549

FSC
www.fsc.org
MIX
Papier | Fördert gute Waldnutzung
FSC® C083411

Kolibri 360 GmbH
Ferdinand-Jühlke-Straße 7
99095 Erfurt, Deutschland
produktsicherheit@kolibri360.de